Computer Games: Development and Technology

Computer Games:
Development and Technology

Edited by Harrison Howard

CLANRYE
INTERNATIONAL
www.clanryeinternational.com

Clanrye International,
750 Third Avenue, 9ᵗʰ Floor,
New York, NY 10017, USA

ISBN: 978-1-63240-946-1

Cataloging-in-Publication Data

Computer games : development and technology / edited by Harrison Howard.
    p. cm.
Includes bibliographical references and index.
ISBN 978-1-63240-946-1
1. Computer games. 2. Computer games--Design. 3. Computer games--Software.
4. Electronic games. I. Howard, Harrison.
GV1469.15 .C66 2020
794.8--dc23

For information on all Clanrye International publications
visit our website at www.clanryeinternational.com

Contents

Permissions

List of Contributors

Index

Preface

Every book is a source of knowledge and this one is no exception. The idea that led to the conceptualization of this book was the fact that the world is advancing rapidly; which makes it crucial to document the progress in every field. I am aware that a lot of data is already available, yet, there is a lot more to learn. Hence, I accepted the responsibility of editing this book and contributing my knowledge to the community.

A computer game is any video game that is played on a personal computer. It is characterized by diverse user-determined gaming hardware and software along with a greater capacity in processing, input and video output. In sophisticated PC gaming, there is a significant investment of processing resources which allows improved visual fidelity of games, better potential fidelity of game simulation, and greater input fidelity owing to compatibility with an array of peripherals. The PC platform is characterized by the absence of centralized control. The benefits of this include increased flexibility, reduced software cost, increased innovation, etc. This book aims to shed light on some of the unexplored aspects of technology and development of computer games and the recent researches in this field. It strives to provide a fair idea about this discipline and to help develop a better understanding of the latest advances within this field. For all those who are interested in computer games development, this book can prove to be an essential guide.

While editing this book, I had multiple visions for it. Then I finally narrowed down to make every chapter a sole standing text explaining a particular topic, so that they can be used independently. However, the umbrella subject sinews them into a common theme. This makes the book a unique platform of knowledge.

I would like to give the major credit of this book to the experts from every corner of the world, who took the time to share their expertise with us. Also, I owe the completion of this book to the never-ending support of my family, who supported me throughout the project.

Editor

Artificial Intelligence in Video Games: Towards a Unified Framework

Firas Safadi, Raphael Fonteneau, and Damien Ernst

Université de Liège, Grande Traverse 10, Sart Tilman, 4000 Liège, Belgium

Correspondence should be addressed to Firas Safadi; fsafadi@ulg.ac.be

Academic Editor: Alexander Pasko

With modern video games frequently featuring sophisticated and realistic environments, the need for smart and comprehensive agents that understand the various aspects of complex environments is pressing. Since video game AI is often specifically designed for each game, video game AI tools currently focus on allowing video game developers to quickly and efficiently create specific AI. One issue with this approach is that it does not efficiently exploit the numerous similarities that exist between video games not only of the same genre, but of different genres too, resulting in a difficulty to handle the many aspects of a complex environment independently for each video game. Inspired by the human ability to detect analogies between games and apply similar behavior on a conceptual level, this paper suggests an approach based on the use of a unified conceptual framework to enable the development of conceptual AI which relies on conceptual views and actions to define basic yet reasonable and robust behavior. The approach is illustrated using two video games, *Raven* and *StarCraft: Brood War*.

1. Introduction

Because artificial intelligence (AI) is a broad notion in video games, it is important to start by defining the scope of this work. A video game can be considered to have two main aspects, the context and the game. The game includes the elements that define the actual challenges players face and the problems they have to solve, such as rules and objectives. On the other hand, the context encompasses all the elements that make up the setting in which these problems appear, such as characters and plot. This work focuses on game AI, that is, AI which is concerned with solving the problems in the game such as defeating an opponent in combat or navigating in a maze. Conversely, context AI would deal with context-specific tasks such as making a character perform a series of actions to advance the plot or reacting to player choices. Thus, the scope of discussion is limited to the game aspect in this work.

Since video games are designed for human beings, it is only natural that they focus on their cognitive skills and physical abilities. The richer and more complex a game is, the more skills and abilities it requires. Thus, creating a truly smart and fully autonomous agent for a complex video game can be as challenging as replicating a large part of the complete human intelligence. On the other hand, AI is usually independently designed for each game. This makes it difficult to create thoroughly robust AI because its development is constrained to the scope of an individual game project. Although each video game is unique, they can share a number of concepts depending on their genre. Genres are used to categorize video games according to the way players interact with them as well as their rules. On a conceptual level, video games of the same genre typically feature similar challenges based on the same concepts. These similar challenges then involve common problems for which basic behavior can be defined and applied regardless of the problem instance. For example, in a first-person shooter one-on-one match, players face problems such as weapon selection, opponent position prediction and navigation. Each moment, a player needs to evaluate the situation and switch to the most appropriate weapon, predict where the opponent likely is or is heading and find the best route to get there. All of these problems can be reasoned about on a conceptual level using data such as the rate of fire of a weapon, the current health of the opponent and the location of health packs. These concepts are common to many first-person shooter games and are enough to define effective behavior regardless of the details of their interpretation. Such solutions already exist for certain navigation problems for instance and are used across many video games. Moreover, human players can often effortlessly use the experience acquired from one video game in another of the same genre. A player with experience in first-person shooter games will in most cases perform better in a new first-person shooter game than one without any experience and can even perform better than a player with some experience in the new game, indicating that it is possible to apply the behavior learned for one game in another game featuring similar concepts to perform well without knowing the details of the latter. Obviously, when the details are discovered, they can be used to further improve the basic conceptual behavior or even override it. It may therefore be possible to create cross-game AI by identifying and targeting conceptual problems rather than their game-specific instances. Detaching AI or a part of it from the development of video games would remove the project constraints that push developers to limit it and allow it to have a continuous and more thorough design process.

This paper includes seven sections in addition to Introduction and Conclusion. Section 2 presents some related work and explains how this work positions itself beside it. Sections 3–6 present a development model for video game AI based on the use of a unified conceptual framework. Section 3 suggests conceptualization as a means to achieve unification. Section 4 discusses the design of conceptual AI while Section 5 discusses conceptual problems. Section 6 then focuses on the integration of conceptual AI in video games. Sections 7-8 include some applications of the development model presented in the previous sections. Section 7 describes a design experiment conducted on an open-source video game in order to concretize the idea of introducing a conceptual layer between the game and the AI. Section 8 then describes a second experiment which makes use of the resulting code base to integrate a simple conceptual AI in two different games. The Conclusion section ends the paper by discussing some of the merits of the proposed approach and noting a few perspectives for the extension of this research.

2. Related Work

Conceptualizing video games is a process which involves abstraction and is similar to many other approaches that share the same goal, namely, that of factoring AI in video games. More generally, abstraction makes it possible to create solutions for entire families of problems that are essentially the same when a certain level of detail is omitted. For example, the problem of sorting an array can take different forms depending on the type of elements in the array, but considering an abstract data type and comparison function allows a programmer to write a solution that can sort any type of array. This prevents unnecessary code duplication and helps programmers make use of existing solutions as much as possible so as to minimize development efforts. Another example of widely used abstraction application is hardware abstraction. Physical components in a computer can be seen as abstract devices in order to simplify software development. Different physical components that serve the same purpose, storage

for example, can be abstracted into a single abstract storage device type, allowing software developers to write storage applications that work with any kind of storage component. Such a mechanism is used in operating systems such as NetBSD [1] and the Windows NT operating system family [2].

The idea of creating a unified video game AI middleware is not new. The International Game Developers Association (IGDA) launched an Artificial Intelligence Interface Standards Committee (AIISC) in 2002 whose goal was to create a standard AI interface to make it possible to recycle and even outsource AI code [3]. The committee was composed of several groups, each group focusing on a specific issue. There was a group working on world interfacing, one on steering, one on pathfinding, one on finite state machines, one on rule-based systems and one on goal-oriented action planning, though the group working on rule-based systems ended up being dissolved [3–5]. Thus, the committee was concerned not only with the creation of a standard communication interface between video games and AI, but with the creation of standard AI as well [6]. It was suggested that establishing AI standards could lead to the creation of specialized AI hardware.

The idea of creating an AI middleware for video games is also discussed in Karlsson [7], where technical issues and approaches for creating such middleware are explored. Among other things, it is argued that when state systems are considered, video game developers require a solution in between simple finite state machines and complex cognitive models. Another interesting argument is that functionality libraries would be more appropriate than comprehensive agent solutions because they provide more flexibility while still allowing agent-based solutions to be created. Here too, the possibility of creating specialized AI hardware was mentioned and a parallel with the impact mainstream graphics acceleration cards had on the evolution of computer graphics was drawn.

An Open AI Standard Interface Specification (OASIS) is proposed in Berndt et al. [8], aiming at making it easier to integrate AI in video games. The OASIS framework is designed to support knowledge representation as well as reasoning and learning and comprises five layers each dealing with different levels of abstraction, such as the object level or the domain level, or providing different services such as access, translation or goal arbitration services. The lower layers are concerned with interacting with the game while the upper layers deal with representing knowledge and reasoning.

Evidently, video game AI middleware can be found in video game engines too. Video game engines such as *Unity* [9], *Unreal Engine* [10], *CryEngine* [11], and *Havok* [12], though it may not be their primary focus, increasingly aim at not only providing building blocks to create realistic virtual environments but realistic agents as well.

Another approach that, albeit not concerned with AI in particular, also shares a similar goal, which is to factor development efforts in the video game industry, is game patterns. Game design patterns allow game developers to document recurring design problems and solutions in such a way that they can be used for different games while helping them understand the design choices involved in developing a game of specific genre. Kreimeier [13] proposes a pattern formalism to help expanding knowledge about game design. The formalism describes game patterns using four elements. These are the name, the problem, the solution and the consequence. The problem describes the objective and the obstacles that can be encountered as well as the context in which it appears. The solution describes the abstract mechanisms and entities used to solve the problem. As for the consequence, it describes the effect of the design choice on other parts of the development and its costs and benefits.

Björk et al. [14] differentiates between a structural framework which describes game components and game design patterns which describe player interaction while playing. The structural framework includes three categories of components. These are the bounding category, which includes components that are used to describe what activities are allowed or not in the game such as rules and game modes, the temporal category which includes components that are involved in the temporal execution of the game such as actions and events, and the objective category which includes concrete game elements such as players or characters. More details about this framework can be found in Björk and Holopainen [15]. As for game design patterns, they do not include problem and solution elements as they do in Kreimeier [13]. They are described using five elements which are name, description, consequences, using the pattern and relations. The consequences element here focuses more on the characteristics of the pattern rather than its impact on development and other design choices to consider, which is the role of the using the pattern element. The relations element is used to describe relations between patterns, such as subpatterns in patterns and conflicting patterns.

In Olsson et al. [16], design patterns are integrated within a conceptual relationship model which is used to clarify the separation of concerns between game patterns and game mechanics. In that model, game mechanics are derived from game patterns through a contextualization layer whose role is to concretize those patterns. Conversely, new patterns can be extracted from the specific implementation of these game mechanics, which in the model is represented as code.

Also comparable are approaches which focus on solving specific AI issues. It is easy to see why, since these approaches typically aim at providing standard solutions for common AI problems in video games, thereby factoring AI development. For instance, creating models for intelligent video game characters is a widely researched problem for which many approaches have been suggested. Behavior languages aim to provide an agent design model which makes it possible to define behavior intuitively and factor common processes. Loyall and Bates [17] presents a goal-driven reactive agent architecture which allows events that alter the appropriateness of current behavior to be recognized and reacted to. ABL, a reactive planning language designed for the creation of believable agents which supports multicharacter coordination, is described in Mateas and Stern [18] and Mateas and Stern [19].

Situation calculus was suggested as a means of enabling high-level reasoning and control in Funge [20]. It allows the character to see the world as a sequence of situations and

understand how it can change from one situation to another under the effect of different actions in order to be able to make decisions and achieve goals. A cognitive modeling language (CML) used to specify behavior outlines for autonomous characters and which employs situation calculus and exploits interval methods to enable characters to generate action plans in highly complex worlds is also proposed in Funge et al. [21], Funge [22].

It was argued in Orkin [23, 24] that real-time planning is a better suited approach than scripting or finite state machines for defining agent behavior as it allows unexpected situations to be handled more naturally. A modular goal-oriented action planning architecture for game agents similar to the one used in Mateas and Stern [18, 19] is presented. The main difference with the ABL language is that a separation is made between implementation and data. With ABL, designers implement the behavior directly. Here, the implementation is done by programmers and designers define behavior using data.

Anderson [25] suggests another language for the design of intelligent characters. The avatar definition language (AvDL) enables the definition of both deterministic and goal directed behavior for virtual entities in general. It was extended by the Simple Entity Annotation Language (SEAL) which allows behavior definitions to be directly embedded in the objects in a virtual world by annotating and enabling characters to exchange information with them [26, 27].

Finally, learning constitutes a different approach which, again, leads to the same goal. By creating agents capable of learning from and adapting to their environment, the issue of designing intelligent video game characters is solved in a more general and reusable way. Video games have drawn extensive interest from the machine learning community in the last decade and several attempts at integrating learning in video games have been made with varying degrees of success. Some of the methods used are similar to the previously mentioned approaches in that they use abstraction or concepts to deal with the large diversity found in video games. Case-based reasoning techniques generalize game state information to make AI behave more consistently across distinct yet similar configurations. The possibility of using case-based plan recognition to reduce the predictability of real-time strategy computer players is discussed in Cheng and Thawonmas [28]. Aha et al. [29] presents a case learning and plan selection approach used in an agent that learns to win against a number of different AI opponents in *Wargus*. In Ontañón et al. [30], a case based planning framework for real-time strategy games which allows agents to automatically extract behavioral knowledge from annotated expert replays is developed and successfully tested in Wargus as well. More work using Wargus as a test platform includes Weber and Mateas [31] and Weber and Mateas [32] which demonstrate how conceptual neighborhoods can be used for retrieval in case-based reasoning approaches.

Transfer learning approaches attempt to use the experience learned from some task to improve behavior in other tasks. In Sharma et al. [33], transfer learning is achieved by combining case-based reasoning and reinforcement learning and used to improve performance over successive games against the AI in *MadRTS*. Lee-Urban et al. [34] also uses

MadRTS to apply transfer learning using a modular architecture which integrates hierarchical task network (HTN) planning and concept learning. Transfer of structure skills and concepts between disparate tasks using a cognitive architecture is achieved in Shapiro et al. [35].

Although machine learning technology may lead to the creation of a unified AI that can be used across multiple games, it currently suffers from a lack of maturity. Even if some techniques have been successfully applied to a few commercial games, it may take a long time before they are reliable enough to become mainstream. On the other hand, video game engines are commonly used and constitute a more practical approach at factoring game development processes to improve the quality of video games. They are however comprehensive tools which developers need to adopt for the entire game design rather than just their AI. Furthermore, they allow no freedom in the fundamental architecture of the agents they drive.

The approach presented in this paper bears the most resemblance to that of creating a unified AI middleware. It is however not an AI middleware, strictly speaking. It makes use of a conceptual framework as the primary component which enables communication between video games and AI, allowing video game developers to use conceptual, game-independent AI in their games at the cost of handling the necessary synchronization between game data and conceptual data. A key difference with previous work is that it makes no assumptions whatsoever on the way AI should be designed, such as imposing an agent model or specific modules. Solutions can be designed for any kind of AI problem and in any way. A clear separation is made between the development of the conceptual framework, that of AI and that of video games. Because AI development is completely separated from the conceptual framework, its adoption should be easier as it leaves complete freedom for AI developers to design and implement AI in whichever way they are accustomed to. Furthermore, the simplicity of the approach made it possible to provide a complete deployment example detailing how an entire video game was rewritten following the proposed design. In addition, the resulting limited conceptual framework prototype was successfully employed to reuse some of the game AI modules in a completely different game.

3. Conceptualize and Conquer

Since video games, despite their apparent diversity, share concepts extensively, creating AI that operates solely on concepts should allow developers to use it for multiple games. This raises an important question however, namely, that of the availability of a conceptual interpretation of video games. In reality, for AI to handle conceptual objects, it must have access to a conceptual view of game data during runtime.

When humans play a video game, they use their faculty of abstraction to detect analogies between the game and others they have played in the past. Abstraction in this context can be seen as a process of discarding details and extracting features from raw data. By recalling previous instances of the same conceptual case, the experience acquired from the other games is generalized and transformed into a conceptual

policy (i.e., conceptualized). For example, a player could have learned in a role-playing game (RPG) to use ranged attacks on an enemy while staying out of its reach. This behavior is known as kiting. Later, in a real-time strategy (RTS) game, that player may be faced with the same conceptual situation with a ranged unit and an enemy. If, at that time, the concept of kiting is not clearly established in the player's mind, they may remember the experience acquired in the RPG and realize that they are facing a similar situation: control over an entity with a ranged attack and the ability to move and the presence of an enemy. The player will thereby conceptualize the technique learned in the RPG and attempt to apply it in the RTS game. On the other hand, if the player is familiar with the concept of kiting, a simple abstraction of the situation will lead to the retrieval of the conceptual policy associated with it, without requiring the recall of previous instances and associated experiences and their conceptualization.

Note that kiting can be defined using only concepts, such as distance, attack range and movement. Distance can have several distinct interpretations, for example yards, tiles or hops. Attack range can be a spell range, a firearm range or a gravity range. Walking, driving and teleporting are all different forms of movement. Kiting itself being a concept, it is clear that concepts can be used to define other concepts. In fact, in order to define conceptual policies, different types of concepts are necessary, such as objects, relationships, conditions and actions. Weapon, enmity, mobility (The condition of being mobile.) and hiding are all examples of concepts.

According to the process shown in Figure 1, conceptual AI, that is AI which operates entirely on concepts, could be used in video games under the premise that three requirements are met. These would be:

(1) the ability to translate game states into conceptual states,

(2) the ability to translate conceptual actions into game actions,

(3) and the ability to define conceptual policies. (A conceptual policy maps conceptual states to conceptual actions.)

Though the third requirement raises no immediate questions, the other two appear more problematic, as translating states and actions needs to be done in real-time and there currently exists no reliable replacement for the human faculty of abstraction. It follows from the latter assertion that this translation must be manually programmed at the time of development. This means that the game developer must have access to a library of concepts during development and write code to provide access at runtime to both conceptual views and conceptual controls of the game for the AI to work with. Using such a process, both the real-time availability and the quality conditions of the translation are satisfied.

As is hinted in Figure 2, rather than translating game states into conceptual states discretely, it is easier to simply maintain a conceptual state in the conceptual data space (CDS). In other words, the conceptual state is synchronized with the game state. Every change in the game state, such as object creation, modification or destruction, is directly

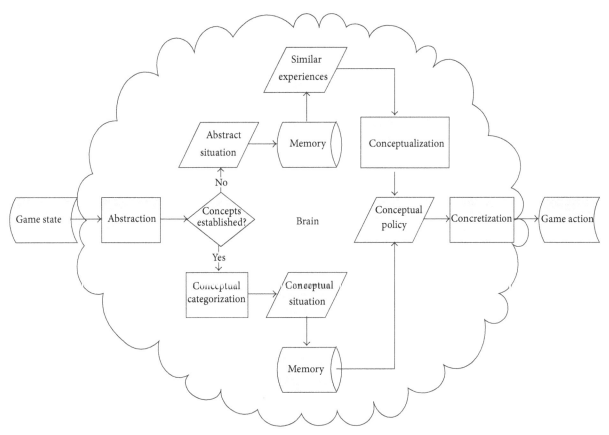

FIGURE 1: Possible process of human decision making in a video game using conceptual policies, as described above. If memory queries do not yield any results, a concrete policy is computed in real-time using other cognitive faculties such as logic or emotion.

propagated to the conceptual state. Note that there is no dynamic whatsoever in the CDS. A change in the CDS can only be caused by a change on the game side, wherein the game engine lies.

Obviously, this design calls for a unified conceptual framework (CF). That is, different developers would use the same conceptual libraries. This would allow each of them to use any AI written using this unique framework. For example, a single AI could drive agents in different games featuring conceptually similar environments, such as a first-person shooter (FPS) arena. This is illustrated in Figure 3.

From a responsibility standpoint, the design clearly distinguishes three actors:

(1) the game developers,

(2) the AI developers,

(3) and the CF developers.

The responsibilities of game developers include deciding which AI they need and adding code to their game to maintain in the CDS the conceptual views required by the AI as well as implementing the conceptual control interfaces it uses to command game agents. Thus, game developers neither need to worry about designing AI nor conceptualizing games. Instead, they only need to establish the links between their particular interpretation of a concept and the concept itself.

On the opposite side, AI developers can write conceptual AI without worrying about any particular game. Using only conceptual elements, they define the behavior of all sorts of agents. They also need to specify the requirements for each AI in terms of conceptual views and controls.

Finally, the role of CF developers is to extract concepts from games (i.e., conceptualize) and write libraries to create and interact with these concepts. This includes writing the interfaces used by game developers to create and maintain conceptual views and by AI developers to access these views and control agents.

Because the CF should be unique and is the central component with which both game developers and AI developers interact, it should be developed using an open-source and extensible model. This would allow experienced developers from different organizations and backgrounds to collaborate and quickly produce a rich and accessible framework. Incidentally, it would allow game developers to write their own AI while extending the framework with any missing concepts.

4. Designing Conceptual AI

From a technical perspective, writing conceptual AI is similar to writing regular AI. That is, developers are free to design their AI any way they see fit. Conceptual AI does not require a specific form. The only difference between conceptual AI and

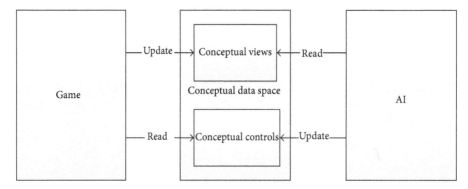

FIGURE 2: Basic architecture of a video game using conceptual AI. The game maintains a conceptual view of its internal state. A conceptual view is the projection of a part of the game state into conceptual space. Based on this conceptual data, the AI controls an agent in the game by issuing conceptual commands, which the game translates back into game actions.

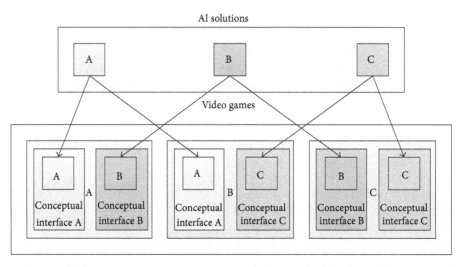

FIGURE 3: Using the same AI in multiple games. AI A can run in games A and B because both implement the conceptual interface A it requires. A conceptual interface is a set of conceptual views and controls.

regular AI is that the former is restricted to the use of conceptual data. Rather than operating on concrete objects, such as knights, lightning guns or fireball spells, it deals with concepts such as melee (Opposite of ranged, can only attack within grappling distance.) tanking units (A tanking unit, or tank, is a unit who can withstand large amounts of damage and whose primary role is to draw enemy attacks in order to ensure the survival of weaker allied units.), long-range hitscan weapons (A hitscan weapon is a weapon that instantly hits the target when fired (i.e., no traveling projectile).) and typed area-of-effect damage projectile abilities. (Area-of-effect abilities target an entire area rather than a single unit.) Likewise, actions involve conceptual objects and properties instead of concrete game elements and can consist in producing an anti-air unit or equipping a damage reduction accessory. This difference is illustrated in Algorithms 1 and 2.

Algorithm 1 shows an excerpt from the combat code of a Fortress Defender, a melee non-player character (NPC) in a RPG. A Fortress Defender can immobilize enemies, a useful ability against ranged opponents who might attempt to kite it. Before commanding the NPC to attack an encountered enemy, the code checks whether the type of opponent is one of those who use a ranged weapon and starts by using its immobilization ability if it is the case.

Algorithm 2 shows a possible conceptualization of the same code. Note how the design remains identical and the only change consists in replacing game elements with conceptual ones. As a result, the new code mimics a more conceptual reasoning. In order to prevent a ranged enemy from kiting the melee NPC, the latter checks whether a movement-impairing ability is available and uses it on the target before moving towards it. Whether the actual ability turns out to slow, immobilize or completely stun the opponent holds little significance as long as the conceptual objective of preventing it from kiting the NPC is accomplished. Although this requires developers to think in a more abstract way, they do retain the freedom of designing their AI however they are accustomed to.

Despite this technical similarity, the idea of conceptualizing video games suggests looking at AI in a more problem-driven way. There are two obvious reasons. First, conceptual AI does not target any game in particular, meaning that it

```
void handle_enemy(pc_t & enemy)
{
    ...
    if (enemy.type() == pc_t::cleric || enemy.type()
        == pc_t::sorcerer || enemy.type() == pc_t::ranger)
      queue_action(use_skill(Skill::root, enemy));
    queue_action(attack(enemy));
    ...
}
```

ALGORITHM 1: Fortress Defender combat code snippet.

```
void handle_enemy(pc_t & enemy)
{
    ...
    if (enemy.ranged() && can_impair_movement())
      queue_action(use_skill(get_skill(SkillType::
        disable_move), enemy));
    queue_action(attack(enemy));
    ...
}
```

ALGORITHM 2: Conceptual combat code snippet.

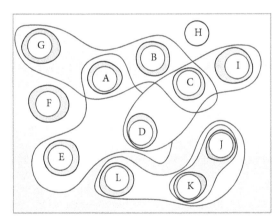

FIGURE 4: Conceptual problems (circles) and solutions (irregular forms). Instead of looking at the whole ADE and CDI problems found in two different games and solving them directly, solving problem D twice in the process, it is more interesting to identify the individual problems A, C, D, E, and I and solve them once first. A solution based on those of the individual problems can then be developed for each game without having to solve them again.

should not be defined as a complete solution for an entire game. Second, with the various interpretation details omitted, AI developers can more easily identify the conceptual problems that are common to games of different genres and target the base problems first rather than their combinations in order to leverage the full factoring potential of conceptualization. The idea of solving the base conceptual problems and combining conceptual solutions is illustrated in Figure 4.

Besides combining them, it can be necessary to establish dependencies between solutions. An AI module may rely

on data computed by another module and require it to be running to function properly. For example, an ability planner module could require a target selection module by planning abilities for a unit or character according to its current target. This can be transparent to game developers when the solutions with dependencies are combined together into a larger solution. When they are not however, game developers need to know whether an AI module they plan on using has any dependencies in order to take into account the conceptual interfaces required by those dependencies. This means that AI developers have to specify not only the conceptual interface an AI solution uses, but also those required by its dependencies. Dependencies in combined and individual AI solutions are illustrated in Figure 5.

It can be argued that problems are actual video game elements. The difference between them and other elements such as objects is that they are rarely defined explicitly. They might be in games where the rules are simple enough to be listed exhaustively in a complete description of the problem the player is facing, but often in video games the rules are complex and numerous and a complete definition of the problems players must face would be difficult to not only write, but also read an understand. Instead, a description of the game based on features such as genres, environments or missions convey the problems awaiting players in a more intuitive way. With such implicit definitions, there can be many ways of breaking down video games into conceptual problems. Different AI developers might consider different problems and compositions. There are no right or wrong configurations of conceptual problems, though some may allow developers to produce AI more efficiently than others, just like the concepts making up the CF. It was suggested that the CF should be developed

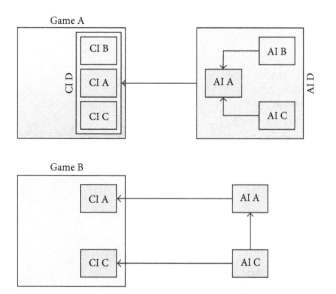

FIGURE 5: AI dependency in combined and individual solutions. Arrows represent requirement. A combination of AI solutions (AI D) has its own conceptual interface (CI D) which includes those of its components, making AI dependency transparent to game developers. In the case of separate AI solutions, a dependency (AI C requires AI A) translates into an additional conceptual interface (CI A) for game developers to provide.

using an open-source model to quickly cover the numerous existing concepts through collaboration and ease the addition of new ones. The same suggestion could be made for conceptual problems. If conceptual problems are listed and organized in the CF, AI developers can focus on solving conceptual problems instead of identifying them. As with concepts, as conceptual problems are identified and included in the CF, they become part of the AI developers' toolkit and allow them to better design their solutions. This task can be added to the responsibilities of CF developers, though since AI developers are the ones facing these conceptual problems and dealing with their hidden intricacies, they are likely to detect similarities between solutions to seemingly distinct problems, and in extension similarities between problems, and could collaborate with CF developers to restructure problems or contribute to the CF directly. Similarly, game developers deal with the details of the explicit elements and may have valuable contributions to make to the CF. In a way, CF developers can include both game and AI developers who could be assuming a double role either as direct contributors or as external collaborators. Such an organization together with the idea of breaking down video games into conceptual problems and using these as targets for conceptual AI is shown in Figure 6. The AI used in a video game could thus be described as solutions to elementary or composite conceptual problems.

5. Identifying Conceptual Problems

Conceptual problems are the heart of this video game AI development model. Indeed, it would serve little purpose to conceptualize video games if the resulting concepts could not

be used to identify problems that are common to multiple games. Problem recurrence in video games is the raison d'être of such a model and why factoring video game AI is worth pursuing. The amount of factoring that can be achieved depends on how well recurring problems are isolated in video games not only of the same genre, but of any genre. This could be used as a measure of the efficiency of the model, as could be the amount of redundancy in AI solutions to disjoint problems. Clearly identifying and organizing conceptual problems is therefore a crucial dimension of this development model.

Problems and their solutions can either be elementary or composite. Elementary problems are problems whose decomposition into lesser problems would not result in any AI being factored. They are the building blocks of composite problems. The latter combine several problems, elementary or composite, into a single package to be handled by a complete AI solution. For example, an agent for a FPS arena deathmatch can be seen as a solution to the problem of control of a character in that setting. This problem could be decomposed into smaller problems which can be found in different settings such as real-time combat and navigation.

Navigation is a popular and well-studied problem found in many video games. Navigation in a virtual world often involves pathfinding. Common definitions as well as optimal solutions already exist for pathfinding problems. Examples include the A^* search algorithm, which solves the single-pair shortest path problem (Find the least-cost path between a source node and a destination node in a graph.), and Dijkstra's algorithm, which solves the single-source shortest path problem (Find the least-cost path between a root node and all other nodes in a graph.). Although standard implementations can be found in developer frameworks and toolboxes, it is not unusual for developers to commit to their own implementation for environment-based customization.

A problem decomposition is often reflected in the AI design of a video game. For example, the AI in a RTS game may be divided into two main components. One component would deal with the problem of unit behavior and define behavior for units in different states such as being idle or following specific orders. This AI component could in turn include subcomponents for subproblems such as pathfinding. Defining autonomous unit behavior involves elements such as the design of unit response to a threat, an attack or the presence of an ally and is a problem that can be found in other games such as RPGs and FPSs. The other main component would deal with the problem of playing the RTS game to make it possible for a human player to face opponents without requiring other human players. This component could be organized in a number of modules to deal with the various tasks a player has to handle in a RTS game. A strategy manager can handle decisions such as when to attack and which units to produce. A production manager can handle construction tasks and assign workers to mining squads. A combat manager can designate assault locations and assign military units to combat squads. Squad managers can handle tasks such as unit formations and coordination and target selection. These AI components can provide insight on the different conceptual problems they attempt to solve and their organization. Coordination between a group of units

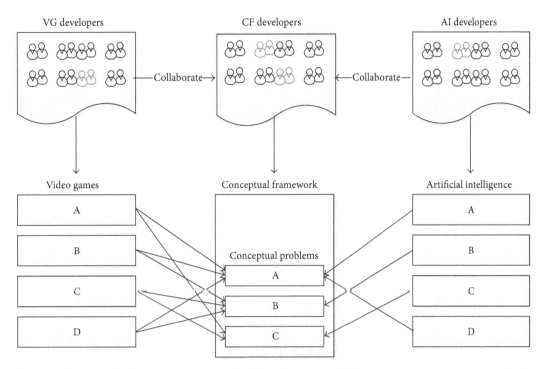

FIGURE 6: Collaboration between developers. Some game and AI developers, possibly large organizations or pioneers, also help developing the CF. Others only use it. Conceptual problems (CP) are listed and organized in the CF. A conceptual problem can be included in multiple games (CP B is included in VG B, C, and D) and can have multiple solutions (AI A and D are two different solutions for CP A).

to select a common target or distribute targets among units and maneuver units can be included in the larger problem of real-time combat which is not exclusive to the RTS genre. On the other hand, production-related decisions could be taken based on generic data such as total air firepower or total ground armor, making it possible for the same conceptual policy to be used for any RTS game providing a conceptual view through which such data can be computed.

More conceptual problems could be derived from these AI components. The real-time combat problem is a complex recurring problem found in many different games and may incorporate problems such as role management, equipment tuning, positioning, target selection and ability planning.

Many such problems have already been studied and the video game AI literature is rich in books which explore common problems in depth. Examples include *Programming Game AI by Example* by Buckland [36], *AI Game Engine Programming* by Schwab [37], *Artificial Intelligence for Games* by Millington and Funge [38], *Artificial Intelligence: A Modern Approach* by Russel and Norvig [39] and the *AI Game Programming Wisdom* books by Rabin [40–43]. More specific publications that focus on positioning for example also exist, such as work from Straatman and Beij [44] and Pottinger [45].

The remainder of this section briefly presents some of these problems and attempts to reason about them conceptually.

5.1. Role Management. Role management in combat is a recurring problem in video games. Role management deals with the distribution of responsibilities, such as damaging,

tanking, healing and disabling, among a group of units or characters fighting together. This problem is often encountered in popular genres such as RPG (e.g., *World of Warcraft*, Blizzard Entertainment 2004), RTS (e.g., *Command & Conquer: Red Alert 3*, Electronic Arts 2008) and FPS (e.g., *Left 4 Dead*, Valve Corporation 2008). Roles can be determined based on several factors, including unit type or character class, attributes and abilities, equipment and items, unit or character state and even player skill or preference. Without targeting any specific game, it is possible to define effective policies for role management using conceptual data only. The data can be static like a sorted list of role proficiencies indicating in order which roles a unit or character is inherently suited for. Such information can be used by the AI to assign roles in a group of units of different type in combat. Dynamic data can also be used to control roles in battle, like current hit points (The amount of damage a unit can withstand.), passive damage reduction against a typed attack and available abilities of a unit. For instance, these can be used together to estimate the current tanking capacity for units of the same type. Naturally, the interpretation of these concepts varies from one game to another. Yet a conceptual policy remains effective in any case.

In a RPG, if a party is composed of a gladiator, an assassin and two clerics, the gladiator may assume the role of tank while a cleric assumes the role of healer and both the assassin and the other cleric assume the role of damage dealers. This distribution can vary significantly however. For example, the gladiator may be very well equipped and manage to assume the double role of tank and damage dealer, or conversely, the assassin may be dealing too much damage and become the target. If the tank dies, the healer may become the target (Healing often increases the aggression level of a monster towards the healer, sometimes more than damaging the monster would.) and assume both the role of tank and healer. In this case, the other cleric may switch to a healer role because the tanking cleric could get disabled by the enemy or simply because the lack of defense compared to a gladiator could cause the damage received to increase drastically, making two healers necessary to sustain enemy attacks. Roles can thus be attributed during combat depending on character affinities and on current state data too.

A similar reasoning process can be used for units in a RTS game. In a squad composed of knights, sorcerers and priests, knights will be assuming the role of tanks and fighting at the frontlines, while priests would be positioned behind them and followed by the sorcerers. Sorcerers would thus be launching spells from afar while knights prevent enemy units from getting to them and priests heal both injured knights and sorcerers. Even among knights, some might be more suited for tanking than others depending on their state. Heavily injured knights should not be tanking lest they not survive a powerful attack. They should instead move back and wait for priests to heal them while using any long range abilities they might have. Unit state includes not only attributes such as current hit points but also status effects (A status effect is a temporary alteration of a unit's attributes such as speed or defense.) and available abilities. Abilities can significantly impact the tanking capacity of a unit. Abilities could create a powerful shield around a unit, drastically increase the health regeneration of a unit or even render a unit completely invulnerable for a short amount of time. Likewise, healing and damage dealing capacities can vary depending on available abilities. The healing or damage dealing capacity of a unit may be severely reduced for some time if the unit possesses powerful but high-cooldown (The cooldown of an ability is the minimum amount of time required between two consecutive activations. It is used to regulate the impact of an ability in a battle.) abilities which have been used recently. If the knights fall, either priests stay at the front and become the tanks or they move to the back and let the sorcerers tank depending on who of the two has the higher tanking capacity. Again, conceptual data can be used to generate operating rules to dynamically assign roles among units.

Algorithm 3 shows a conceptual AI function which can be used to determine the primary tank in a group. The primary tank is usually the unit or character that engages the enemy and is more likely to initiate a battle. Algorithm 4 details a possible implementation of the scoring function. It estimates the total amount of damage a unit could withstand based on its hit points and the overall damage reduction factor it could benefit from that can be expected during the battle given the abilities of both sides. A damage reduction factor is just one way of conceptualizing defensive attributes such as armor or evasion. The `dmgred_abilities` function could create a list of available damage reduction abilities and average their effects. For each ability, the amount of reduction it contributes to the average can be estimated using the reduction factor it adds, the duration of the effect, the cooldown of the ability as well as its cast time. In the case of conflicting abilities

(i.e., abilities whose effects override each other), the average reduction bonus could be estimated by spreading the abilities over the cooldown period of the one with the strongest effect. The `dmgamp_abilities` function could work with damage amplification abilities in a similar way. It could also take into account the unit's resistance to status effects.

Any form of distribution of responsibilities between units or characters fighting together can be considered role management. Role management does not assume any objective in particular. Depending on the goal of the group, different distribution strategies can be devised. The problem of role management in combat can therefore be described as follows. Given an objective, two or more units or characters and a set of roles, define a policy which dynamically assigns a number of roles to each unit or character during combat in a way which makes the completion of the objective more likely than it would be if units or characters each assumed all responsibilities individually. An example of objective is defeating an enemy unit. Roles do not have to include multiple responsibilities. They can be simple and represent specific responsibilities such as acting as a decoy or baiting the enemy.

5.2. Ability Planning. Another common problem in video games is ability planning. It can be found in genres such as multiplayer online battle arena (MOBA) (e.g., *League of Legends*, Riot Games 2009 and *Dota 2*, Valve Corporation 2013) and RPG (e.g., *Aion: The Tower of Eternity*, NCsoft 2008 and *Diablo III*, Blizzard Entertainment 2012). Units or characters may possess several abilities which can be used during combat. For instance, a wizard can have an ice needle spell which inflicts water damage on an enemy and slows it for a short duration, a mana shield spell which temporarily causes damage received to reduce mana points (Also called magic points or ability points. Using abilities usually consumes mana points.) instead of health points and a dodge skill which can be used to perform a quick sidestep to evade an attack. Each of these abilities is likely to have a cost such as consuming a certain amount of mana points or ability points and a cooldown to limit its use. Units or characters thus need to plan abilities according to their objective to know when and in what order they should be used. As with role management, both static and dynamic data can serve in planning abilities. For example, if the enemy's class specializes in damage dealing, disabling abilities or protective abilities could take precedence over damaging abilities because its damage potential may be dangerously high. However, if the enemy's currently equipped weapon is known to be weak or its powerful abilities are known to be on cooldown, the use of protective abilities may be unnecessary.

Although abilities can be numerous, the number of ability types is often limited. These may include movement abilities, damaging abilities, protective abilities, curative abilities, enhancing abilities, weakening abilities and disabling abilities. Evidently, it is possible for an ability to belong to multiple categories. Abilities can be described in a generic way using various conceptual properties such as damage dealt, travel distance, conceptual attribute modification such as increasing hit points, effect duration, conceptual attribute cost such as action point cost, and cooldown duration. Abilities could also

```
void set_tank(UnitList & grp)
{
  //Get a list of the enemies the group is fighting
  UnitList enemies = get_nearby_threats(grp);
  Unit* toughest = NULL;
  double score = 0;
  //For each unit in the group, estimate its toughness against the enemy
  UnitList::iterator u;
  for (u = grp.begin(); u != grp.end(); ++u)
  {
    double cs = score_tanking(*u, grp, enemies);
    if (cs > score)
    {
      toughest = *u;
      score = cs;
    }
  }
  //Assign the role of tank to the toughest unit in the group
  if (score > 0)
    set_role(toughest, Role::tank);
}
```

ALGORITHM 3: Primary tank designation. This function could be used to determine which unit or character should engage the enemy.

```
double score_tanking(Unit* u, UnitList & grp, UnitList & enemies)
{
  //Set the base score to the current unit hit points
  double score = u->hitpts();
  //Get primary damage type of enemy
  DamageType dt = get_primary_dtype(enemies);
  //Get current damage reduction of the unit
  double dr = u->dmgred(dt);
  //Factor in average reduction bonus from ally abilities
  dr += dmgred_abilities(u, grp, dt);
  //Factor in average amplification bonus from enemy abilities
  dr -= dmgamp_abilities(u, enemies, dt);
  if (dr >= 1.0)
    return numeric_limits<double>::infinity();
  //Estimate effective hit points
  score *= 1.0/(1.0 - dr);
  return score;
}
```

ALGORITHM 4: Tanking capacity estimation. This function could be used to evaluate how fit of a tank a unit or character is.

be linked together for chaining, such as using an ability to temporarily unlock another. Ability planning can then be achieved without considering the materialization of the abilities in a particular world. Even special abilities used under certain conditions, such as a boss attack that is executed when the hit points of the boss fall under a specific threshold, can be handled by conceptual policies. For instance, a powerful special ability of a boss monster can be unavailable until a condition is met. At that point, a policy that scans abilities and selects the most powerful one available would automatically result in the use of the special ability. If the ability must be used only once, a long cooldown can stop subsequent uses

assuming cooldowns are reset if the boss exits combat (This is to ensure that the boss can use the special ability again in a new battle in case its opponents are defeated or run away.).

Abilities can be planned according to some goal. For example, the goal could be to maximize the amount of damage dealt over a long period of time, also called damage per second (DPS). Maximizing DPS involves determining a rotation of the most powerful abilities with minimum downtime (A state where all useful abilities are on cooldown.). Conversely, the goal could be maximizing the amount of damage dealt over a short period of time, or dealing as much damage as possible in the shortest amount of time, also called

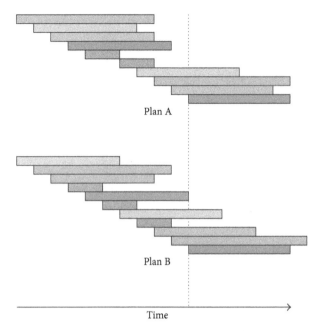

FIGURE 7: Ability planning using a burst strategy (Plan A) and a DPS strategy (Plan B). Rectangles represent cooldown periods of abilities. Each color corresponds to a different ability. Cast time is represented by a delay between the use of two consecutive abilities.

burst damage. A burst plan is compared to a DPS plan in Figure 7. While the burst strategy (Plan A) obviously deals more damage at the beginning, it is clear that the DPS strategy (Plan B) results in more damage over the entire period. The DPS plan orders long-cooldown abilities in a way that avoids simultaneous cooldown resets because these powerful abilities need to be used as soon as they are ready to make the most out of them, which is not possible if multiple ones become ready at the same time. It also avoids the downtime between the two consecutive uses of the purple ability in Plan A by better interleaving its casts throughout the time period. This leads to a higher output overall. Note that the burst strategy eventually converges towards the the DPS strategy.

When combat is largely based on abilities, predicting and taking into account enemy abilities becomes crucial for effective ability planning. If a lethal enemy attack is predicted, a unit or character can use a protective ability such as casting a shield just before the attack is launched to nullify its effect. Alternatively, it can use a disabling ability to prevent the enemy from using the ability or interrupt it. Known enemy abilities could be evaluated in order to predict the enemy's likely course of action and plan abilities accordingly. Just like role management, ability planning can be dealt with by defining interesting conceptual policies for various frequently encountered objectives.

In Algorithm 5, the DPS of an ability chain is estimated by adding up the damage and duration of each ability in the chain. Ability chains can be useful to represent linked abilities, for example when an ability can only be activated after another. They can also be used to generate different versions of the same ability in cases where using an ability after a specific one alters the attributes of the ability. If activating

ability Y after X increases the damage of Y by 100% or reduces its use time by 50%, X and Y may be interesting from a DPS standpoint in cases where they otherwise are not when considered individually. The attribute values of Y can then be different from their default ones depending on the chain in which they appear. Of course, this function only estimates a theoretical damage and is more useful to generate all-purpose ability rotations than to plan abilities against a specific enemy. DPS can be more accurately estimated by factoring in the attributes and status effects of both the user and the target. If the target is very resistant against a particular type of damage, powerful abilities of this type may be outranked by less powerful ones dealing a different type of damage. The attributes or the status effects of the user can also affect the effectiveness of different abilities in different ways. One ability may have a high base damage value but gain nothing from the strength of the user, while another ability may have a low base damage but greatly benefit from the strength attribute and end up out-damaging the former. Use time can also vary depending on the user's attributes. Note that the use time corresponds to the total time during which the user is busy using an ability and cannot use another. Some abilities may involve both a cast time (i.e., a phase where the user channels energy without the ability being activated) and an activation duration (i.e., the time between the activation of the ability and the time the user goes back to an idle state). This function does not calculate other costs either. If abilities cost ability points or mana points to use in combat, these additional costs can be estimated for the chain together with the time cost since they usually cannot be ignored during a battle.

The concept of abilities is used in several genres. They usually correspond to actions that can be taken in addition to base actions, such as moving, at a cost. Given an objective and a set of abilities, the problem of ability planning is to produce a sequence of abilities which leads to the completion of the objective. Note that the set of abilities does not have to belong to a single entity. Like in role management, the objective can be fairly abstract and common, such as running away, disabling an enemy or protecting an ally.

5.3. Positioning. A frequently encountered problem in video games is positioning in the context of combat. Many genres include it, such as action-adventure (AA) (e.g., *The Legend of Zelda: Ocarina of Time*, Nintendo 1998), RTS (e.g., *StarCraft II: Wings of Liberty*, Blizzard Entertainment 2010) and RPG (e.g., *TERA: Rising*, Bluehole Studio 2011). Maneuverable units or characters have to continuously adjust their position according to their role or plan. A character whose role is to defend other characters will move to a position from which it can cover most of its allies from enemy attacks. An archer will attempt to stay outside the range of its enemies but close enough to reach them. A warrior with strong melee area-of-effect (AoE) attacks must move to the center of a group of enemies so as to hit as many of them as possible with each attack. An assassin may need to stick to the back of an enemy in order to maximize its damage. A specialized unit with poor defense could remain behind its allies in order to easily retreat in case it becomes targeted. This kind of behavior results from conceptual reasoning and needs not be specific to any one game.

```
double calc_dps(AbilityChain & ac)
{
  double dmg = 0;
  double dur = 0;
  AbilityChain::iterator a;
  //Add up the damage and duration of each ability in the chain
  for (a = ac.begin(); a != ac.end(); ++a)
  {
    dmg += (*a)->damage();
    dur += (*a)->usetime();
  }
  //DPS = total damage/total execution time
  if (zero(dmg))
    return 0;
  if (zero(dur))
    return numeric_limits<double>::infinity();
  return dmg/dur;
}
```

ALGORITHM 5: DPS estimation of an ability chain. This function can be useful for creating optimal DPS plans.

While navigation deals with the problem of traveling from one position to another, positioning is more concerned with finding new positions to move to. New positions can be explicitly designated for a unit or character or they could be implicitly selected by adjusting movement forces. For example, a unit may need to step outside the range of an enemy tower by moving to a specific position, or it could avoid bumping into a wall while chasing another unit by adding a force that is normal to the direction of the wall to its steering forces instead of selecting a position to move to. When positions are explicitly calculated, navigation may be involved to reach target positions. This can lead to a dependency between solutions to positioning problems and solutions to navigation problems.

Algorithm 6 shows a function which moves a unit out of the attack range of a group of enemies. For each enemy, it creates a circular area based on the enemy's attack range and centered on its predicted position. The latter is simply calculated by adding the enemy's current velocity to its position. This function ignores enemies that are faster than the unit because even if the unit is currently outside their range, it would eventually fall and remain within their reach. This could be delayed however. A list of immediate threats is thus created and used to compute a force to direct the unit away from the center of threats as quickly as possible. Note that this code does not differentiate between threats. It can be improved by weighting each position in the calculation of the center according to an estimation of the danger the threat represents. The more dangerous the threat, the larger the weight can be. This would cause the unit to avoid pressing threats with higher priority. This function could be used for kiting.

The code in Algorithm 7 shows how a straight line projectile can be dodged by a unit. A ray is created from the current position of the projectile and used to determine whether a collision with the unit is imminent. If this is the case, the unit is instructed to move sideways to avoid collision. The bounding radius of the projectile as well as that of the unit are used to determine the distance which must be traveled. The side on which the unit moves depends on its relative position vis-à-vis the projectile course. Of course, this function does not take into account the speed of the projectile and could therefore be better. If the projectile is slow compared to the unit, the movement could be delayed. On the other hand, if it is too fast, dodging may be impossible and the unit would not need to waste any time trying to do that.

Clearly, both code examples presented above follow a purely conceptual reasoning and could apply to a multitude of video games. They operate solely on conceptual objects and properties such as units, positions, velocities, steering forces and distances. Creating a comprehensive collection of general policies to deal with positioning problems can be time-consuming, making it unlikely to be profitable for a video game developer. When the solutions are conceptual and target all video games however, they may become profitable, providing incentive for AI developers to undertake the challenge.

Like role management and ability planning, positioning exists within the context of an objective. It is possible to design conceptual yet effective positioning policies for generic objectives such as maximizing damage dealt or minimizing damage received. Given an objective, the problem of positioning is to control the movement of a maneuverable entity in a way which serves the completion of the objective. Note that objectives could automatically be derived from roles. Depending on the space and the type of movement, different positioning problems could be considered. For example, it may be more interesting to consider 2D positioning and 3D positioning separately than to consider a single multidimensional positioning problem.

6. Integrating Conceptual AI in Video Games

Since conceptual AI is designed independently from games, an integration mechanism is necessary for it to be used by game developers. Game developers must be able to choose

```
void stay_safe(Unit* u, UnitList* enemies)
{
  UnitList threats;
  UnitList::iterator e;
  //Iterate on enemies to detect immediate threats
  for (e = enemies.begin(); e != enemies.end(); ++e)
  {
    //Ignore enemies that can't be outrun
    if (u->maxspeed() > (*e)->maxspeed() &&
      distance(u->position(), (*e)->position() + (*e)
        ->velocity()) <= (*e)->maxrange())
      threats.add(*e);
  }
  //Get the center of the threats
  Vector c = center(threats);
  //If the unit is located at the center, drop one of the threats
  if (c == u->position())
    c = center(remove_weakest(threats));
  //Create a force that pulls the unit away from the center
  Vector dir = u->position() - c;
  //Add a steering force of maximum magnitude
  u->addforce(dir*u->maxforce()/dir.norm());
}
```

ALGORITHM 6: Avoiding enemy attacks by staying out of range. This function can be used for kiting.

```
void dodge_projectile(Unit* u, Projectile* p)
{
  //Create a ray for the projectile course
  Ray r(p->position(), p->velocity());
  //Get a list of objects intersecting the ray
  ObjectList is = intersection(r, p->radius());
  //Only dodge if u is the first object to intersect the ray
  if (is.front() == u)
  {
    //Is u exactly on the projectile course?
    if (r.passthru(u->position()))
    {
      //Move perpendicularly by a distance equal to the sum of bounding radiuses
      u->move(u->position() + r.normal()*(p->radius() + u->radius()));
      return;
    }
    //Project the unit position on the projectile course
    Vector pr = r->project(u->position());
    //Get a normal to the projectile course with a norm equal to the distance between
    //  the unit position and its projection
    Vector mv = u->position() - pr;
    //Rescale it to the width of the intersection
    mv *= (p->radius() - (mv.norm() - u->radius()))/mv.norm();
    //Follow the normal to avoid collision
    u->move(u->position() + mv);
  }
}
```

ALGORITHM 7: Dodging a straight line projectile. This function assumes that the projectile is not penetrating.

and connect AI solutions to a game. This is achieved by registering AI controllers with conceptual objects. To assign control, partial or complete, of an entity in the game to a particular AI, the corresponding controller must be instantiated and registered with the projection of the entity in CDS. The AI then controls the conceptual entity, effectively controlling the entity in the game. For example, a game developer could use two AI solutions for a racing game, one for controlling computer opponents on the tracks and another for dynamically adjusting the difficulty of a race to the player's performance. Each time a computer opponent is added to the race, a new instance of the driving AI is created and registered with its conceptual projection. As for the difficulty AI, it can be created at the beginning of the race and registered with a real-time player performance evaluation object.

For each controllable conceptual object defined by the CF developers, a controller interface is defined together with it. This interface describes functions the AI must implement in order to be able to properly assume control over the conceptual object. These are not to be confused with the conceptual controls, also defined by the CF developers, which the AI can use to control the conceptual object and which are implemented by the game developers. Figure 8 illustrates the distinction.

It is possible for multiple controllers to share control of the same object. For example, a NPC could be controlled by different AI solutions depending on its state. It may have a sophisticated combat AI which kicks in only when the NPC enters a combat state and otherwise remains on standby, while a different AI is used when the NPC is in an idle state to make it roam, wander or rest. Multiple controllers however may lead to conflict in cases with overlapping control. One way to resolve conflicts is for AI controllers to have a table indicating a priority level for each conceptual control. Conceptual control calls would then be issued by controllers with their respective priorities and queued for arbitration. Of course, when multiple AI controllers are integrated into a complete solution, this issue can be handled by the author of the solution in whatever way they may choose and only the complete controller can be required to provide a priority table for conceptual controls.

Figure 9 shows how multiple controllers can be registered with a conceptual object. First, an object in the game, an Undead Peon, is created. Following this, its projection in CDS, a NPC, is created and linked to the Undead Peon. Finally, several independent AI controllers, one for generating idle behavior when the Undead Peon is idle, another for generating social behavior when the Undead Peon is around other Undead Peons and other types of NPCs and another for generating combat behavior when the Undead Peon is facing enemies, are created and registered with the NPC in CDS. In this case, there is no overlap in the control of the NPC by the different AI solutions. Using this registration mechanism, an AI controller can also verify that its dependencies are running and access them via the conceptual object.

Examples of functions found in controller interfaces are an update function and event handlers. An update function is used to update the internal state of the AI and can be called every game cycle or at an arbitrarily set update rate.

This function is illustrated in Figure 10. Note how the NPC in CDS has no internal state update cycle. This is because there is no dynamic in the CDS. Objects in CDS are projections of game objects and are only modified as a result of a change in game objects. Event handlers are used to notify AI controllers of game events, such as a unit being killed by another. When an event occurs in the game, a conceptual projection is fired at the projection of the involved game object. The events that can involve a conceptual object are determined by the CF developers and used to create the controller interface. An AI controller does not necessarily need to handle all events. This is obvious for partial controllers. Therefore, it is possible for AI controllers to ignore some events. Event handlers are illustrated in Figure 11. Other examples are functions for suspending and resuming the controller.

When game developers link AI solutions to their games, they can either link them statically at build time or load them dynamically at runtime. Loading AI at runtime makes it easier to test different AI solutions and can also allow players to hook their own AI to the game. Typically, the AI would be running within the video game process, though it can be interesting to consider separating their execution. Deploying the AI in a separate process means it can run on a different machine. The latter could be optimized for AI processing or it could even be on the Internet, making it possible for AI developers to offer AI as a service. A multiprocess design can easily be imagined, as shown in Figure 12.

7. Graven: A Design Experiment

7.1. Description. The Graven experiment consists in rebuilding an open-source video game called *Raven* according to the design presented in the previous sections. (See Figure 2.) Namely, the AI is separated from the game and a conceptual layer is added in between. The AI is adapted to interact with the conceptual layer rather than directly with the game and the latter is modified to maintain a conceptual view in memory and use the conceptual AI. Albeit basic, Raven involves enough concepts to use as a decent specimen for conducting experiments relating to the deployment and use of a CF. The goal of the experiment is twofold.

(1) Concretize the design architecture as well as key processes in a working example.

(2) Obtain a code base to use as a limited prototype for testing conceptual AI in multiple games.

Note that the Graven experiment does not directly aim at demonstrating the efficiency of conceptual AI.

7.2. Raven. Raven is an open-source game written by Mat Buckland. A detailed presentation of the game as well as the code can be found in *Programming Game AI by Example* Buckland [36], where it is used to demonstrate a number of AI techniques such as path planning, goal-driven behavior, and fuzzy logic. It is a single-player, top-down 2D shooter featuring a deathmatch mode.

Maps are made of walls and doors and define spawn locations for players as well as items. When players die,

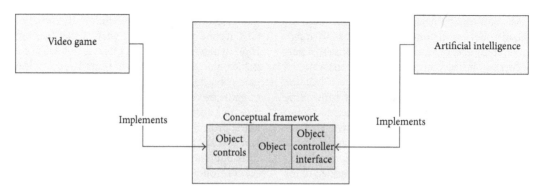

FIGURE 8: Conceptual controls and controller interface. Both are defined by the CF developers. Conceptual controls have to be implemented by game developers while the controller interface has to be implemented by AI developers.

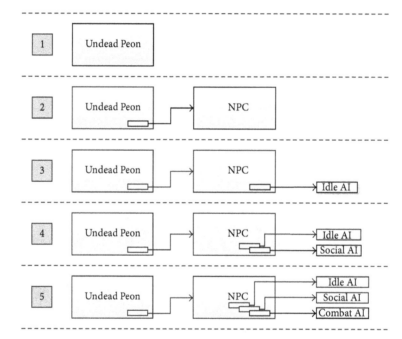

FIGURE 9: Registering multiple controllers with a conceptual object. Depending on its state, the Undead Peon is controlled by one of the three AI solutions.

they randomly respawn at one of the fixed spawn locations. Items also respawn at fixed time intervals after they are picked up. There are two types of items in Raven, weapons and health packs. Three weapons can be picked up. These are the Shotgun, the Rocket Launcher and the Railgun. A fourth weapon, the Blaster, is automatically included in every player's inventory at spawn time.

Each weapon is characterized by a unique set of features such as a firing rate and the maximum quantity of ammunition that can be carried for it. The Blaster is a basic projectile weapon with unlimited ammo. The Shotgun is a hitscan weapon which fires several pellets that spread out. The Rocket Launcher is a projectile weapon which fires rockets that deal AoE damage when they explode either on impact or after traveling a certain distance. The Railgun is a hitscan weapon which fires penetrating slugs that are only stopped by walls. Players can pick up weapons they already have. In that case, only the additional ammo is added to their inventory.

Initially, a default number of bots are spawned depending on the map. Bots can then be added to and removed from the game. The player can possess one of the existing bots to participate in a match. The left and right mouse buttons can be used to fire and move respectively, while numbers on the keyboard can be used to switch weapons. Despite their adorable look, these bots will compute the shortest paths to navigate the map, avoid walls, pick up ammo and health when needed, estimate their opponent's position to aim projectiles properly, use the most appropriate weapon depending on the situation, remember where they last saw or heard an opponent, chase or run away from an opponent, perform evasive maneuvers and, of course, kill. A preview of the game is shown in Figures 13 and 14.

The world in a Raven game is essentially composed of a map, bots and projectiles. The map is composed of walls and includes a navigation graph used for pathfinding as well as triggers. Triggers are used to define item pick up locations as

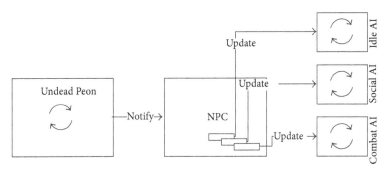

FIGURE 10: Updating the internal state of AI controllers when game objects update theirs. Note how objects in CDS do not have an update cycle.

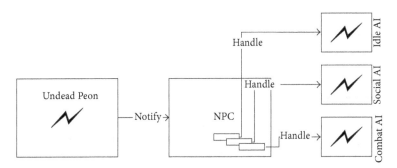

FIGURE 11: Event handling by AI controllers. Game events are projected into CDS before being pushed to AI controllers.

well as temporary sound sources. This composition is illustrated in Figure 15. The bot AI is primarily made of 6 interdependent modules, as shown in Figure 16. The brain module handles abstract goals and takes decisions such as attacking the current target or retrieving an item. The steering module manages steering forces resulting from multiple simultaneous behaviors such as avoiding a wall while seeking an enemy. The path planner module handles navigation requests by computing paths between nodes in the navigation graph. The sensory memory module keeps track of all the information the bot senses and remembers, such as visible enemies, hidden enemies and gunshot sound locations. The target selection module is used to select a target among a group of enemies. Finally, the weapon system module handles aiming and shooting and also includes per-weapon specific modules to evaluate the desirability of each weapon given the current situation.

7.3. Overview of the Code Structure. The code structure in Graven comprises five categories of components:

(1) the Raven classes,

(2) the conceptual view classes,

(3) the conceptual AI classes,

(4) the conceptual controls,

(5) and the Raven control classes.

The Raven classes are the game classes and an adaptation of the original code where all the AI components are removed and code to synchronize the conceptual view with the game

state is added. The second category is a library of objects representing concepts corresponding to the Raven objects. The conceptual AI classes are a modification of the original AI code in which the AI is made to interact with the conceptual layer rather than the game. The fourth category includes a set of conceptual controls used by the conceptual AI to control bots. Finally, the Raven control classes implement these conceptual controls. Note that from a design perspective, the conceptual controls belong in the conceptual layer classes and their implementation in the game classes. They are separated in the code structure for the purpose of clarity.

7.4. Conceptualization. Raven is primarily composed of generic elements, as can be seen in Figure 15. A 2-dimensional world, projectiles, or walls are concepts commonly found in many video games. The added conceptual layer thus largely consists of clones of the objects in Raven. Unlike their Raven counterpart, however, conceptual objects are entirely static and do not update their own state. Instead, their state is only modified as a result of a modification on the game side. This is illustrated in Algorithm 8.

In Algorithm 8, the Raven_Weapon class declares a ShootAt function which is used to fire the weapon and which is implemented by each of the four Raven weapon classes. It also defines an IncrementRounds function which is used to update the number of rounds left for the weapon when a bot picks up additional ammo. In the corresponding CptWeapon class, the ShootAt function has been removed, and the IncrementRounds function has been replaced with

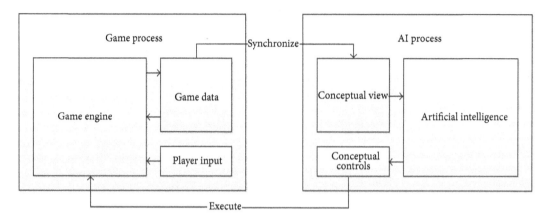

FIGURE 12: Running AI in a separate process. Synchronizing a conceptual view with game data requires an inter-process communication mechanism such as sockets or remote procedure call (RPC) systems. The mechanism is also required for using conceptual controls.

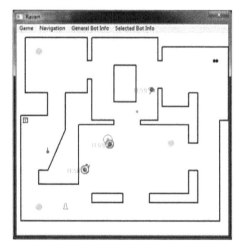

FIGURE 13: Screenshot taken from the Raven game. Player spawn locations are drawn in gray. On the top right corner is a Shotgun in black. At the bottom is a Rocket Launcher. At the left are a Railgun and a health pack. Each bot has its current hit points drawn next to it.

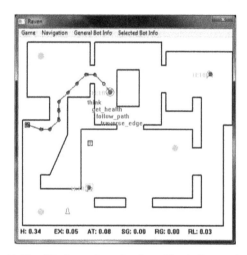

FIGURE 14: The AI information of a selected bot in Raven. Are shown are the goal stack, the path the bot is currently following, the current target of the bot (shown as a colored square around another bot) as well as a number of numerical desirabilities which indicate how important some of the actions the bot is thinking about are. From left to right, these are getting health, exploring, attacking the current target, getting a Shotgun, getting a Railgun and getting a Rocket Launcher.

a `SetNumRoundsLeft` function which can be used by the game to update the number of rounds left for the weapon in CDS. The synchronization process is detailed in a subsequent section.

Four conceptual controls have been defined. These are used by the conceptual AI to control the bots in Graven and are shown in Algorithm 9. The `ApplyForce` function can be used to apply a steering force to a bot and control its movement. The `RotateToward` function can be used to rotate a bot and control the direction of its field of view. The `EquipWeapon` function can be used to switch a bot's weapon to any of those it holds in its inventory. Lastly, The `ShootAt` function can be used to fire a bot's equipped weapon. These conceptual controls can be applied to a `CptMvAgent2D` object, the conceptual projection of a Raven bot in CDS. They are implemented game-side.

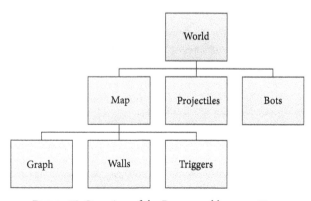

FIGURE 15: Overview of the Raven world composition.

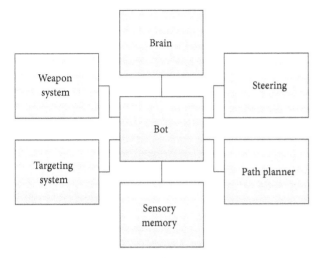

FIGURE 16: Overview of the Raven bot AI structure. Concrete actions such as firing a weapon or applying a steering force are taken by the green modules.

On the AI side, a CptMvAgent2D represents a controllable object and therefore the class comes with a controller interface. For an AI to be recognized as a valid controller by the game, it has to implement this interface. The interface is shown in Algorithm 10. It includes six functions. The KilledBy_Handler function is called whenever a bot is killed by an opponent and allows the controller to retrieve information about the killer. The HeardSound_Handler function is called when a bot hears a gunshot and can be used by the AI to find the origin of the sound. The BotRemoved_Handler function is called when a player removes a bot from the game via the main menu and can be used to notify other bots that the removed bot no longer exists. The Suspend and Resume functions serve to temporarily disable the controller when a bot is possessed by the player. The last Update function is used to allow the AI to update its state every game cycle.

Functionally, the AI in Graven is the same as the original Raven AI. It slightly differs in its structure, however. In Raven, the Raven_WeaponSystem class serves as a weapon inventory and handles weapon switching and also aiming and shooting, whereas weapon selection and aiming and shooting are separated in Graven. The central AI module through which other AI modules interact is the CptBot class. It resembles the original Raven_Bot class, though there are two significant differences. One, it interacts solely with the conceptual layer instead of the game. Two, it does not host any game state data such as current position and velocity, which is found in the CptMvAgent2D it controls. The AI state is thus clearly separated from the game state.

7.5. Creating a Conceptual View. The following process is used to synchronize the conceptual view with the Raven game state. For each class representing an object in the Raven game which has some projection in the CDS, a pointer to an object of the corresponding conceptual class is added to its data members. Then, following each statement that directly

modifies a member of the class (without calling a function), a second operation is added to update the conceptual object accordingly. The conceptual object is created at the beginning of the class constructor and destroyed at the end of its destructor. By confining the synchronization code of an object to its class, its synchronization is done only once and never mixed with that of other objects. This idea is illustrated in Algorithm 11.

One problem with this technique is that it cannot be used directly with virtual classes because, even if they have corresponding conceptual classes, they do not represent actual objects with an independent projection in the CDS. The projection of a virtual class only exists as a part of the projection of a concrete class (i.e., a conceptual concrete class) and can only be accessed through this conceptual concrete class. A remedy for this problem is using a pure virtual getter implemented by its concrete subclasses, as shown in Algorithm 12. This involves another problem however, since virtual functions cannot be called in the constructor. (In C++, the virtual table of an object is only initialized after its construction is complete.) This is solved by moving the synchronization code in the constructor into an additional sync function for each class. This applies even to concrete classes. The sync function in a subclass always starts by calling the sync function of its superclass, ensuring that the synchronization code of an object remains confined within its class definition. A call to the sync function is added immediately after the creation of a conceptual object in the constructor of a concrete class, effectively executing the synchronization code of all its superclass constructors.

In order to properly synchronize certain template classes in Raven, it is necessary to use additional data type parameters to accommodate conceptual data types associated with the base parameters. For example, the Trigger_Respawning template class in Raven takes an entity type parameter which determines the type of game object that can activate the trigger. The class Trigger_WeaponGiver which extends Trigger_Respawning uses a Raven_Bot as parameter. However, its conceptual projection, a CptTrigger WeaponGiver, requires a CptMvAgent2D parameter. For this reason, the Trigger_Respawning class takes two parameters in Graven, one for the game data type and one for the corresponding conceptual data type.

7.6. Registering the Conceptual AI. The CptBot class implements the CptMvAgent2D_Controller interface and provides the AI functionality of the original Raven. The CptMvAgent2D class defines an AddController function which can be used by the game to register CptMvAgent2D_Controller objects with its instances. All registered controllers are updated and notified through the CptMvAgent2D instance. This is shown in Algorithm 13.

A DMController module can be used to instantiate and register CptBot objects without exposing the class to the game. Algorithm 14 shows how a controller is registered in the constructor of the Raven_Bot class. After creating and synchronizing a corresponding CptMvAgent2D, the RegisterDMController function is used to relegate the control of the bot to the conceptual AI.

```
class Raven_Weapon
{
    ...
    //this discharges a projectile from the weapon at the given target position (provided
        the weapon is ready to be discharged... every weapon has its own rate of fire)
    virtual void ShootAt(Vector2D pos) = 0;
    void IncrementRounds(int num)
    {
        m_iNumRoundsLeft += num;
        Clamp(m_iNumRoundsLeft, 0, m_iMaxRoundsCarried);
        //Synchronize rounds in CDS
        GetCptWeapon()->SetNumRoundsLeft(m_iNumRoundsLeft);
    }
    ...
};
class CptWeapon
{
    ...
    //Removed
    //virtual void ShootAt(Vector2D pos) = 0;
    void SetNumRoundsLeft(int n)
    {
        m_iNumRoundsLeft = n;
    }
    ...
};
```

ALGORITHM 8: Modifications in the conceptual copy of a Raven class. No game behavior is defined in CDS, which hosts nothing more than a projection of the game state.

```
//Applies a steering force to a bot
void ApplyForce(int agent_id, Vector2D force);
//Rotates the facing direction of a bot
void RotateToward(int agent_id, Vector2D position);
//Switches the equipped weapon of a bot
void EquipWeapon(int agent_id, int weapon_type);
//Fires the equipped weapon of a bot
void ShootAt(int agent_id, Vector2D position);
```

ALGORITHM 9: Conceptual controls used by the AI in Graven. In order, these are used by the conceptual AI to send commands to apply a steering force to a bot, to rotate a bot toward a certain position, to switch the currently equipped weapon of a bot, and to fire a bot's weapon at a given position. Together, these conceptual controls are sufficient to replicate the intricate behavior from the original code.

8. Using the Graven Targeting AI in StarCraft

8.1. Description. Following the Graven experiment which produced a limited CF prototype as well as a number of conceptual AI solutions, a second experiment was conducted to assess the work involved in using a simple conceptual AI solution in different games. Two games were used in this experiment, *Raven* and *StarCraft: Brood War* (BW), a real-time strategy game developed by Blizzard Entertainment. Albeit very different, these two games share a common conceptual problem, namely, target selection. Target selection in combat deals with deciding which enemy should be targeted in the presence of multiple ones. In Raven, a bot may face multiple opponents at the same time. Likewise in BW, a unit may face multiple enemy units on the battlefield.

This experiment consists in using the same solution to this targeting problem in both Raven and BW, resulting in having the exact same code drive the targeting behavior of both bots in Raven and military units in BW.

8.2. StarCraft and the Brood War API. Although BW is not open-source, hackers have long been able to tamper with the game process by breaking into its memory space. Eventually, a development framework was built on top of this hacking. The Brood War Application Programming Interface (BWAPI) [46] is an open source C++ framework which allows AI developers to create custom agents by providing them with means to access the game state and issue commands. More information regarding the features and the design of the API can be found on the project's web page.

```
class CptMvAgent2D_Controller
{
protected:
  CptMvAgent2D* m_pOwner;
public:
  virtual ~CptMvAgent2D_Controller() {}
  //Called when a bot is killed by an opponent
  virtual void KilledBy_Handler(CptMvAgent2D* attacker) = 0;
  //Called when a bot hears a gunshot
  virtual void HeardSound_Handler(CptMvAgent2D* source) = 0;
  //Called when the player removes a bot from the game
  virtual void BotRemoved_Handler(CptMvAgent2D* bot) = 0;
  //Called when the player takes control of a bot
  virtual void Suspend() = 0;
  //Called when the player hands back control to a bot
  virtual void Resume() = 0;
  //Called every game update cycle
  virtual void Update() = 0;
};
```

ALGORITHM 10: The controller interface of a CptMvAgent2D. These functions are used by the CptMvAgent2D class to relay events to the AI.

```
void Raven_Bot::Spawn(Vector2D pos)
{
  ...
  //Direct modification: sync!
  m_iHealth = m_iMaxHealth;
  cpt->SetHealth(m_iHealth);
  //Function call: don't sync, already done in function definition!
  SetAlive();
  //Different class: don't sync, WeaponSystem has its own sync code!
  m_pWeaponSys->Initialize();
  ...
}
```

ALGORITHM 11: Conceptual data synchronization in Graven. Synchronization code in a class is added whenever its members are modified directly.

8.3. Targeting in Graven. The targeting system module in Graven, CptTargetingSystem, is used by the main AI module CptBot. To function, it requires another module, the sensory memory module CptSensoryMemory, which determines which enemies the bot currently senses. The targeting system works by setting an internal target variable which the bot module can read to find out which enemy it should aim at.

The original AI selects targets based on their distance to the bot and prioritizes closer enemies. It was modified to instead select targets based on their health and prioritize weaker enemies, a more interesting strategy for this experiment because the default unit AI in BW also uses distance as the primary factor in target selection. The main module function is shown in Algorithm 15. The vision update function in the sensory module is shown in Algorithm 16.

8.4. Completing the Graven Conceptual Layer. In terms of conceptual view, the requirements of the targeting module

include those of its dependencies (i.e., the sensory memory module). The solution requirements can quickly be determined by looking at Algorithms 15 and 16. It requires a 2D world with the list of targetable entities that exist in it as well as a list of vision-blocking obstacles such as walls typically defined in a map. The entities must have their position, facing direction, field of view and health attributes synchronized. All of these concepts are already defined in the conceptual layer used in Graven.

In addition to those, BW involves three more concepts which are not present in Raven and which need to be defined. First, the concept of entity ownership is required to specify the player a unit belongs to. In Raven, a player is associated with a single bot. In BW, a player is associated with multiple units. Therefore, an owner property is required for units to differentiate between allies and enemies. The second concept is that of sight range. In Raven, a bot has a 180 degree field of view but its vision range is only limited by obstacles. In BW, a unit has a 360 degree field of view but can only

```
class MovingEntity: public BaseGameEntity
{
  ...
  //Virtual accessor – Retrieves the conceptual projection of this entity
  virtual CptMvEntity2D* GetCptMvEntity2D() const = 0;
  ...
  void SetVelocity(const Vector2D & NewVel)
  {
    m_vVelocity = NewVel;
    //Velocity changed, update conceptual data
    GetCptMvEntity2D()->SetVelocity(m_vVelocity);
  }
  ...
}
class Raven_Bot: public MovingEntity
{
protected:
  //The conceptual projection
  CptMvAgent2D* cpt;
  ...
public:
  //Returns the entire conceptual projection of this bot
  CptMvAgent2D* GetCptMvAgent2D() const { return cpt; }
  //Returns the conceptual projection of the MovingEntity part of this bot
  CptMvEntity2D* GetCptMvEntity2D() const { return cpt; }
  //Returns the conceptual projection of the BaseGameEntity part of this bot
  CptEntity2D* GetCptEntity2D() const { return cpt; }
  ...
}
```

ALGORITHM 12: Synchronization with virtual classes. The virtual class MovingEntity uses a pure virtual getter implemented by its concrete subclass Raven_Bot for its synchronization code.

```
class CptMvAgent2D: public CptMvEntity2D
{
private:
  //List of registered controllers
  std::list<CptMvAgent2D_Controller*> controllers;
  ...
public:
  //Registers a new controller
  void AddController(CptMvAgent2D_Controller* c)
  {
    controllers.push_back(c);
  }
  //Notifies controllers that a bot has been removed from the game
  void BotRemoved(CptMvAgent2D* bot)
  {
    std::list<CptMvAgent2D_Controller*>::iterator it;
    for (it = controllers.begin(); it != controllers.end(); ++it)
    {
      (*it)->BotRemoved_Handler(bot);
    }
  }
  ...
}
```

ALGORITHM 13: Controller management in the CptMvAgent2D class.

```
Raven_Bot::Raven_Bot(Raven_Game* world,Vector2D pos):
        ...
{
    //Create the conceptual projection
    cpt = new CptMvAgent2D(world->GetCptWorld2D());
    //Synchronize initialization
    sync();
    ...
    //Instantiate and register a DMController
    RegisterDMController(cpt);
}
```

ALGORITHM 14: Conceptual AI registration in Graven. The `RegisterDMController` function is defined in the `DMController` module and is used to instantiate the `CptBot` class.

```
void CptTargetingSystem::Update()
{
    int LowestHPSoFar = MaxInt;
    m_pCurrentTarget = 0;
    //grab a list of all the opponents the owner can sense
    std::list<CptMvAgent2D*> SensedBots;
    SensedBots = m_pOwner->GetSensoryMem()->GetListOfRecentlySensedOpponents();
    std::list<CptMvAgent2D*>::const_iterator curBot = SensedBots.begin();
    for (curBot; curBot != SensedBots.end(); ++curBot)
    {
        //make sure the bot is alive and that it is not the owner
        if ((*curBot)->isAlive() && (*curBot != m_pOwner->GetAgent()))
        {
            int hp = (*curBot)->Health();
            if (hp < LowestHPSoFar)
            {
                LowestHPSoFar = hp;
                m_pCurrentTarget = *curBot;
            }
        }
    }
}
```

ALGORITHM 15: Modified target selection in Graven. Health is compared instead of distance.

see up to a certain radius. A sight range property is thus required. The third concept is the plane. The world in BW is two-dimensional but there are ground and air units. Ground units are not always able to attack air units and vice versa. A property to indicate the plane in which a unit exists and which planes it can target is thus needed. As a result, five new members are added to the CptMvAgent2D class, a player ID, a sight range, a plane flag, and two plane reach flags. Note that the sensory memory module is slightly modified to take into account this information, though this has no impact on its functionality in Raven.

As far as conceptual controls are concerned, the aiming and shooting controls in Graven are not necessary for BW. When a unit in BW is given an order to attack another unit, the target only needs to be within firing range to be automatically attacked continuously. Only one conceptual control, an attack command, is required for this experiment and added to the conceptual framework.

8.5. Integrating the Targeting AI in StarCraft. In order to use the targeting AI from Graven in BW, there are a few tasks that need to be completed. These are

(1) adding code to the game to maintain in memory a conceptual view including the elements mentioned above,

(2) implementing the attack conceptual control,

(3) and creating an AI solution which makes use of the targeting AI to control units.

8.5.1. Conceptual View. The conceptual view is maintained using 3 callback functions provided by the BWAPI, the onStart function which is called at the beginning of a BW game, the onEnd function which is called at the end of the game and the onFrame function which is called every game frame. The code added in each of these functions is shown

```
void CptSensoryMemory::UpdateVision()
{
    //for each bot in the world test to see if it is visible to the owner of this class
    const std::list<CptMvAgent2D* > & bots = m_pOwner->GetWorld()->GetAllBots();
    std::list<CptMvAgent2D* >::const_iterator curBot;
    for (curBot = bots.begin(); curBot != bots.end(); ++curBot)
    {
        //make sure the bot being examined is not this bot
        if (m_pOwner->GetAgent() != *curBot)
        {
            //make sure it is part of the memory map
            MakeNewRecordIfNotAlreadyPresent(*curBot);
            //get a reference to this bot's data
            CptMemoryRecord & info = m_MemoryMap[*curBot];
            //test if there is LOS between bots
            if (m_pOwner->GetWorld()->isLOSOkay(m_pOwner->GetAgent()->Pos(), (*curBot)->Pos()))
            {
                info.bShootable = true;
                //test if the bot is within FOV
                if (isSecondInFOVOfFirst(m_pOwner->GetAgent()->Pos(),
                        m_pOwner->GetAgent()->Facing(),
                        (*curBot)->Pos(), m_pOwner->GetAgent()->FieldOfView()))
                {
                    info.fTimeLastSensed = Clock->GetCurrentTime();
                    info.vLastSensedPosition = (*curBot)->Pos();
                    info.fTimeLastVisible = Clock->GetCurrentTime();
                    if (info.bWithinFOV == false)
                    {
                        info.bWithinFOV = true;
                        info.fTimeBecameVisible = info.fTimeLastSensed;
                    }
                }
                else
                {
                    info.bWithinFOV = false;
                }
            }
            else
            {
                info.bShootable = false;
                info.bWithinFOV = false;
            }
        }
    }//next bot
}
```

ALGORITHM 16: Vision update in the Graven sensory memory module.

in Algorithms 17, 18, and 19, respectively. The syncUnit function is shown in Algorithms 20.

Because the source code of BW is not available, the synchronization process is different from the one used in the Graven experiment. Every game cycle, the game state is scanned and new and destroyed units are added to and removed from the conceptual view and the states in CDS are synchronized with unit states in the game.

8.5.2. Conceptual Controls. The Attack conceptual control is easily implemented using the basic attack command players

can give to units in BW. The implementation is shown in Algorithms 21.

8.5.3. Conceptual AI. For units capable of attacking, an attack AI is added to the list of controllers of their projection using the RegisterDMController function. This function instantiates the CptBot class, which is similar to the one in Graven but which has been modified to only use the sensory memory and targeting system modules. The update function of the CptBot module is shown in Algorithms 22. Note that the sensory memory module only registers reachable enemy units. Allied units are ignored.

```
void GravenAIModule::onStart()
{
   ...
   //Create 2D world
   cptWorld = new CptWorld2D();
   //Add an empty map
   cptWorld->pSetMap(new CptMap2D());
   //Set map dimensions
   cptWorld->GetMap()->pSetSizeX(Broodwar->mapWidth() * 32);
   cptWorld->GetMap()->pSetSizeY(Broodwar->mapHeight() * 32);
}
```

ALGORITHM 17: Conceptual view code in the onStart callback function. Map dimensions in BW are given in build tiles, each build tile representing a 32 by 32 area.

```
void GravenAIModule::onEnd(bool isWinner)
{
   ...
   //Destroy world
   delete cptWorld;
}
```

ALGORITHM 18: Conceptual view code in the onEnd callback function. The conceptual world destructor also destroys associated objects.

8.6. Results. The same targeting AI was successfully used in both Raven and BW, as shown in Figures 17 and 18. Unsurprisingly, the CF prototype (more specifically the CptMvAgent2D class) built from Raven, a very simple 2D shooter, had to be slightly extended for this experiment. Even so, the effort required to integrate the Graven targeting AI in BW was minimal. Of course, the AI was minimal too. This shows however that the work involved in creating conceptual AI that can be used in different games does not have to grow significantly with the number of games it can be applied to and that when a conceptual problem is clearly identified, it can be solved independently of the game it appears in.

Obviously, though it may not have been the goal of the experiment, the modified unit AI performs better in combat than the original one for ranged units, since it uses a better a strategy. In the presence of enemies, the original unit AI acquires a target by randomly selecting one within firing range. The modified unit AI on the other hand selects among targets within its sight radius the one with the lowest health. Because the sight range of a ranged unit is often close to its firing range, this behavior is similar to the original one in the sense that the unit does not move to reach a target when another target that is already in firing range exists. The behavior is therefore close but the unit does target weak enemies first in order to reduce their firepower as fast as possible. Moreover, setting a short memory span in the CptSensoryMemory class prevents units from remembering runaway targets for too long and starting to look for them. This helps maintain similarity between the original and modified unit AI. That way, the original

TABLE 1: Units lost in each battle for each group with the modified and original unit AI.

Battle	1	2	3	4	5	6	7	8	9	10
Units lost										
Modified AI	3	3	1	3	2	3	3	4	4	3
Original AI	5	5	5	5	5	5	5	5	5	5

unit behavior is maintained, making it harder for players to notice any difference other than the improved targeting strategy. Needless to say, the targeting AI remains completely unchanged. Note that modifying the sensory module to pick up targets that are within firing range rather than sight range makes the strategy work for melee units as well.

The modified unit AI was tested using 10 battles of 5 Terran Ghosts versus 5 Terran Ghosts, one group being controlled by the modified unit AI and the other by the original unit AI. Ghosts are ranged ground units. The group with the modified unit AI won every battle. The number of Ghosts lost during each battle is reported in Table 1.

9. Conclusion

The main contribution of this research is an approach for the development of AI for video games based on the use of a unified conceptual framework to create a conceptual layer between the game and the AI. (The AI referred to here is game related and does not include context related AI as specified at the beginning of this work.) This approach is inspired by an interpretation of human behavior. Human players have the ability to detect analogies between games and generalize, or conceptualize, the knowledge acquired in one game and apply it in another. By conceptualizing video games and asking game developers to create conceptual views of their games using a unified framework, it becomes possible to create solutions for common conceptual problems and use them across multiple video games. Developing solutions for conceptual problems rather than specific video games means that AI design is no longer confined to the scope of individual game projects and can be more efficiently refined over time. Such conceptual AI can then serve as a core engine

```
void GravenAIModule::onFrame()
{
  ...
  //For each unit visible to the player
  Unitset units = Broodwar->getAllUnits();
  for (Unitset::iterator u = units.begin(); u != units.end(); ++u)
  {
    //Ignore neutral units which include mineral fields and critters
    if (u->getPlayer()->isNeutral())
      continue;
    //Get the projection of the unit in CDS
    CptMvAgent2D* cptUnit = dynamic_cast<CptMvAgent2D*>(cptEntityMgr->GetEntityFromID
      (u->getID()));
    //Projection found, synchronize state and update controllers
    if (cptUnit)
    {
      syncUnit(cptUnit, *u);
      cptUnit->Update();
    }
    //Projection not found, create one
    else if (u->exists() && u->isCompleted())
    {
      cptUnit = new CptMvAgent2D(cptWorld);
      syncUnit(cptUnit, *u);
      cptWorld->pAddBot(cptUnit);
      cptEntityMgr->RegisterEntity(cptUnit);
      //If the unit can attack, register the targeting AI
      if (u->getPlayer() == Broodwar->self() && u->canAttack())
      {
        RegisterDMController(cptUnit);
      }
    }
  }
  //Remove projections of units that no longer exist in the game
  std::list<CptMvAgent2D*> cptUnits = cptWorld->GetAllBots();
  for (std::list<CptMvAgent2D*>::iterator c = cptUnits.begin(); c != cptUnits.end(); ++c)
  {
    if (!Broodwar->getUnit((*c)->ID()) || !Broodwar->getUnit((*c)->ID())->exists())
    {
      cptEntityMgr->RemoveEntity(*c);
      cptWorld->pRemoveBot((*c)->ID());
    }
  }
}
```

ALGORITHM 19: Conceptual view code in the onFrame callback function. The RegisterDMController creates a CptBot, which uses the Graven targeting AI to attack enemies, and adds it to the list of controllers of the CptMvAgent2D.

for driving agents in a variety of video games which can be complemented by game developers specifically for each game. This would both reduce AI redundancy and facilitate the development of robust AI.

Such an approach can result in a number of advantages for game developers. First, it means that they no longer need to spend a lot of resources to design robust game AI unless they want to and can simply use existing AI solutions. Even though they have to add code for the creation of conceptual views, not having to worry about game AI can result in significant cuts in development time. For example, they would not even need to plan for coordination mechanisms between multiple

agents in the game. Moreover, they do not need to use conceptual AI for all tasks. They can select the problems they want to handle using conceptual AI and use regular AI for other tasks. Story and environment related AI, which this approach does not apply to, can be designed using existing tools and techniques, such as scripting engines and behavior trees, which make it easy to implement specific behavior. In addition, the continuous development of conceptual AI is likely to yield better quality solutions over time than what can be achieved through independent game projects. It may also be that clearly identifying and organizing the conceptual problems that make up the challenges offered by video games

```
void GravenAIModule::syncUnit(CptMvAgent2D* u, Unit unit)
{
  //Synchronize CptEntity2D attributes
  u->SetID(unit->getID());
  u->SetEntityType(cpttype_bot);
  u->SetScale(1);
  u->SetBRadius(MAX(unit->getType().height() / 2, unit->getType().width() / 2));
  u->SetPos(Vector2D(unit->getPosition().x, unit->getPosition().y));
  //Synchronize CptMvEntity2D attributes
  u->SetHeading(Vector2D(unit->getVelocityX(), unit->getVelocityY()));
  u->SetVelocity(Vector2D(unit->getVelocityX(), unit->getVelocityY()));
  u->SetMass(1);
  u->SetMaxSpeed(unit->getType().topSpeed());
  u->SetMaxTurnRate(unit->getType().turnRadius());
  u->SetMaxForce(unit->getType().acceleration());
  //Synchronize CptMvAgent2D attributes
  u->SetMaxHealth(unit->getType().maxHitPoints() + unit->getType().maxShields());
  u->SetHealth(unit->getHitPoints() + unit->getShields());
  u->SetScore(unit->getKillCount());
  u->SetPossessed(false);
  u->SetFieldOfView(360);
  u->Face(Vector2D(unit->getVelocityX(), unit->getVelocityY()));
  u->SetWorld(this->cptWorld);
  u->SetStatus(unit->exists() ? CptMvAgent2D::alive: CptMvAgent2D::dead);
  u->SetPlayer(unit->getPlayer()->getID());
  u->SetSightRange(unit->getType().sightRange());
  u->SetPlane(unit->isFlying());
  u->SetAirReach(unit->getType().airWeapon() != WeaponTypes::None);
  u->SetGroundReach(unit->getType().groundWeapon() != WeaponTypes::None);
}
```

ALGORITHM 20: Synchronizing conceptual unit state. Some attributes are not required by the targeting AI and only serve as illustrations.

could allow game developers to compose new challenges more easily.

Since this approach allows AI development to progress independently of video games, it could lead to the birth of a new game AI business. AI developers could compete to create the best AI solutions and commercialize them or they could collaborate to design a solid open-source AI core which would be perfected over time. Additionally, machine learning techniques would be more straightforward to apply with a unified conceptual representation of game elements. These techniques can be used to learn specialized behavior for each game which can enhance the basic generic behavior. This is similar to the way humans tune their generic experience as they learn specific data about a video game they are playing to improve their performance in that particular game.

With an open-source unified conceptual framework, incentive for both game developers and AI developers to contribute to the development of the framework and the conceptualization of video games would exist. AI developers would benefit from a better conceptual framework because it would help factor AI better and allow more efficient AI development, resulting in better quality AI which benefits game developers directly when they integrate it in their games to create smarter, more challenging and more realistic agents.

Because the conceptual layer constitutes a sort of middleware, a new version of the conceptual framework may not be compatible with AI developed prior to its update. Even if it is, legacy AI may require an update in order to benefit from the improved conceptual framework. Another disadvantage of the approach is that it requires more computational resources in order to maintain a conceptual view in memory during runtime, though this may not represent a major obstacle with mainstream hardware featuring increasingly more processing cores and system memory. Other issues may also arise from the separation of AI from video games. Indeed, game developers could lose some control over the components of their games and subsequently over the ability to balance them. For instance, it may be necessary to design new mechanisms to allow game developers to retain control over the difficulty of the game and adjust the skill level of their agents. Furthermore, although machine learning techniques such as imitation learning could benefit from a larger learning set as a unified conceptual representation would give them access to data from many games, they would require a translation process to project human actions into conceptual data space since, unlike AI actions, those are not conceptual. In other words, without a translation process, conceptual game states could only be linked to concrete game actions.

Though an implementation of the approach was presented to illustrate some applications, alternative implementations can easily be imagined. For example, even if the AI code was compiled alongside the game code in Graven, it

```
void Attack(int agent_id, int target_id)
{
  Unit u = Broodwar->getUnit(agent_id);
  Unit v = Broodwar->getUnit(target_id);
  // Don't attack under explicit move orders
  if (u->getOrder().getID() == Orders::Move)
    return;
  // Already attacking that target
  if (u->getLastCommand().getTarget() != NULL && u->
      getLastCommand().getTarget()->getID() == target_id)
    return;
  if (v->getType().isFlyer())
  {
    if (u->getType().airWeapon() != WeaponTypes::None)
      u->attack(v);
    return;
  }
  else
  {
    if (u->getType().groundWeapon() != WeaponTypes::None && u->exists())
      u->attack(v);
    return;
  }
}
```

ALGORITHM 21: Implementation of the `Attack` conceptual control in BW. Because the targeting AI only selects targets the unit can attack, the test to see whether the unit is flying could be discarded.

```
void CptBot::Update()
{
  //if the bot is under AI control but not scripted
  if (!GetAgent()->isPossessed())
  {
    //examine all the opponents in the bots sensory memory and select one
    //to be the current target
    if (m_pTargetSelectionRegulator->isReady())
    {
      m_pTargSys->Update();
    }
    //update the sensory memory with any visual stimulus
    if (m_pVisionUpdateRegulator->isReady())
    {
      m_pSensoryMem->UpdateVision();
    }
    //Attack
    if (m_pAttackRegulator->isReady() && m_pTargSys->isTargetPresent())
    {
      Attack(m_pOwner->ID(), m_pTargSys->GetTarget()->ID());
    }
  }
}
```

ALGORITHM 22: The update function of the `CptBot` class. The function uses the `Attack` conceptual control to issue commands to the units in the game.

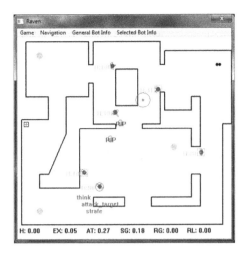

FIGURE 17: Raven with the modified targeting AI. The selected bot can be seen aiming at the enemy with low health (31), instead of the one close to it.

FIGURE 18: StarCraft: Brood War with the modified unit AI. The selected Goliaths are prioritizing Dragoons instead of the Archons in front of them because of their lower health.

was designed to be independent. AI modules can be compiled independently from game code and either linked to the game statically or dynamically loaded at runtime. An implementation using the latter option would benefit from easier testing of different AI solutions. When deployed, it would allow players to switch between different solutions too. This may not be desirable however, as untested solutions may result in unexpected behavior. A security mechanism could be added to prevent the game from loading unverified AI modules.

Perhaps the most exciting extension to this research would be a study of the world of conceptual problems found in video games. Both the video game industry and the scientific community would benefit from tools for describing and organizing problems using a set of convenient standards, perhaps a bit like game design patterns. This would help better categorize and hierarchically structure problems and result in a clearer view and understanding of the complexity of video games.

References

[1] The NetBSD Foundation, "Portability and supported hardware platforms," http://netbsd.org/about/portability.html.

[2] Microsoft, Windows NT Hardware Abstraction Layer (HAL), http://support.microsoft.com/kb/99588.

[3] A. Nareyek, N. Combs, B. Karlsson, S. Mesdaghi, and I. Wilson, "The 2003 report of the IGDA's artificial intelligence interface standards committee," Tech. Rep., International Game Developers Association, 2003, http://www.igda.org/ai/report-2003/report-2003.html, http://archive.org/web/.

[4] A. Nareyek, N. Combs, B. Karlsson, S. Mesdaghi, and I. Wilson, "The 2004 report of the IGDA's artificial intelligence interface standards committee," Tech. Rep., International Game Developers Association, 2004, http://www.igda.org/ai/report-2004/report-2004.html.

[5] A. Nareyek, N. Combs, B. Karlsson, S. Mesdaghi, and I. Wilson, "The 2005 report of the IGDA's artificial intelligence interface standards committee," Tech. Rep., International Game Developers Association, 2005, http://www.igda.org/ai/report-2005/report-2005.html, http://archive.org/web/.

[6] B. Yue and P. de Byl, "The state of the art in game AI standardisation," in Proceedings of the 2006 International Conference on Game Research and Development, pp. 41–46, Murdoch University., 2006.

[7] B. F. F. Karlsson, "Issues and approaches in artificial intelligence middleware development for digital games and entertainment products," CEP 50740:540, 2003.

[8] C. Berndt, I. Watson, and H. Guesgen, "OASIS: an open AI standard interface specification to support reasoning, representation and learning in computer games," in Proceedings of the Workshop on Reasoning, Representation, and Learning in Computer Games (IJCAI '05), pp. 19–24, 2005.

[9] Unity Technologies, "Unity—Game Engine," http://unity3d.com/.

[10] Epic Games, Unreal Engine Technology — Home, https://www.unrealengine.com/.

[11] Crytek, CRYENGINE: The complete solution for next generation game development by Crytek, http://cryengine.com/.

[12] Havok, http://www.havok.com/.

[13] B. Kreimeier, The case for game design patterns, 2002, http://www.gamasutra.com/view/feature/132649/the_case_for_game_design_patterns.php?print=1.

[14] S. Björk, L. Sus, and H. Jussi, "Game design patterns," in Proceedings of the Level Up-1st International Digital Games Research Conference, Utrecht, The Netherlands, November 2003.

[15] S. Björk and J. Holopainen, "Describing games—an interaction-centric structural framework," in Level Up: Proceedings of Digital Games Research Conference, 2003.

[16] C. M. Olsson, S. Björk, and S. Dahlskog, "The conceptual relationship model: understanding patterns and mechanics in game design," in Proceedings of the DiGRA International Conference (DiGRA '14), 2014.

[17] A. B. Loyall and J. Bates, "Hap: a reactive, adaptive architecture for agents," Tech. Rep. CMU-CS-97-123, Carnegie Mellon University, School of Computer Science, 1991.

[18] M. Mateas and A. Stern, "A behavior language for story-based believable agents," IEEE Intelligent Systems and Their Applications, vol. 17, no. 4, pp. 39–47, 2002.

[19] M. Mateas and A. Stern, "A behavior language: joint action and behavioral idioms," in Life-Like Characters, Cognitive Technologies, pp. 135–161, Springer, Berlin, Germany, 2004.

[20] J. D. Funge, "Making them behave: cognitive models for computer animation," 1998.

[21] J. Funge, X. Tu, and D. Terzopoulos, "Cognitive modeling: knowledge, reasoning and planning for intelligent characters," in *Proceedings of the 26th Annual Conference on Computer Graphics and Interactive Techniques*, pp. 29–38, ACM Press/Addison-Wesley, 1999.

[22] J. Funge, "Representing knowledge within the situation calculus using interval-valued epistemic fluents," *Reliable Computing*, vol. 5, no. 1, pp. 35–61, 1999.

[23] J. Orkin, "Symbolic representation of game world state: toward real-time planning in games," in *Proceedings of the AAAI Workshop on Challenges in Game Artificial Intelligence*, 2004.

[24] J. Orkin, "Agent architecture considerations for real-time planning in games," in *Proceedings of the Artificial Intelligence and Interactive Digital Entertainment (AIIDE '05)*, pp. 105–110, 2005.

[25] E. F. Anderson, "Scripting behaviour—towards a new language for making NPCs act intelligently," in *Proceedings of the zfxCON05 2nd Conference on Game Development*, 2005.

[26] E. F. Anderson, "SEAL—a simple entity annotation language," in *Proccedings of zfxCON05-2nd Conference on Game Development*, pp. 70–73, Stefan Zerbst, Braunschweig, Germany, 2005.

[27] E. F. Anderson, "Scripted smarts in an intelligent virtual environment," in *Proceedings of the Conference on Future Play: Research, Play, Share*, pp. 185–188, ACM, 2008.

[28] D. C. Cheng and R. Thawonmas, "Case-based plan recognition for real-time strategy games," in *Proceedings of the 5th International Conference on Computer Games: Artificial Intelligence, Design and Education (CGAIDE '04)*, pp. 36–40, 2004.

[29] D. W. Aha, M. Molineaux, and M. J. V. Ponsen, "Learning to win: case-based plan selection in a real-time strategy game," in *Proceedings of the 6th International Conference on Case-Based Reasoning (ICCBR '05)*, pp. 5–20, August 2005.

[30] S. Ontañón, K. Mishra, N. Sugandh, and A. Ram, "Case-based planning and execution for real-time strategy games," in *Case-Based Reasoning Research and Development: 7th International Conference on Case-Based Reasoning, ICCBR 2007 Belfast, Northern Ireland, UK, August 13–16, 2007 Proceedings*, vol. 4626, pp. 164–178, Springer, Berlin, Germany, 2007.

[31] B. Weber and M. Mateas, "Conceptual neighborhoods for retrieval in case-based reasoning," in *Proceedings of the 8th International Conference on Case-Based Reasoning (ICCBR '09)*, pp. 343–357, 2009.

[32] B. G. Weber and M. Mateas, "Case-based reasoning for build order in real-time strategy games," in *Proceedings of the 5th Artificial Intelligence and Interactive Digital Entertainment Conference (AIIDE '09)*, pp. 106–111, October 2009.

[33] M. Sharma, M. Holmes, J. Santamaria, A. Irani, C. Isbell, and A. Ram, "Transfer learning in real-time strategy games using hybrid CBR/RL," in *Proceedings of the 20th International Joint Conference on Artificial Intelligence (IJCAI '07)*, pp. 1041–1046, January 2007.

[34] S. Lee-Urban, H. Muñoz-Avila, A. Parker, U. Kuter, and D. Nau, "Transfer learning of hierarchical task-network planning methods in a real-time strategy game," in *Proceedings of the 17th International Conference on Automated Planning & Scheduling (ICAPS '07), Workshop on AI Planning and Learning (AIPL)*, 2007.

[35] D. Shapiro, T. Könik, and P. O'Rorke, "Achieving far transfer in an integrated cognitive architecture," in *Proceedings of the 23rd National Conference on Artificial Intelligence (AAAI '08)*, pp. 1325–1330, July 2008.

[36] M. Buckland, *Programming Game AI by Example*, Jones & Bartlett Learning, 2004.

[37] B. Schwab, *AI Game Engine Programming*, Cengage Learning, 2008.

[38] I. Millington and J. Funge, *Artificial Intelligence for Games*, CRC Press, Boca Raton, Fla, USA, 2009.

[39] S. Russel and P. Norvig, *Artificial Intelligence: A Modern Approach*, Prentice Hall, 2009.

[40] S. Rabin, *AI Game Programming Wisdom*, Charles River Media, 2002.

[41] S. Rabin, *AI Game Programming Wisdom 2*, Cengage Learning, 2003.

[42] S. Rabin, *AI Game Programming Wisdom 3*, Cengage Learning, Boston, Mass, USA, 2006.

[43] S. Rabin, *AI Game Programming Wisdom 4*, Charles River Media Group, 2008.

[44] R. Straatman and A. Beij, "Killzone's AI: dynamic procedural combat tactics," in *Proceedings of the Game Developers Conference*, 2005.

[45] D. Pottinger, "Implementing coordinated movement," *Game Developer Magazine*, pp. 48–58, 1999.

[46] bwapi—An API for interacting with Starcraft: Broodwar (1.16.1)—Google Project Hosting, https://code.google.com/p/bwapi/.

Using the Revised Bloom Taxonomy to Analyze Psychotherapeutic Games

Priscilla Haring ⓘ,[1] **Harald Warmelink,**[2] **Marilla Valente,**[3] **and Christian Roth ⓘ**[4]

[1]*Media psychology, Amsterdam, Netherlands*
[2]*NHTV Breda University of Applied Sciences, Netherlands*
[3]*Dutch Game Garden, Netherlands*
[4]*HKU University of the Arts, Utrecht, Netherlands*

Correspondence should be addressed to Priscilla Haring; priscillaharing@hotmail.com

Academic Editor: Hock S. Seah

Most of the scientific literature on computer games aimed at offering or aiding in psychotherapy provides little information on the relationship between the game's design and the player's cognitive processes. This article investigates the use of Bloom's taxonomy in describing a psychotherapeutic game in terms of knowledge level and cognitive processing. It introduces the Revised Bloom Taxonomy and applies this to five psychotherapeutic games (Personal Investigator, Treasure Hunt, Ricky and the Spider, Moodbot, and SuperBetter) in a two-round procedure. In the first round consensus was reached on the Player Actions with Learning Objectives (PALOs) in each game. The second round sought to determine what level of knowledge and cognitive processing can be attributed to the PALOs by placing them in the taxonomy. Our low intercoder reliability in the second round indicates that Bloom's Revised Taxonomy is not suitable to compare and contrast content between games.

1. Introduction

Over the past decade we have observed the emergence of a modest amount of psychotherapeutic games. With the term psychotherapeutic games, we refer to computer games aimed at offering or aiding in therapy for any psychological disorders or conditions (most often the precursors of depression or anxiety). The use of psychotherapeutic board games as well as existing entertainment computer games during therapy is already widely regarded as good practice in many situations [1]. Innovative game-based therapy has shown a higher chance of engaging younger target audiences than traditional conversational and "paper-based" methods [2]. It is therefore surprising to find only limited information concerning psychotherapeutic videogames in the scientific literature relating to design and content [2, 3]. Horne-Moyer et al. focused their review on high-order design characteristics (games for health-related behaviours or individual therapy, versus games for entertainment used in individual or group therapy) and their general effectiveness [4]. Fleming et al. offered a more comprehensive review but kept their review of the games' designs still quite basic by only briefly commenting on each game's "rule, goals and game objectives"; "outcomes and feedback to the user"; "conflict, competition, challenge or opposition"; "interaction"; and "representation or story" [5].

A lack of insight into the design intricacies, gameplay, and their cognitive processes is problematic. It makes it hard to compare content across several games and thus discuss the state of the art of this field amongst designers, researchers, and practitioners beyond any specific game. Finally, having insight into what cognitive processes are addressed within gameplay would make it easier to spot missed opportunities for effective psychotherapeutic game design.

We set out to test the application of an analytical tool for labelling the cognitive elements of a psychotherapeutic game. We first present the tool itself—the Revised Bloom Taxonomy—and describe our approach in using this taxonomy for the analysis of five psychotherapeutic games: Personal Investigator, Treasure Hunt, Ricky and the Spider, Moodbot, and SuperBetter. We evaluated the content of these games independently, which allowed us to perform an intercoder reliability analysis and rigorously evaluate the reliability of applying the taxonomy. We conclude with a critique on Bloom's Revised Taxonomy, answers to our three research questions, and limitations of our own approach.

This paper builds on an earlier exploration of using Bloom's Revised Taxonomy as an analytical framework to identify whether psychotherapeutic games include metacognition in their games [6]. From this earlier exploration we hypothesized that Bloom's Revised Taxonomy might be useful in different ways. This paper seeks to extend this earlier work by testing the robustness of Bloom's Revised Taxonomy as an analytical framework. We wish to explore whether the framework will be useful to designers, researchers, and psychologists using psychotherapeutic games. Thus our research questions are as follows:

(1) For designers: can Bloom's Revised Taxonomy be used as a checklist during the design of a psychotherapeutic game?

(2) For researchers: can Bloom's Revised Taxonomy allow researchers to make a more objective description of game content and allow for comparisons across psychotherapeutic games?

(3) For psychologists: can Bloom's Revised Taxonomy support psychologists in making a more informed choice concerning psychotherapeutic games that might be included in their therapy?

2. Methodology

2.1. Choosing Bloom's Revised Taxonomy. Bloom's Revised Taxonomy has already been considered as the "most popular cognitive approach to Serious Game evaluation" [7]. Bloom's original taxonomy [8] stems from the field of education and consisted of categories for Knowledge, Comprehension, Application, Analysis, Synthesis, and Evaluation. Bloom's original taxonomy was a popular tool for objectives-based evaluation as it allowed for a high level of detail when stating learning objectives [9].

However, the original taxonomy was criticized resulting in various revisions by different authors. See de Kock, Sleegers, and Voeten for a classification of learning environments, containing reviews of the revisions [10]. The revision of Anderson et al. [11] as well as Pintrich [12] improves the original taxonomy by including the category of metacognition. They also distinguish between two dimensions: a Knowledge dimension and a Cognitive Process dimension. We feel the inclusion of the metacognition knowledge level reflects the ongoing insight in the field of psychotherapy where Cognitive Behavioural Therapy (CBT) is currently advancing into its "third wave." The first wave of CBT started in the 1950s and applied classical conditioning and operant learning. The second wave applied information processing and brought CBT to its current worldwide status. Now, a third wave of psychotherapies is developing "…a heterogeneous group of treatments, including acceptance and commitment treatment, behavioural activation, cognitive behavioural analysis system of psychotherapy, dialectical behavioural therapy, metacognitive therapy, mindfulness-based cognitive therapy and schema therapy" [13]. These

three waves in CBT can be seen to move up along both dimensions of our taxonomy. Different therapy forms in CBT's third wave are aimed at the metacognitive level and include all the cognitive processing steps up to and including Creation as part of their treatment.

By applying Bloom's Revised Taxonomy to analyze the content of psychotherapeutic games, we are approaching these games as educational content. We see all therapeutic interaction as part of a learning process; often knowledge is to be acquired, emotions are revised, and behaviour is changed during psychotherapy.

2.2. Bloom's Revised Taxonomy. Bloom's revised taxonomy consists of two dimensions with several levels each. The levels within the dimensions have a hierarchical nature, meaning that every higher level presupposes the presence of the lower levels.

On the knowledge dimension, the taxonomy distinguishes between the following levels:

(1) Factual Knowledge: the basic elements that students must know to be acquainted with a discipline or solve problems in it.

  (a) Knowledge of terminology

  (b) Knowledge of specific details and elements

(2) Conceptual Knowledge: the interrelationships between the basic elements within a larger structure that enable them to function together.

  (a) Knowledge of classifications and categories

  (b) Knowledge of principles and generalizations

  (c) Knowledge of theories, models, and structures

(3) Procedural Knowledge: how to do something, methods of inquiry, and criteria for using skills, algorithms, techniques, and methods.

  (a) Knowledge of subject-specific skills and algorithms

  (b) Knowledge of subject-specific techniques and methods

  (c) Knowledge of criteria for determining when to use appropriate procedures

(4) Metacognitive Knowledge: knowledge of cognition in general as well as awareness and knowledge of one's own cognition.

  (a) Strategic knowledge

  (b) Knowledge about cognitive tasks, including appropriate contextual and conditional knowledge

  (c) Self-knowledge

On the cognitive process dimension, the taxonomy distinguishes between the following levels:

TABLE 1: Taxonomy Table.

The Cognitive Process Dimension						
The Knowledge Dimension	(1) Remember	(2) Understand	(3) Apply	(4) Analyze	(5) Evaluate	(6) Create
(A) Factual Knowledge						
(B) Conceptual Knowledge						
(C) Procedural Knowledge						
(D) Metacognitive Knowledge						

(1) Remember: retrieving (recognizing, recalling) relevant knowledge from long-term memory.

(2) Understand: determining (interpreting, exemplifying, classifying, summarizing, inferring, comparing, and explaining) the meaning of instructional messages, including oral, written, and graphic communication.

(3) Apply: carrying out (executing) or using (implementing) a procedure in a given situation.

(4) Analyze: breaking material into its constituent parts and detecting how the parts relate to one another and to an overall structure or purpose (differentiating, organizing, and attributing).

(5) Evaluate: making judgments (checking, critiquing) based on criteria and standards.

(6) Create: putting elements together (generating, planning, and producing) to form a novel, coherent whole or make an original product.

Seen together these two dimensions can be visualized in the Taxonomy (Table 1) [14].

2.3. Five Psychotherapeutic Games. We applied the Revised Bloom Taxonomy to five psychotherapeutic games: Personal Investigator, Treasure Hunt, Ricky and the Spider, Moodbot, and SuperBetter. These five games have been specifically selected, as they have been published in scientific journals and are explained in sufficient detail for us to perform an analysis [15–20]. We wanted to perform an analysis that could exist outside of the game—not playing the game ourselves or observing the gameplay of the intended players. This approach allows us to compare games by not starting from the individual perspective—creating more bias—as well as providing a very practical limitation in research effort. Our approach is intended to be performed based on the (design) description of the game content, preferably including the goals of the game designers and/or the therapeutic goals the game content is based on.

2.4. First Round of Analysis. In order to try and answer our three research questions we provide a robust measurement that might support designers and can be used to compare and contrast game content by both researchers and psychologists. In this paper we investigate the application of Bloom's revised taxonomy by going through the process of applying it and looking for intercoder reliability. Our process started with the following steps:

(1) Use coders with a background in psychology and (serious) game design.

(2) Select and read literature concerning Bloom's revised taxonomy.

(3) Select and read literature concerning the psychotherapeutic games.

(4) Provide instruction on applying the taxonomy.

(5) Apply the taxonomy individually.

(6) Present and discuss results at a face-to-face intercoder meeting.

All four authors of this paper have backgrounds in psychology and/or social science, with experience in game research, in game design, and in education. We started by independently reading the selected literature describing the taxonomy [6, 11, 14] and the selected literature describing our five psychotherapeutic games [15–20]. The instructions provided to classify the games consisted of three steps per game:

(1) Describe the possible actions by the player needed to proceed in the game.

(2) Place actions in the taxonomy and provide a short argument why you place it there. Please note any reservations, questions, and comments that arise while you do this.

(3) Create one Taxonomy Table per game.

All coders independently went through these three steps.

When we presented the results to each other in a face-to-face meeting, it became evident that our process had yielded wildly different results concerning the identified player actions and their respective placement in the Taxonomy Table. Our subsequent discussion focused on elaborating and clarifying the diverse interpretations of the categories in Bloom's Revised Taxonomy. Our biggest discrepancy concerned the knowledge dimension, especially the difference in classifying an action as conceptual, procedural, or metacognitive knowledge. For the categories in the cognitive process dimension we found it easier to align our interpretations by using concrete examples. We reaffirmed that any discussion of the cognitive processing or knowledge levels can only discuss the lower bound, i.e., the minimal requirement in knowledge acquisition or application to fulfil what the game is asking of the player. Every assignment in a game could be approached from a higher knowledge level, processed with a deeper understanding and a more overt strategy than where we allocated them in the Taxonomy Table. There is no way of knowing this upper bound without measuring every individual during gameplay. We judged the described game content for what knowledge levels and processes were necessary (lower bound) to fulfil its assignment and can therefore be predicted. In our discussion, this perspective was an important anchoring necessary to make any judgement.

There was also discussion on the interpretation of "self-knowledge" as it might be argued that the subject of therapy is the "self" and therefore all therapeutic interactions deal with self-knowledge. To resolve this, we turned to the description of "metacognitive knowledge is knowledge of [one's own] cognition and about oneself in relation to various subject matters..." [11]. The "knowledge of cognition" here goes beyond the identification of feelings and thoughts that is core to the CBT approach, where the patient is made an observer of his/her own (internal) behaviours. This makes the minimal requirement for most CBT self-observation and not necessarily self-knowledge as meant in the metacognitive definition. We concluded that questions concerning experiences and thoughts might be placed in the Taxonomy Table at the Factual Knowledge level, if the questions do not go beyond self-observation.

2.5. Second Round of Analysis. We did not use the results in the Taxonomy Tables of this first round of assessment for further analysis. To see if Bloom's Revised Taxonomy can be used as a basis for comparison, intercoder reliability must be established. If we can establish that the same data will be coded in the same way by different observers, we can be confident that objective comparisons can be made. In order to perform any intercoder reliability analysis, we had to accumulate an agreed upon list with the same amount of player actions per game.

We decided to leave actions that are only necessary as part of the game literacy out of the assessment—such as retrieving a key in a game to open a game object. Overall, the activity of playing a game can be seen as belonging to Applying Process Knowledge in the Taxonomy Table "students who successfully play or operate a game are showing understanding of process and task and application of skills" [21].

In search of more homogenous way to describe game content and player actions we returned to the literature, where we found the stipulation that the taxonomy is meant as a structure for learning objectives. This provided a structured way of forming a description. Stating a learning objective requires a verb and an object, where the verb refers to the intended cognitive process and the object refers to the knowledge level that must be acquired or constructed [11]. We decided to use this verb/object structure to formulate Player Actions with a Learning Objective (PALO) and structured our consolidated list accordingly.

In our second round of assessment our process consisted of three steps:

(1) Create a consolidated list of PALOs per game.

(2) Each coder individually places the PALOs in a Taxonomy Table.

(3) Establish intercoder reliability by means of statistical analysis.

Leaving pure game actions out of the scope, merging similar descriptions through open discussion and rephrasing our descriptions of player actions lead to an agreed upon list of PALOs for every game. These PALOs were independently encoded by placing them in the Taxonomy Table and the results were shared in order to calculate intercoder reliability. We now offer a basic description and the PALOs of our five selected psychotherapeutic games.

2.6. Personal Investigator. Personal Investigator is a game based on Solution Focused Therapy (SFT) and aimed at adolescent psychological patients. Coyle et al. [15] present SFT as "a structured rather than a freeform therapeutic model," similar to CBT. The game is meant to help adolescent patients go through five different conversational steps with their therapists. These five steps are translated into five main areas in the 3D game world, where the player interacts with nonplaying characters. Initial trials proved promising, but further trials would be required to further test the game's validity [15].

The game is a single-player 3D computer game with role-playing characteristics. In the game the player becomes the personal investigator that "hunts for solutions to personal problems," keeping a notebook along the way to keep a record of the hunt and the solutions found. It is played over roughly three therapy sessions, taking just over half of the one-hour session each time. During the sessions, the player plays the game on the computer, while the therapist observes and offers explanations if requested.

After discussion a consensus of 13 PALOs was reached:

(1) The player is asked to give a detective name to his/her avatar.

(2) The player is asked to write down a problem he/she has that they would like to work on in the detective notebook.

(3) The player is asked to turn a problem into a goal they would like to achieve—this becomes the goal of the game.

(4) The player is encouraged to think about situations in which the problem that is opposite of the goal is absent or less prevalent.

(5) The player is encouraged to understand (but we do not know how) what they are doing differently when the problem is absent or less prevalent.

(6) The player is asked to set goals for repeating the behaviours that result from action 5 more often.

(7) The player is asked to write about how he/she copes with difficult situations.

(8) The player is asked to write about positive, active ways of coping that draw on their strengths and interests.

(9) The player is asked to identify people that can help achieve the goal (in real life).

(10) The player is asked to think about personal strengths and write down in the detective notebook things they are good at and past successes.

(11) The player is asked to draw the answer to the Miracle Question in their detective notebook.

(12) The player is asked to write down what they and others would think, feel, and do differently after the Miracle.

(13) The player is asked to rate on a scale of 1-10 how close they are to achieving this new future.

2.7. Treasure Hunt. Treasure Hunt is a game meant to support CBT for children with both internalizing (e.g., depression, anxiety) and externalizing (e.g. oppositional defiant disorder, conduct disorder) psychological disorders [2]. It specifically supports therapy "by offering electronic homework assignments and rehearsing basic psychoeducational parts of treatment" [16]. Players experience CBT support by going through six levels during gameplay, each corresponding to a certain step of the therapy. Again, initial tests proved promising, but further rigorous trials would be required to test the game's validity [16].

The game is a single-player, 2.5D adventure computer game on an old ship inhabited by Captain Jones, Felix the ship's cat, and Polly the ship's parrot. The captain has found an old treasure map that he needs to decipher. The player helps by completing tasks to obtain sea stars, which will eventually allow him/her and the captain to read the map. Finally, after receiving a certificate signed by the captain and the therapist and summarizing what he/she has learnt, the player will find the treasure. The player plays one level per therapy session, lasting roughly 20 minutes.

The literature provides a very limited description of play. It does provide a clear translation between the cognitive behavioural concepts and the game metaphors chosen. The paper also stipulates the importance of the guidance of the therapist and that the game is not meant as self-help but must be embedded in therapy.

After discussion a consensus of six PALOs was reached:

(1) The player receives "psycho-education" within the game. The basic psychological foundations of CBT are laid out: one's personality is made up of thoughts, feelings, and behaviour; one's thoughts influence one's feelings; four basic feelings can be distinguished, i.e., anger, fear, happiness, and sadness.

(2) The player is asked to distinguish between helpful and unhelpful thoughts in general.

(3) The player is asked to distinguish between helpful and unhelpful thoughts specific to the player.

(4) The player is asked to shoot unhelpful thoughts in the form of fish.

(5) The player is asked to replace unhelpful thoughts with helpful thoughts in the form of fish.

(6) The player is asked to summarize the gameplay on a "sailor certificate" that is then signed by Captain Jones and the therapist.

2.8. Ricky and the Spider. Ricky and the Spider is a game based on CBT for treating obsessive compulsive disorder (OCD) amongst children. Brezinka presents the game as "not a self-help game" but one that "should be played under the guidance of a therapist" [17]. The game's design foundation is a "child-friendly metaphor" for understanding both OCD and the CBT approach, thereby combining "psycho-education, externalizing techniques and exposure with response prevention." Players experience the therapy by going through eight levels during gameplay. Data gathered from therapists and patients who purchased the game revealed promising results, but, further, rigorous trials would be required to test the game's validity more convincingly [17].

The game is a single-player, 3D adventure computer game. In the game the player is confronted by Ricky the Grasshopper and Lisa the Ladybug who (without saying it explicitly) suffer from OCD and need to confront The Spider who has been making demands that they cannot meet. They ask Dr. Owl for advice, who in turn requires the player's help. There are eight levels of gameplay in which Dr. Owl, Ricky, and/or Lisa explain certain theories and tools and give certain tasks that the player must apply and fulfil. The first four levels are all psychoeducational. The latter four levels are focused on exposure tasks that are called "courage tasks" in the game. With the therapist observing, the player plays one level at the beginning of a therapy session, which takes approximately 15 minutes, and recounts the content of the level after which therapy session continues from there.

After discussion a consensus of seven PALOs was reached:

(1) The player receives "psycho-education" within the game. The well-established metaphor for OCD is the thought-stream, which is discussed. As well as the four-leaf-clover with strategies for behaviour.

(2) The player is asked to give the Spider (antagonist) a silly nickname.

(3) The player is asked to make his/her own compulsion map with courage tasks to complete.

(4) The player is asked to practice the easiest courage task multiple times a day (outside of gameplay).

(5) The player is asked to support Lisa in performing additional courage tasks.

(6) The player is asked to motivate Ricky to do additional courage tasks with the four-leaf-clover strategies.

(7) The player is asked to recount the gameplay in interaction with the therapist.

2.9. Moodbot. Moodbot is a game for adult psychological patients recovering from conditions such as psychosis and attempts to prevent them from relapsing [18]. As such the game is not tied to a single form of psychotherapy but is a more general psychotherapeutic aid. As a relapse prevention aid, the game is based on two assumptions. The first is that "communication between a patient and his/her healthcare worker about the patients' mental state is important for the patient's path towards recovery." The second is that patients exhibit various, unique signs that indicate whether they are likely to relapse that need to be recorded in so-called "alert schemes" so that they may be used to help prevent relapse. Moodbot is therefore primarily a way of identifying and communicating mental states and any indicative signs from a patient to his/her therapist between therapy sessions. The game is apparently being trialled in professional psychotherapeutic practice. As yet, there is no further information available to ascertain the game's validity.

The game is an online, multiplayer 2D computer game, although the interaction with other players is indirect (similar to well-known online, social games such as FarmVille). In the game the player is on board a highly imaginative ship (a large fish) and has to help keep it moving and steer it towards certain islands [19]. The player can overview all the rooms of the ship and visit individual rooms where he/she can perform specific actions that might earn him/her points (dust bunnies) that can be spent to get the ship moving and to steer it towards an island. The game is played daily for approximately five to ten minutes per day [18]. In doing so the player offers daily updates of his/her mental state as well as signs that could be indicative of a relapse that the therapist can access in a backend interface at any time.

After discussion a consensus of four PALOs was reached:

(1) Before gameplay the future player is asked to decide—together with their therapist and based on their alert scheme and goals—on the labels of the dashboard.

(2) The player is asked to express how they feel that day by adjusting their moodbot, moodtube, and dashboard.

(3) The player has the opportunity to go into other players' rooms and observe their mood-state. It is possible to leave comments (tips and advice) in these rooms.

(4) The game can stipulate real world challenges, provided and monitored by the therapist, which bring in-game fulfilment in the shape of a plant.

2.10. SuperBetter. SuperBetter is a game (or gamified platform) that is available as a web-based tool and an app for mobile devices. It appropriates game mechanics in order to provide a new narrative for accomplishing challenging health and wellbeing related goals [22]. SuperBetter is not specifically designed as a psychotherapeutic game. However, in a random controlled trial SuperBetter proved itself effective in decreasing depressive symptoms in comparison with a waitlist group [20].

In SuperBetter players give themselves a superhero-secret-identity based on their "favourite heroes." Players then select a goal to work toward and are awarded "resilience points" throughout the game (physical, mental, emotional, and social resilience) and level up. Gameplay ends when the goal is achieved and can be continued by setting new goals. Players can take steps towards achieving their goal by performing Quests: actions that share a common theme. SuperBetter has predetermined Quests that players can select or design their own or select Quests designed by other players. Players can also undertake mood-enhancing activities (power-ups), which are simple and instantly possible actions such as drinking a glass of water or hugging yourself. The platform provides Bad guys to battle. These Bad guys

belong to certain Quests or can be copied from other players or designed by the player. Finally, players gather social support (invite allies). Players can invite friends through the SuperBetter platform to help them. SuperBetter offers a mail contact form and a Facebook plug-in to do this. If the friend becomes an Ally they have access to the players' Quests, Power-Ups, and Bad guys and can suggest new ones.

After discussion a consensus of nine PALOs was reached:

(1) The player is asked to create a superhero identity to play the game with.

(2) The player is asked to state a goal (epic win).

(3) The player has the opportunity to select and perform Quests—a series of actions that help achieve their goal.

(4) The player has the opportunity to create and perform a Quest—a series of actions that help achieve their goal.

(5) The player has the opportunity to select and perform a Power-Up—simple mood-enhancing activities.

(6) The player has the opportunity to create and perform a Power-Up—simple mood-enhancing activities.

(7) The player has the opportunity to select and battle Bad Guys—behaviours that are counterproductive to achieving a Quest.

(8) The player has the opportunity to create and battle Bad Guys—behaviours that are counterproductive to achieving a Quest.

(9) The system asks players to invite Allies as in-game social support through social networks or e-mail.

2.11. PALOs and Intercoder Reliability. In this section, we describe the results of placing the PALOs in Bloom's Revised Taxonomy Table. The similarity in overall assessment is low. Only one PALO is scored exactly the same by all four coders (PALO 4 of Ricky and the Spider) and on five PALOs three out of four coders agreed (PALOs 1 and 5 from Ricky and the Spider, PALO 1 from Treasure Hunt, PALO 5 from Personal Investigator, and PALO 8 from SuperBetter), twelve PALO showed two coder agreements, and the remaining twenty-one PALOs had no exact agreement between coders.

Concerning the attribution of a Knowledge level, the PALOs of Treasure Hunt, Personal Investigator, and Superbetter were most frequently scored as Conceptual Knowledge. Ricky and the Spider and MoodBot were most frequently scored as Procedural Knowledge.

On the attribution of a Cognitive Processing level, the PALOs of Treasure Hunt and Personal Investigator were most frequently scored as "Understand," while Ricky and the Spider and MoodBot were scored as "Apply" most and SuperBetter had most PALOs scored as "Create."

When looking at the selection within dimensions, Knowledge level had three PALOs for which all four coders chose the same knowledge level (PALOs 4-6 from Ricky and the Spider), fourteen had three coder agreements, twenty-one had two coder agreements, and only one had no agreement

TABLE 2: PALO encoding results.

Datapoints in Taxonomy Table	Krippendorff' reliability	95% CI LL / UL
All PALO	$\alpha = .0753$	.0293 / .1259
Knowledge level of PALO	$\alpha = .1309$	.0422 / .2196
Cognitive processing of PALO	$\alpha = .1737$	.0986 / .2488
All analyses done with 5000 bootstrapping sample, concerning 39 units, 4 observers and 234 pairs.		

(PALO 9 from Personal Investigator). Within the cognitive processing dimension three PALOs (PALO 4 from Ricky and the Spider, PALO 5 from Personal Investigator, and PALO 1 from SuperBetter) had complete agreement, twelve had three coder agreements, twenty-one had two coder agreements, and three (PALO 3 from Treasure Hunt, PALO 4 from Personal Investigator, and PALO 3 from Moodbot) had no agreement.

Having arrived at an equal amount of data points, an inference concerning the intercoder reliability could be calculated. The Taxonomy Tables were merged into a single matrix, containing a unique identifying number for each cell in the table per game, making the data suitable for the calculation of Krippendorff's alpha [23, 24]. This is a statistic that represents the reliability of a variable and its encoding process, which is suitable for cases with any number of coders and variables of all measurement levels (nominal in our case) [25]. Running a Krippendorff analysis for intercoder reliability of all the PALOs resulted in a very low alpha (see Table 2). This indicates that intercoder reliability is virtually nonexistent as the four observers rarely agree on any exact placement in the Taxonomy Table. A Krippendorff alpha of exactly zero would mean that there are no differences between the encoding results and attributing random values to the data. The alpha statistic can also be negative, in which case the encoding results are worse than random and indicate a structural error. In our results we are encoding somewhat above pure chance ($\alpha = .00$) but not at the level of the norm for a good reliability test ($\alpha = $ between .60 and .80) [25]. Our results indicate a lot of room for subjectivity and interpretation in the placement of our 39 PALOs in the Taxonomy Table. Agreement on encoding within both dimensions was a little higher than overall agreement but provided no intercoder reliability (see Table 2).

All the analyses were rerun while excluding one coder consecutively. Although the Krippendorff alpha does alter slightly by excluding any one coder, there is no indication for a structural error and the reliability remains far below acceptable. This supports the notion that there is actual disagreement between the encoders and it is distributed equally.

The overall results from the analysis indicate that there is no error in the methodology and that the results are not pure chance but that the encoding by this taxonomy is too subjective to be considered reliable.

3. Discussion

In this article we demonstrated the application of the Revised Bloom Taxonomy in the analysis of five psychotherapeutic games. In a two-round process, we managed to come to a consensus on the *Player Actions with Learning Objectives* (PALOs) that each game contains in its design. All four researchers coded each PALO of each game independently and compared the results and an intercoder reliability statistic was subsequently calculated.

The process of assessing game content through the lens of the Revised Bloom Taxonomy turned out to be open to interpretation and resulted in such a great variability in statements after the first round that no sensible comparison of assessment could be made. However, a consolidated version of what PALOs should be assessed was achieved during discussion. We found that applying Bloom's Revised Taxonomy to our five games provided a structured discussion of player actions in relation to cognitive processes, knowledge levels, and design goals. We feel that such discussions would be useful in the design process of psychotherapeutic games. Describing possible player actions in terms of a PALO provided an interesting perspective on the translation of (therapeutic) goals into game content.

The intercoder reliability statistic revealed that no consensus could be achieved on how to interpret the game content within the Revised Bloom Taxonomy. The rating is prone to subjectivity, making it challenging to assign PALOs to appropriate cells in the Taxonomy Table. The work of Karpen and Welch [26] also suffered from low interrater reliability ($r = 0.25$) and accuracy (46%) when assigning exam questions to the appropriate Bloom cells. Accuracy improved (81.8%) when limiting the encoding to three levels instead of six "a three-tier combination of the Bloom's levels that would optimally improve accuracy: Knowledge, Comprehension/Application, and Analysis/Synthesis/Evaluation."

4. Conclusion

4.1. For Designers (RQ1)

Can Bloom's Revised Taxonomy Be Used as a Checklist during the Design of a Psychotherapeutic Game? Our discussion to formulate PALOs provided a structured way of describing how game design connects player actions to certain objectives and might provide support during the design process of a psychotherapeutic game. Attempting to place these PALOs in the taxonomy establishes a discussion of the game content on the level of cognition. Although categorization of content based on Bloom's Revised Taxonomy is too subjective to be used as a design checklist, we do feel the process facilitates a discussion of high value.

4.2. For Researchers (RQ2)

Can Bloom's Revised Taxonomy Allow Researchers to Make a More Objective Description of Game Content and Allow for Comparisons across Psychotherapeutic Games? The low intercoder reliability indicates that applying the Revised Bloom Taxonomy to psychotherapeutic games does not provide a robust structure for objectivity. The classification of game content remains very open to interpretation and the descriptions it provides should not be used to compare content across different psychotherapeutic games. In order to be useful as a means of comparison, the taxonomy needs to be further developed into a protocol in which designers, researchers, and therapists need to be involved until the process yields an acceptable intercoder reliability. We estimate a lot of effort needs to be applied before Bloom's Revised Taxonomy would be suitable, and it is advisable to first investigate if other models or taxonomies might be of more value.

4.3. For Psychologists (RQ3)

Can Bloom's Revised Taxonomy Support Psychologists in Making a More Informed Choice Concerning Psychotherapeutic Games That Might Be Included in Their Therapy? By describing content in terms of Player Actions with Learning Objectives, the designers provide a better insight into how their choices relate to the intended processing by the player and the desired overall outcome of gameplay. This gives any therapist a better insight into the level of cognitive engagement envisioned (lower bound) for different game content, which would support a more informed choice. Unfortunately, placing these PALOs in Bloom's Revised Taxonomy has not provided a reliable classification of game content and cannot be seen as valuable information.

4.4. Overall Conclusion. We have established that Bloom's Revised Taxonomy cannot be used as an objective classification of game content for psychotherapeutic games due to very low intercoder reliability. We have found the process of describing Player Actions with Learning Objectives of value, as it forces game designers to formalize their intentions.

We remain confident in the usefulness of trying to find a common language between game designers, researchers, and psychologists to describe the content of psychotherapeutic games beyond the level of any individual game.

4.5. Limitations. One of the limitations of this paper is that we only describe five games. Although this analysis is by no means exhaustive, we believe that an overview such as this paper can already be helpful to game designers or practitioners in the field of psychotherapeutic gaming. Moreover, analysis of game content can and should also be extended to include psychotherapeutic VR games.

We are also aware that we do not provide an in-depth analysis where knowledge and actions during gameplay are minutely observed, described, and categorized. As every gameplay is a unique experience to some degree, we expect that when encoding would be based on game-play subjectivity would increase and intercoder reliability would decrease.

References

[1] T. A. Ceranoglu, "Video Games in Psychotherapy," *Review of General Psychology*, vol. 14, no. 2, pp. 141–146, 2010.

[2] V. Brezinka, "Computer games supporting cognitive behaviour therapy in children," *Clinical Child Psychology and Psychiatry*, vol. 19, no. 1, pp. 100–110, 2014.

[3] T. Fovet, J.-A. Micoulaud-Franchi, G. Vaiva et al., "Le serious game : applications thérapeutiques en psychiatrie," *L'Encéphale*, vol. 42, no. 5, pp. 463–469, 2016.

[4] H. L. Horne-Moyer, B. H. Moyer, D. C. Messer, and E. S. Messer, "The Use of Electronic Games in Therapy: a Review with Clinical Implications," *Current Psychiatry Reports*, vol. 16, no. 12, 2014.

[5] T. M. Fleming, C. Cheek, S. N. Merry et al., "Juegos serios para el tratamiento o la prevención de la depresión: una revisión sistemática," *Revista de Psicopatología y Psicología Clínica*, vol. 19, no. 3, p. 227, 2015.

[6] P. Haring and H. Warmelink, "Looking for Metacognition," in *Games and Learning Alliance*, pp. 95–106, Springer International Publishing, 2016.

[7] A. De Gloria, F. Bellotti, and R. Berta, "Serious Games for education and training," *International Journal of Serious Games*, vol. 1, no. 1, 2014.

[8] B. S. Bloom, M. D. Engelhart, E. J. Furst et al., *Taxonomy of educational objectives: Handbook I: Cognitive domain*, vol. 56(19), 1956.

[9] J. Marzano and S. Kendall, "The need for a revision of Blooms taxonomy," in *The New Taxonomy of Educational Objectives, Chapter: 1*, pp. 1–20, Corwin Press, 2006.

[10] A. De Kock, P. Sleegers, and M. J. M. Voeten, "New learning and the classification of learning environments in secondary education," *Review of Educational Research*, vol. 74, no. 2, pp. 141–170, 2004.

[11] L. W. Anderson, D. R. Krathwohl, and B. S. Bloom, *A taxonomy for learning, teaching, and assessing: A revision of Bloom's taxonomy of educational objectives*, Allyn & Bacon, 2001.

[12] P. R. Pintrich, "The role of metacognitive knowledge in learning, teaching, and assessing," *Theory Into Practice*, vol. 41, no. 4, pp. 219–225, 2002.

[13] K. G. Kahl, L. Winter, and U. Schweiger, "The third wave of cognitive behavioural therapies: what is new and what is effective?" *Current Opinion in Psychiatry*, vol. 25, no. 6, pp. 522–528, 2012.

[14] D. R. Krathwohl, "A revision of bloom's taxonomy: an overview," *Theory Into Practice*, vol. 41, no. 4, pp. 212–218, 2002.

[15] D. Coyle, M. Matthews, J. Sharry et al., "Personal Investigator: A therapeutic 3D game for adolecscent psychotherapy," *Interactive Technology and Smart Education*, vol. 2, no. 2, pp. 73–88, 2005.

[16] V. Brezinka, "Treasure Hunt-a serious game to support psychotherapeutic treatment of children," in *eHealth beyond the horizon - Get IT there*, S. K. Andersen, Ed., vol. 136, pp. 71–76, IOS Press, Amsterdam, The Netherlands, 2008.

[17] V. Brezinka, "Ricky and the Spider - A Video Game to Support Cognitive Behavioural Treatment of Children with Obsessive-Compulsive Disorder," *Clinical Neuropsychiatry*, vol. 10, no. 3, 2013.

[18] M. Hrehovcsik and L. van Roessel, "Using Vitruvius as a Framework for Applied Game Design," in *Games for Health*, B. Schouten, S. Fedtke, T. Bekker et al., Eds., pp. 131–152, Wiesbaden: Springer Fachmedien Wiesbaden, 2013.

[19] Gainplay Studio. (2016). *Moodbot*. Last accessed September 30, 2016. http://www.gainplaystudio.com/moodbot/.

[20] A. M. Roepke, S. R. Jaffee, O. M. Riffle, J. McGonigal, R. Broome, and B. Maxwell, "Randomized Controlled Trial of SuperBetter, a Smartphone-Based/Internet-Based Self-Help Tool to Reduce Depressive Symptoms," *Games for Health Journal*, vol. 4, no. 3, pp. 235–246, 2015.

[21] A. Churches, "Bloom's digital taxonomy," in *Educational Origami*, vol. 4, 2009.

[22] J. McGonigal, *SuperBetter: A Revolutionary Approach to Getting Stronger, Happier, Braver and More Resilient*, Penguin Press, New York, NY, USA, 2015.

[23] A. F. Hayes and K. Krippendorff, "Answering the call for a standard reliability measure for coding data," *Communication Methods and Measures*, vol. 1, no. 1, pp. 77–89, 2007.

[24] K. Krippendorff, "Computing Krippendorff's alpha reliability," *Departmental papers (ASC)*, vol. 43, 2007.

[25] K. De Swert, *Calculating inter-coder reliability in media content analysis using Krippendorff's Alpha*, Center for Politics and Communication, 2012.

[26] S. C. Karpen and A. C. Welch, "Assessing the inter-rater reliability and accuracy of pharmacy faculty's Bloom's Taxonomy classifications," *Currents in Pharmacy Teaching and Learning*, vol. 8, no. 6, pp. 885–888, 2016.

## 3

Little Botany: A Mobile Game Utilizing Data Integration to Enhance Plant Science Education

Suphanut Jamonnak and En Cheng

Department of Computer Science, College of Arts and Sciences, University of Akron, Akron, OH 44325-4003, USA

Correspondence should be addressed to En Cheng; echeng@uakron.edu

Academic Editor: Michela Mortara

Mobile devices are rapidly becoming the new medium of educational and social life for young people, and hence mobile educational games have become an important mechanism for learning. To help school-aged children learn about the fascinating world of plants, we present a mobile educational game called Little Botany, where players can create their own virtual gardens in any location on earth. One unique feature of Little Botany is that the game is built upon real-world data by leveraging data integration mechanism. The gardens created in Little Botany are augmented with real-world location data and real-time weather data. More specifically, Little Botany is using real-time weather data for the garden location to simulate how the weather affects plants growth. Little Botany players can learn to select what crops to plant, maintain their own garden, watch crops to grow, tend the crops on a daily basis, and harvest them. With this game, users can also learn plant structure and three chemical reactions.

1. Introduction

School-aged children worldwide are growing up immersed in a media-rich, "always connected" world. New technology has brought with it new tools for learning, and research has shown that the educational potential of mobile games resonates with teachers and students [1]. Game is an important element for healthy child development including learning development. Mobile educational games provide an opportunity for players to learn through simulated environments; these games are not necessarily a distraction from learning; rather they can be an integral part of learning and intellectual development [2–5]. Mobile devices are rapidly becoming the new medium of educational and social life for young people, and hence mobile educational games [6–8] are a key topic for researchers and software developers. It is worth mentioning that the strengths of the mobile platform include its portability, context sensitivity, connectivity, and ubiquity, which make it ideal for educational games in elementary, secondary, university, and lifelong education.

Despite its apparent simplicity, gardening is actually a complex system involving the emergent interaction of multiple parameters. Successful gardeners usually need to juggle highly technical knowledge about a plant's sunlight and shade requirements, water needs, and what plants grow well together when placed near each other in a plot. To help school-aged children learn about the fascinating world of plants, we present a mobile educational game called Little Botany, where players can create their own dream gardens in any location on earth. The principal environmental requirements for plant growth include adequate space for root and canopy development, sufficient light, water, oxygen, carbon dioxide, and mineral elements, and temperature suitable for essential physiological processes [9]. Weather plays a major role in the healthy growth and development of plants. To simulate how the weather affects plants growth, the virtual gardens created in Little Botany are using real-time weather data for the garden location. The game also teaches users how to care for the plants on a daily basis. For instance, an adequate amount of water is essential for plant growth and maintenance of essential plant processes. With this game, users can discover where our food comes from and learn how to tend and harvest crops.

This paper is based upon a previous work [8], but the main contribution with respect to this work can be found in Related Work, Game Design, and Evaluation. The

TABLE 1: Numbers of installations for five gardening games from Google Play Store.

Game name	Number of installations
Farm Story	10,000,000–50,000,000
Inner Garden	1,000,000–5,000,000
Flower House	500,000–1,000,000
Sweet Garden	500,000–1,000,000
Dream Garden	100,000–500,000

remainder of this paper is structured as follows: Section 2 presents some related work; Section 3 describes the game design of Little Botany; Section 4 presents the three-layered system architecture of Little Botany; Section 5 describes three service agents, which are backend support for Little Botany; Section 6 illustrates the main functionalities provided by Little Botany; Section 7 presents evaluation results for Little Botany; Section 8 concludes the paper with discussions and future work.

2. Related Work

The primary mobile game market consists of Apple Store for iOS devices such as iPhone and iPad and Google Play Store for Android devices such as Samsung Galaxy and Nexus. In this section, we review five mobile gardening games that have been released on Google Play Store, because Google Play Store provides the total user installations for each game. Table 1 summarizes the number of installations for each game, which is useful for identifying the potential of user's interest in gardening games.

Farm Story [10] provides over 150 varieties of delicious fruits, veggies, and beautiful flowers. Farm Story allows players to design and decorate their farms with fences and building. Moreover, Farm Story allows players to have animals such as cows, sheep, and chicken. Players can visit their neighbors and view their friends' garden over social networks.

Inner Garden allows players to design and decorate their own garden [11]. Players can also take a photo of their garden and share it with their friends over social networks. It contains a realistic art in 2D world, which consists of recognizable plant species for children and adults.

Flower House [12] provides 139 unique flowers and 10 different characters. The game has approximately 500 thousand to 1 million installations. Flower House allows players to decorate unique interior garden with various flowerpots and statuettes. It provides functionality for players to sell their flowers and send them as a gift to their friends over the social network.

Sweet Garden [13] is one of the unique applications that allow players to add flower as a widget over the mobile screen. It creates an interactive flower over mobile user interface in real time. Furthermore, it also generates different characteristics and scenarios of flowers over the mobile interface.

Dream Garden [14] allows players to dress up their gardener's outfit and wear some favorite clothes. Dream Garden has approximately 100 thousand to 500 thousand installations. Dream Garden also provides gardening techniques. For instance, players will regularly water the plants with a watering can, prune their plants with scissors, trim the grass around the fence, or cut the lawn in the garden.

Our study of these five gardening games on the Google Play Store indicates the popularity of garden-themed games. To help school-aged children learn about the fascinating world of plants, Little Botany [8] attempts to leverage real-world location data and real-time weather data to create a virtual reality garden for users. More specifically, Little Botany is using real-time weather data for the garden location to simulate how weather affects plants growth. Little Botany players can learn to plan their own garden, select what crops to plant, watch crops to grow, tend the crops on a daily basis, and harvest them. With this game, users can also track plant growth and learn plant structure.

3. Game Design

3.1. Functionality Design. Storyboard is commonly used to illustrate the ideas and activities of a game. At the early design stage of Little Botany, we followed the strategies for serious game design proposed by the researchers [15–17] to accomplish functionality design for Little Botany. The activities in Figure 1 show the sequential actions performed by a game player. For example, if a player wants to create a garden, he can first select a location and choose a starting date for his garden.

Scenes and modules are used to illustrate the functional components of Little Botany. Figure 2 shows the scenes and modules designed for Little Botany. Virtual garden scene focuses on simulating plants growth in different stages, different locations, and different weather. Moreover, it also plays an important role in teaching players about how to take care of their plants. For instance, players need water and spray pesticide to protect their plants in a garden. Educational scene consists of two different modules, which are plant structures and plant chemical reaction. These two modules focus on teaching players about plant anatomy, photosynthesis, respiration, and transpiration.

3.2. Usability Design. The usability design in Little Botany focuses on user interface (UI) and gestures. Users can play our game by using gestures such as swiping, rotating, scaling, and drag-and-drop. We designed UI to support two mobile operating systems including iOS and Android. We have designed the UI in Little Botany according to the graphical areas of usage in landscape view. The areas over the mobile's UI contain light pink, light blue, and burlywood colors, which can be represented as the reachable areas including easy, normal, and difficult, respectively, in Figure 3.

Figure 4 illustrates the UI layout of Little Botany in landscape view. We started by providing the "home" button on the top-right corner. Players need to stretch their finger in order to reach the "home" button. In contrast, we put "gardening tool" buttons in the center-bottom area of the screen for easier access.

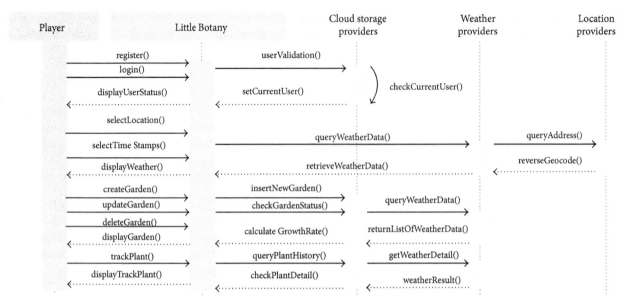

FIGURE 1: An illustration of player activities in Little Botany.

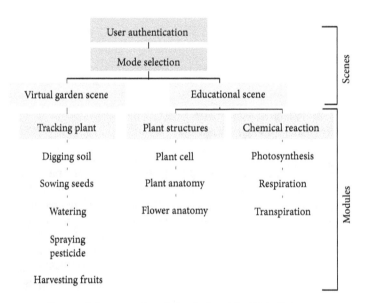

FIGURE 2: Scenes and modules designed for Little Botany.

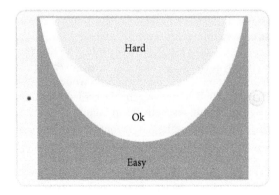

FIGURE 3: Graphical usages of mobile UI in landscape view.

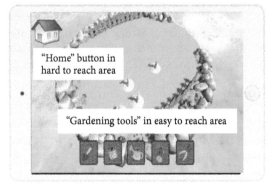

FIGURE 4: Little Botany UI design.

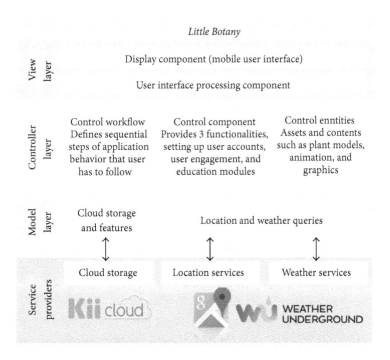

FIGURE 5: The system architecture of Little Botany.

Touch gestures are the combination of finger movements and clicks. In this project, we designed our application to recognize different touch gestures and events such as pointing, panning, zooming, rotating, and swiping. For example, one common gesture is to use one finger in a downward or upward motion to scroll. With the touch functions provided by Unity3D, we provide several gestures that can be used to interact with multitouch devices such as smartphones and tablets.

4. System Architecture

The system architecture of Little Botany has three layers including view layer, controller layer, and model layer. The Unity3D game engine [18] is the development framework for Little Botany. We used Unity3D to implement game mechanisms in C# and JavaScript programming languages. To generate 3D models and assets in our game, we use Autodesk Maya [19], 3D computer graphics software that runs on Windows, OS X, and Linux. Figure 5 illustrates the system architecture of Little Botany.

4.1. View Layer. The view layer contains the components for building user interface and managing user interaction. Unity3D new UI system provides an efficient approach to create UI components, such as buttons, input fields, images, panels, and texts, which are placed and displayed on the top of the game's canvas. Moreover, Unity3D also supports user input from multiple devices. Users can play our game by using gestures such as swiping, rotating, scaling, and drag-and-drop.

4.2. Controller Layer. In Little Botany, controller layer has three components: control workflow, control components,

and control entities. We explain the roles and responsibilities of each component as follows.

(i) Control Workflow. Users usually take multiple steps to accomplish a task. The steps must be performed in a correct order and orchestrated. For example, users need to select a location and a specific date before creating their garden or users need to follow the gardening steps by digging the soil first before sowing seeds.

(ii) Control Components. Little Botany provides three control components, which are (1) setting up user accounts, (2) user engagement, and (3) education modules:

(1) *Setting up user accounts*: users are required to set up their accounts before creating gardens

(2) *User engagement*: the component provides the entertainment content for users. The goal is to motivate users to play the game and learn how to grow plants. In addition, users can simulate plant development and track their plant growth

(3) *Education modules*: the component contains in-depth knowledge about gardening and plant growth. Users can learn about plant structure and plant growth factors including photosynthesis, respiration, transpiration, light, temperature, and water

(iii) Control Entities. Game objects such as plant models, gardens, images, and colors are drawn under the Unity3D graphic pipeline. Ultimately, Little Botany can have twenty plants for users to choose. Each plant has thirty static models represented as plant development stages.

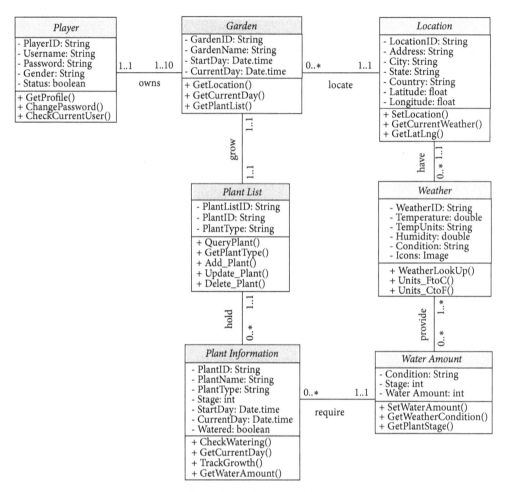

FIGURE 6: Database schema of Little Botany.

4.3. Model Layer. Model layer stores each user's game data in Little Botany. Model layer plays an important role in the three-layer architecture. Controller layer cannot function properly without accurate data provided by model layer. Model layer includes data management and service agent described as follows.

(i) Data Management. This component centralizes the data access functionality, which makes the application easy to configure and maintain. In Little Botany, game data is stored in the cloud storage named "Kii Cloud" [20]. This cloud storage provides us the ability to develop our game application without worrying about server-side implementation and operations.

(ii) Service Agent. Controller layer is built upon multiple external service agents, which provide data for business components' implementation. In this component, we develop the code to manage and communicate with external services. To provide weather and location for a user, we have selected external services including wunderground.com [21] for weather data and Google Maps Geocoding API [22] for location data.

5. Services

5.1. Mobile Backend as a Service (MBaaS). MBaaS [23] provides various server-side features such as user authentication, data management, application analytics, and push notification. With MBaaS, we can develop our mobile application without burden by server-side implementation and operations. We considered several MBaaS providers [24]. In the end, we found Kii Cloud [20] provided by Kii Corporation, which can fulfill the requirements for Little Botany.

Using Kii Cloud, We implemented server-side logic and applications for Little Botany. In addition, our application uses Kii Cloud to allow users to store game data on the server or share data among multiple devices. Figure 6 illustrates the schema designed for Little Botany using UML diagram. Kii Cloud lets us manage our server 24 hours a day and 365 days a year. It also enables us to react quickly to the issue and recover our service promptly. Furthermore, Kii Cloud is also enabling us to develop and distribute our application along with their provided Unity SDK.

For developers, Kii Unity SDK is easy to work with in terms of developing server-side logic. This SDK consists of KiiObject, Bucket, User, Scope, and Push Notification. In

TABLE 2: A sample of weather data.

Time SGT	Temperature (F)	Dew point (F)	Humidity	Sea level pressure	Visibility (MPH)	Wind direction	Wind speed (MPH)	Events	Conditions	Date UTC
12:00 AM	84.2	73.4	70	29.86	6.2	SSE	6.9	N/A	Mostly cloudy	2014-10-09, 16:00:00
12:30 AM	84.2	73.4	70	29.86	6.2	SE	6.9	N/A	Mostly cloudy	2014-10-09, 16:30:00
1:00 AM	84.2	75.2	74	29.86	6.2	SE	6.9	N/A	Mostly cloudy	2014-10-09, 17:00:00
1:30 AM	82.4	75.2	79	29.86	6.2	SE	6.9	N/A	Mostly cloudy	2014-10-09, 17:30:00
2:00 AM	83	74	69	29.84	9	SE	6.9	N/A	Hazy	2014-10-09, 18:00:00

Little Botany, we use KiiObject for storing application data. We can store values and string using key-value pair, and these key-value pairs are stored as JSON format. We also use Bucket to organize multiple KiiObjects, which act like a container for KiiObjects.

5.2. Location Services. Little Botany provides users the flexibility to choose any location on earth to start a garden. To provide an easy way for users to choose a location, users can touch a spherical globe designed in Little Botany. With the Unity3D game engine, Little Botany can retrieve user-touched position in 3-dimensional world and convert it to the geographic coordinates with latitude and longitude values. Giving the geographic coordinates as inputs, we need to use web services to retrieve a specific location. In Little Botany, we use Google Maps Geocoding API [22] provided by Google Inc. This API has the capability of converting latitude and longitude values to human-readable address. The returned addresses have four different formats. Given 40.714224 in latitude and 73.961452 in longitude as inputs, we illustrate how Google Maps Geocoding API retrieves a specific location as follows.

Input: Google Maps Geocoding API (40.714224 in Latitude and 73.961452 in Longitude)

> http://maps.googleapis.com/maps/api/geocode/json?latlng=40.714224,-73.961452

Output: Different Formatted Address

> "formatted_address": "277 Bedford Avenue, Brooklyn, NY 1121, USA",
>
> "formatted_address": "Grand St/Bedford Av, Brooklyn, NY 11211, USA",
>
> "formatted_address": "Grand St/Bedford Av, Brooklyn, NY, 11249, USA",
>
> "formatted_address": "Bedford Av/Grand St, Brooklyn, NY 11211, USA",

> "formatted_address": "Brooklyn, NY 11211, USA",
>
> "formatted_address": "Williamsburg, Brooklyn, NY, USA",
>
> "formatted_address": "Brooklyn, NY, USA",
>
> "formatted_address": "New York, NY, USA",
>
> "formatted_address": "New York, USA",
>
> "formatted_address": "United States",

For Little Botany, it is sufficient to use a simple address format, which consists of city and country.

5.3. Weather Services. Users can have their garden not only in different locations but also in different weather conditions. In Little Botany, users have an option to select historical time. For instance, users can have their garden in 2012. To retrieve weather condition for a specific location, we considered several weather provider sites [25]. In order to select a suitable weather provider site, we have considered API call limit, cost, and data provided by the site. As a result, we discovered that weather information can be retrieved over HTTP requests instead of calling their APIs and paying for services.

In the end, we selected Weather Underground [21] as the service that provides weather information to users. Weather Underground allows developers to query both current and historical weather data using HTTP links. Table 2 illustrates the retrieved weather data from wunderground.com on October 9, 2014, from 12:00 AM to 2:00 AM in Singapore airport. The link used for retrieving the data is

> https://www.wunderground.com/history/airport/SIN/2014/10/10/DailyHistory.html?format=1

For Little Botany, we extract five attributes from Table 2 to describe weather condition for a specific location. The five attributes are time, temperature, humidity, events, and condition.

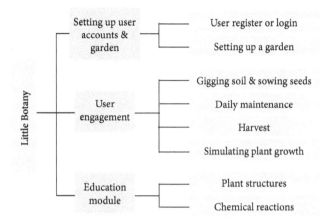

FIGURE 7: Little Botany's functionality diagram.

FIGURE 8: Start-game scene in Little Botany.

6. Functionalities

By playing with Little Botany, users can learn to grow and maintain their plants in different locations and weather conditions. Users can also track their plant growth. In addition, Little Botany provides an education module that teaches about in-depth gardening such as plant structure and factors affecting plant development. Figure 7 illustrates Little Botany functionalities diagram.

6.1. Setting Up User Accounts and Garden

6.1.1. User Register or Login. After a user installs Little Botany on a mobile device, he/she must create his/her account if he/she wants to start the game and create a garden. Figure 8 shows a snapshot of starting game scene in Little Botany. Players can click on the "Let's grow" button to start the game. After the game is started, the player can create his account by selecting the "Create new account" option or provide his username and password to login to the game, which are illustrated in Figure 9.

Little Botany authenticates username and password using Kii Cloud services. More importantly, Little Botany offers Single Sign-On feature with the support of Kii Cloud services, because Kii Cloud can automatically authenticate users by checking the current user's account or the user's session that appeared on the system.

FIGURE 9: User login or register scene.

FIGURE 10: Select-location scene in Little Botany.

6.1.2. Setting Up a Garden. Users can create their dream gardens in different locations. Once users want to create their garden, Little Botany brings users to the location selection scene shown in Figure 10.

In Figure 10, users can select location by touching or clicking on the spherical globe. With the Unity3D game engine, we can retrieve user-touched position in 3-dimensional world and convert it to the geographical coordinates with latitude and longitude values. This technique can be achieved by using the formulas (see (1)) to convert Cartesian to spherical coordinates, where $r \in [0, \infty)$, $\theta \in [0, \pi]$, $\varphi \in [0, 2\pi)$, by

$$r = \sqrt{x^2 + y^2 + z^2}$$

$$\theta = \arccos\left(\frac{z}{\sqrt{x^2 + y^2 + z^2}}\right) = \arccos\left(\frac{z}{r}\right) \quad (1)$$

$$\varphi = \arctan\left(\frac{y}{x}\right).$$

The Cartesian coordinate (x, y, z) can be converted to spherical coordinate of a point in the ISO convention (radius r, inclination θ, and azimuth φ). Azimuth angle φ and inclination or polar angle θ are basically the same as *latitude* and *longitude* values.

The latitude and longitude values are used to retrieve both weather information and location information. In addition, we also provide calendar for our users to select a specific day for starting a garden. After users have selected their location and a date from the calendar, our game will bring users to

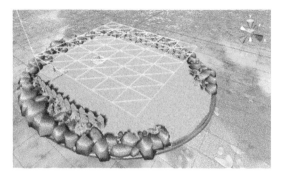

FIGURE 11: Little Botany garden with tile map structure.

FIGURE 13: Gardening tools.

y-axis	(0,1)	(1,1)	(2,1)	(3,1)	(4,1)
	(0,0)	(1,0)	(2,0)	(3,0)	(4,0)

x-axis

FIGURE 12: (5×2) tile map structure.

FIGURE 14: Digging-soil scene.

their garden. Users are able to grow plants and vegetables by selecting a specific tile in this scene. We have designed user's garden using 2-dimensional tile map as shown in Figure 11. The tile map is structured in (x, y) axis. Figure 12 shows how Little Botany stores positions in the tile map system.

Users start growing their plants and vegetables by selecting gardening tools. After sowing the tomato seed to the soil, users can track the tomato plant's development and user's activity logs and learn about the structure of tomato plant. Little Botany displays a detailed description for each plant, which includes health condition, water amount, plant state, and plant type.

6.2. User Engagement. In Little Botany, we provide five gardening tools, shovel, seed can, water pitcher, pesticide spray, and scissor, which are shown at the bottom of the snapshot in Figure 13. The gardening tools are important components for plant maintenance. We describe the roles and functionalities of each tool with snapshots as follows:

(a) *Shovel*: to use a shovel for digging soil, users can interact with the game by swiping their fingers. Each swipe will play the digging animation and is being counted

(b) *Seed can*: users can select a specific seed from Little Botany's seed store and start sowing the seed by holding the button until the progress bar has filled

(c) *Watering*: users hold on the watering button until watering gauge reaches the required amount. In some cases, plant will display a message if it still needs more water

(d) *Pesticide spray*: users can interact with the game by destroying harmful insects. Users can spray pesticide

FIGURE 15: Sowing-seed scene.

to the insect, and the insect will be eliminated from the plant

(e) *Scissor*: users use a scissor to harvest the fruit from a plant. Users pick a specific fruit and put it into a basket. Users will earn money by selling those fruits they picked.

(1) Digging Soil and Sowing Seeds. Users will start digging the soil by performing the swipe gesture; after that, users will start sowing plant seeds by selecting their favorite plant they would like to grow. Figures 14 and 15 show a snapshot of digging soil and sowing seeds in Little Botany, respectively.

In beta version of Little Botany, we provide three vegetables: tomatoes, carrots, and onions. We plan to provide twenty common plants and vegetables in the near future. The list of

FIGURE 16: Watering scene.

FIGURE 17: Spraying-pesticide scene.

FIGURE 18: Harvesting scene.

most common plants and vegetables that users can grow on Little Botany in the near future is as follows:

Apples

Onions

Potato

Spinach

Peaches

Tomatoes

Asparagus

Blueberries

Grapes

Lettuce

Celery

Avocado

Egg plant

Watermelon

Peppers

Strawberries

Cabbage

Kale

Kiwi

Pine apple

(2) Garden Daily Maintenance. Little Botany requires users to water and spray pesticide to their plants and vegetables. Tomatoes are susceptible to insect pests, especially tomato hornworms and whiteflies. Users should maintain their plants on a daily basis. Figures 16 and 17 show a snapshot of watering tomato and spraying pesticide, respectively. If some weather events have occurred, the maintenance activities will be adjusted accordingly. For example, if it rains on a specific day, users do not need water plants in their gardens.

(3) Harvest. When a plant reaches its final growing season, users can harvest the vegetable or fruit from the plant. Figure 18 shows a snapshot of harvesting tomato. Harvest time for tomatoes will occur at the end of its growing season, once the tomatoes are at their mature green stage. Users will start picking about 60–85 days after planting seedlings in the garden.

Playing with Little Botany, users can learn how to grow their plants and vegetables. Moreover, users can learn to take care of their garden in different seasons and locations. After harvest, users can sell the fruit for money and then buy seeds for a new plant.

(4) Simulating Plant Growth. The principal environmental requirements for plant growth include adequate space for root and canopy development, sufficient light, water, oxygen, carbon dioxide, and mineral elements, and temperature suitable for essential physiological processes. An adequate amount of water is essential for plant growth. To simulate plant growth and development, we use Growing Degree-Day (GDD) formula (see (2)) to calculate a plant's development rate based upon real-time weather data. For tomato plant, GDD formula is defined as follows:

$$\text{GDD} = \frac{T_{\max} + T_{\min}}{2} - T_{\text{base}}. \tag{2}$$

$T_{\max}$ is maximum temperature, $T_{\min}$ is minimum temperature, and T_{base} is usually equal to $50°\text{F}$.

Each plant in the garden has a timestamp, which records the plant's starting date. The game automatically calculates how long the plant has been growing based upon the timestamp. Then the game calculates the amount of water that each plant requires so that users can provide an adequate growing environment for the plant. Table 3 shows water amount based upon tomato stages and weather conditions.

TABLE 3: Water amount based upon tomato stages and weather conditions.

| Tomato plant stage | Stage description | Days of development | Weather condition (mm = millimeters) | | | | | |
| | | | Day time | | | Night time | | |
			Clear	Cloudy	Rain, snow, thunder	Clear	Cloudy	Rain, snow, thunder
1	Establishment	1–3 days	7	6	0	5	4	0
2	Establishment	3–5 days	12	11	0	10	9	0
3	Establishment	5–7 days	17	16	0	15	14	0
4	Development and vegetable growth	7–10 days	22	21	0	20	19	0
5	Development and vegetable growth	10–14 days	27	26	0	25	24	0
6	Fruit flowering and fruit set	14–28 days	32	31	0	30	29	0
7	Fruit flowering and fruit set	28–35 days	37	36	0	35	34	0
8	First phase of fruit development	35–40 days	42	41	0	40	39	0
9	Harvest initiation	40–45 days	47	46	0	45	44	0
10	Full harvest	45–60 days	52	51	0	50	49	0

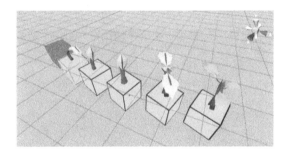

FIGURE 19: Five development stages of tomatoes.

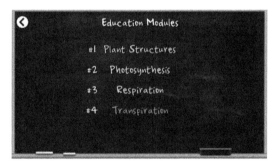

FIGURE 21: Content of education modules scene.

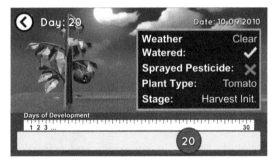

FIGURE 20: Tracking plant scene.

Figure 19 illustrates five models of tomatoes, each model represented as one development stage.

(5) Tracking Plant Growth. Users should perform daily activities to take care of the plants in their garden. Activities such as watering and spraying pesticide will be stored in the activity log. Users can keep track of all plant development since the first day the plant has been planted. In order to track a specific plant, Little Botany uses the scroll bar. For example, a user started growing his tomato on January 11, 2010. When the user logs in Little Botany on January 15, 2010, he can drag the scroll bar within five days, view his daily activities, and check plant's status. Figure 20 shows a snapshot of the tracking-plant-growth scene.

Little Botany uses activity logs to keep track of users' activities and plant's development. Activity data including watering, spraying pesticides, and plant health data is recorded in the activity logs. Therefore, when a user drags the scroll bar, Little Botany displays all the activities the user has performed in his garden.

6.3. Education Module. In addition to tracking plants' development, Little Botany can also teach users about plant structure, photosynthesis, respiration, and transpiration, which are listed in Figure 21. Plant structure is divided into two

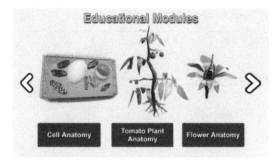

FIGURE 22: Plant structures-selection scene.

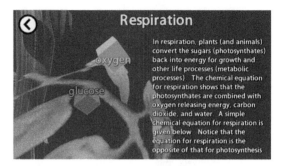

FIGURE 24: Respiration scene.

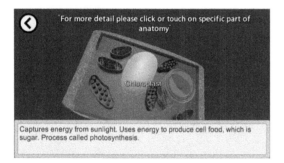

FIGURE 23: Cell-anatomy scene.

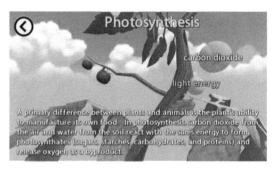

FIGURE 25: Photosynthesis scene.

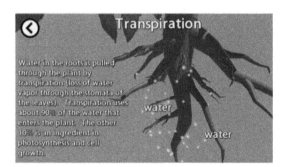

FIGURE 26: Transpiration scene.

parts: external structure and internal structure. External parts consist of root, stem, leaf, flower, fruit, and seed. Internal parts consist of plant cell and plant tissue. When a user touches on a specific part of the plant, a detailed description of the functions for the touched part will be displayed to the user.

Using tomato plant as an example, Figure 22 illustrates the plant-structures-selection scene where users can select different topics such as plant cell anatomy, tomato plant anatomy, and flower structures. Figure 23 shows a snapshot of cell anatomy scene. This scene provides a free rotation of objects. Thus, users can interact with the plant in a 360-degree view. Moreover, users can learn a specific part of anatomy by touching on an individual part. Figure 24 shows a snapshot of respiration scene; Figure 25 shows a snapshot of photosynthesis scene; and Figure 26 shows a snapshot of transpiration scene.

7. Evaluation

The primary characteristics of a mobile game which make it enjoyable are its content, storyboard, rewards, graphics, sound effects, and user experience. Korhonen and Koivisto [26] have defined heuristics termed as playability heuristics to evaluate mobile games. These heuristics are divided into three modules: game usability, mobility, and gameplay. The game usability module covers the game controls and interface through which the player interacts with the game. Also, it contains common usability aspects that help the player to get into the game and interact with it. Mobility module deals with the characteristics of mobile devices and their context

that can influence the design of games. The gameplay module deals with issues that arise when the player interacts with the game's mechanics and story. The playability heuristics discussed by Korhonen and Koivisto [26] were summarized in Tables 4, 5, and 6.

7.1. User Study Design. In our design and evaluation, our main priority has been usability and playability rather than a dense educational content. Assessing playability and usability in such a game is essential as it will determine if and for how long the children will be using it, which is an important factor for ensuring learning success.

A total of 28 school-aged children including 12 females and 16 males were purposely recruited from Sunday school at The Chapel in Akron. Participants were asked to have experience of using mobile devices (including smartphones and tablets). We manually installed the game on either

TABLE 4: Heuristics for evaluating game usability.

#	Game usability heuristics
1	Audiovisual representation supports the game
2	Screen layout is efficient and visually pleasing
3	Device UI and game UI are used for their own purposes
4	Indicators are visible
5	The player understands the terminology
6	Navigation is consistent, logical, and minimalist
7	Control keys are consistent and follow standard conventions
8	Game controls are convenient and flexible
9	The game gives feedback on the player's actions
10	The player cannot make irreversible errors
11	The player does not have to memorize things unnecessarily
12	The game contains help

TABLE 5: Heuristics for evaluating mobility.

#	Mobility heuristics
1	The game and play sessions can be started quickly
2	The game accommodates with the surroundings
3	Interruptions are handled reasonably

TABLE 6: Heuristics for evaluating gameplay.

#	Gameplay heuristics
1	The game provides clear goals or supports player created goals
2	The player sees the progress in the game and can compare the results
3	The players are rewarded and rewards are meaningful
4	The player is in control
5	Challenge, strategy, and pace are in balance
6	The first-time experience is encouraging
7	The game story supports the gameplay and is meaningful
8	There are no repetitive or boring tasks
9	The players can express themselves
10	The game supports different playing styles
11	The game does not stagnate
12	The game is consistent
13	The game uses orthogonal unit differentiation
14	The player does not lose any hard-won possessions

TABLE 7: The statements used in questionnaire to evaluate usability.

#	Statements
Q_1	Screen layout is efficient and visually pleasing.
Q_2	The symbols and words on screen were easy to understand.
Q_3	The amount of information displayed on screen was appropriate.
Q_4	The information displayed on screen was consistent.
Q_5	Navigation is consistent and logical.
Q_6	The game and play sessions can be started quickly.
Q_7	Game controls are convenient and flexible.
Q_8	The game gives feedback on the player's actions.
Q_9	The player does not have to memorize things unnecessarily.
Q_{10}	The help contained in the game is useful.

TABLE 8: The statements used in questionnaire to evaluate playability.

#	Statements
Q_1	The first-time experience is encouraging.
Q_2	The game provides clear goals.
Q_3	The player sees the progress in the game.
Q_4	The player is rewarded and rewards are meaningful.
Q_5	The player feels that challenge and pace are in balance.
Q_6	The game story supports the gameplay and is meaningful.
Q_7	There are no repetitive or boring tasks.
Q_8	The game does not stagnate.
Q_9	The player improved his/her knowledge about gardening.
Q_{10}	The player became more interested in real-world gardening.

participant's or their parent's mobile devices. 18 participants play the game on tablets, and 10 participants play the game on smartphones. We had a quick presentation session to teach participants how to play the game. We asked participants to play Little Botany for a period of three weeks. During this time, players were asked to play with Little Botany at least 3 times a week. After playing the game for three weeks, participants were asked to complete questionnaires regarding usability and playability. The questionnaire we used in our user study is adapted from the playability heuristics proposed

by Korhonen and Koivisto [26]. The ten statements used to measure game's usability and playability are listed in Tables 7 and 8, respectively.

7.2. Results. Participants were asked to answer to what extent they agree to the statements in Tables 7 and 8. We use a 5-point Likert scale ranging from strongly disagree to strongly agree. The results of experiments evaluating usability are shown in Figure 27.

We were interested to know if players find the game's controls and interface pleasing. We were also interested to know if the players think the content, graphics, and sound effects are enjoyable. As shown in Figure 27, Little Botany shows a high level of usability according to the responses of participants (the average score is greater than 3.9 for all parameters). To really give a game player what he/she wants, we have to understand what is important to him/her: we have to care about what he/she cares about and think how he/she thinks. One of the main challenges with Little Botany is to provide players with experience that they feel the existence of virtual gardens in the real world. Participants reported that they felt they were maintaining a real garden in Little Botany.

The results of experiments evaluating playability are shown in Figure 28.

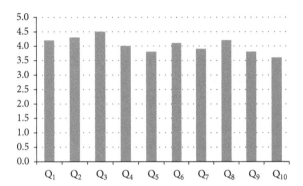

FIGURE 27: The average score of statements in Table 7 answered by participants to measure usability.

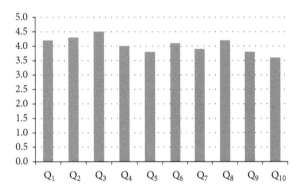

FIGURE 28: The average score of statements in Table 8 answered by participants to measure playability.

We were interested to know if players think the storyboard and user experience are enjoyable. We were also interested to know if the game improved the players' knowledge about gardening. As shown in Figure 28, Little Botany shows a high level of playability according to the responses of participants (the average score is greater than 4.0 for all parameters). Although the overall score is acceptable, the average scores for Q_9 (the player improved his/her knowledge about gardening) and Q_{10} (the player became more interested in real-world gardening) are somehow low in comparison to other questions. We argue that three weeks is not long enough to measure the educational effectiveness of our game. Therefore, we plan to perform additional long-term experiments to measure the educational effectiveness of Little Botany.

8. Conclusion

Games are important for learning development. In this paper, we present a mobile educational game for gardening to enhance plant science learning and improve student content retention. Using Little Botany, users can create their dream garden in any place in the world. More importantly, Little Botany is using real-time weather data for the garden location (e.g., South America) to simulate how the weather affects plants growth. Weather plays a major role in the healthy

growth and development of plants. To engage users, Little Botany has plant daily maintenance component which requires users' daily involvement with the game. With this game, users can discover where our food comes from and learn how to tend and harvest crops and learn about insects and pollinators. The current virtual garden in Little Botany is simulated based upon soil gardening, but we plan to add indoor hydroponic system to our game in the near future. Hydroponic gardening [27] uses considerably less water than soil gardening because of the constant reuse of the nutrient solutions. Mobile devices are rapidly becoming the new medium of educational and social life for young people, and hence mobile educational games are a key topic for learning.

References

[1] J. Paul Gee, *What Video Games Have to Teach Us about Learning and Literacy*, vol. 1 of *Theoretical and Practical Computer Applications in Entertainment*, 2003.

[2] T. M. Connolly, E. A. Boyle, E. MacArthur, T. Hainey, and J. M. Boyle, "A systematic literature review of empirical evidence on computer games and serious games," *Computers and Education*, vol. 59, no. 2, pp. 661–686, 2012.

[3] M. Virvou and E. Alepis, "Mobile educational features in authoring tools for personalised tutoring," *Computers and Education*, vol. 44, no. 1, pp. 53–68, 2005.

[4] F. Ke, "A case study of computer gaming for math: engaged learning from gameplay?" *Computers and Education*, vol. 51, no. 4, pp. 1609–1620, 2008.

[5] I. Boada, A. Rodriguez-Benitez, J. M. Garcia-Gonzalez, S. Thió-Henestrosa, and M. Sbert, "30: 2: a game designed to promote the cardiopulmonary resuscitation protocol," *International Journal of Computer Games Technology*, vol. 2016, Article ID 8251461, 14 pages, 2016.

[6] J. P. Gee, "Learning by design: good video games as learning machines," *E-Learning*, vol. 2, no. 1, pp. 5–16, 2005.

[7] H. J. Hsu, "The potential of kinect in education," *International Journal of Information and Education Technology*, vol. 1, no. 5, pp. 365–370, 2011.

[8] S. Jamonnak and E. Cheng, "Little botany: a mobile educational game for gardening," in *Proceedings of the 15th International Conference on e-Learning, e-Business, Enterprise Information Systems, and e-Government (EEE '16)*, Las Vegas, Nev, USA, 2016.

[9] N. Castilla and J. Lopez-Galvez, "Vegetable crop responses in improved low-cost plastic greenhouses," *Journal of Horticultural Science*, vol. 69, no. 5, pp. 915–921, 1994.

[10] TeamLava Games, "Google play store: Farm story," https://play.google.com/store/apps/details?id=com.teamlava.farmstory.

[11] Google play store: inner garden, https://play.google.com/store/apps/details?id=com.dustflake.innergarden.

[12] Gameinsight, "Google play store: flower house," 2016, https://play.google.com/store/apps/details?id=com.gameinsight.flower-houseandroid.

[13] SPRING GAMES, "Google play store: sweet garden," 2016, https://play.google.com/store/apps/details?id=toast.sweetgarden.

[14] TutoTOONS Kids Games, "Google play store: dream garden," https://play.google.com/store/apps/details?id=air.com.tutotoons.app.dreamgarden.

[15] P. Rooney, "A theoretical framework for serious game design: exploring pedagogy, play and fidelity and their implications for the design process," *International Journal of Game-Based Learning*, vol. 2, no. 4, pp. 41–60, 2012.

[16] L. A. Annetta, "The 'I's' have it: a framework for serious educational game design," *Review of General Psychology*, vol. 14, no. 2, pp. 105–112, 2010.

[17] M. De Sá and L. Carriço, "Designing and evaluating mobile interaction: challenges and trends," *Foundations and Trends in Human-Computer Interaction*, vol. 4, no. 3, pp. 175–243, 2010.

[18] "Unity3D Game Engine," https://unity3d.com/.

[19] Autodesk Maya, http://www.autodesk.com/products/maya/overview-dts?s_tnt=69290:1:0.

[20] "Kii Cloud," https://en.kii.com/.

[21] "Weather Underground API," http://www.wunderground.com/.

[22] Google Geocode API, https://developers.google.com/maps/documentation/geocoding/intro.

[23] Mobile Backend as a Service (MbaaS), https://en.wikipedia.org/wiki/Mobile_backend_as_a_service.

[24] Best MbaaS, http://forum.unity3d.com/threads/best-mbaas-solutions.252863/.

[25] Top 10 Weather API, http://www.programmableweb.com/news/top-10-weather-apis/analysis/2014/11/13.

[26] H. Korhonen and E. M. I. Koivisto, "Playability heuristics for mobile games," in *Proceedings of the 8th International Conference on Human-Computer Interaction with Mobile Devices and Services (MobileHCI '06)*, pp. 9–16, Helsinki, Finland, September 2006.

[27] M. H. Jensen and W. L. Collins, "Hydroponic vegetable production," in *Horticultural Reviews*, J. Janick, Ed., vol. 7, John Wiley & Sons, Hoboken, NJ, USA, 1985.

## 4

How Color Properties can be used to Elicit Emotions in Video Games

Erik Geslin,[1,2] **Laurent Jégou,**[3] **and Danny Beaudoin**[4]

[1]UCO Laval 3Di, LICIA, 25 rue du Mans, 53000 Laval, France
[2]Arts et Métiers ParisTech, LAMPA, 2 Boulevard du Ronceray, 49000 Angers, France
[3]Maître de Conférences, Department of Geography and UMR LISST, Toulouse Jean-Jaurès University, 5 allée Antonio Machado, 31058 Toulouse Cedex 9, France
[4]Psychology Department, Faculty of Social Sciences, Université Laval, Pavillon Félix-Antoine-Savard, 2325 rue des Bibliothèques, Quebec City, QC, Canada G1V 0A6

Correspondence should be addressed to Erik Geslin; erik.geslin@gmail.com

Academic Editor: Manuel M. Oliveira

Classifying the many types of video games is difficult, as their genres and supports are different, but they all have in common that they seek the commitment of the player through exciting emotions and challenges. Since the income of the video game industry exceeds that of the film industry, the field of inducting emotions through video games and virtual environments is attracting more attention. Our theory, widely supported by substantial literature, is that the chromatic stimuli intensity, brightness, and saturation of a video game environment produce an emotional effect on players. We have observed a correlation between the RGB additives color spaces, HSV, HSL, and HSI components of video game images, presented to $n = 85$ participants, and the emotional statements expressed in terms of arousal and valence, recovered in a subjective semantic questionnaire. Our results show a significant correlation between luminance, saturation, lightness, and the emotions of joy, sadness, fear, and serenity experienced by participants viewing 24 video game images. We also show strong correlations between the colorimetric diversity, saliency volume, and stimuli conspicuity and the emotions expressed by the players. These results allow us to propose video game environment development methods in the form of a circumplex model. It is aimed at game designers for developing emotional color scripting.

1. Introduction

It is widely accepted today that emotions are a key element in the success of video games. They can create a variety of experiences that players will encounter, and these can usually be described using a formal taxonomy, such as flow [1], presence [2], immersion [3], and fun [4]. Producing emotions through environments or narration is a key challenge in this industry. Human emotions have been studied in literature since antiquity, and they were initially opposed to reason [5]. Scientific research on emotions, in the fields of neuroscience and psychology, has recently shown that if their role is primarily to take part in the survival of the species, contributing to preservation and reproduction, they are not provided exclusively as reflexes and relayed only to limbic brain but are

also cognitive [6]. Many phenomena and contextual stimuli result in the production of complex emotions, which can be classified into categories with 5 basic emotions [7] and 21 known combinatorial emotions [8], or with a dimensional space based on their valence and activation level [9]. The literature has shown for several years strong links between visual stimuli and emotions [10]. Effects of colors on emotions were studied several times and although there are diverging results about which colors promote a positive or negative mood, these works show a strong correlation between colors, hue, saturation, and brightness with emotional arousal, valence, and dominance [11]. Several studies show that the human brain (or the macaque's, as reference) is much more active in environments of colors like red compared to yellow [12]. A 23-culture semantic differential study of affective

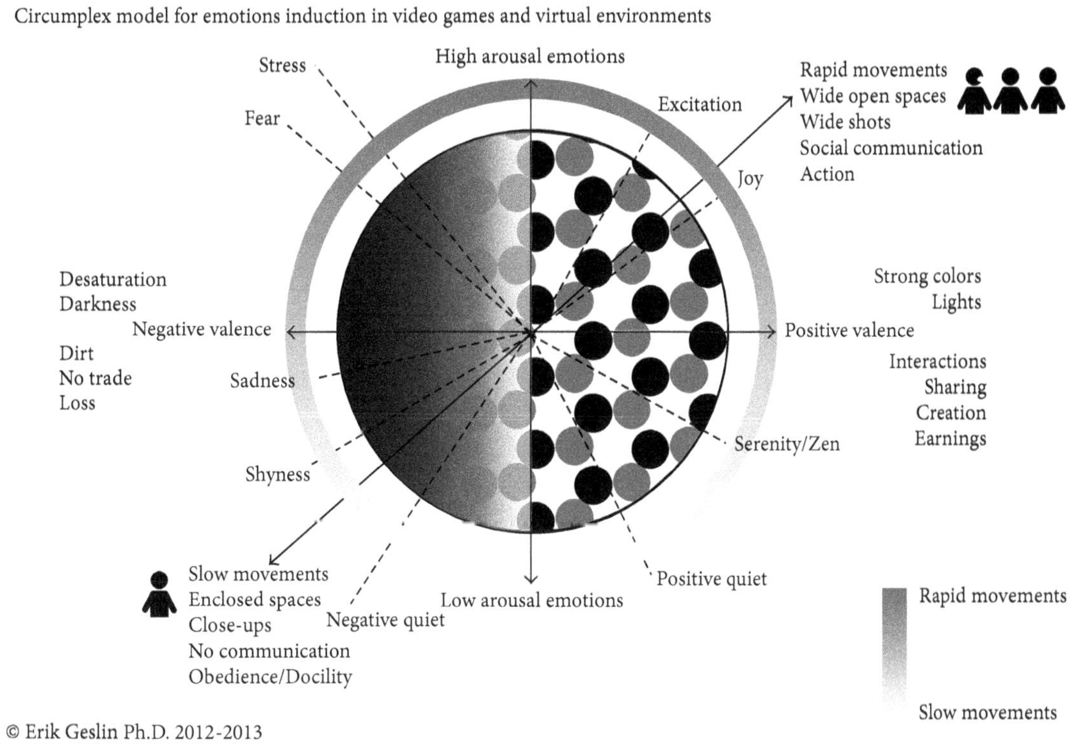

Circumplex model for emotions induction in video games and virtual environments

© Erik Geslin Ph.D. 2012-2013

FIGURE 1: Circumplex model of induction of emotions in video games [15].

meanings also reveals cross-cultural similarities in emotional color perception [13]. We will not discuss the case of each color in a virtual environment, but we will instead focus on the general effects of hue, saturation, and lightness on the emotions of players. We present a study involving $n = 85$ participants on the correlations between the RGB hue, saturation, and value components of 24 frames of video game environments and the emotional effects collected in a semantic subjective questionnaire, which was based on the IAPS survey [14]. This method is based on a schematic circumplex dimensional model of emotions in a virtual reality context [15]. This model is included in an evolutionary perspective of cognitive overgeneralization; it does not take into account the personal experiences of players which inevitably lead to an idiosyncratic positioning. We do not question the strength of these environmental aspects but we seek to define a more general methodology.

This method allows game designers to create emotional environments in accordance with the curves of interest (script pacing) to keep players in an optimal state of flow, depending on the ratios of challenge, boredom, and engagement [16]. Since the flow experience in games is accepted as being related to the emotional involvement of the player [17–19], emotions are therefore seen as an essential part of the production of a video game. These emotions are the result of both gameplay and narrative but can also be produced by games with active environments. This is the kind of emotional environment that we offer to help build with color scripting via our circumplex model of emotion induction (Figure 1).

2. Methods

2.1. Image Analysis. There has been many studies on emotional colors (term defined below), both isolated or combined in pairs [20–22], and they have been in use for a long time in areas such as advertisement design. However, studies on the emotional impact of complex images are more rare. Both the difficulties of the choice of semantic subjective interpretation models and also of contextualizing complex images make this work fascinating and difficult. Most of these studies use clustering principles that segment images into small regions of homogeneous color [23]. However, excluding this segmentation allows for a more comprehensive analysis of the emotional picture. In a 2007 study, Gao et al. have shown that, in the context of a multicultural study (eight groups from different international regions), participants showed a strong importance on lightness and chroma as emotional colors [24]. It seemed interesting to us to study the emotional influences of colors in the paradigms of video games taken as a whole context. We therefore selected 24 still images from video games categorized into different genres, using the Elverdam and Aarseth dynamic classification to ensure a wide range [25]: Racing, FPS, RPG, Casual, Strategic, and Experimental. For each of these six themes, four still images from video games were selected. These four images were randomly selected in a real-time footage database comprising 20 frames. All these still images were produced by the studios that own them. The 120 preselected video games are from the video games database rewarded by the Academy of Interactive Arts & Sciences. We have calculated the RGB value of each still image by adding up the red, green, and blue values. Color analysis showed 4 color groups: Group 1 = total RGB $[400; +\infty[$ and HSV total $] - \infty; 200]$; Group 2 = total RGB $[350; 400]$ and total HSV $[150; 200]$; Group 3 = total RGB $[180; 350]$ and total HSV $[100; 150]$; Group 4 = RGB $] - \infty; 180]$ and HSV $] - \infty; 100]$. These analyses aim to show images with homogeneous color values. All images are presented as standardized 800×450 pixels 72 dpi JPEG compressed ISO/CEI 10918-1 UIT-T T.81 in an online questionnaire. Our random selection of images, drawn among the 120 initial images corresponding to the 6 selected categories of video games, allows us to avoid a subjective selection through the presence of contextual stimuli such as emotional facial expressions or contextual actions. We chose an online questionnaire to help in reaching a larger number and a better diversity of participants. This method implies, however, that we were not able to control the quality of the color reproduction on the participant's screens. It should be noted however that the color reproduction quality to web users today is considered good enough to propose visual online surveys. For example, browser statistics show that more than 99% of the visitors of a well-known web coding site, W3Schools, are using 24-bit or 32-bit color mode (cf. http://www.w3schools.com/browsers/browsers_Display.asp) (also known as "16.7 million" colors). Numerous online surveys either on color perception or with emphasis on color have been conducted for several years (e.g., [26]).

Figure 2 shows the chromatic analysis applied to each image of groups 1 to 6. We analysed the colors of each image in the RGB additive color space, HSV, HSL, and HSI, and were thus able to determine the perceptual uniformity thereof. We chose to compare image values in many colors spaces because there is no consensus regarding the way of measuring image lighting, color, or saturation, except on CIE guide models [27]. Some terms are synonyms. We have computed the hue from RGB as described by Preucil [28]:

$$h_{\text{rgb}} = \text{atan2}\left(\sqrt{3} \cdot (G - B), 2 \cdot R - G - B\right). \quad (1)$$

Hue is defined technically as "*the degree to which a stimulus can be described as similar to or different from stimuli that are described as red, green, blue, and yellow*" [29]. Brightness is "*an attribute of visual perception in which a source appears to be radiating or reflecting light*" [27]. In the RGB color space, it can be determined using

$$\mu = \frac{R + G + B}{3}. \quad (2)$$

Chroma is the "*purity*" of a color in relation to saturation; the lower the chroma level is, the more the colors are washed out [30]. We have calculated the average picture Chroma as follows [31]:

$$
\begin{aligned}
M &= \max (R, G, B), \\
m &= \min (R, G, B), \\
C &= M - m.
\end{aligned}
\quad (3)
$$

Medium faded green

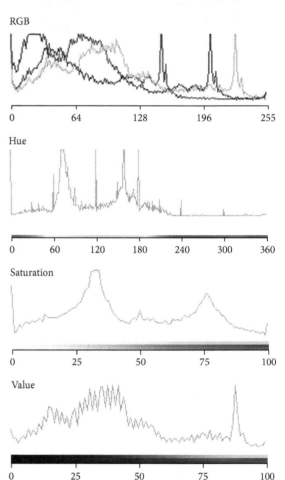

FIGURE 2: Video game frame color analysis.

Value is defined as the largest component of a color; it is described by Smith in the HSV "Hexcone" model by this simple formula [32]:

$$V = M = \max (R, G, B). \quad (4)$$

Lightness is the midpoint between the minimum and maximum R, G, and B values: the intensity average of the R, G, and B values. In an HSI color space, lightness intensity and color saturation are given by

$$
\begin{aligned}
I_{\text{HSI}} &= \frac{R + G + B}{3}, \\
S_{\text{HSI}} &= I - \frac{3 \min (R + G + B)}{R + G + B}.
\end{aligned}
\quad (5)
$$

For a second method of image analysis, we used a color segmentation method based on a component difference threshold [33]. The difference threshold is the limit beyond which the color is considered belonging to a new group, not assigned to an existing one. The higher the threshold, the smaller the number of color groups that will be created by the analysis. The lower the threshold, the smaller the groups of similar color created by the analysis. The calculation of the color difference is the combined difference between the color model components used (RGB, HSV, or, for a more perceptually adapted model, CIE $L*u*v$). To minimize color groups in our analysis, we used a difference threshold of 40 with a CIE $L*u*v$ model.

The data are visualized on 2D and 3D hue and saturation spaces with colored proportional circles and balls representing the size of each group. (The tool is freely available online at: https://www.geotests.net/couleurs/frequs_svg.html?l=en.) All the data are saved in a CSV file. The analysis presents the hierarchy of color groups in the image (number of pixels) and their relations in terms of color components (gradients, oppositions, etc.). We are trying to establish whether a correlation exists between the volume of color groups in each image and the emotions described by participants. It is possible to refine the analysis of the image's colored areas by estimating a visual saliency map of the image. Salience is a concept from cognitive psychology and robotics, which involves estimating the areas of the image that will attract attention quickly and hold it. Thus, one can identify which parts of the image will actually be viewed and perceived by users and determine their color composition. In the context of a game where the images are changing rapidly, this can be particularly important. Several algorithmic methods for highlighting areas of image saliency exist. One of the most cited algorithms of salience modeling is the iLab Neuromorphic Vision C++ Toolkit or INVT [34]. It was developed by the iLab Laboratory at USC Los Angeles. Another, more recent, algorithm seems efficient: it is referred to as "Image Signature" [35]. However, the most common model used (in more than 100 scientific articles) seems to be the Walther and Koch model, an evolution of previous Walther and Koch work [36]. We chose to use this model with the MATLAB software [37]. We then tested if a correlation existed between the volume of pixels considered salient in each of the images and the valence and activation of the emotions of the players. We analysed the saliency maps rather than highly targeted rescaled binary shape maps because our research is not focused on the analysis of the supposed major point of interest in each image (Figure 4), but rather on the potential link between the number of stimuli and emotional state of the players. We have specifically chosen to measure the volume of salient pixels in the Intensity Conspicuity Map for each image (Figure 5).

Images are analysed with the same method as for the first test: we used a color segmentation method based on a component difference threshold. Data are saved in a CSV file. We then calculate all the pixels in the projecting selection by removing rgb(0, 0, 0) black pixels. These values are then compared to values obtained in the subjective semantic questionnaires.

2.2. Questionnaire Subjective Semantics.

Many studies have shown that the influence of colors can be affected by age and sex, as well as nationality and cultural backgrounds. However, studies also showed that, regardless of ethnic and geographical origin, humans experience some common emotions when faced with the same colors [24, 38, 39]. In most questionnaires of the previous experiments, participants were asked to define emotions that were more or less important from their point of view. Our approach is different: we did not use categorical classifications of emotions, but rather a dimensional classification of valence and arousal [9]. The IAPS survey is used to study image emotional impact on pleasure, arousal, and dominance. Initially, the IAPS system was developed to suggest a set of emotional pictures for psychological investigations on emotions and attention, but we did not use this set of emotional pictures. We used the IAPS scale semantic subjective questionnaire for measuring emotional impact from our own selected video game environments still images. The questionnaire is an online web form sent to participants via social networks. Filling the questionnaire is relatively long (35 minutes on average); this represents a real investment both in terms of attention and time, avoiding voluntarily erratic responses. The questionnaire is presented in English and French. The first page explains the terms of the measurement:

> "HAPPY-UNHAPPY scale. At one extreme of the scale, you felt happy, pleased, satisfied, contented and hopeful. If you felt completely happy while viewing the picture, you can indicate this by placing a "Black Point" over the left. The other end of the scale is when you felt completely unhappy, annoyed, unsatisfied, melancholic, despaired, bored. EXCITED versus CALM dimension is the second type of feeling displayed here. At one extreme of the scale you felt stimulated, excited, frenzied, jittery, wide-awake, aroused. If you felt completely aroused while viewing the picture, place a "Point" over the number 0 at the left of the row. On the other hand, at the other end of the scale, you felt completely relaxed, calm, sluggish, dull, sleepy, unaroused. CONTROLLED versus IN-CONTROL. At one end of the scale you have feelings characterized as completely controlled, influenced, cared-for, awed, submissive, guided. Please indicate feeling controlled by placing a "Point" over the 0 number at the left. At the other extreme of this scale, you felt completely controlling, influential, in control, important, dominant, and autonomous."

Then the instructions text invites the participant to rate the pictures: "*Please rate each one as you actually felt while you watched the picture.*" First, the participant must evaluate a practice picture and then he begins the questionnaire. Pictures are presented randomly. There are 6 pages to evaluate, each containing 4 pictures and their 3 evaluation scales from 1 to 10. Each participant's unique IP address can only rate one

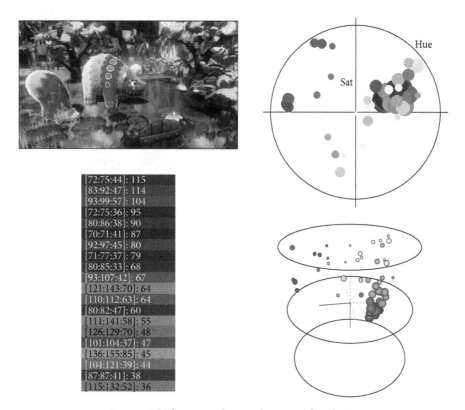

FIGURE 3: Video games frame colors second analysis.

questionnaire. Personal information is not stored about the participants, except their age and sex.

3. Results

We recruited $n = 85$ participants on the web by the use of social networks. They have answered the semantic subjective questionnaire via their web browser (Google Forms). We have temporarily kept the user's IP to avoid bounced questionnaires; all the IP addresses have been erased after this verification. Regarding the time taken to answer the questionnaire (generally more than 25 minutes), we argue that this delay helped avoid made-up answers. The group was composed of 31 females and 54 males, with an average age of 32 years. The participants answered the semantic subjective questionnaire after observing each of the 24 video game frames randomly presented (Figure 3). This method allowed us to collect data in a single online database. Since a difference of emotional sensitivity in video games has been shown to correlate to the participant's level of knowledge of the media [40], we only asked participants playing video games for more than 2 hours per week to participate in the experiment.

The correlations between feelings of joy versus sadness are all strong in testing results related to the following: brightness: $R = -0.085$, $p = 0.009$, the value: $R = -0.84$, $p = 0.007$, chroma $R = -0.85$, $p = 0.000$, and lightness: $R = -0.80$, $p = 0.01$. The correlation is low regarding the links between hue and happy/unhappy (see Table 1).

TABLE 1: Happiness correlation.

	Happy/unhappy		
N	Input	R specific	p
24	Brightness	−0.85	**0.009**
24	Hue	0.21	0.041
24	Value	−0.84	**0.007**
24	Chroma	−0.85	**0.000**
24	Lightness	−0.80	**0.013**

TABLE 2: Arousal correlation.

	Arousal		
N	Input	R specific	p
24	Brightness	−0.39	0.007
24	Hue	−0.04	0.033
24	Value	−0.37	0.006
24	Chroma	−0.43	0.000
24	Lightness	−0.33	0.011

The emotional activity collected in the subjective semantics questionnaire, by asking between calm versus excitement, produces only low correlations. The values are not significant, respectively, for brightness $R = -0.39$, $p = 0.007$, hue $R = -0.04$, $p = 0033$, value $R = -0.37$, $p = 0.006$, chroma $R = -0.43$, $p = 0.000$, and lightness $R = 0.33$, $p = 0.011$ (see Table 2).

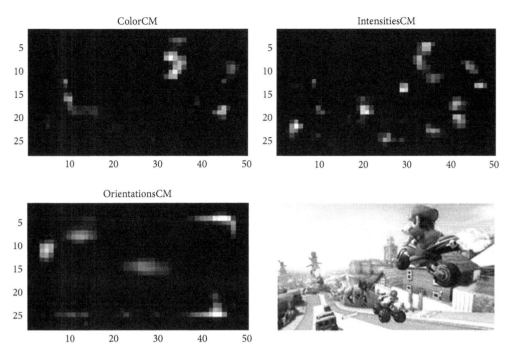

FIGURE 4: One of the images and its saliency map.

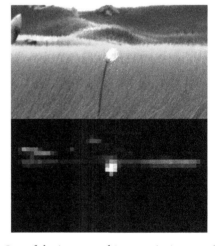

FIGURE 5: One of the images and its conspicuity map, Sony Computer Entertainment. Thatgamecompany, Bluepoint Games, 2009.

TABLE 3: Valence correlation.

N	Input	R specific	p
	Controlled/dominant		
24	Brightness	**0.68**	**0.004**
24	Hue	−0.10	0.017
24	Value	**0.64**	**0.003**
24	Chroma	**0.62**	**0.000**
24	Lightness	**0.69**	**0.006**

TABLE 4: Color number correlation.

	Happ	Arr	Contr
Color diversity			
Corr	**−0.667**	**−0.58**	0.404
Sig. b	**0.000**	**0.003**	0.050
N	24	24	24

The values of controlled versus dominant to assess feelings of fear or confidence of the players are, like the feelings of joy versus sadness, significantly and positively correlated: brightness $R = 0.68$, $p = 0.004$, value $R = 0.64$, $p = 0.003$, and chroma $R = 0.62$, $p = 0.000$, as correlations with joy and sadness, hue has a weak negative correlation $R = −0.1$, $p = 0.017$ (see Table 3).

We tested if the amount of chromatic diversity in the images was significantly correlated with the different emotional states identified in semantic subjective questionnaire. Pearson's correlations between volume chromatic diversity and the sense of joy versus sadness show strong correlation with $R = −0.66$, Sig. $= 0.000$ but also with arousal (corresponding to emotions calm versus excitement) with $R = −0.58$, Sig. $= 0.003$. The correlation is low contrast regarding emotions controlled versus dominant as fear or confidence (see Table 4).

We finally evaluate the correlations between the assumed number of salient pixels in each image identified after MATLAB analysis and removing rgb$(0, 0, 0)$ pixels. This showed stronger correlation with the evaluated emotions of sadness Joy $R = −0.79$, Sig. $= 0.000$ and also with the emotions of fear confidence $R = 0.56$, Sig. $= 0.004$. On the other hand, the correlation between the volume of saliency and arousal was low (see Table 5).

TABLE 5: Pixel saliency correlation.

	Happ	Arr	Contr
PxNb saliency			
Corr	**−0.793**	−0.483	**0.560**
Sig. b	**0.000**	0.017	**0.004**
N	24	24	24

4. Discussion

The results of our research imply that links exist between feelings of joy/sadness and environment properties: brightness, value, saturation, chroma, and lightness. For the brightness of images, the greater the color Saturation is, the more positive the valence of these feelings is. This corroborates previous studies which also showed that images leading to the perception of joy tend to be brighter, more saturated, and having more colors than images of sadness in a virtual environment [41]. The same links are observed with feelings of fear/confidence, with questions in the survey, as controlled/dominant. It also seems that if the video game environments are less saturated, the negative valence and the feeling of fear are higher. This is also true for the luminosity density: lower brightness induces a sense of fear, while high brightness seems to make players have more confidence. In all initial conditions related to brightness, chroma, value, or lightness, we have not observed, at this stage of the experiment, links with emotional arousal. However, a correlation was observed between arousal (a player's emotional excitement or relative calm) and the chromatic diversity. We can assume that if an image has more sources of different colors, there could be increased neuronal activity related to observation [42], thereby generating the conditions for greater emotional activity [43]. This high color diversity also allows the generation of a positive sense of joy, which is also correlated with the number of observable saliency points in an environment. Salient elements require more activation of the rods of the visual system, as joy and fear require more awakeness. It is likely that in both cases the large volume of stimuli elements may indeed generate great neuronal analysis, leading to cognitive positive or negative valence. Several studies have shown that evolutionary selective pressures have resulted in slightly higher spatial acuity rather than increased chromatic sensitivity [44]. This could explain why color diversity produces lower emotional activity except for happiness and sadness. The pixel saliency number is more indicative of the volume of stimuli producing emotional activity. In our experiments we did not test the correlation between motion stimuli and emotion because several studies have already shown the very high influence of movement stimuli on emotional activation or the relative calm produced by the slow movement of these same stimuli [45, 46].

The circumplex model for colors design is defined as an analysis of evolutionary cognitive overgeneralization, not really within an idiosyncratic ecological context. However, we recognize that the thresholds of emotional activities are also linked to the personal experiences of each player; they are not

discussed here. We obviously do not conclude that a saturated color environment could not induce an emotion such as fear or sadness. Other contextual factors and stimuli explain the induction of emotion.

In an upcoming experiment, we will test participants in a unique interactive virtual game. In this environment, we will change colors, lights, and saturation as suggested by our circumplex model to try to induce several emotions. The context will remain unchanged and we will not intervene on the stimuli of different participants, except for the color diversity variations, lightness, saturation, and perspective view (stimuli saliency). In the same way, stimuli motion speed will differ.

5. Conclusion

5.1. General Conclusion. Our research was conducted in order to design a tentative tool for the essential emotional phase in video game design: color scripting. The color design defines the chromatic aspects of each scene according to the emotions that the authors want to suggest. This tool was designed according to the previous circumplex model [15]. Our study is an analytical study proposing a methodology for defining the chromatic atmosphere of interactive environments based on a wide range of inducible emotions. The circumplex model could allow for the generation of emotions based on their positive or negative valences, but also according to their arousal: game designers can use volume of chromatic diversity, color saturation, brightness, and even motion speeds.

Making this tentative tool available to the gaming community is a priority for our team. We hope to contribute to increasing the quality of emotional experiences in the future of the gaming industry.

5.2. How to Use the Circumplex Model. To use the tentative circumplex model tool, we recommend first defining in advance what kind of emotion the environment should induce and then setting this emotional valence and arousal in the circumplex model (Figure 6). The positioning of the emotion in the schema defines the color, light, intensity, and motion speed to use. The top right area defines a large chromatic diversity: it does not specify a particular color, but the more distant the selected emotion is from the center, the more the virtual environment must contain a high number of colors. The lower right area defines poor chromatic diversity, the colors are organized in monochrome, and their kind depends on untreated or subjective cultural context here. If the chosen emotion is far away from the center of the diagram, the gradation will be less colourful. The bottom left area uses the same concepts of shades, but if the cursor moves away from the center of the diagram, the colors will appear less saturated and less bright. The top left area will use a variety of colors like the upper right area, but if the chosen emotion is far from the center, these colors will also be desaturated and low lighting. In the lower half of the circle, stimuli motions are slower, and the lower the chosen emotion in the circle is, the slower the stimuli will be. In the

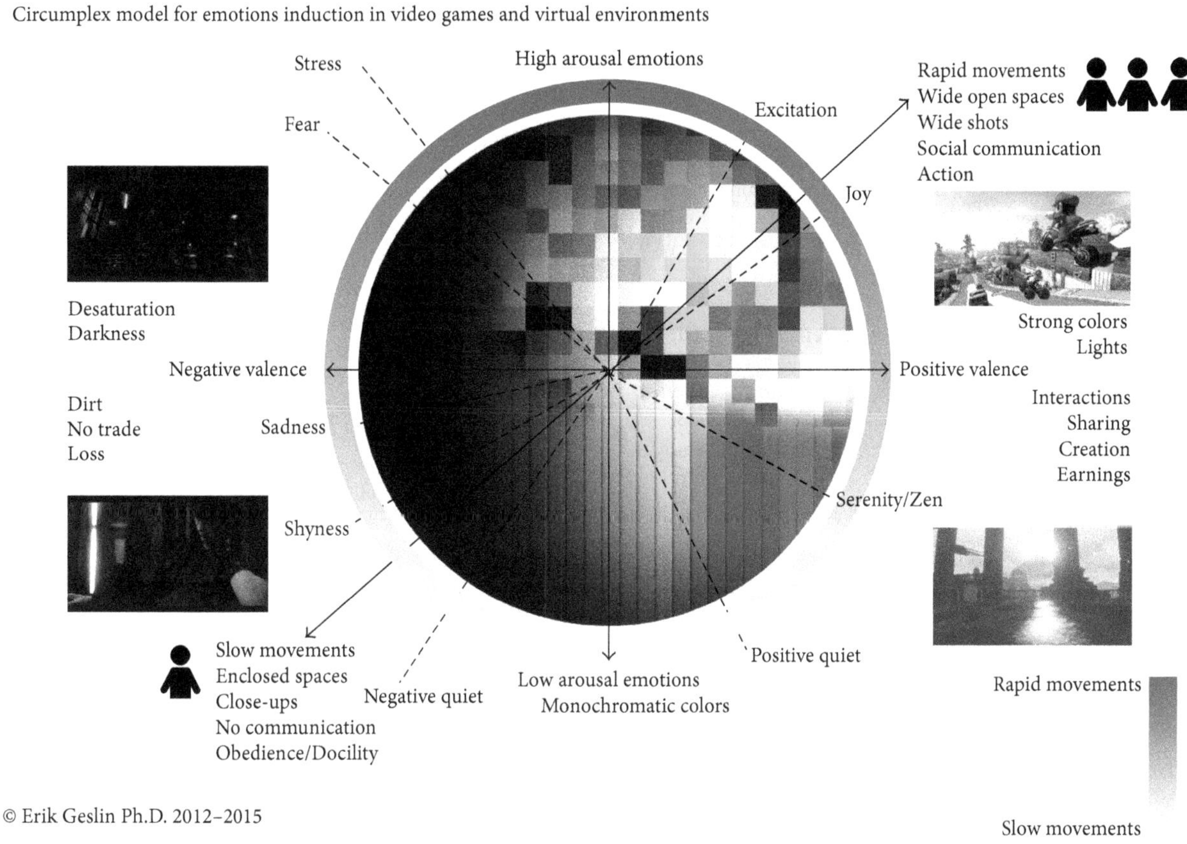

Circumplex model for emotions induction in video games and virtual environments

© Erik Geslin Ph.D. 2012–2015

FIGURE 6: A tentative circumplex model for color scripting in video game.

top half quarter, the more the emotion is at the top of the ordered axis, the faster the visual stimuli will be. The volume of salient stimuli is determined by a cutting plane, dividing the circle at 45 degrees, with emotions located at the top right and farthest from the center of the diagram area having the highest volume of stimuli. In contrast, the emotions of low farthest left of the center area will be those that show the least amount of visual stimuli.

Acknowledgments

The authors wish to thank all the participants of the experiment for the time spent on their research. Special thanks are due to Andrea Trapnell for her time spent.

References

[1] B. Cowley, D. Charles, M. Black, and R. Hickey, "Toward an understanding of flow in video games," *Computers in Entertainment*, vol. 6, no. 2, article 20, 2008.

[2] M. Slater, "Place illusion and plausibility can lead to realistic behaviour in immersive virtual environments," *Philosophical Transactions of the Royal Society B: Biological Sciences*, vol. 364, no. 1535, pp. 3549–3557, 2009.

[3] C. Jennett, A. L. Cox, P. Cairns et al., "Measuring and defining the experience of immersion in games," *International Journal of Human-Computer Studies*, vol. 66, no. 9, pp. 641–661, 2008.

[4] R. Koster, *Theory of Fun for Game Design*, O'Reilly Media, 2013.

[5] Platon, *Les Lois*, GF Flammarion, Paris, France, 2006.

[6] J. LeDoux, *The Emotional Brain*, W&N, London, UK, 1999.

[7] P. Ekman, *Emotions Revealed*, Owl Books, 2003.

[8] S. Du, Y. Tao, and A. M. Martinez, "Compound facial expressions of emotion," *Proceedings of the National Academy of Sciences of the United States of America*, vol. 111, no. 15, pp. E1454–E1462, 2014.

[9] J. A. Russell, "A circumplex model of affect," *Journal of Personality and Social Psychology*, vol. 39, no. 6, pp. 1161–1178, 1980.

[10] S.-Y. Yoon and K. Wise, "Reading emotion of color environments: computer simulations with self-reports and physiological signals," in *Industrial Applications of Affective Engineering*, pp. 219–232, Springer, Basel, Switzerland, 2014.

[11] P. Valdez and A. Mehrabian, "Effects of color on emotions," *Journal of Experimental Psychology: General*, vol. 123, no. 4, pp. 394–409, 1994.

[12] M. Li, F. Liu, M. Juusola, and S. Tang, "Perceptual color map in macaque visual area V4," *The Journal of Neuroscience*, vol. 34, no. 1, pp. 202–217, 2014.

[13] F. M. Adams and C. E. Osgood, "A cross-cultural study of the affective meanings of color," *Journal of Cross-Cultural Psychology*, vol. 4, no. 2, pp. 135–156, 1973.

[14] P. J. Lang and M. M. Bradley, *International Affective Picture System (IAPS): Affective Ratings of Pictures and Instruction Manual*, NIMH, Center for the Study of Emotion & Attention, 2005.

[15] E. Geslin, *Processus d'Induction d'Émotions dans les Environ-*

nements Virtuels et le Jeu Vidéo, Ecole Nationale Superieure d'Arts et Metiers (ENSAM), 2013.

[16] J. Chen, "Flow in games (and everything else)," *Communications of the ACM*, vol. 50, no. 4, pp. 31–34, 2007.

[17] D. Choi and J. Kim, "Why people continue to play online games: in search of critical design factors to increase customer loyalty to online contents," *Cyberpsychology & Behavior*, vol. 7, no. 1, pp. 11–24, 2004.

[18] A. E. Voiskounsky, O. V. Mitina, and A. A. Avetisova, "Playing online games: flow experience," *PsychNology Journal*, vol. 2, no. 3, pp. 259–281, 2004.

[19] D. Weibel, B. Wissmath, S. Habegger, Y. Steiner, and R. Groner, "Playing online games against computer- vs. human-controlled opponents: effects on presence, flow, and enjoyment," *Computers in Human Behavior*, vol. 24, no. 5, pp. 2274–2291, 2008.

[20] L.-C. Ou, M. R. Luo, A. Woodcock, and A. Wright, "A study of colour emotion and colour preference. Part I: colour emotions for single colours," *Color Research & Application*, vol. 29, no. 3, pp. 232–240, 2004.

[21] L.-C. Ou, M. R. Lou, A. Woodcock, and A. Wright, "A study of colour emotion and colour preference. Part II: colour emotions for two-colour combinations," *Color Research & Application*, vol. 29, no. 4, pp. 292–298, 2004.

[22] B. Manav, "Color-emotion associations and color preferences: a case study for residences," *Color Research & Application*, vol. 32, no. 2, pp. 144–150, 2007.

[23] W.-N. Wang and Y.-L. Yu, "Image emotional semantic query based on color semantic description," in *Proceedings of the International Conference on Machine Learning and Cybernetics (ICMLC '05)*, IEEE, Guangzhou, China, August 2005.

[24] X.-P. Gao, J. H. Xin, T. Sato et al., "Analysis of cross-cultural color emotion," *Color Research & Application*, vol. 32, no. 3, pp. 223–229, 2007.

[25] C. Elverdam and E. Aarseth, "Game classification and game design: construction through critical analysis," *Games and Culture*, vol. 2, no. 1, pp. 3–22, 2007.

[26] H. P. Anderson and J. Ward, "Principle component analyses of questionnaires measuring individual differences in synaesthetic phenomenology," *Consciousness and Cognition*, vol. 33, pp. 316–324, 2015.

[27] R. B. Gibbons, *Official Recommendations on Uniform Color Spaces, Color Difference Equations, and Metric Color Terms*, Supplement no. 2 to CIE Publication no. 15, Colorimetry, Commission Internationale de L'Eclairage (CIE), Paris, France, 1976.

[28] F. Preucil, "Color hue and ink transfer—their relation to perfect reproduction," in *TAGA Proceedings*, pp. 102–110, 1953.

[29] M. D. Fairchild, *Color Appearance Models*, John Wiley & Sons, 2013.

[30] A. H. Munsell, *A Color Notation*, Munsell Color Company, 1919.

[31] M. K. Agoston, *Computer Graphics and Geometric Modeling*, Springer, Berlin, Germany, 2005.

[32] A. R. Smith, "Color gamut transform pairs," *ACM SIGGRAPH Computer Graphics*, vol. 12, no. 3, pp. 12–19, 1978.

[33] L. Jégou and J. P. Deblonde, "Vers une visualisation de la complexité de l'image cartographique," *Cybergeo: European Journal of Geography*, 34 pages, 2012.

[34] L. Itti and C. Koch, "Computational modelling of visual attention," *Nature Reviews Neuroscience*, vol. 2, no. 3, pp. 194–203, 2001.

[35] X. Hou, J. Harel, and C. Koch, "Image signature: highlighting sparse salient regions," *IEEE Transactions on Pattern Analysis and Machine Intelligence*, vol. 34, no. 1, pp. 194–201, 2011.

[36] D. Walther and C. Koch, "Modeling attention to salient proto-objects," *Neural Networks*, vol. 19, no. 9, pp. 1395–1407, 2006.

[37] MathWorks, *MATLAB*, MathWorks, 2014.

[38] L. Sivik, "Connotations and perceptual variables," in *Tagungs-Bericht Compte Rendu. Proceedings. Internationale Farbtagung. International Colour Meeting*, vol. 69, pp. 1064–1072, Muster-Schmidt, Göttingen, Germany, 1970.

[39] C. E. Osgood, "The cross-cultural generality of visual-verbal synesthetic tendencies," *Behavioral Science*, vol. 5, no. 2, pp. 146–169, 1960.

[40] E. Geslin, S. Bouchard, and S. Richir, "Gamers' versus non-gamers' emotional response in virtual reality," *Journal of CyberTherapy & Rehabilitation*, vol. 4, no. 4, pp. 489–493, 2011.

[41] C. M. De Melo and J. Gratch, "The effect of color on expression of joy and sadness in virtual humans," in *Proceedings of the 3rd International Conference on Affective Computing and Intelligent Interaction and Workshops (ACII '09)*, pp. 1–7, IEEE, Amsterdam, The Netherlands, September 2009.

[42] C. Ware, *Information Visualization: Perception for Design*, Elsevier, 2012.

[43] K. R. Gegenfurtner and L. T. Sharpe, *Color Vision: From Genes to Perception*, Cambridge University Press, Cambridge, UK, 2001.

[44] G. Gagin, K. S. Bohon, A. Butensky et al., "Color-detection thresholds in rhesus macaque monkeys and humans," *Journal of Vision*, vol. 14, no. 8, article 12, 2014.

[45] B. H. Detenber and B. Reeves, "A bio-informational theory of emotion: motion and image size effects on viewers," *Journal of Communication*, vol. 46, no. 3, pp. 66–84, 1996.

[46] R. F. Simons, B. H. Detenber, T. M. Roedema, and J. E. Reiss, "Emotion processing in three systems: the medium and the message," *Psychophysiology*, vol. 36, no. 5, pp. 619–627, 1999.

5

The Relationship between Player's Value Systems and their In-Game Behavior in a Massively Multiplayer Online Role-Playing Game

Chaoguang Wang and Gino Yu

Digital Entertainment Lab, Hong Kong Polytechnic University, Hung Hom, Kowloon, Hong Kong

Correspondence should be addressed to Gino Yu; gino.yu@polyu.edu.hk

Academic Editor: Hanqiu Sun

This study examines the relationship between player's value systems and their actions in playing a massively multiplayer online role-playing game. Online survey data from 1,577 players were paired with their behavioral metrics within the game. A number of correlations were found between the scores of value system and the in-game metrics. Participants that scored high on the Red value system tend to spend more real money in the game, level up their character and ability as quickly as possible, and seek other achievements in the forms offered by game world. These characteristics for fun, power, and immediate gratification are also predicted by the Red value system. The finding provides valuable information on how to better design, evaluate, and understand enjoyment in games. The results also show the possibility of using the game as a platform in inferring players' value systems and in training people to develop certain skills.

1. Introduction

MMORPGs (massively multiplayer online role-playing games) have become the most popular game genre, representing a revolution of social, cultural, and considerable financial impact. The total gaming market revenue of China increased to US$18.5 billion in 2014, and MMORPGs accounted for about a third of it [1].

Understanding player characteristics is an essential part of game design and also has important implications for increasing games' potential for positive impact on society. The personality, which reflects the behaviors that define and characterize each individual, has been recognized as one of the key components to understanding both the uses and effects of video games. The diversity of player behaviors within game world also offers unique opportunities to study the relationship between personality and game playing, and MMORPGs are "a gold mine of personality data" [2].

However, the personality characteristics of players as a group are still not well understood, and there has been relatively little research involving personality of players and their

in-game behavior. What is more, most of the current gaming research tends to be based on self-reported data obtained from the players using interviews, surveys, or ethnographic observations. To address these limitations, we should pay more attention to longitudinal data collected directly from games, which provides us with a solid empirical foundation to better understand these complex virtual worlds [3]. Studies about China MMORPGs players are also still scarce, and a better knowledge of them is to be hoped, given that China players are the largest MMORPGs user group in the world.

In the present study, we examine the relationship between player personalities as conceptualised by Graves [4] and their behavior in a MMORPG in China. The findings will help to gain insight about the audience in order to fulfil the needs of the specific player and enable game industry to create more engaging and targeted games.

1.1. Personality and Player Behavior. Personality is defined as the organized totality of characteristics or qualities that makes a person different from others. It combines attitudes, motivations, needs, and emotions and influences how people think, behave, and approach internal and external situations [5]. There have been numerous studies about the factors that may affect leisure activity of a given group, community, and population, such as age, education, income, sex, occupation, and social class [6]. However, for predicting leisure behavior, the traditional demographic variables have proven to be weak, and, as suggested before, personality may be a better predictor of choice than demographics for experiential products [7].

The response to video game is primarily based upon the relationship between the presentation of the game content and the interpretation occurring within the mind of the player. The personality has a strong influence on how people think and behave in the real world and should, therefore, also influence their in-game behavior as well. Existing research has also demonstrated players behaved much the same in online games as they do in the real world [8]. The patterns of neurons arising from virtual experiences are very similar to those arising from physical threats [9]. Since the players are personally invested in their avatars and the environment, the game playing is thought to be a personally revealing activity [10].

There have been a number of attempts to apply the personality to investigate playing styles of game users and explore the relationship between the personality and in-game behaviors. Using Myers-Briggs Type Indicator (MBTI) test, Bateman and Boon explored personality as a way to better understand game playing and how such information can affect game design [11]. In their research, 16 personality types of MBTI were grouped into four playing styles with different tastes and needs: conqueror, manager, wanderer, and participant. By conducting a Five-Factor Model personality test and a value survey, Griebel found both personality traits and values correlated with specific game play behavior in the game of Sims 2 [12]. Van Lankveld et al. correlated the game behavior within the game of Neverwinter Nights to scores in the personality questionnaire and demonstrated that all five traits of the Five-Factor Model have an effect on players' in-game behavior [13]. Tekofsky et al. investigated the correlations between Five-Factor Model personality traits and playing behavior of Battlefield 3 provided by a database of their game statistics and found that play style correlated significantly to players' personality [14].

The existing research has also revealed several meaningful correlations between personality traits and in-game behaviors in MMORPGs. Yee et al.'s study examined the link between personality and playing behaviors in World of Warcraft and found many behavioral cues in the game were related to personality traits of the Five-Factor Model [10]. For example, Extraverts prefer group activities over solo activities, and players that scored higher on Openness have more characters and complete more exploration achievements. In contrast, McCreery et al. found no significant correlations between Five-Factor personality traits and corresponding sets of in-game behavior in World of Warcraft, such as correlation between the Agreeableness trait and a set of predefined "agreeable" behaviors [15]. However, as acknowledged by McCreery et al., the validity of the behavior sets they defined was not analyzed, and it is not clear whether the items

in each set form appropriate and reliable scales. Also the sample size (n = 39) in their study may be too small to have a generalized conclusion. In a more recent study, Worth conducted a survey on players' personalities of World of Warcraft and their different behaviors within the game [16]. Significant correlations were found between HEXACO (Honesty-Humility, Emotionality, Extraversion, Agreeableness, Conscientiousness, and Openness to Experience) personality traits and in-game behavior. For instance, Social Player-versus-Environment activities positively correlated with Extraversion.

In summary, a considerable amount of research about the player personality has narrowly focused on the horizontal psychological typologies, such as the Five-Factor Model. McLuhan stated that games are collective and social reactions to the main drive or action of a specific culture, and when cultures change, so do previously accepted patterns of games [17]. The horizontal psychological typologies, such as the Five-Factor Model, or the Myers-Briggs personality type system, merely identify stylistic differences and are unable to explain players' changing tastes in relation to their personality. There is a strong need to address the personality features of players using a developmental and hierarchical model. Additionally, the limited volume of research available for studying personality and in-game behavior overlooks more precise information related to game mechanics. Much research relied on self-edited game level or public database of game to record and analyze players' behavior but did not use commercial game data (also live player data sets).

1.2. Value Systems Model and Measurement Instrument. Graves performed decades of empirical research between the 1950s and the 1970s regarding what is mature human personality and concluded with a framework of human development he named the Emergent Cyclical Levels of Existence Theory [4]. Graves' academic achievements were adapted to the model of Spiral Dynamics, the most authoritative theory on value systems, and introduced to a wider audience by his students and successors Beck and Cowan [18]. In the meantime, a considerable number of other studies and books have appeared, referring to Graves' model or Spiral Dynamics, and described a wide range of extensive applications in which the value systems could be used [19].

Graves pointed out that human nature is an open, constantly evolving system and humans construct new conceptual model of the world in response to the interaction of external conditions with internal neuronal systems [4]. Graves referred to these states of equilibrium between environmental problems of living and neurological coping systems as levels of existence or value systems. The value systems are the primary term we used here, which are considered to be modes of adjustment for coping with the perception of the reality of the world.

Graves identified eight core value systems consisting of a set of world views, a hierarchy of needs, and corresponding behavior. The development of value systems occurs in a fixed order as shown in Table 1. Each value system is designated by pairs of letters from Graves's original terminology, while the first letter stands for the neurological system and the second

TABLE 1: Summary of value systems.

Level and label	Means values	Nature of existence	Basic theme
1th AN (Beige)	None	Automatic	Express self as if it were just another animal according to the dictates of one's imperative psychological needs
2th BO (Purple)	Traditionalism	Ttribalistic	Sacrifice self to the way of your elders
3th CP (Red)	Exploitation	Egocentric	Express self, to hell with the consequences, lest one suffer the torment of unbearable shame
4th DQ (Blue)	Sacrifice	Deferentialistic	Sacrifice self now in order to receive reward later
5th ER (Orange)	Scientism	Materialistic	Express self for what self desires, but in a fashion calculated not to bring down the wrath of others
6th FS (Green)	Sociocentricity	Personalistic	Sacrifice now in order to get acceptance now
7th GT (Yellow)	Accepting	Cognitivistic	Express self for what self desires, but never at the expenses of others and in a manner that all life, not just my life, will profit
8th HU (Turquoise)	Experiencing	Experientialistic	Adjust to the realities of one's existence and automatically accept the existential dichotomies as they are and go on living

for the existential problems [4]. Beck and Cowan designated a different color for each value as symbol in their Spiral Dynamics Model, which has been widely accepted and used [18].

And, in the development process, the new value systems will merely establish subordination of the older ones, not eradicate them. For example, when the Purple system takes over, the Beige is still there and subordinated in it. The new value system includes and transcends the previous ones, thus forming a natural hierarchy, and there is a mixture of value systems at work in each person all the time.

As indicated by Graves, when in a certain development state, a human would have opened only certain systems for coping and has their own hierarchy of needs around a core value system [4]. They would think, feel, and be motivated in manners appropriate to the state of his centralization and have biochemical characteristics and a state of neurological activation particular to it.

Graves' theory has evident implication in the analysis of responses to video game, and its substance resides on revealing different sets of world views players place on their decisions and actions. What is more, Graves' theory suggested the value of individual is an evolving and always-open-to-change system, which moves beyond the assessment of fixed horizontal dimensions and type indicators of the individual personality. For example, according to Graves' model, we not only know that a person is operating on the Blue but that he came from the Red and could move up to the Orange. Compared with Five-Factor Model or other personality theory, this valuable information permits us to understand the player personality in relation to not only current game playing but also their changing tastes.

A number of efforts have been made to develop instruments for assessing a person's position in the levels of Human Existence hierarchy. The CultureView (http://5deep-vitalsigns.com/products/instruments/cultureview-series/) is derived from the original work of Graves and built upon the work of Don Beck. It was developed and owned by Don Beck and originated in paper form in 1997. Beck first met Graves in 1975 shortly after his Emergent Cyclical theory was published in 1974. He worked with Graves closely until Graves' death in 1986 and then continued to spend many years adapting the work of Graves. CultureView developed by Don Beck, therefore, seemed one of the most qualified instruments to assess individual's value system based on Graves' theory. Since 2001, the CultureView instrument has over 12,000 electronic completions globally and has been translated to many different language versions including English (UK), Dutch, Korean, German, and Spanish.

2. Methods

With an innovative mixed methodology, this study brings together methodological approaches from self-report survey and game metric technique. Participants recruited from the game Ghost II firstly completed an initial survey about value systems and then the value profile was paired with their behavioral metrics within the game world.

2.1. Chinese Translation of the CultureView and Verification. We employed a Chinese translation of the CultureView to assess six value systems from Purple to Yellow. Table 2 lists a representative question of CultureView and illustrates how participants respond to it in a 7-point Likert scale. The

TABLE 2: Representative statements of six value systems, from survey question of CultureView.

| | | What matters most to me... | | | | | | |
Value systems	Representative statement	1	2	3	4	5	6	7
Purple	Be Safe by staying close to friends and family							
Red	Be Strong by taking charge and calling the shots							
Blue	Be Dependable by doing what is right and responsible							
Orange	Be Successful by setting goals and getting ahead							
Green	Be Sensitive by experiencing feelings and promoting harmony							
Yellow	Be Authentic by integrating natural functions and flows							

response options ranged from 1 (very disagreeable) to 7 (very agreeable).

After translating to Chinese, the CultureView was tested among people who can speak both fluent English and Chinese. 10 participants firstly completed the English or Chinese version randomly and then were invited to complete the other corresponding version. After each testing, the correlation was calculated between English and Chinese items, computing Pearson Correlation for the items of continuous variables and Chi-Square Tests for the items of nominal variables. If the result is not significant ($p > 0.05$), the translation of those items will be revised and be brought to one more tested again with another 10 participants. Totally, 4 sessions of testing were conducted to make sure that the item translated to Chinese is significantly correlated with the original English item.

The high correlation between Chinese and English items has indicated that we can retain the validity and reliability of the CultureView. The original CultureView is known to have high validity as verified by the expert review and shown through the personal interview in coaching process. We then examined the test-retest reliability of the Chinese version with 20 participants, and they completed the CultureView twice with an interval of one week. 87.65% of items were significantly correlated between two tests, showing a good reliability of the questionnaire. Finally, an online version of CultureView with Chinese items translated and tested was created and used to assess the value systems of Chinese players in the present study.

2.2. Ghost II.
Ghost II (http://nie.163.com/en/qn2.html#aw, NetEase Inc., China), a 3-dimension Real-Time MMORPG, is currently the widely popular online game available commercially in China. Early in 2011, just 131 days after it was released, the total number of registered players was announced as over 12 million. And Ghost II was ranked as one of the Top Ten Domestic MMORPGs in 2012 and 2013 by Chinese game media.

As shown in Figure 1, the game playing of Ghost II is designed around a huge number of different quests or raids, which refer to a specific in-game adventure or endeavor. There are countless objectives and game contents for players

FIGURE 1: A screenshot of Ghost II.

to achieve and explore, such as getting to the next level, acquiring rare items, and being part of a story. Ghost II not only allows task related activities for achievement but also provides a rich context for social experience. Players are encouraged in different ways to communicate and collaborate with other players and regroup in massive guilds. PvP (player-versus-player) activities are also provided from one-to-one duels to large 20-versus-20 battlegrounds.

2.3. Administration of the Online Survey and Game Metric.
With the permission of the NetEase Company that developed and runs Ghost II, the linkage of CultureView survey was presented to the player within the game world directly, and all data was automatically collected and stored via the online survey system of NetEase.

The data collection took place over a period of one week, and all respondents were not paid or compensated for their participation. As shown in Figure 2, when players first logged in during this period, a message appeared and invited them to complete the online survey. When clicking the link to the survey included in this message the participants were taken to a website to submit their data online. The message appeared only once and was not presented again when this character logged on next time. Also this research limited the survey and invitation message to characters above 15 levels in order to ensure we could gain sufficient information about in-game behavior from the higher level characters

TABLE 3: In-game behavior in Ghost II.

	Variables	Description
(1)	Time played	Amount of time (minutes) logged onto the game since the character was created
(2)	Consumption	Amount of real money (China Yuan) spent in game for virtual items since the character was created
(3)	Character level	Level of current character
(4)	Magic stone level	Level of magic stone, an item for enhancing equipment
(5)	Character ability score	Reflecting comprehensive ability of character
(6)	Achievement Point	Total number of achievements player has completed
(7)	Ranking of ability among friends	Ranking among the friends list player added
(8)	Equipment score	Sum of all equipment item scores
(9)	Ability Practice	Number of times player has leveled up character skill and ability
(10)	Number of friends	Total number of present friends added
(11)	Goodwill point	Gaining through grouping and helping lower level player
(12)	Guild level	Level of guild belonged to
(13)	Guild point	Contribution to guild by finishing quest or activities
(14)	Dueling point	Number of winning in duel with players
(15)	Player killing point	Number of killing other player maliciously
(16)	Battleground score	Gaining through Killing against other player and winning a battle in battleground
(17)	Pet score	Pet is a little functional but largely decorative companion
(18)	House score	Reflecting player house's construction that is mainly for decorating and vanity
(19)	Narrative point	Count of completing main storyline quests
(20)	Marriage	Married or not
(21)	Mentorship	In a mentorship or not
(22)	Character Class	Character class participant chooses

FIGURE 2: Survey Invitation Message in Ghost II.

and also not to interrupt the game play of new players. The data form collected in this study contained the following: items of CultureView questionnaire, gender, age, income, areas of residence, occupation, education background, character identity number of player, IP address of respondent, and completion time.

This research had access to the official database of Ghost II in order to collect data of the participant's actual in-game behavior. Player character ID was used as the key for game metrics retrieval, and the players' self-report data containing demographic and value system variables was paired with their character profile created by data mining. Overall, what a player says and does at all times is precisely recorded in MMORPGs, and we can track nearly all actions through the analysis of game logs. In addition, video games vary widely in terms of the kinds of game play and action they offer. However, we cannot extract all possible variables for analysis in this research, and a basic grasp of core game mechanics is necessary.

This study limits the game metrics to a meaningful and manageable subset of longitudinal behavioral data related to the core play dynamics of Ghost II. Like other MMORPGs, Ghost II is achievement oriented and the game design encourages players to progress, gain power, and accumulate wealth and status in game world. The in-game behavior data reviewed here was the key performance statistics of playing in Ghost II and also covered a wide range of behaviors, such as the character level, playing time, the quality of equipment, achievement score, the amount of PvP activities, friendship, and guild membership. A full list and description of the behaviors recorded and analyzed here have been presented in Table 3. All the metrics data recorded here were tracked since the character was first created and were cumulative over a long time.

TABLE 4: Correlations between value systems and player behavior.

	Variables	Purple	Red	Blue	Orange	Green	Yellow
(1)	Time played	−0.003	0.036	0.047	0.005	0.036	0.020
(2)	Consumption by time	0.041	**0.101****	0.035	**0.090***	0.015	0.035
(3)	Character level	0.017	**0.064***	0.034	0.034	0.028	0.028
(4)	Magic stone level by time	0.018	**0.061****	−0.018	0.049	−0.038	0.042
(5)	Character ability score	0.011	**0.063***	0.039	0.035	0.049	0.037
(6)	Achievement Point	0.004	0.042	0.031	0.007	**0.058***	0.026
(7)	Ranking by time	0.000	−0.014	0.007	0.010	−0.027	0.036
(8)	Equipment score by level	0.020	**0.050***	0.041	0.028	0.053*	0.034
(9)	Ability practice by time	0.007	**0.051***	0.011	0.047	0.047	0.007
(10)	Friends number by time	0.013	0.007	−0.008	0.023	−0.033	0.016
(11)	Goodwill point by level	−0.007	0.017	**0.064***	0.022	0.033	0.018
(12)	Guild level by level	0.027	0.033	0.000	0.033	0.010	0.005
(13)	Guild point by level	0.009	−0.011	0.013	0.034	−0.025	−0.005
(14)	Dueling point by time	0.021	0.022	0.017	0.037	−0.002	0.014
(15)	Killing point by time	0.015	0.023	−0.015	0.013	−0.024	−0.005
(16)	Battleground score by time	0.002	0.018	−0.015	−0.006	−0.010	−0.004
(17)	Pet score	0.010	**0.061***	0.031	0.042	0.047	0.043
(18)	House score by level	0.018	0.018	0.021	0.000	**0.056****	0.021
(19)	Narrative point by level	−0.006	**0.053****	0.015	0.017	0.029	0.007
(20)	Marriage	−0.012	−0.015	0.004	0.018	−0.024	0.010
(21)	Mentorship	−0.020	−0.019	−0.013	−0.017	0.010	0.017

Notes. $^*p < 0.05$. $^{**}p < 0.01$.

3. Results

3.1. Participant Demographics. The majority of respondents (58.8%, $n = 1{,}577$) are male, and over one-third of them (36.5%) are aged between 19 and 22 years, and 29.5% study for or achieved a bachelor degree. Overall, 28.2% of participants registered as a full-time student, 7.6% worked in technology or research occupations, 5.9% worked in sales occupations, and 5.7% worked in production occupations. 31.1% of them earned no monthly income, and 23.4% had a monthly income between 3,001 and 5,000 RMB (China Yuan).

Most participants had extensive prior experience with online games. More than 40 percent had played online game over 4 years, 18.1% from 2 to 3 years, and 16.1% from 3 to 4 years. The game experience of participants covered nearly all popular MMORPGs available in the Chinese market. Prior to Ghost II, over 10 percent played League of Legends mostly, 9.1% played Fantasy Journey to the West 2 mostly, 8.3% played CrossFire mostly, and about 5 percent played World of Warcraft mostly.

3.2. Correlation Analysis between Value Systems and In-Game Behavior. The game metrics need to be normalized. For example, a player who played for one year would spend more money in the game than a player who played just three months. But there was not one variable that all metrics could be normalized against. Most in-game behaviors were normalized against the time played, including consumption, magic stone level, ability practice, number of friends, dueling point, player killing point, battleground score, ranking of ability

among friends, and guild point. Some metrics that were highly dependent on character level were normalized against character level accordingly, such as equipment score, house score, goodwill point, narrative point, and guild level. For example, a level 60 character can be easily accepted as a member by a higher level guild than a level 20 character. For metrics that could not be normalized, their original numbers were calculated, including character level, character ability score, achievement point, pet score, marriage, mentorship, and class.

A series of Pearson's r correlation tests was performed between scores on the six value systems measured by Culture-View and 15 continuous player behavior variables recorded by game metrics. Pearson's r analysis was also applied to determine the correlations between the score of value systems and 2 dichotomous variables of marriage and mentoring relationship of players, since we can use Pearson's r to calculate point biserial correlation. Table 4 lists the total number of significant correlations per value system. The correlations with $p < 0.05$ are considered to be significant.

The significant results revealed by value systems will be described in the following sections. No significant correlations were found between in-game behavior and scores on the Purple or Yellow value systems, all $p > 0.05$.

3.2.1. Red. Of the six value systems measured here, Red provides the most and strongest correlations with in-game behavior of the player. As defined by Graves, the theme of Red state is to express self and to hell with the consequences. The people operating at the Red level are "egocentric, impulsive

TABLE 5: Multiple regressions on six value systems.

Variables	R	R^2	Adjusted R^2	F	P
Purple	0.074	0.005	−0.002	0.775	0.666
Red	0.128	**0.016****	0.009	2.328	0.007
Blue	0.092	0.009	0.002	1.221	0.267
Orange	0.130	**0.017****	0.010	2.438	0.005
Green	0.089	0.008	0.001	1.126	0.336
Yellow	0.081	0.007	0.000	0.932	0.508

Notes. $^{**}p < 0.01$.

and hedonistic" and "for him the best answer to any problem is the one that brings him immediate pleasure regardless of what happens to anyone else" [4]. The motivation is for power, fun, and control, and the belief is "might-is-right."

Players who scored high on Red tend to advance in the game as quickly as possible. They spent more real money to buy in-game items (2), which is the main indicator of devotion to the game for a free-to-play game. Their character level (2) increases gradually with the scoring on the Red. They had a higher magic stone level (4) and equipment score (8), showing that they seek to become powerful and acquire rare items that other players may never have. The magic stone is a core game mechanic of Ghost II, which can be used to level up the property value of equipment and items, and so contributes a lot to promote the total ability of the character. Players can buy magic stones by paying real money directly within the game and can also acquire them through completing some quests and raids.

Such players enjoy making constant progress and gaining priority in the forms offered by the game. They completed a higher number of ability practices (9), and their ability score (5) was also high, which means they spent a lot of time and money to improve or optimize their own character. They completed the main storyline and gained more narrative points (19), which can be used to level up present skills or acquire new skills. They even had a high score on their pet (17), which provides some help in fighting but mainly as a customization.

3.2.2. Blue. The primary value of the Blue state is to sacrifice now to get reward later. People here control their impulses and easily defer to a higher authority. They also follow certain rules which are considered to offer a clear sense of right and wrong.

Individuals who scored high on the Blue value system gained more goodwill points (11), which is a reward for grouping with a lower level player and helping them to kill monsters or complete quests.

3.2.3. Orange. According to Graves' model, the people of Orange state seek self-achievement and try to find the best solution through rational thought. They value the accomplishments and enjoy the process of competition.

In terms of game playing performance, the individual who scored high on the Orange value system also spent more real money within the game (2). No other significant

correlations were found between Orange score and other achievement indicators of virtual behaviors such as character level or equipment score.

3.2.4. Green. As seen by Graves, in the Green state, people are concerned with inner peace and group recognition. They are derived by the need for community, equality, and unity. Individuals that scored high on Green had a high score of achievement points (6) and equipment (8), showing they have a diversity of interests within game. They were also attracted by the house system (18) of the game, which is mainly used for customization and display purpose.

Beside the correlation analysis, the impact of character class on value systems was assessed using a one-way analysis of variance (ANOVA). The analyses revealed that there was a significant difference on the score of Red across ten character classes, $F = 1.90$, $df = 9$, $n = 1,577$, and $p = 0.048 < 0.05$. For example, Swordsman scored highest on the Red followed by the archer; both are classes of material attack.

The correlation coefficient, such as Pearson's r, only reveals the relationship between two variables, and a multiple regression could allow us to better examine the value system in its relation to more than one behavioral variable. Six linear multiple regressions were conducted on each of the value systems with 11 behavioral variables as predictors that correlated significantly with value system. We used an Entry method, which forces all 11 predictor variables into the model simultaneously. As the results in Table 5 indicate, the multiple regressions for Red ($p < 0.01$) and Orange ($p < 0.05$) were significant, and the other four regression models were not significant.

It is suggested that we can infer a player's Red or Orange value system statistically using playing behaviors in the game world. For instance, the best predictor of Red value system was the magic stone level ($\beta = 3.10$, $p < 0.001$) followed by the total consumption ($\beta = 2.77$, $p < 0.005$). However, the regression value is low, and only 1.6% of variance in Red or 1.7% of variance in Orange scores can be predicated by 11 playing behavioral variables.

4. Discussion

Through pairing players' value systems from self-report data with their actual behaviors recorded by game metrics, we explore and explain the relationships between value systems and playing behavior in a MMORPG. To date, the current study is the first attempt to investigate the links between

Graves' construct and players' in-game behavior. With this work, we show that there is a correlation between in-game behavior and real-life behavioral attitudes as modeled by the ECLET. Participants that scored high on the Red value system tend to spend more real money in the game, level up their character and ability as quickly as possible, and seek other achievements in the forms offered by game world. These characteristics for fun, power, and immediate gratification are also predicted by the Red value system. The results also show the possibility of using the game as a platform in inferring players' value systems.

A number of significant correlations were observed between the score of value systems and the in-game metrics. The consumption in the game has a positive relationship with Red and Orange, which means that increases in the scores of those two value systems correspond to more real money spent for the virtual items contained within Ghost II. Both Red and Orange value systems are viewed as externally oriented (expression self to control the world) and strive for self-achievement, and so, a possible explanation for them purchasing virtual items is that the items give users a performance advantage. As shown by other researchers, there is a link between the virtual item purchases with real money and motivations of playing for advancement and advantage in competitive settings and self-expression, and enhancing playing performance is regarded as the main driver of real-money spending in games [20].

There is also a positive relationship between goodwill points (gained through grouping with players who are 15 levels lower than themselves) and the Blue value system, where higher scoring of Blue corresponds to an increase in helping others. A key characteristic of Blue value system that seems to be supported by this preference is caring about other people and giving support. Both achievement points and house score have a positive relationship with the Green value system. Regarding the positive relationship of achievement points, the people that scored higher on Green have a wide range of different interests because the achievement point is the sum of total achievements of leveling up characters, completing quests, competing with others, making friends, joining guilds, and exploring new maps. Such players also show interest in the house system which has more decorative value than functional value. All these suggested that players who scored higher on Green (internally oriented) pay more attention on their own inner interest and uniqueness as anticipated by the ECLET.

We find that up to eight playing behaviors are positively correlated with the score of Red value system, which accounted for the largest number of significant relationships between the value system and playing features, covering nearly all key game performances from consumption, character level, magic stone, character ability, equipment, ability practice, and pet system to narrative points. This finding reveals that the Red value system is the most important one to explain and anticipate game playing. Players who scored high on the Red value system tend to commit a considerable amount of money on the game, seek powerful items and equipment, and level up their character and skills as quickly as possible. Beck and Cowan previously noted that video games

are a safe place where the Red can go for fun and adventure [18] because the game environment allows them to behave as they would normally do in real life and create a scenario with settings that support who they are and how the world works for them. The features of the Red value system, such as preferring instant gratification, valuing violence, and no sense of shame, match the core play dynamics of video games well, where advancement, competition with monsters or other players, impatience, and impulsive reactions are presented and reassure the behaviors, feelings, and tendencies of Red value. As we discovered here, only significant relationships between Red and achievement within the game were found, and no significant links were observed between Red and social interaction or casual playing such as making friends, joining guilds, and pet or house system.

Content personalization and system customization based on a user's personality factors have long been interests of the game development [21]. This finding has important implication for game design, since it provides valuable information for game designers to understand and meet the need of target users as accurately as possible. The links between value systems and online consumption can be applied to the designing of virtual items that ultimately generate the revenues for the game and help to determine who would potentially be the customer for the virtual items in question and how to better satisfy their needs and wants. This has become a main concern of game designers and player model research [22]. For example, for the user that scored high on Red, the virtual goods should be presented in a simple, concrete, and visual manner. The short-term benefits they will bring immediately must be stressed.

Another possibility directly applicable to game design would be to use inferred learning styles of players as modeled by their certain value system to minimize the learning curve involved to master game play. Every game starts with a training session in which the participants learn how to perform the various actions that are necessary to play the game. The design of these tutorials is essential for retaining new users and, to a certain extent, can determine the success of a commercial game. As is shown above, the players express more characteristics of Red value system within their game playing. As maintained by Graves, the people operating at the Red state cannot learn by punishment, because they do not feel or comprehend punishment [4]. They find their way through learning only by positive reinforcement, and the learning takes place best when the reward is presented soon after they do what we want them to do. As for designing game tutorials, we should not give any punishment such as death of character or deduction of experience points if an error is made by the new player. Designers should simply ask the player to start again until the desired operation is achieved and then award them immediately. Also, the individuals tend to have a very short attention span, and you must have everything structured [4]. The tutorials design should ensure every minute is laid out and always put something in front of a player in order to hold them right there. They move from a 60-second playing session to the next playing session and if there is any pause in this flow, it will distract their attention and they may leave the game.

Except for feeding the industry, the long term implications of this research will be huge. The results show the possibility of inferring users' value systems based on their activity traces within the game. Traditional personality assessment methods such as behavioral measurement, observation, and questionnaire may suffer from many weaknesses including ambiguity, high cost, and reliability. The games could be used as an alternative method of establishing personality profiles of the individual [13]. Video game combined the strengths of traditional personality assessment tools by quantifying behavior, automating observations and side-stepping self-report, and, what is more, it offered a high ecological validity [14]. Yee et al. believed that MMORPGs are a platform to develop unobtrusive personality assessment tools [10].

The game experience can also be further used to facilitate personal transformation on their level of existing as defined by Graves, while game content can engage the user's awareness and belief. Griebel indicated that skills used in a virtual world would be naturally translated into real lives of players and suggested that the game might be a useful instrument in training people to develop certain skills [12]. And role-play games are considered to be particularly effective in exploring individual's personal development. As admitted by Graves, the difficulty in training the Red man is that we do not have someone there to "give them an immediate reward when they do what we want them to do" [4]. But, in a digital game, players can be rewarded immediately once they achieve the goal set by the game designer. Instead of placing the individual in potentially mortal danger, the game will highlight the underlying negative belief structures in a safe way. By storing awareness acquired through game experience, individuals can slightly moderate their future value system and world view in real world situations which have the same underlying structure and pattern.

The findings indicate that the value system is only moderately related to their playing features within game. We noted the correlations calculated here are low, and, according to the effect size classified by Cohen, most of our findings would be "small effect" ($r \leq 0.10$) [23]. Although statistical relations were obtainable, the personality of a player may be at best one variable among many that needed to be considered for explaining gaming behavior.

However, the effect sizes of our findings are of enough magnitude and are equal to or greater than the effect sizes reported in other similar research. Yee discovered that over 60 percent of significant correlations between scores on five personality traits of FFM with behavior variables in World of Warcraft were at $r < 0.10$ with only three correlations with $r > 0.15$. For example, the number of deaths in dungeons correlated significantly with score on Extraversion at $r = 0.06$ [10]. In line with this, Tekofsky et al. noted almost all significant correlations they revealed between the 100 IPIP (International Personality Item Pool) scores of FFM and the 173 playing behavior variables in Battlefield 3 have a small effect size of $r < 0.1$, and only the 17 correlations were at $0.10 < r < 0.15$ among all 4,442 significant correlations yielded in their result [14]. Harari et al. investigated whether avatars in World of Warcraft convey information about players'

personalities and observed very weak relations ($r = 0.03$) [24].

There are multiple sources that influence players' actions within a game, including peer pressure, previous experience, time available, friendship, and cultural background. Higher effect sizes may be found between personality and playing behavior in future study if we take into account more variables and have a better controlled experiment process. The small effect sizes of correlations may be partly due to the large sample size of present research, while the research conducted with small sample has lower statistical power and often yields higher effect sizes. To sum up, even though at first sight the correlations revealed might be seen as low, considering the broader complexity involved here, thus the proportions covered by value system factors should not be minimized.

One major limitation of the present study is that the results may be slightly biased by recruiting participants and gaining metrics from only one game. It is unclear whether the relationship we found here can also be generalized to other game players. More studies are recommended to gather data from additional games to increase the generalization. Another limitation may be the bias of cultural influences, since only the data of Chinese players was collected [25]. In any future study, it would be helpful to do a cross-cultural comparison within game players. And, finally, we relied on the set of variables that Ghost II recorded. It is possible that other unrecorded variables, such as logged chat, may be even more predictive of value systems.

References

[1] China gaming industry report (Abstract), (2014), accessed 18th May 2015, http://cdn.cgigc.com.cn/report/2014/game_report_2014_brief.pdf.

[2] N. Yee, "The psychology of MMORPGs: Emotional investment, motivations, relationship formation, and problematic usage," in *Avatars at Work And Play: Collaboration and Interaction in Shared Virtual Environments*, vol. 34, pp. 187–207, Springer-Verlag, London, UK, 2006.

[3] S. De Castell, N. Taylor, J. Jenson, and M. Weiler, "Theoretical and methodological challenges (and opportunities) in virtual worlds research," in *Proceedings of the 2012 Foundation of Digital Games Conference, FDG 2012*, pp. 134–140, USA, June 2012.

[4] C. W. Graves, *The Never Ending Quest*, ECLET Publishing, Santa Barbara, CA, USA, 2005.

[5] W. Mischel, Y. Shoda, and R. E. Smith, *Introduction to Personality: Toward an Integration*, John Wiley and Sons, New York, NY, USA, 2004.

[6] G. Bammel and L. L. Burrus-Bammel, *Leisure and Human Behavior*, Brown and Benchmark, Madison, WIS, USA, 3rd edition, 1996.

[7] L. A. Barnett, "Accounting for leisure preferences from within: The relative contributions of gender, race or ethnicity, personality, affective style, and motivational orientation," *Journal of Leisure Research*, vol. 38, no. 4, pp. 445–474, 2006.

[8] F. Bayraktar and H. Amca, "Interrelations between virtual-world and real-world activities: Comparison of genders, age groups, and pathological and nonpathological internet users," *Cyberpsychology, Behavior, and Social Networking*, vol. 15, no. 5, pp. 263–269, 2012.

[9] J. Blascovich and J. Bailenson, *Infinite Reality: Avatars, Eternal Life, New Worlds, and the Dawn of the Virtual Revolution*, William Morrow and Co, New York, NY, USA, 2011.

[10] N. Yee, N. Ducheneaut, L. Nelson, and P. Likarish, "Introverted elves & conscientious gnomes: The expression of personality in World of Warcraft," in *Proceedings of the 29th Annual CHI Conference on Human Factors in Computing Systems*, pp. 753–762, 2011.

[11] C. Bateman and R. Boon, *21st Century Game Design (Game Development Series)*, Charles River Media, Cambridge, Mass, USA, 2005.

[12] T. Griebel, "Self-portrayal in a simulated life: Projecting personality and values in the sims 2," *Game Studies*, vol. 6, no. 1, article no. 5, 2006.

[13] G. Van Lankveld, P. Spronck, J. Van Den Herik, and A. Arntz, "Games as personality profiling tools," in *Proceedings of the 2011 7th IEEE International Conference on Computational Intelligence and Games, CIG 2011*, pp. 197–202, Republic of Korea, September 2011.

[14] S. Tekofsky, P. Spronck, A. Plaat, J. Van Den Herik, and J. Broersen, "Play style: Showing your age," in *Proceedings of the 2013 IEEE Conference on Computational Intelligence in Games, CIG 2013*, Canada, August 2013.

[15] M. P. McCreery, S. Kathleen Krach, P. G. Schrader, and R. Boone, "Defining the virtual self: Personality, behavior, and the psychology of embodiment," *Computers in Human Behavior*, vol. 28, no. 3, pp. 976–983, 2012.

[16] N. C. Worth and A. S. Book, "Personality and behavior in a massively multiplayer online role-playing game," *Computers in Human Behavior*, vol. 38, pp. 322–330, 2014.

[17] M. McLuhan, *Understanding Media: The Extensions of Man*, MIT Press, London, UK, 1st edition, 1994.

[18] D. E. Beck and C. Cowan, *Spiral Dynamics: Mastering Values, Leadership and Change*, Blackwell Publishing, Malden, MA, USA, 1996.

[19] K. Wilber, *A Theory of Everything*, Shambhala, Boston, Mass, USA, 2001.

[20] V. Lehdonvirta, "Virtual item sales as a revenue model: Identifying attributes that drive purchase decisions," *Electronic Commerce Research*, vol. 9, no. 1-2, pp. 97–113, 2009.

[21] C. T. Tan and H.-L. Cheng, "Tactical agent personality," *International Journal of Computer Games Technology*, Article ID 107160, 2011.

[22] J. Hamari and J. Tuunanen, "Player Types: A Meta-synthesis," *Transactions of the Digital Games Research Association*, vol. 1, no. 2, 2014.

[23] J. Cohen, "A power primer," *Psychological Bulletin*, vol. 112, no. 1, pp. 155–159, 1992.

[24] G. M. Harari, L. T. Graham, and S. D. Gosling, "Personality Impressions of World of Warcraft Players Based on Their Avatars and Usernames: Consensus but No Accuracy," *International Journal of Gaming and Computer-Mediated Simulations*, vol. 7, no. 1, pp. 58–73, 2015.

[25] C. Wang and G. Yu, "The relationship between players value systems and their In-game behavior in a massively multiplayer online role playing game," in *Proceedings of the 2nd Annual Conference of Chinese DiGRA*, Beijing, China, 2015.

## 6

Development of a Car Racing Simulator Game using Artificial Intelligence Techniques

Marvin T. Chan, Christine W. Chan, and Craig Gelowitz

Software Systems Engineering Program, Faculty of Engineering and Applied Science, University of Regina, Regina, SK, Canada S4S 0A2

Correspondence should be addressed to Christine W. Chan; christine.chan@uregina.ca

Academic Editor: Manuel M. Oliveira

This paper presents a car racing simulator game called *Racer*, in which the human player races a car against three game-controlled cars in a three-dimensional environment. The objective of the game is not to defeat the human player, but to provide the player with a challenging and enjoyable experience. To ensure that this objective can be accomplished, the game incorporates artificial intelligence (AI) techniques, which enable the cars to be controlled in a manner that mimics natural driving. The paper provides a brief history of AI techniques in games, presents the use of AI techniques in contemporary video games, and discusses the AI techniques that were implemented in the development of *Racer*. A comparison of the AI techniques implemented in the Unity platform with traditional AI search techniques is also included in the discussion.

1. Introduction

Games have become an integral part of everyday life for many people. A traditional game often presents a situation where "players engage in an artificial conflict, defined by rules and results in a quantifiable outcome" [1]. Such artificial conflicts are often represented as a puzzle or a challenge, and having the puzzle solved or the challenge resolved provides a real-world purpose to the game players [2]. This type of games is sometimes referred to as "serious" games [3]. However, this kind of traditional or "serious games" has been increasingly replaced by electronic games, especially for the so-called "game generation" [4]. This generation typically consists of "digital natives," who, in contrast to the "digital immigrants" [4] of the older generation, grew up playing a lot of games and who are trained in skills such as "dealing with large amounts of information quickly even at the early ages, using alternative ways to get information, and finding solutions to their own problems through new communication paths" [5].

The artificial intelligence (AI) community has witnessed a similar transition from the "classical AI games" such as Samuel's Checker Player [6] and Waterman's Poker Player [7] to the contemporary AI techniques adopted in electronic games. The objective of the game is no longer a quantifiable outcome of beating the opponent in a checker or poker game. Instead, a contemporary game contains changing environments, multiple objectives, and dynamic aspects of the game that are revealed to the game player as the game unfolds. The objective is to offer to the human player an enjoyable experience through his or her interaction with the game, and this does not involve any specific quantifiable outcome.

The game *Racer* is a contemporary video game, and its objective is to offer the player a challenging and enjoyable experience in a car race against a game-controlled car. Although the player's goal within the game is to win the race against the game-controlled car, the AI techniques adopted in the game are primarily designed to give the player an enjoyable time racing his or her car. In other words, the objective of winning by either side is not given the highest priority.

This paper proceeds as follows. Section 2 provides some background literature relevant to the work. Section 3 presents the design of the software system of *Racer*. Section 4 presents implementation of the game software system using some AI techniques. Section 5 gives a sample execution of the game system. Section 6 presents some discussion on the AI techniques adopted in *Racer* and its performance, and

Section 7 includes the conclusion and some ideas on future directions of the work.

2. Background Literature

There has been substantial research work that focuses on developing AI-controlled components of game systems, which can approximate or emulate human game playing styles. These components are often referred to as "bots." The motivation for developing the "bots" is that a human player's enjoyment in the gaming experience will be higher if he or she can be led to believe that the opponents in the game are other human players. An example of this type of game is the popular multiplayer first person shooter game Counter-Strike [8], in which the objective is to eliminate all players on the enemy or opponent team.

Similar AI-controlled components or "bots" also appear in the early video game of PacMan; the computer-controlled ghosts in the maze are able to move towards the player-controlled characters because the former incorporated some path finding algorithms [9]. Other AI algorithms that were adopted by games include finite state machines, fuzzy state machines, and decision trees. Decision trees are used to represent the decision making process involved in games like Checkers or Chess. A decision tree can specify a number of possible game states given a current state and support a search process for a goal state, where the human player is defeated provided the AI-controlled game can identify the path to the goal state more efficiently than the human player.

In addition to decision trees, other AI techniques are also used for building bots so that they would mimic or emulate human behavior. Khoo and Zubek discussed their use of a behavior-based action selection technique in the software development kit (SDK) of Flexbot for developing an AI-controlled bot, called Groo [10]. Based on Groo, 32 bots were developed and can run simultaneously on a single machine, and human players who played against the bots believed the bots effectively emulated human behavior [10]. Similarly, Tatai and Gudwin [11] discussed the use of semiotics in their development of a bot, which can assist or attack the human player in the game of Counter-Strike. The objective of their work was to design the AI system so that the bot can entertain and challenge the human player and not simply to defeat him or her. Therefore, the performance of the bot is measured not by its efficiency in killing its opponents, but by its "capability to emulate as close as possible all the activities commonly performed by a human player" [11]. This consideration also means that the bot cannot be seen to be waiting because human players expect bots to be continuously working. Hence, the bot's reaction time was one of the criteria in measuring its performance [11].

Similarly, in driving and racing games, human players expect to control their cars by making small adjustments to the car's direction while driving, just like how they would control a car in real life. Therefore, the race car bot must make continuous adjustments to its car's direction as opposed to simply driving in a straight line and turning only when a curve in the road approaches. To ensure the race car bot can mimic human behavior in this manner, some AI techniques

FIGURE 1: Waypoints at key positions on the racetrack are shown as (red) spheres.

were used for implementing the bots in *Racer*, which are explained in detail in the following section.

3. Game System Design

The design of the *Racer* game software involved three contemporary game AI concepts and techniques, which are presented as follows.

3.1. Waypoint System with Vector Calculations. The first technique used was the simple waypoint system used for controlling the car. The waypoint system includes a set of waypoints and each waypoint is a coordinate in 3D space that represents a key position on the racetrack. This system was used by many early car racing games because of its effectiveness and simplicity. In *Racer*, waypoints are stored as a sorted list of positions in 3D space using the List generic class from the System.Collections.Generic namespace [12]. The game software system reads this list of waypoints as input and then iterates through the list until all the waypoints have been passed by the game-controlled car. The game system only iterates to the next waypoint in the list when it detects that the game-controlled car is within a specified distance from its current waypoint. The (red) spheres along the racetrack in Figure 1 indicate the waypoints at key positions on the track.

In order to turn the car towards its current waypoint, the game system performs a series of vector calculations, which determine the amount of steering the game system needs to provide to the car. These calculations are based on an initial vector created by both the position of the current waypoint and the current position of the car itself. This series of calculations produces an output vector, which provides the bases for the steering and braking output levels of the car. However, during development of the game, it was found that using only the method of waypoints with vector calculations was ineffective in controlling the car. Due to the nonlinear relationship between the input and output vectors, the car could not be controlled using this method alone, and, therefore, the conditional monitoring system was adopted to augment the method of waypoints with vector calculations.

3.2. Conditional Monitoring System. Due to the nonlinear relationship between the input and output vectors, the steering and braking output levels of the game-controlled car could not be determined solely from the calculated output vector in the waypoints system. It was necessary for the

FIGURE 2: The race car and its associated trigger detection area are highlighted in the (green) wireframe mesh.

FIGURE 3: The interface of the Unity editor.

game system to also employ a conditional monitoring system that can further refine the steering and braking output levels applied to the car. In other words, depending on the values of the initial calculated output vector produced from the waypoint system's vector calculations, the steering and braking output levels applied to the car are adjusted by the conditional monitoring system. When the foundational waypoint system was enhanced with the conditional monitoring system, the car was able to traverse the track with satisfactory results.

Instead of adding the conditional monitoring system, the alternative design of deriving and incorporating a nonlinear mathematical function into the game system was also considered. Since this may require complex mathematical manipulations or modeling of the mathematical function using techniques like artificial neural networks, this alternative was abandoned.

3.3. Artificial Environment Perception. The second method that the game system employs in controlling the car is the use of trigger detection and artificial environment perception. Trigger detection is a popular mechanism used in contemporary video games, and it supports detecting a specific game object when it is within the vicinity of another game object. This method can determine if the game-controlled car may run into some object such as a wall. To prevent the collision from happening, the game system can adjust the steering and braking output levels applied to the car. The mechanism that supports this feature is the trigger area added to the car. If a wall enters into this trigger area, the game system becomes aware of where the wall is with respect to the car and it would adjust the output levels accordingly so as to steer the car away from the wall. With this addition of the trigger area, the game system is able to control the car so that it can navigate the track satisfactorily. The car in the middle of Figure 2 highlighted in the (green) wireframe mesh has a trigger detection area defined as the (green) rectangle around it. When an obstacle or another car enters into the trigger detection area, the output levels of the highlighted car will be adjusted so as to steer the highlighted car away from the obstacle.

An alternative technique considered for implementing this environment perception component of the game was the ray-casting technique. Ray-casting is a mechanism commonly used in contemporary video games, which involves drawing a ray or line from an object towards a specified direction, which, in the *Racer* game, would be the direction the car is heading. This drawn line would be used to determine if the car is about to collide with another object. However, the ray-casting mechanism is inadequate in that it can only detect collisions in one direction while the trigger detection mechanism can detect collisions in all directions.

4. Implementation of Game System

The component technologies that function as the higher-level abstraction programming tools and implemented the design of the game system described in the previous section are presented as follows.

4.1. Unity Game Engine. The game's 3D environment was built using the Unity game engine developed by Unity Technologies [13]. Unity is a game development engine combined with an integrated development environment (IDE) that is capable of creating applications for Windows, Mac OS X, Linux, and other mobile platforms [13]. The Unity game engine can perform graphical rendering and physics calculations, thereby enabling game developers to focus on the creation and development of the game software. Using the Unity engine, developers can position, scale, and add realistic physics to objects in the game system. Figure 3 shows the Unity editor's interface. The left panel shows a list of defined game objects, the middle visualization shows the game objects in the 3D space of the racetrack, the right panel shows the attributes of a selected game object, and the bottom panel consists of icons of the scripts, each of which defines the behavior of a game object.

4.2. MonoDevelop. The Unity game engine works in conjunction with MonoDevelop for controlling the behavior of objects. MonoDevelop is an open source Integrated Development Environment or IDE developed by Xamarin and the Mono community [14], which is primarily used for development in the C# programming language. With MonoDevelop, developers are able to write scripts in C#, JavaScript, or Boo and attach them to objects in the Unity engine; these scripts enable developers to control the logic and behaviors of objects within the Unity environment [13]. For example, if a developer was implementing the braking system on the wheels of the player-controlled car, she/he would write and attach a script that takes keyboard input from the user and applies the input value to the wheel's velocity. In this way, the combined tools of Unity and MonoDevelop enable developers to focus on the development of the AI components

FIGURE 4: An excerpt of the script developed with the MonoDevelop IDE interface.

FIGURE 5: The start screen of *Racer*.

FIGURE 6: A screenshot of *Racer* during gameplay.

of the game rather than on issues related to 3D graphics rendering and physics calculations. Figure 4 shows the script inside one of the icons shown on the bottom panel of the Unity editor; development of the script was supported by the MonoDevelop IDE.

4.3. Programming Languages and Data Structures. The primary programming language used for writing the scripts to control the behaviors of objects was C#. C# was chosen because it is object-oriented and class-based. Also, it has a variety of libraries and frameworks built specifically for development with Unity, which contain many generic classes and interfaces such as the List, Stack, and Dictionary [13]. These built-in classes have been optimized and are accessible with online documentation. For example, the List generic class from the System.Collections.Generic namespace was adopted during development to become an integral part of the game's waypoint system.

4.4. Detailed Implementation of Racer Game System

4.4.1. Player-Controlled Car Module. The player-controlled car module consists of four submodules: (i) the body, (ii) the wheels, (iii) the heads-up-display (HUD), and (iv) the player controller script. The body of the car is the 3D model that the player sees in the game environment; this submodule also contains the colliders, which enable the car to collide with objects in the game environment. The wheels of the car contain wheel colliders, which enable the wheels to make contact with the road and drive the car forward. The wheels submodule also contains a script which animates the rotation of the wheels as the car moves. The HUD component of the car is controlled by the HUD.cs script, which handles displaying the current speed, position, and lap of the car to the player. Lastly, the submodule of the player-controller script, called PlayerCarController.cs, handles the user input from the keyboard and applies the appropriate steering, accelerating, and braking output levels of the player-controlled car.

4.4.2. Game-Controlled Car Module. The game-controlled car (or the AI-controlled car) consists of four submodules: (i) the body, (ii) the wheels, (iii) the trigger area, and (iv) the AI controller script. The body and wheels of the game-controlled car are identical to the body and wheel components of the player-controlled car. The trigger area component

of the car is controlled by the CarSensor.cs script and detects when a wall enters into the trigger area. When this happens, the AI controller script is informed so that it would slightly adjust its control of the car. The AI controller script, called AICarController.cs, contains all the implemented AI techniques and algorithms that handle the driving of the game-controlled car so that it can effectively race against the player-controlled car.

4.4.3. Environment Module. The environment module consists of two submodules: (i) the racetrack and (ii) the waypoints system. The racetrack is the road within the game environment on which the cars race, and the waypoints system represents the key positions around the racetrack. The latter enables the game-controlled cars to navigate around the racetrack.

5. Sample User Run of *Racer* Game System

To control the player car, the user inputs commands to the car through the keyboard: the "W" key is pressed to accelerate, the "S" key is pressed to use the brake, the "D" key is pressed to steer right, and the "A" key is pressed to steer left. The player needs to finish three laps of the racetrack in order to win. Figure 5 shows the start screen of the game. Figure 6 shows the *Racer* game during gameplay. Figure 7 shows the indicators of the game components, which include the two game-controlled cars or "AI Car" in the background, the player-controlled car or "player car" in the foreground, and the "heads-up display" or HUD that indicates the status of the "player car": (i) speed or SPD at 90 km/hr, (ii) position or POS at 4/4, which means the car is at the fourth position among four cars, and (iii) lap or LAP at 0/1, which means the "player car" is in the first lap.

FIGURE 7: The game interface with indicators of the game components.

6. Discussion

Development of the game system was made easier because of the implementation tools. The Unity game engine supports effective development of the game system of *Racer* with its high-level abstraction programming tools and intuitive user interface. These features support developers in implementation of AI concepts so that they can focus on the game logic and ignore lower level development details such as graphics rendering and physics calculations. The combined tools of MonoDevelop and Unity support the implementation processes because MonoDevelop consists of autocorrection features for many libraries and SDKs used in Unity. For example, the combined tools support the developer in implementation of the waypoint system because the Unity engine supports positioning waypoints in 3D space. Hence, the developer can use the waypoint system instead of more traditional AI search techniques in determining a path for the race car on the track.

Compared to traditional AI search techniques, the waypoint system in the Unity platform enables the car racing system of the game to be more efficiently developed. If the Unity platform was not used, the racetrack would be mapped to a set of coordinates or nodes, which represent the 3D search space that covers the track. Then the path that the race car follows on the racetrack can be determined using either a blind or heuristic search algorithm, which identifies the nodes to be included in the path in the 3D space of the racetrack. In a blind search, the car will proceed to the next node in either a breadth-first or depth-first manner, and the node chosen as the subsequent node at each step will be the one that advances the car furthest along the track. In a heuristic search method such as the A^* search algorithm, the next node will be determined with an evaluation function that combines the length of the path traversed and the length of the path that has yet to be taken. Since the path traversed is not of interest for the race car, the evaluation function can consist of only the length of the path that has yet to be taken, which will move the car farthest along the track in a direction towards the destination. In implementing either search method in the game's 3D space, it is important that the set of nodes included in the path, through which the car traverses, represents a smooth trajectory that mimics human driving. In other words, the path should neither include any sharp turns nor float above or below the track, for a race car is expected to cruise along the racetrack smoothly.

This would require substantial calculation of the angle between two succeeding nodes on the path so that, for example, the car would not be seen to be following a zigzagging path along the track. The car also needs to travel on top of the track and any zigzagging along the z-axis would also be unacceptable. Moreover, since this is a racing game, determining the path has to be fast.

The Unity platform provides built-in components that can satisfy these requirements of a smooth path along the track and its fast determination. Instead of representing the racetrack as a set of nodes, through which the race car searches for a smooth path, the Unity platform supports the developer in defining the waypoints at key positions along the 3D racetrack so that the race car can follow that path of waypoints. This path of waypoints is indicated with the (red) spheres shown in Figure 1. This substantially reduces the search space and effort. Unity has a default gravity function to ensure the car would travel on the road and that the car does not zigzag along the z-axis. It also provides functions that support vector calculations between two nodes along a path so that the race car can avoid sharp turns on its path. With the waypoint system and the built-in gravity and vector calculation functions, the development effort involved in implementing the race cars that could mimic human driving and traverse the racetrack smoothly was substantially minimized.

Other features of Unity also support the development effort. For controlling the car, the system of conditional monitoring was adopted instead of developing the nonlinear mathematical functions. In terms of collision prevention, the trigger detection technique was used instead of ray-casting for artificial environment perception, because the former is more effective than the latter in that the technique of ray-casting only supports artificial environment perception in one single direction per casted ray. By comparison, the trigger detection technique allows for simultaneous perception in all directions surrounding the car. The Unity engine has built-in high-level abstractions for trigger detection, which also reduced implementation efforts.

7. Conclusion and Future Work

Racer was tested by over twenty users, who all reported that they thoroughly enjoyed the game. It was observed that there was approximately equal number of players who were able to win the race against the game-controlled cars. This suggests that not only did the game provide an entertaining gaming experience, it also provided a reasonably engaging and challenging gameplay.

In general, it can be concluded that the Unity platform supported efficient development of the race car game. The Unity platform supports implementing the race car's search for a path on the racetrack with its components of the waypoint system, the physics engine, and vector calculation functions, all of which are not available if the implementation was done using traditional AI search techniques. With these Unity components, the developer was able to implement the race car's search for a path on the track with less effort and more efficiently, and the developed race car can successfully mimic human driving behavior.

Future work would involve incorporating other path finding techniques into the existing game system so that it can be more exciting. The waypoint system can be used to support a different implementation of the search for the race car's path such that it is more dynamically determined based on its current position. This would make it more difficult for the human players to predict the behavior of the game-controlled cars. This unpredictable behavior would mean a more challenging gameplay for the user. Furthermore, while this game was designed for entertainment, the software can be extended to become a driver simulator for educational purposes. By modifying some of the parameter values of the car, such as the braking coefficients and torque values, and by modifying the game environment to resemble that of a municipal road system, *Racer* can be adapted to become a simulation software for learner-level drivers or for familiarizing drivers with the roadway layouts and traffic laws of foreign or unknown cities.

Acknowledgment

The first author wishes to acknowledge the generous support of the Graduate Studies Scholarship of the Faculty of Graduate Studies and Research, University of Regina, Regina, SK, Canada.

References

[1] K. Salen and E. Zimmerman, *Rules of Play: Game Design Fundamentals*, vol. 1, MIT Press, 2004.

[2] Y. Liu, T. Alexandrova, and T. Nakajima, "Gamifying Intelligent Environments," http://www.dcl.cs.waseda.ac.jp/~yefeng/yefeng/pubs/2011/ubimui11_yefeng.pdf.

[3] L. C. Wood and T. Reiners, "Gamification in logistics and supply chain education: extending active learning," in *Proceedings of the IADIS International Conference on Internet Technologies & Society (ITS '12)*, P. Kommers, T. Issa, and P. Isaias, Eds., pp. 101–108, IADIS Press, Perth, Australia, November 2012.

[4] M. Prensky, "Digital natives, digital immigrants part 1," *On the Horizon*, vol. 9, no. 5, pp. 1–6, 2001.

[5] G. K. Akilli, "Games and simulations: a new approach in education?" in *Games and Simulations in Online Learning: Research and Development Frameworks*, D. Gibson, C. Aldrich, and M. Prensky, Eds., pp. 1–3, Information Science Publishing, London, UK, 2007.

[6] A. L. Samuel, "Some studies in machine learning using the game of checkers. II—recent progress," *IBM Journal of Research and Development*, vol. 11, no. 6, pp. 601–617, 1967.

[7] D. A. Waterman, "Generalization learning techniques for automating the learning of heuristics," *Artificial Intelligence*, vol. 1, no. 1-2, pp. 121–170, 1970.

[8] Counter-Strike: Source, http://www.valvesoftware.com/games/css.html.

[9] J. DeNero and D. Klein, "Teaching Introductory Artificial Intelligence with Pac-Man," http://www.aaai.org/ocs/index.php/EAAI/EAAI10/paper/viewFile/1954/2331.

[10] A. Khoo and R. Zubek, "Applying inexpensive AI techniques to computer games," *IEEE Intelligent Systems*, vol. 17, no. 4, pp. 48–53, 2002.

[11] V. K. Tatai and R. R. Gudwin, "Using a semiotics-inspired tool for the control of intelligent opponents in computer games," in *Proceedings of the International Conference on Integration of Knowledge Intensive Multi-Agent Systems*, pp. 647–652, IEEE, Boston, Mass, USA, September-October 2003.

[12] Microsoft Developer Network, http://msdn.microsoft.com/en-US/.

[13] Unity—Game Engine, http://unity3d.com.

[14] MonoDevelop, http://monodevelop.com.

## 7

Gamification Assisted Language Learning for Japanese Language using Expert Point Cloud Recognizer

Yogi Udjaja [1,2]

[1]Computer Science Department, School of Computer Science, Bina Nusantara University, Jl. K. H. Syahdan, No. 9, Kemanggisan, Palmerah, Jakarta 11480, Indonesia
[2]Ekspanpixel, Jl. K. H. Syahdan, No. 37R, Kemanggisan, Palmerah, Jakarta 11480, Indonesia

Correspondence should be addressed to Yogi Udjaja; yogi.udjaja@binus.ac.id

Academic Editor: Michael J. Katchabaw

Starting from people limitations to understand Japanese, education and social life of those people in Japan can be hindered. Therefore, a game is needed that allows one to understand Japanese using Gamification Assisted Language Learning (GALL) method, involving the introduction of Japanese language implementation using expert point cloud ($EP) recognizer. This method is used to stimulate the sensory and motor nervous system and motivate students (players) to study harder. This can be evidenced by increase in players ability from 20% to 100%.

1. Introduction

Gamification emerged in the late 1960 [1]. Because researchers see the effectiveness of gamification use, it has become a major highlight since the early 2010 [2]. Gamification is a method to implement by which a boring activity is converted into a fun activity, to attract interest and attention and motivate and improve performance in certain activities. It is widely used in the fields of education, economics, social studies, culture, politics, health, business ecology, and many more related fields [3–8].

In general, gamification changes person's perception of nongame activity into games [9]. In this case, the game can also serve to stimulate different sensory and motor systems for each person [10], so as to enhance person's understanding and memory [11]. Then it can activate the brain cells as one of its functions can improve the ability of person language [12, 13]. Human intuitive theories explain the development of brain cells in the game because one can explain the world of the game, analyze some examples, and generate counterfactual thinking and produce effective plans [14].

On the other hand, some countries use language as one of the main conditions for continuing education and obtaining citizenship and residence [15]. In a study conducted by [16] on language education policy in China, Indonesia, Japan, the Philippines, and Vietnam, one of the countries that rejected internal linguistic diversity was Japan. It is governed by the myth of Japanese identity monoethnicity that is largely derived from the assimilation of Japanese norms that reinforce a monolingual as well as monoculture ideal of the Japanese state itself. Then at the Meiji restoration in 1868 began an educational revolution, where foreign language was the focus of education in Japan.

Currently, according to statistics from Japan Student Service Organization (JASSO) through articles written in Student Guide to Japan 2016/2017, the value of production per person (Gross Domestic Product) is the 3rd highest in the world, and Japan ranks the 7th in the world and number 1 in Asia because 24 Japanese nationals received Nobel prizes in 2016. These things make more and more people interested in continuing education in Japan, which can be seen from the data of 2011-2016: the number of international students is increasing (see Figure 1); then data as of May 1, 2016, explains that the number of international students continuing their education in Japan is 239287 people and that dominates from Asia, that is, 222627 people (see Figure 1) [17]. If viewed

TABLE 1: Number of International Students Based on Nations.

No.	Country/Region	Number of Students					
		2016	2015	2014	2013	2012	2011
1	China	98483	94111	94399	81884	86324	87533
2	Vietnam	53807	38882	26439	6290	4373	4033
3	Nepal	19471	16250	10448	3188	2451	2016
4	Republic of Korea	15457	15279	15777	15304	16651	17640
5	Taiwan	8330	7314	6231	4719	4617	4571
6	Indonesia	4630	3600	3188	2410	2276	2162
7	Sri Lanka	3976	2312	1412	794	670	737
8	Myanmar	3851	2755	1935	1193	1151	1118
9	Thailand	3842	3526	3250	2383	2167	2396
10	Malaysia	2734	2594	2475	2293	2319	2417
11	U.S.A.	2648	2423	2152	2083	2133	1456
12	Mongolia	2184	1843	1548	1138	1114	1170
13	Bangladesh	1979	1459	948	875	1052	1322
14	Philippines	1332	1028	753	507	497	498
15	France	1299	1122	957	793	740	530
16	Other	15264	13881	12243	42291	33313	34098
	Total	**239287**	**208379**	**184155**	**168145**	**161848**	**163697**

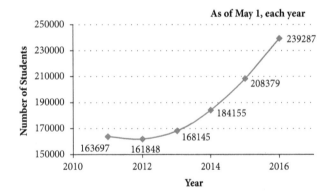

FIGURE 1: Movement of number of international students in Japan from 2011-2016.

statistically from a survey conducted by JASSO, by 2016 the number of Indonesian international students is ranked 6th after Taiwan (see Table 1) [18, 19].

Along with the increase of international students, Japan is also the 6th most popular country with many devotees to continue education. On the other hand, the increasing number of international students and the popularity of the country resulted in various problems and challenges that must be faced. According to [20], one of the factors which is a common problem often found against international students in Japan is the language skills. Of the 100 international students studying in Japan, 81% say that Japanese is hard to understand [20]. Based on these results, preferably before continuing education to Japan, prospective students must learn Japanese first, so as to facilitate life in Japan, and students who are interested in continuing education in

Japan are easier to be accepted in schools or universities in destination (schools or universities that have the main terms of Japanese as a language of daily learning).

In the process of learning, Japanese has several elements that must be considered: the letters (*moji*), vocabulary (*goi*), and grammar (*bunpo*). One of the first elements to be learned in Japanese is to memorize letters such as hiragana, katakana, and kanji, because Japanese letters model is different from the alphabetic language in general [21]. In fact, it is quite difficult to memorize Japanese because of its form and complex writing. Therefore, many researchers are comparing several methods of learning Japanese language so that someone better understand the language.

One of the learning models is conventional or using textbooks. In general, conventional Japanese learning makes it difficult for a person to understand the material given [22]. Ref. [22] said that Japanese language learning methods that use multimedia elements can attract motivation and encourage someone to continue learning Japanese to understand the use of the grammar. Meanwhile, the problem when using multimedia elements is that the learner focuses more on the effects raised of the multimedia elements provided instead of focusing on Japanese content, such as graphics, animation, or other multimedia elements. Therefore, gamification is made using Japanese as the most important part of the game.

In its implementation, this educational game uses point cloud ($P) recognizer algorithm developed by [23], because the $P recognizer has fast computing and high accuracy. On the other hand, the weakness of the algorithm is that it can only detect the result of the pattern that has been made, so it cannot detect the process of making it. Then the algorithm is developed again into expert point cloud ($EP) recognizer for the player who can learn to write Japanese well and truly.

Symbol	Description
n	Number of sampled points
T	Number of training samples per gesture type
R	Number of iterations required
S	Number of strokes in a multistroke
$S!.2^s$	Number of different permutations of stroke ordering and direction

2. Related Work

2.1. Game Development Live Cycle (GDLC). The main stages in game development are design, prototype, production, and testing. Based on research conducted by [9, 24], GDLC has several processes, scilicet, initiation, preproduction, production, testing, beta, and release done iteratively to enable flexibility during the development process, resulting in good game quality. The quality can be measured from 5 criteria, namely, fun, functional, balanced, internally, and accessible.

2.2. Computer-Assisted Language Learning (CALL). CALL was born in the 1960s. Fundamentals of CALL framework are always doing mutual relationship between development, implementation, and evaluation so that CALL can always evolve [25]. Then in the evaluation several considerations are involved; that is,

(i) Can users understand what the application is doing?

(ii) What kind of content of the lesson that is created is compatible with current technological interactions? For example, in terms of reading, writing, or listening.

(iii) How well are the design elements with understanding of user?

According to [26] in general CALL is used audiolingually, where the students listen to a recording and then learner is asked to retell the recorded tape by saying or typing an answer that has been programmed by computer. Then in 2016 CALL was developed using game. The game has a Role-Playing Game Simulators gameplay (RPG Sims), where the inference gained by the game can be used to facilitate learning Japanese language, as it produces fairly good learning outcomes, and RPG Sims has a high potential to motivate learners too [27].

Once reviewed, game still adopts the conventional way of learning and then converts to digital. Things that become attraction or how to motivate learners to learn can be developed again by making the learning content as the main game content. Then according to [28], computer studies need to analyze linguistic input from learners to detect errors and provide corrective feedback and have contextual instructional guidance.

2.3. $-Family Recognizer. **Unistroke ($1) Recognizer** is a 2D gesture recognizer algorithm designed to read patterns quickly. As the name implies, $1 algorithm can only be used to read a single pattern (stroke) or it can be said to have 2

permutations [23, 29]. Characteristics of the $1 algorithm are rotation invariant and size invariant. Rotation invariant is a pattern formed by slope of angle created by user; if it is in accordance with the order of formation of the same pattern, it will produce same reading. Subsequently size invariant is a pattern formed with a certain size created by the user, where reading is done by adjusting the size of the data created, resulting in same reading. Here is the complexity algorithm of $1:

$$\$1 = O\left(n.T.R\right) \tag{1}$$

Multistroke ($N) Recognizer is an algorithm that reads more than one pattern (stroke) but uses a lot of memory resulting in a slow process, because of the permutation of each stroke [23]. Here is the complexity algorithm of $N:

$$\$N = O\left(n.S!.2^s.T\right) \tag{2}$$

Because this algorithm produces a slow process, the point cloud recognizer algorithm is developed.

Point Cloud ($P) Recognizer is to optimize the $N algorithm that reads a pattern based on a stroke made; then $P is based on the relationship between the points so it does not require permutation or the number of patterns does not affect the complexity level of the algorithm. This algorithm produces accuracy above 99% and the process is faster than $N [23].

Characteristics possessed by the $P algorithm are the size invariant and direction invariant. The size invariant of $P equals $1, while the direction invariant is a pattern formed in a different order that will produce the same reading, if pattern is formed according to existing datasets. Here is the complexity algorithm of $P:

$$\$P = O\left(n^{2.5}.T\right) \tag{3}$$

The explanation of the $-Family algorithm can be seen in Table 2.

2.4. Game Experience. Game experience is judged based on emotion, thought, reaction, and behavior from players because it is influenced by the functionality, content, service, player affinity, and value of the player, where there are some elements that become benchmarks, namely, user interface (UI), user experience (UX), gameplay experience (GX), and game balancing. That matter will be evaluated using game experience questionnaire.

The benchmark adopts research undertaken by. [30–38], specifically,

(i) User Interface (UI)

(1) Usability: UI can be said to be usable when all features work properly and have informative feedback.

(2) Consistent: UI can be said to be consistent when an event used is also used elsewhere with the same model, thereby reducing short-term memory.

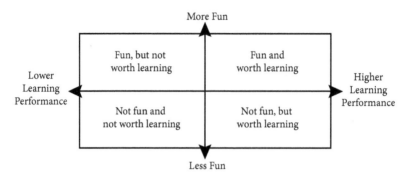

FIGURE 2: Gameplay Experience Evaluation for Learning Performance [30].

(ii) User Experience (UX)

(1) Useful: UX can be said to be useful if it can meet basic needs of player or game has benefits for player.

(2) Usable: UX can be said to be usable if it can be used efficiently and easily learned.

(3) Desirable: UX can be said to be desirable if it can contribute to user satisfaction by having a design with attractive aesthetic value.

(iii) Gameplay Experience (GX)

Based on research [35], there are 2 main factors that can be formed through cognitive and affective person, namely, beliefs and feelings, which are derived from a combination that is expected by someone to an object where it becomes something fun for player. Then besides fun, [30] adds a review for gamification where the content contained therein is worthy of studying (see Figure 2).

(iv) Game Balancing

(1) Game is fair: every action taken has an appropriate impact on the game. Any success and failure experienced by player can be understood rationally.

(2) Different skill levels: this is needed to determine the satisfaction of players, where there are challenges that have different levels of difficulty in every quest faced.

3. Propose Method

3.1. Gamification Assisted Language Learning (GALL). In general, the process of CALL is to change the learning of language conventionally to digital. When collaborated with gamifications, these high potentials can be maximized, since gamification has the following elements:

(i) Like games, the main requirement of gamification is to make a person feel happy and satisfied, and there are intrinsic elements of the contribution of knowledge in it.

(ii) Have goals to achieve.

(iii) Limiting game with the rules that apply to achieve the goal.

(iv) Provide information about progress of achievements that have been made to achieve the objectives.

(v) Have psychological elements to motivate players. Ref. [39] says there are 6 principal perspectives on motivation that closely relate to gamification, namely, trait perspective, behavioral learning perspective, cognitive perspective, perspective of self-determination, perspective of interest, and perspective of emotion.

Because Computer Assisted Language Learning (CALL) can be developed into Gamification Assisted Language Learning (GALL), GALL can maximize player interest to learn compared to CALL.

3.2. Datasets Japanese Language. Before recognizing Japanese writing required datasets are used as a measuring tool for the assessment standards of the games to be used as learning. These datasets are created by projecting the initial process of line formation to produce the final form of a point, where the datasets are stored in the xml format containing the position (x, y) of the writing. As seen in Figure 3, for example, this research has canvas of 5×5 and letter written is *Ku*. The letter is cut in accordance with the existing coordinates and then processed with the resample algorithm of $1 and $P where $1 each scratch generates 64 points with the same distance between points and $P each letter produces 32 points with the same distance between points. Visualization of datasets model made can be seen in Tables 3 and 4. The table describes the correct sequence of writing and the number of strokes contained in the Japanese language.

3.3. Expert Point Cloud ($EP). Generally, the $-Family Recognizer has a deficiency of reading a pattern based on the results that have been formed, not based on the manufacturing process. To learn Japanese, the process of writing the letter is very important, because the pattern of writing symbolizes the balance and neatness of writing someone; therefore a method is required that can read the process of making Japanese from beginning to end.

To accomplish this, the $P algorithm was developed again into an expert point cloud ($EP) recognizer, where the algorithm used is a combination and modification of expert

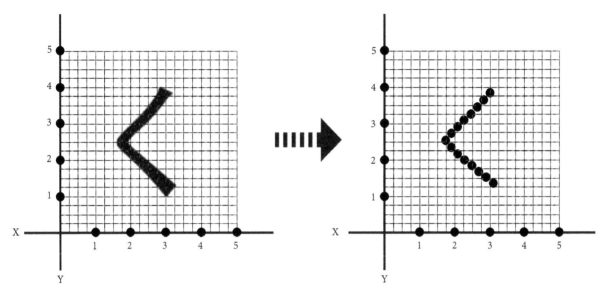

FIGURE 3: Example formation of dataset coordinates.

TABLE 3: Hiragana Letter.

	A	I	U	E	O
	あ	い	う	え	お
K	か	き	く	け	こ
S	さ	し	す	せ	そ
T	た	ち	つ	て	と
N	な	に	ぬ	ね	の
H	は	ひ	ふ	へ	ほ
M	ま	み	む	め	も
Y	や		ゆ		よ
R	ら	り	る	れ	ろ
W	わ				を
N	ん				

TABLE 4: Katakana Letter.

	A	I	U	E	O
	ア	イ	ウ	エ	オ
K	カ	キ	ク	ケ	コ
S	サ	シ	ス	セ	ソ
T	タ	チ	ツ	テ	ト
N	ナ	ニ	ヌ	ネ	ノ
H	ハ	ヒ	フ	ヘ	ホ
M	マ	ミ	ム	メ	モ
Y	ヤ		ユ		ヨ
R	ラ	リ	ル	レ	ロ
W	ワ				ヲ
N	ン				

system methods, unistroke ($1) recognizer from [29] and point cloud ($P) recognizer from [23].

Expert systems are used to make Japanese recognition systems sequentially, so that writing procedure from beginning to end can be properly written (see Tables 3 and 4). Subsequently, to detect every stroke (striation), $1 algorithm is used by doing resample, rotation, scale, and translation. After all strokes formed into letter, the $P algorithm is used to detect writing as a whole, by doing greedy cloud match, resample, scale, and translation. Examples of model illustrations of $1 and $P modified to form $EP can be seen in Figures 4–7 and explanation of the algorithm can be seen in Tables 5–11. Subsequently, overall algorithm flow can be seen in Figure 8.

3.3.1. Unistroke ($1) Recognizer Algorithm Model. The following are stages of $1 algorithm:

(1) Resample. Based on the illustration of Figure 4, step (a) describes the player being asked to create a Japanese letter; then systematically input from the player is processed to find out whether language is true or not. Letter processing starts from step (b); step (b) explains that the input made by player will change to N point in accordance with the coordinates of writing. After that at step (c) the calculation of the distance

TABLE 5: Description of Formula Resample.

Symbol	Description
$\text{avg } D$	Average distance
d	Distance between starting points
D	d plus distance to the next point
p_i	Current point position
p_{i-1}	Position point to i minus 1
q_x	New coordinates of x-axis
q_y	New coordinates of y-axis

is done between the points until all points passed all and the results can be seen in step (d). Step (e) describes N-th distance divided into 64 points. Here is the formula used in the resample stages:

(a) Formula for calculating the average distance:

$$\text{avg } D = \sum_{i=1}^{n} \sqrt{\left(p_i - p_{i-1}\right)^2 + \left(p_i - p_{i-1}\right)^2} \qquad (4)$$

(b) For each point, if $\text{avg } D \geq 1$ then the following equation is used:

$$d = p_i + p_{i-1} \qquad (5)$$

TABLE 6: Description of Formula Rotation.

Symbol	Description
c_x	Coordinates of midpoint against the x-axis
c_y	Coordinates of midpoint against the y-axis
x_0	Starting point coordinates to x-axis
x_1	Coordinate 1st point of x-axis
x_n	Coordinates of n-point of x-axis
y_0	Starting point coordinates to y-axis
y_1	Coordinate 1st point of y-axis
y_n	Coordinates of n-th point of y-axis
k	Sum of all points
θ	Angle formed by θ
x'	Coordinate posts after rotation of x-axis
y'	Coordinate posts after rotation of y-axis

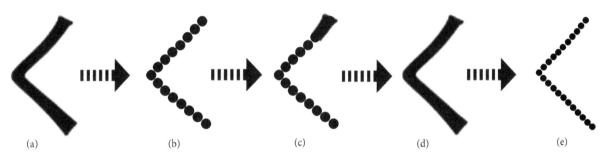

(a) (b) (c) (d) (e)

FIGURE 4: Resample Stages.

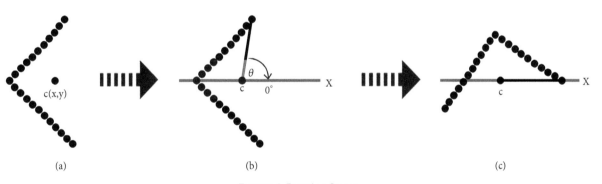

(a) (b) (c)

FIGURE 5: Rotation Stages.

Subsequently if $(D + d) \geq I$ then the following equation is used:

$$q_x = P_{i-1_x} + \left(\frac{\text{avg } D - D}{d} \right) \times \left(P_{i_x} - P_{i-1_x} \right) \quad (6)$$

$$q_y = P_{i-1_y} + \left(\frac{\text{avg } D - D}{d} \right) \times \left(P_{i_y} - P_{i-1_y} \right) \quad (7)$$

If $(D + d) \leq I$ then the following equation is used:

$$D = D + d \quad (8)$$

(2) Rotation. In this step, Figure 5 describes step (a) where the midpoint of the writing is processed by resample. Then in step (b) withdrawal line is done from the midpoint to starting point of writing, after that the angle of θ is determined. In step (c) a rotation is performed on the x-axis until θ reaches angle of 0^0. This matter is done so that writing can still be detected even though writing canvas is upside down. Here is the formula used in the rotation stages:

(a) Formula to determine the midpoint:

$$c_x = \frac{x_0 + x_1 + \cdots + x_n}{k} \quad (9)$$

$$c_y = \frac{y_0 + y_1 + \cdots + y_n}{k} \quad (10)$$

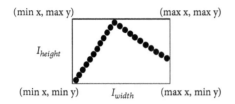 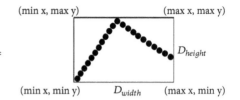

FIGURE 6: Scale Stages.

(b) Formula for determining angular tilt:

$$\theta = \text{atan}\left(c_y - x_0, c_x - y_0\right) \quad \text{for } -\pi \leq \theta \leq \theta \quad (11)$$

(c) Formula for rotation:

$$x' = \left(x_n - c_x\right)\cos\theta - \left(y_n - c_y\right)\sin\theta + c_x \quad (12)$$

$$y' = \left(x_n - c_x\right)\sin\theta + \left(y_n - c_y\right)\cos\theta + c_x \quad (13)$$

(3) Scale. In this step, scaling is performed to determine the equalization of the large or small size of inputs made to existing datasets. Initially, there is formation of a bounding box by drawing line perpendicularly from the coordinates of min (x, y) and max (x, y) so as to form a box that has coordinates (min x, max y), (max x, max y), (minx, min y), and (max x, min y) (see Figure 6). Then, bounding box of player posts compared to datasets. If bounding box player is not the same as bounding box dataset, then calculation is done using the following formula:

$$q_x = P_x\left(\frac{I_{width}}{D_{width}}\right) \quad (14)$$

$$q_y = P_y\left(\frac{I_{height}}{D_{width}}\right) \quad (15)$$

(4) Translation. At this step is the determination of center point of writing player and datasets, so that center point of both writing models is in position (0, 0). It means writing of player coincides with writing of datasets. Then look for all difference distance between point of player and dataset (see Figure 7). Here is formula used in the translation stages:

(a) Formula to determine center point of writing:

$$q_x = P_x - c_x \quad (16)$$

$$q_y = P_y - c_y \quad (17)$$

(b) Formula to determine average distance between points:

$$d_i = \frac{\sum_{k=1}^{N}\sqrt{\left(I[k]_x - D_i[k]_x\right)^2 + \left(I[k]_y - D_i[k]_y\right)^2}}{N} \quad (18)$$

TABLE 7: Description of Formula Scale.

Symbol	Description
q_x	New coordinates of x-axis
q_y	New coordinates of y-axis
P_x	current coordinates of x-axis
P_y	current coordinates of y-axis
I_{width}	length of bounding box of player input
I_{height}	Size of bounding box width of player input
D_{width}	length of bounding box of dataset
D_{width}	Size of bounding box width of dataset

TABLE 8: Description of Formula Translation.

Symbol	Description
q_x	Center point of x-axis
q_y	Center point of y-axis
P_x	Coordinate point input player against x-axis
P_y	Coordinate point input player against y-axis
c_x	Coordinate point datasets against x-axis
c_y	Coordinate point datasets against y-axis
d_i	Average distance
I	Input made by player
D_i	Dataset to i
k	Point to k
N	Total number of points

(5) Score. Calculation accuracy of ratio is calculated from 0 to 1 with the following formula:

$$s = 1 - \frac{d_i^*}{(1/2)\sqrt{I_{height}^2 + I_{width}^2}} \quad (19)$$

3.3.2. Point Cloud Recognizer ($P) Algorithm Model. In $P algorithm steps taken are not much different from $1; for the resample stage, the scale and translation remain the same as $1, which distinguishes it is the N-distance calculation which is divided into 32 points and calculated using greedy cloud match and $P algorithm does not have a rotation.

Greedy which is conducted by $P is looking for minimum distance that is compared between input player and datasets. In greedy usage there is distance calculation using cloud distance. Cloud distance uses variable weight to determine level of accuracy of a comparison. If a point in input player is paired to the nearest datasets point, then weight variable will

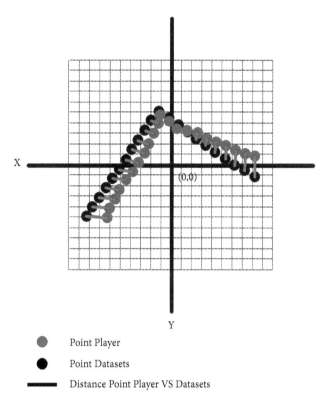

Point Player

Point Datasets

Distance Point Player VS Datasets

FIGURE 7: Translation Stages.

TABLE 9: Description of Formula Score.

Symbol	Description
s	Score
d_i^*	Distance to i
I_{height}	Size of bounding box width of player input
I_{width}	length of bounding box of player input

TABLE 10: Description of Formula Greedy Cloud Distance.

Symbol	Description
w	Weight
w_i	Weight to i
i	$1 \cdots n$
p_0	Coordinate starting point
n	Number of points already paired
I_i	Coordinate point input player to i
I_{i_x}	Coordinate point input player to i against x-axis
I_{i_y}	Coordinate point input player to i against y-axis
D_j	Coordinate point datasets to j
D_{j_x}	Coordinate point datasets to j against x-axis
D_{j_y}	Coordinate point datasets to j against y-axis

TABLE 11: Description of Formula Score Final ($EP).

Symbol	Description
F	Score final
$s\$1$	Score $1
$s\$1_1$	Score $1 to 1
$s\$1_n$	Score $1 to n
$s\$P$	Score $P
n	Number of strokes plus overall stroke that make up the writing

In addition, within cloud distance there is an Euclidean distance that is used for distance calculation at point cloud. Here is formula used for calculating distance of point cloud:

$$\sum_{i=1}^{n} \left\| I_i - D_j \right\| = \sum_{i=1}^{n} \sqrt{\left(I_{i_x} - D_{j_x} \right)^2 + \left(I_{i_y} - D_{j_y} \right)^2} \qquad (21)$$

$$\sum_i w_i \cdot \left\| I_i - D_j \right\| \qquad (22)$$

3.3.3. Score Final Expert Point Cloud ($EP) Recognizer. For assessment of overall accuracy, the following formula is used. If stroke = 1 then the following equation is used:

decrease. Here is the formula used for calculation of variable weight:

$$w = 1 - \frac{\left((i - p_0 + n) \mod n \right)}{n} \qquad (20)$$

$$F = s\$1 \qquad (23)$$

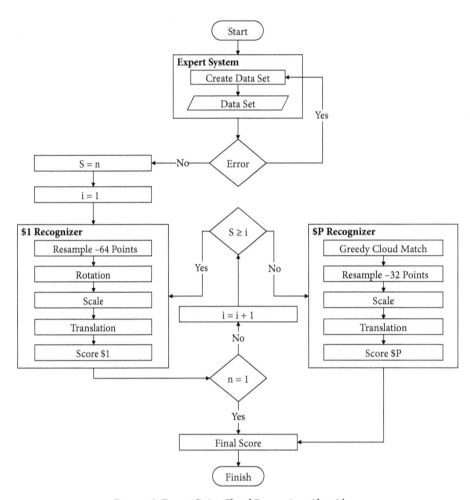

FIGURE 8: Expert Point Cloud Recognizer Algorithm.

If stroke > 1 then the following equation is used:

$$F = \frac{s\$1_1 + \cdots + s\$1_n + s\$P}{n} \qquad (24)$$

$EP algorithm is used as the standardization of writing of language performed, since the input of the player will be compared with datasets that have been created, where it will affect accuracy of assessment.

4. Results and Discussion

In created RPG game, the battle system is lifted using turn based and has an active time battle (ATB), where, when the battle is done, the player and enemy alternately attack in accordance with the ATB that has been determined. Then to attack the player must write the Japanese language correctly, and damage is obtained by enemy in accordance with the accuracy of the writing.

In general, order of Japanese writing system can be seen in Figure 8. That figure explains the process of making datasets with algorithm process that runs up to get the accuracy of the writing player.

Then, after the game has been made, the game experience evaluation and pretest and posttest are given to 150 players to see players ability improvement, where there are 2 player categories: 46 players have learned Japanese and 104 player never learned Japanese. Test is done by asking player to make all the letters contained in Tables 3 and 4 along with the romaji.

On the other hand, to conduct game experience evaluation, a game experience questionnaire (GEQ) is made below:

(1) Are the features in this game is running well?

    (a) Yes (100%)
    (b) No (0%)

(2) Whether in-game display of buttons, portals, and all displays on each screen with the same model can make it easier to remember the function of interface used?

    (a) Yes (100%)
    (b) No (0%)

(3) Do tutorial and help feature can help you in playing?

    (a) Yes (100%)

    (b) No (0%)

(4) Is the system in the game easy to learn?

    (a) Yes (100%)

    (b) No (0%)

(5) How do you think about aesthetics are displayed in this game?

    (a) Attractive (97%)

    (b) Not attractive (3%)

(6) Does game you have played help you understand Japanese?

    (a) Yes (100%)

    (b) No (0%)

(7) How do you think difficulty level of the game after played?

    (a) Appropriate (100%)

    (b) Not appropriate (0%)

(8) Whether achievements and punishments provided matches the effort you are providing?

    (a) Appropriate (100%)

    (b) Not appropriate (0%)

(9) Is overall learning content provided worthy to be learn?

    (a) Worth learning (100%)

    (b) Not worth learning (0%)

(10) How do you think a game you have played?

    (a) Fun (100%)

    (b) Not fun (0%)

From GEQ it can be concluded that conditions found in the game experience have been met. For aesthetic problems, it is a matter of taste of player, because the developer cannot force someone to like aesthetics of the game made.

Before performing GEQ do pretest and posttest, where pretest is done before playing and posttest is done after playing, in which case player is asked to play for one week. Here are pretest results with 150 players: 10 players answered all questions correctly, 36 players answered with an average of 30%-50% wrong answers, and 104 players did not answer end answer but all wrong answers.

Subsequently, here are posttest results from the same person with pretest: there are 10 players who answered all the answers correctly (same player with pretest) and 134 people answered the correct average answer of 20%-100 %, while 6 players answered questions with all wrong answers.

5. Conclusions

Inference of this research is as follows:

    (i) Japanese datasets are based on expert knowledge.

    (ii) Currently $-Family has a new family of Expert Point Cloud Recognizer ($EP).

    (iii) RPG game battle system using turn-based and ATB plus attack system using $EP can attract players to learn to write Japanese.

    (iv) A game that is made already meets rules of game experience.

    (v) Increased ability of a person is based on the capability of the person, because everyone has different capabilities. It can be said that the more diligent a person is to learn, the more science is absorbed.

    (vi) A good game is a game that makes player feel happy to play it and unknowingly player can understand the science implicit in it.

    (vii) Overall GALL in a matter of a week can increase players ability from 20% to 100%.

References

[1] A. Deif, "Insights on lean gamification for higher education," *International Journal of Lean Six Sigma*, vol. 8, no. 3, pp. 359–376, 2017.

[2] M. Sailer, J. U. Hense, S. K. Mayr, and H. Mandl, "How gamification motivates: An experimental study of the effects of specific game design elements on psychological need satisfaction," *Computers in Human Behavior*, vol. 69, pp. 371–380, 2017.

[3] C. J. Costa, M. Aparicio, and I. M. S. Nova, "Gamification: Software Usage Ecology," *Online Journal of Science and Technology*, vol. 8, no. 1, 2018.

[4] J. Kasurinen and A. Knutas, "Publication trends in gamification: A systematic mapping study," *Computer Science Review*, vol. 27, pp. 33–44, 2018.

[5] H. Korkeila and J. Hamari, "The Relationship Between Player's Gaming Orientation and Avatar's Capital: a Study in Final Fantasy XIV," in *Proceedings of the Hawaii International Conference on System Sciences*.

[6] L. E. Nacke and S. Deterding, "The maturing of gamification research," *Computers in Human Behavior*, vol. 71, pp. 450–454, 2017.

[7] F. Xu, D. Buhalis, and J. Weber, "Serious games and the gamification of tourism," *Tourism Management*, vol. 60, pp. 244–256, 2017.

[8] L. J. Hilliard, M. H. Buckingham, G. J. Geldhof et al., "Perspective taking and decision-making in educational game play: A mixed-methods study," *Applied Developmental Science*, vol. 22, no. 1, pp. 1–13, 2018.

[9] Yanfi, Y. Udjaja, and A. C. Sari, "A Gamification Interactive Typing for Primary School Visually Impaired Children in Indonesia," *Procedia Computer Science*, vol. 116, pp. 638–644, 2017.

[10] F. E. Gunawan, A. Maryanto, Y. Udjaja, S. Candra, and B. Soewito, "Improvement of E-learning quality by means of a recommendation system," in *Proceedings of the 11th International Conference on Knowledge, Information and Creativity Support Systems, KICSS 2016*, Indonesia, November 2016.

[11] M. B. Armstrong and R. N. Landers, "An Evaluation of Gamified Training: Using Narrative to Improve Reactions and Learning," *Simulation & Gaming*, vol. 48, no. 4, pp. 513–538, 2017.

[12] J. S. Hong, D. H. Han, Y. I. Kim, S. J. Bae, S. M. Kim, and P. Renshaw, "English language education on-line game and brain connectivity," *ReCALL*, vol. 29, no. 1, pp. 3–21, 2017.

[13] M. E. D. M. Pérez, A. P. Guzmán Duque, and L. C. F. García, "Game-based learning: Increasing the logical-mathematical, naturalistic, and linguistic learning levels of primary school students," *Journal of New Approaches in Educational Research*, vol. 7, no. 1, pp. 31–39, 2018.

[14] P. A. Tsividis, T. Pouncy, J. L. Xu, J. B. Tenenbaum, and S. J. Gershman, "Human learning in Atari," in *Proceedings of the 2017 AAAI Spring Symposium Series, Science of Intelligence: Computational Principles of Natural and Artificial Intelligence*, 2017.

[15] E. Shohamy, *Critical language testing*, Language Testing and Assessment, 2017.

[16] A. Kirkpatrick and A. J. Liddicoat, "Language education policy and practice in East and Southeast Asia," *Language Teaching*, vol. 50, no. 2, pp. 155–188, 2017.

[17] JASSO, "Student Guide to Japan 2017-2018," 2017, http://www.jasso.go.jp/en/study_j/_icsFiles/afieldfile/2017/05/22/sgtj_2017_e.pdf.

[18] JASSO, "International Students in Japan 2016," 2017, http://www.jasso.go.jp/en/about/statistics/intl_student/_icsFiles/afieldfile/2017/03/29/data16_brief_e.pdf.

[19] JASSO, "Student Guide to Japan 2016-2017," 2017, http://www.jasso.go.jp/id/study_j/_icsFiles/afieldfile/2016/11/30/sgtj_2016_id_2.pdf.

[20] J. S. Lee, "Challenges of international students in a Japanese university: Ethnographic perspectives," *Journal of International Students* , vol. 7, no. 1, pp. 73–93, 2017.

[21] T. Ogino, K. Hanafusa, T. Morooka, A. Takeuchi, M. Oka, and Y. Ohtsuka, "Predicting the reading skill of Japanese children," *Brain & Development*, vol. 39, no. 2, pp. 112–121, 2017.

[22] M. C. Chan, *Multimedia Courseware for Learning Japanese Language Level 1 [Ph.D. thesis]*, UTAR, 2016.

[23] R.-D. Vatavu, L. Anthony, and J. O. Wobbrock, "Gestures as point clouds: A $p recognizer for user interface prototypes," in *Proceedings of the 14th ACM International Conference on Multimodal Interaction, ICMI 2012*, pp. 273–280, USA, October 2012.

[24] R. Ramadan and Y. Widyani, "Game development life cycle guidelines," in *Proceedings of the 2013 5th International Conference on Advanced Computer Science and Information Systems, ICACSIS 2013*, pp. 95–100, Indonesia, September 2013.

[25] P. Hubbard, "Foundaton of Computer-Assisted Language Learning," 2017, https://web.stanford.edu/~efs/callcourse2/CALL1.htm.

[26] N. Gunduz, "Computer assisted language learning," *Journal of Language and Linguistic Studies*, vol. 1, no. 2, 2005.

[27] S. J. Franciosi, "Acceptability of RPG Simulators for Foreign Language Training in Japanese Higher Education," *Simulation & Gaming*, vol. 47, no. 1, pp. 31–50, 2016.

[28] T. Heift and M. Schulze, "Tutorial computer-assisted language learning," *Language Teaching*, vol. 48, no. 4, pp. 471–490, 2015.

[29] J. O. Wobbrock, A. D. Wilson, and Y. Li, "Gestures without libraries, toolkits or training: A $1 recognizer for user interface prototypes," in *Proceedings of the 20th Annual ACM Symposium on User Interface Software and Technology, UIST 2007*, pp. 159–168, USA, October 2007.

[30] S. Kim, K. Song, B. Lockee, and J. Burton, *Gamification in Learning and Education*, Springer International Publishing, Cham, 2018.

[31] D. P. Kristiadi, Y. Udjaja, B. Supangat et al., "The effect of UI, UX and GX on video games," in *Proceedings of the 2017 IEEE International Conference on Cybernetics and Computational Intelligence (CyberneticsCom)*, pp. 158–163, Phuket, November 2017.

[32] E. Adams, *Fundamentals of game design*, Pearson Education, 2014.

[33] E. C. Contreras and I. I. Contreras, "Development of Communication Skills through Auditory Training Software in Special Education," in *Encyclopedia of Information Science and Technology*, pp. 2431–2441, IGI Global, 4th edition, 2018.

[34] D. Lightbown, *Designing the user experience of game development tools*, CRC Press, 2015.

[35] M. Kors, E. D. Van der, Spek., and B. A. Schouten, "A Foundation for the Persuasive Gameplay Experience," *FDG*, 2015.

[36] Y. Udjaja, "Ekspanpixel Bladsy Stranica: Performance Efficiency Improvement of Making Front-End Website Using Computer Aided Software Engineering Tool," *Procedia Computer Science*, vol. 135, pp. 292–301, 2018.

[37] H. Joo, "A Study on Understanding of UI and UX, and Understanding of Design According to User Interface Change," *International Journal of Applied Engineering Research*, vol. 12, no. 20, pp. 9931–9935, 2017.

[38] Y. Udjaja, V. S. Guizot, and N. Chandra, "Gamification for Elementary Mathematics Learning in Indonesia," *International Journal of Electrical and Computer Engineering (IJECE)*, vol. 8, no. 6, 2018.

[39] M. Sailer, J. Hense, H. Mandl, and M. Klevers, "Psychological Perspectives on Motivation through Gamification," *Psychological Perspectives on Motivation through Gamification*, vol. 19, pp. 28–37, 2013.

## 8

Turn-Based War Chess Model and its Search Algorithm per Turn

Hai Nan,[1,2] **Bin Fang,**[1] **Guixin Wang,**[2] **Weibin Yang,**[3] **Emily Sarah Carruthers,**[4] **and Yi Liu**[5]

[1]College of Computer Science, Chongqing University, Chongqing 400044, China
[2]Department of Software Engineering, Chongqing Institute of Engineering, Chongqing 400056, China
[3]College of Automation, Chongqing University, Chongqing 400044, China
[4]College of International Education, Chongqing University, Chongqing 400044, China
[5]PetroChina Chongqing Marketing Jiangnan Company, Chongqing 400060, China

Correspondence should be addressed to Bin Fang; fb@cqu.edu.cn

Academic Editor: Michela Mortara

War chess gaming has so far received insufficient attention but is a significant component of turn-based strategy games (TBS) and is studied in this paper. First, a common game model is proposed through various existing war chess types. Based on the model, we propose a theory frame involving combinational optimization on the one hand and game tree search on the other hand. We also discuss a key problem, namely, that the number of the branching factors of each turn in the game tree is huge. Then, we propose two algorithms for searching in one turn to solve the problem: (1) enumeration by order; (2) enumeration by recursion. The main difference between these two is the permutation method used: the former uses the dictionary sequence method, while the latter uses the recursive permutation method. Finally, we prove that both of these algorithms are optimal, and we analyze the difference between their efficiencies. An important factor is the total time taken for the unit to expand until it achieves its reachable position. The factor, which is the total number of expansions that each unit makes in its reachable position, is set. The conclusion proposed is in terms of this factor: Enumeration by recursion is better than enumeration by order in all situations.

1. Introduction

Artificial intelligence (AI) is one of the most important research fields in computer science, and its related algorithms, technologies, and research results are being widely used in various industries, such as military, psychological, intelligent machines and business intelligence. Computer games, known as "artificial intelligence's drosophila," are an important part of artificial intelligence research. With the increasing development of computer hardware and research methods, artificial intelligence research in traditional board games has seen some preliminary results. Alus et al. [1] have proven that Go-Moku's AI, provided it moves first, is bound to win against any (optimal) opponent by the use of threat-space search and proof-number search. The Monte Carlo Tree Search (MCTS) method, based on UCT (UCB for tree search), has improved the strength of 9 × 9 Go, close to the level of a professional Kudan [2].

Computer game based on artificial intelligence is a sort of deterministic turn-based zero-sum game, containing certain information. Man-machine games can be classified into two categories: two-player game and multiplayer game, according to the number of game players. Most traditional chesses, such as the game of Go and Chess, belong to the two-player game category, to which α-β search based on min-max search and its enhancement algorithms such as Fail-Soft α-β [3], Aspiration Search [4], Null Move Pruning [4], Principal Variation Search [5], and MTD(f) [5] are usually applied. On the contrary, Multiplayer Checkers, Hearts, Sergeant Major, and so forth belong to the multiplayer game category [6] which runs according to a fixed order of actions, with participants fighting each other and competing to be the sole winner of the game. Its search algorithm involves Max^n search [7], Paranoid [6], and so forth. The α-β search previously mentioned based on min-max search is a special case based on the Max^n search and shadow pruning algorithms [7]. Man-machine

(a) Wargaming

(b) SLG game "Battle Commander"

FIGURE 1: Wargaming and SLG game.

FIGURE 2: SLG game "Heroes of Might & Magic."

games can also be classified into two categories: classic board games and new board games, according to the game content. Classic board games involve Go, chess, backgammon, checkers, and so forth, which are widespread and have a long history. While other board games such as Hex [8], Lines of Action [9], and Scotland Yard [10] are ancient games, with the rapid development of modern board games and mobile client applications they have been accepted by more and more players until their prevalence is comparable to that of the classic board game. The machine game algorithms of the board games listed above are all based on α-β search and their enhancement algorithms. The MCTS algorithm has developed rapidly in recent years, being used increasingly in these board games and getting increasingly satisfactory results [8–10].

However, not all board games can be solved with the existing algorithms. Turn-based strategy games (TBS), as well

as turn-based battle simulation games (SLG) (hereinafter collectively referred to as turn-based strategy games), originated from the wargames [11] that swept the world in the mid-19th century (Figure 1(a) shows an example of a wargame). With the introduction of computer technology, this new type of game, turn-based strategy game, has flourished (Figure 1(b) shows a famous TBS game called "Battle Commander," and Figure 2 shows the popular SLG game "Heroes of Might & Magic"). Now, TBS games have become the second most famous type of game after RPGs (role-playing games). With the blossoming of mobile games, TBS games will have greater potential for development in the areas of touch-screen operation, lightweight, fragmented time, and so on. The content of a TBS game generally comprises two levels: strategic coordination and tactical battle control. The latter level, whose rules are similar to those of board games, for example, moving pieces on the board, beating a specified enemy target for victory, and turn-based orders, is called the turn-based war chess game (TBW). The artificial intelligence in TBW is an important component of TBS games. The AI of modern TBS games is generally not so intelligent, of which the fundamental reason is that the AI in its local battle (TBW) is not so intelligent. How to improve the TBW's artificial intelligence, thus improving the vitality of the entire TBS game industry, is an urgent problem that until now has been overlooked.

Currently, the study of artificial intelligence in turn-based strategy games is mainly aimed at its macro aspect, and the research object is primarily the overall macro logistics, such as the overall planning of resources, construction, production, and other policy elements. The main research contents involve planning, uncertainty decisions, spatial reasoning, resource management, cooperation, and self-adaptation. However, studies on artificial intelligence for a specific type of combat in TBS are scarce, and the attention paid to researching the TBW units' moves, attacks, and presentation of the game round transformation, whose AI is precisely the worst of all parts of the AI in a large number of TBS games, is not enough. At present, the research related to TBW's behavior involves spatial reasoning techniques. Bergsma and Spronck [12] divided the AI of TBS (NINTENDO's Advanced Wars) into tactical and strategic modules. The tactical module essentially has to decide where to move units and what to attack. It accomplishes this by computing influence maps, assigning a value to each map tile to indicate the desirability for a unit to move towards the tile. This value is computed by an artificial neural network. However, they unfortunately do not provide any detail on how such a mechanism would work. Paskaradevan and Denzinger [13] presented a shout-ahead architecture based on two rule sets, one making decisions without communicated intentions and one with these intentions. Reinforcement learning is used to learn rule weights (that influence decision making), while evolutionary learning is used to evolve good rule sets. Meanwhile, based on the architecture, Wiens et al. [14] presented improvements that add knowledge about terrain to the learning and that also evaluate unit behaviors on several scenario maps to learn more general rules. However, both approaches are essentially based on rules for the artificial intelligence, resulting in a lack of flexibility of intelligent behaviors, a lack of generality as they depend on a game's custom settings, and, moreover, a lack of reasoning for more than one future turn, similar to common chess games.

At present, research on TBW's AI from the perspective of the multiround chess game method is scarce because a TBW's player needs to operate all his pieces during each round, which is an essential difference with other ordinary chess games. Thus, the number of situations generated by permutation grows explosively such that, from this perspective, the TBW's AI can hardly be solved during regular playtime by the game approach described previously.

This paper attempts to study TBW's AI from the perspective of the chess game method. This is because the TBW's rules have many similarities with other chess games, and the decision made every turn in a TBW can be made wisely as in other chess games. In this paper, we propose two enumeration methods in a single round: dictionary sequence enumeration

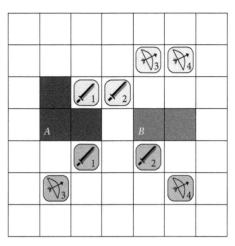

FIGURE 3: An example of TBW: Here are four red units and four blue units belonging to two players, respectively, on a square board. The units are divided into sword men and archers. The number written in the bottom right of each unit is the unit index. White tilts mean their terrain can be entered. However, ochre ones marked by "A" illustrate hilly areas no unit can enter. The dark green tilts marked by letter "B" illustrate lakes or rivers, which also cannot be entered, but archers can remotely attack the other side of the tilts.

and recursive enumeration, which is the fundamental problem in our new framework. The improvement in TBW's AI can not only bring more challenges to game players but also bear a new series of game elements, such as smart AI teammates, which will provide players with a new gaming experience.

A TBW game is essentially the compound of combinational optimization laterally and game tree search vertically (Section 3.2), which can be regarded as a programming problem of multiagent collaboration in stages and can be seen as a tree search problem with huge branching factor. Thus, the expansion and development of the traditional systems hidden behind TBW games will make the research more meaningful than the game itself.

This paper first summarizes the general game model for TBW and illustrates its key feature, that is, that the branching factor is huge in comparison with traditional chess games. Then, it puts forward two types of search algorithms for a single round from different research angles: the dictionary sequence enumeration method (Algorithm 2) and the recursive enumeration method (Algorithm 5). Ensuring invariability of the number of branches, Algorithm 5 has less extension operation of pieces than Algorithm 2 under a variety of conditions. The experiments also confirmed this conclusion.

2. Game Module of Turn-Based War Chess

2.1. Rules. TBW is played on a square, hexagonal, or octagonal tile-based map. Each tile is a composite that can consist of terrain types such as rivers, forests, and mountains or built up areas such as bridges, castles, and villages (Figure 3). Each tile imposes a movement cost on the units that enter them. This movement cost is based on both the type of terrain and the

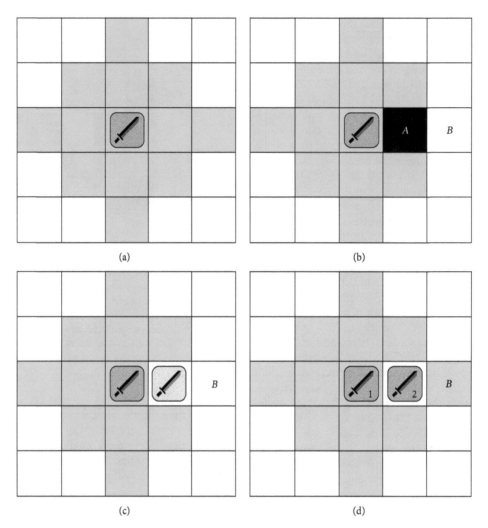

FIGURE 4: Green tilts illustrate the movement range of a swordsman, whose movement point is 2. The movement cost of each tilt is 1. (a) No obstacle. (b) Tilt A is an obstacle and thus tilt B is out of the movement range. (c) The swordsman cannot pass the enemy to reach tilt B. (d) The swordsman can pass units of the same side to reach tilt B.

type of unit. Each tile is occupied by only one unit at the same time.

Each player in a TWB game controls an army consisting of many units. All units can either move or attack an enemy unit. Each unit has an allotted number of movement points that it uses to move across the tiles. Because different tiles have different movement costs, the distance that a unit can travel often varies. All of the tiles the unit can travel to compose a union of them called movement range (Figure 4), including the tile occupied by the unit itself. The movement range can generally be calculated by some algorithm such as breadth first search [18].

In addition to the movement point, each unit has its own health point (Hp) and attack power (ATK), which are numerical values and are various among the different units. Like movement range, a unit's attack range is another union of tiles to which the unit can attack from its current tile (Figure 5). Commonly, a unit's attack range is determined by its attack technique. Melee units, such as swordsmen, generally only attack adjacent units, and thus their attack range looks like

that shown in Figure 5(a). Ranged attacking units, such as archers, can attack enemies as far as two or more tiles away (Figure 5(b)). Special units' attack range is also a special one. If a unit attacks another unit, it forfeits all of its movement points and cannot take any further actions that turn; therefore, if a unit needs to be moved to a different tile, it must perform the move action prior to performing an attack action. A unit also has the option not to take any attack action after its movement or even not to take any action and stay on its current tile.

Each unit attacked by its enemy must deduct its Hp by the attacking unit's ATK, which indicates the damage. When a unit's Hp is deducted to or below 0, this indicates that it is dead and must be removed from the board immediately. The tilt it occupied becomes empty and can be reached by other following units.

A game of TBW consists of a sequence of turns. On each turn, every player gets their own turn to perform all of the actions for each of their side's units. This is unlike ordinary board games, such as chess, where turns are only for selecting

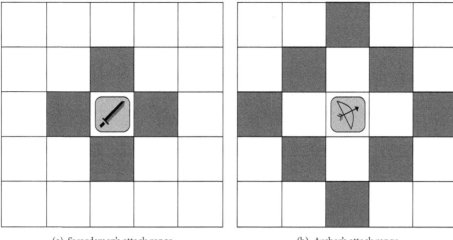

(a) Swordsmen's attack range (b) Archer's attack range

FIGURE 5: Units' attack range.

a pawn to move. The opposing side does not get to perform its actions until the current side has finished. A player wins the game if all of the units or the leader units of the other player have died.

2.2. Setup and Notation. TBW is composed of the board and pieces (units). The board is considered as an undirected graph $G(V, E)$, where V is the set of vertices (tilts) and E is the set of edges that connect the neighboring tilts. Units are divided into two parties A (*Alex's*) and B (*Billie's*) according to which player they belong to. The sizes of the two parties are denoted as n_A and n_B, respectively, and the indexes of the units in the two parties are $1, 2, \ldots, n_A$ and $1, 2, \ldots, n_B$, respectively. Let $n = n_A + n_B$ be the total number of units. An assignment $M : [1, n] \to V$ places the units in unique tilts: $\forall i, j \in [1, n]$, $j \neq i : M(i) \in V, M(j) \in V, M(i) \neq M(j)$. For each unit, there is a movement range $R \subseteq V$, where $r = |R|$, and an attack range R_{atk}, where $r_{atk} = |R_{atk}|$.

Let Ord^C be a sequence of elements in set C such that Ord_i^C is the ith element of this sequence. We denote $n = |C|$, and thus $Ord_i^C \in C$ and $\forall i, j \in [1, n], j \neq i : Ord_i^C \neq Ord_j^C$.

Let Q^C be a set of all sequences of the elements in set C such that $Q^C = \{Ord^C\}$. Thus, $|Q^C| = P_n^n$.

Without loss of generality, let Ord^A be an action sequence of units in *Alex's* turn such that Ord_i^A expresses the index of the unit doing the ith action, where $i \in [1, n_A]$.

2.3. Game Tree Search. We try to use game tree search theory to research the AI of TBW. Game tree search is the most popular model for researching common chess games. In the game tree (Figure 6), nodes express states of the game board. Branches derived from nodes express selections of the move method. The root node is the current state, and the leaf nodes are end states whose depths are specifically expanded from the root. Both sides take turns. Even layer nodes belong to the current player (squares), while odd layer nodes belong to the other side (circles). If the leaf node is not able to give

a win-lose-draw final state, an evaluation on a leaf node is needed to select the expected better method from the current state; this is the function of game tree search. Game tree search is based on min-max search, which is used to find the best outcome for the player and the best path leading to this outcome (Principal Variation) and, eventually, to find the corresponding move method in the root state (Root Move), that is, the best move for the player's turn [19].

It is not difficult to see that the evaluation and search algorithm are the most important parts of the game tree. For TBW, the evaluation factor of the state generally involves powers, positions, spaces, and motilities of units. The most common algorithms of game tree search are Alpha-Beta search [20] and Monte Carlo Tree Search [21], which can also be, although not directly, applied to TBW's search. This is because the branching factor of the search tree for TBW is huge and the common algorithms applied to TBW's search cause a timeout.

3. Features and Complexity Analysis

3.1. Complexity Analysis. A game of TBW consists of a sequence of turns. During each turn, every player gets their own turn to perform all of the actions for each of their side's units, which is the most important feature of TBW. The sequence of actions is vital. This is because the units cannot be overlapped; moreover, a different sequence of actions will also have a different state when a unit of another side is eliminated (Figure 7). Thus, during each side's turn, all of the plans of actions for its units are calculated by a permutation method. The amount of plans is estimated from both the worst and best situations (e.g., in the case of *Alex's* turn).

Step 1. Determine the sequence of actions: the total number is $P_{n_A}^{n_A} = n_A!$.

Step 2. Calculate the number of all plans of action in a specified action sequence.

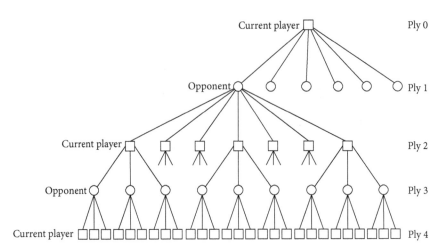

FIGURE 6: Game tree expanding to ply 4.

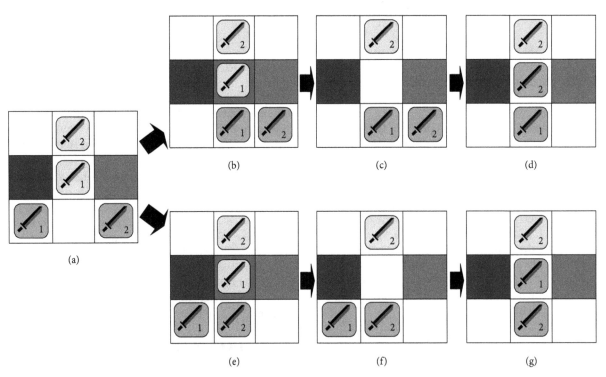

FIGURE 7: Effect of actions sequence. (a) The initial state of red side's turn. (b–d) Red swordsman number 1 acts and eliminates blue swordsman number 1, followed by red swordsman number 2. (e–g) Red swordsman number 2 acts and eliminates blue swordsman number 1, followed by red swordsman number 1.

Let R_i be the movement range of unit number i such that $r_i = |R_i|$. For simplicity, we assume that $r_1 = r_2 = \cdots = r_{n^A} = r$. In the worst case, the movement ranges of all of Alex's units are independent without overlapping each other; that is, $\forall i, j \in [1, n_A], j \neq i : R_i \cap R_j = \varnothing$. Moreover, in the attack phase, the amount of enemies that fall into each of Alex's units reaches maximum. For example, on a four-connected board, a melee unit has at most four adjacent tilts around it, which are full of enemies. Then, the number of attack plans is at most five (including a plan not to attack any enemy), that is, $r_{atk} + 1$.

According to the multiplication principle, the number of states expanding under a specified actions sequence is

$$[r(r_{atk} + 1)]^{n_A}. \tag{1}$$

According to Step 1, the number of actions sequences is $P_{n_A}^{n_A} = n_A!$ and thus, in the worst situation, the number of plans is

$$S_{worst} = [r(r_{atk} + 1)]^{n_A} \times n_A!. \tag{2}$$

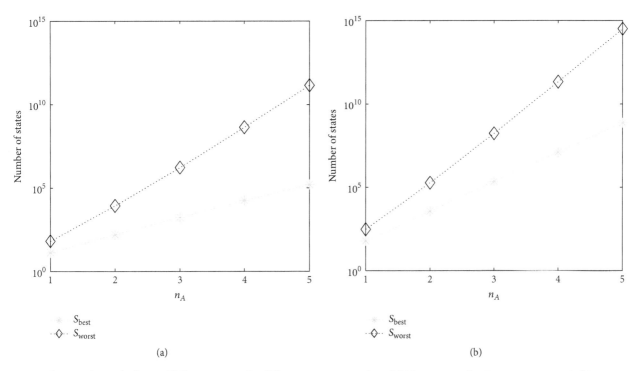

FIGURE 8: The growth trend of states S following n_A under different movement points. (a) Movement point: 2, movement cost: 1; (b) movement point: 5, movement cost: 1.

In the best situation, the movement ranges of all units overlap completely such that $R_1 = R_2 = \cdots = R_{n^A} = R$. Moreover, there are no enemies in the attack range of every unit. Thus, the amount of states can be calculated by the arrangement number $P_r^{n_A}$ such that we can select n_A from r positions to make all of the arrangements of the units. Therefore, the number of plans in the best situation is

$$S_{\text{best}} = \frac{r!}{(r - n_A)!}. \tag{3}$$

Above all, the total number of plans under all action sequences, denoted by S, is

$$S_{\text{best}} < S \leq S_{\text{worst}}. \tag{4}$$

In the following examples, we calculate the actual values of the total plans S. For "Fire Emblem," a typical ordinary TBW game, both sides have five units, and in the open battlefield, the movement range of each unit can reach at most 61 tilts (in that map, each tilt is adjacent to four other tilts, the movement point is 5, the movement cost of each tilt is 1, and there is no obstacle). Thus, $S_{\text{best}} \approx 710$ million and $S_{\text{worst}} \approx 317$ trillion. Assuming that the average computing time for searching a plan is 200 nanoseconds, searching all plans for one side's turn will then take from 2.4 minutes to approximately two years. Note that in the formula n_A is a key factor such that as it increases, the number of plans will dramatically expand (Figure 8). For a large-scale TBW, such as "Battle Commander," whose units may amount to no less than a dozen or dozens, the search will be more difficult.

TABLE 1: Branching factors comparison between TBW game and other board games.

	Branching factor	Comment
Chess [15]	≈ 30	Maximum branching factor is 40.
Go [16]	≈ 100	
Amazons [17]	≈ 1500	There are 2176 branches in the first turn.
TBW	710 million~317 trillion	Suppose that the movement point is 5, the movement cost is 1, and the amount of units is 5 for each side.

3.2. Features and Comparison. Compared with TBW games, other board games (such as chess, checkers, etc.) only require selecting a unit to perform an action in a single round, which not only results in fewer single-round action plans but also makes the number of plans linear with increasing numbers of units (for the chess type played by adding pieces, such as Go and Go-Moku, the number of plans is linear with increasing amounts of empty grids on the board). The number of single-round action plans corresponds to the size of the game tree branching factor. Table 1 shows a comparison between TBW games and some other ordinary board games that have more branching factors. A large branching factor and a rapidly expanding number of units are the key features by which the TWB games are distinguished from other board games.

A TBW game is essentially the compound of combinational optimization laterally and game tree search vertically

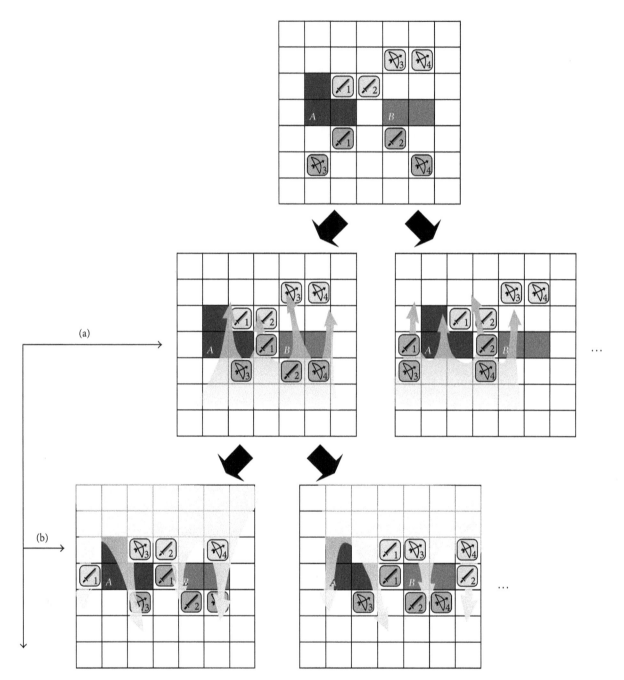

FIGURE 9: Search tree of TBW game: (a) red side's turn; (b) blue side's turn.

(Figure 9). Vertically, it can be seen as a tree search problem with a huge branching factor. Laterally, the relationship between layers is a series of phased combination optimizations, which is like a programming problem of multiagent collaboration. Therefore, the new game model generated by the expansion of the explosive branches needs to be researched by new algorithms.

Because the large number of states in a single round is the key problem by which the TBW games are distinguished from other board games, the optimization search and pruning of a single round have become the most important issues and processes for solving TBW games. That the search of a single round can be efficiently completed guarantees that the entire game tree can be extended. In the following, we propose two single-round search algorithms and compare them.

4. Single-Round Search Algorithms

4.1. Algorithm 2: Dictionary Sequence Enumeration Algorithm. Each side of a TBW game (hereafter, unless otherwise stated, referring specifically to Alex's side) wants to achieve a single turn search. Based on Section 3.1, we need to first determine the sequence of actions of n_A units and then enumerate all of the action plans of the units in each sequence.

Input: the original permutation sequence
$$Ord = Ord_1 Ord_2 \cdots Ord_{j-1} Ord_j Ord_{j+1} \cdots Ord_{k-1} Ord_k Ord_{k+1} \cdots Ord_n$$
(1) find $j = \max\{i \mid Ord_i < Ord_{i+1}\}$
(2) **if** j doesn't exist **then**
(3)   **exit**, and next permutation sequence doesn't exist.
(4) **else**
(5)   find $k = \max\{i \mid Ord_i > Ord_j\}$
(6)   **swap**(Ord_j, Ord_k)
(7)   reverse the sub-sequence $Ord_{j+1} \cdots Ord_{k-1} Ord_j Ord_{k+1} \cdots Ord_n$
(8)   **Output**: $Ord' = Ord_1 Ord_2 \cdots Ord_{j-1} Ord_k Ord_n \cdots Ord_{k+1} Ord_j Ord_{k-1} \cdots Ord_{j+1}$ is the
   next permutation sequence.
(9) **end if**

ALGORITHM 1: *next_permutation(Ord)*.

---

(1) initialize a sequence Ord which is the first sequence in dictionary sequences
(2) **while** Ord exists **do**
(3)   call $Search(1)$
(4) $Ord \leftarrow next\_permutation(Ord)$
(5) **end while**

ALGORITHM 2: Dictionary sequence enumeration algorithm.

4.1.1. Action Sequence of Units Algorithm. Determining an action sequence of n_A units requires a permutation algorithm. There are some famous permutation algorithms, such as the recursive method based on exchange, the orthoposition trade method, the descending carry method, and the dictionary sequence method [22–25]. Their execution strategies are different, their time and space complexities vary, and they have been used in different problems. We first apply the dictionary sequence method, whose time complexity is lower. The idea of all permutation generation from n elements (e.g., $\{1, 2, \ldots, n\}$) is that with the beginning of the first sequence $(123 \cdots n)$ a series of subsequent larger sequences are generated lexicographically until reaching the reverse order $(n \cdots 321)$. The algorithm, called *next_permutation*, which generates the next sequence from an original one, is illustrated as in Algorithm 1.

For example, 754938621 is a sequence of numbers 1–9. The next sequence obtained by this algorithm is 754961238.

4.1.2. Algorithm 2: Dictionary Sequence Enumeration Algorithm. Enumerate all of the plans of units' actions in a particular order. Because the search depth is limited (equal to the number of units), depth-first search is an effective method. Because the depth is not great, realizing the depth-first search by the use of recursion requires smaller space overhead, which leads to the sequential enumeration algorithm with permutation and recursion, as in Algorithm 2.

Here $Search(i)$ is the algorithm for enumerating all of the action plans of the ith unit (see Algorithm 3).

4.2. Algorithm 5: Recursive Enumeration Algorithm. Algorithm 2 comes from a simple idea that always starts enumeration from the first unit in every search for the next

sequence. However, compared with the previous sequence, the front parts of units whose orders are not changed are not required to be enumerated again, which creates redundant computing and reduces efficiency. For example, when the search of sequence $Ord_1, Ord_2, \ldots, Ord_i, \ldots, Ord_j, \ldots, Ord_n$ is finished, if the next sequential order is adjusted only from the ith to the jth unit, then in the recursive enumeration phases the units from the first one to the $i - 1$th can directly inherit the enumeration results of the previous sequence and we only need to enumerate the units from the ith to the last one recursively. On the basis of this feature, we switch to the recursive permutation algorithm to achieve the arrangement so that the recursive algorithm combines with the recursive depth-first search algorithm for the purpose of removing the redundant computation, which is the improved algorithm called the *recursive enumeration algorithm* illustrated as in Algorithm 4.

In Algorithm 4, n is the size of our sequence (lines (1), (6)). With respect to the predefined procedure, we generate the permutations from the ith to the last unit in the sequence by calling the function *recursive_permutation(i)*. The latter is realized using the subpermutations from the $i + 1$th to the last unit in the sequence, which are generated by calling function *recursive_permutation(i + 1)* recursively (lines (5)–(11)). The index j points to the unit swapped with the ith unit (line (7)) in every recursive call, after which the two units must resume their orders (line (9)), for the next step.

By initializing the sequence Ord and running the function *recursive_permutation(1)*, we can obtain a full permutation of all the elements.

Based on the above, the improved single-round search algorithm, called the recursive enumeration algorithm, is described as in Algorithm 5.

```
(1) if i > n then
(2)     return
(3) else
(4)     for each action plan of the ith unit
(5)         execute the current plan
(6)         call Search(i + 1)
(7)         cancel this plan and rollback to the previous state
(8)     end for
(9) end if
```

ALGORITHM 3: *Search(i)*.

```
(1) if i ≥ n then
(2)     output the generated sequence Ord₁, Ord₂, ..., Ordₙ
(3)     return
(4) else
(5)     j ← i
(6)     while j ≤ n do
(7)         swap(Ordᵢ, Ordⱼ)
(8)         call recursive_permutation(i + 1)
(9)         swap(Ordᵢ, Ordⱼ)
(10)        j ← j + 1
(11)    end while
(12) end if
```

ALGORITHM 4: *recursive_permutation(i)* (enumerate sequences from *i*th to the last element).

The framework of this new algorithm is similar to that of the *recursive_permutation* algorithm, where n is the number of units. In the new algorithm, all the action plans of the ith unit, which involve selecting targets for attack, are enumerated and executed separately (lines (7)-(8)) after the required swap process. Then, after solving the subproblem using the recursive call *Plans_Search(i+1)*, a rollback of the current plan is necessary and the state needs to be resumed (line (10)).

To enumerate the actions plans of all the units, the sequence *Ord* is initialized, and then the function *Plans_Search(1)* runs.

From step (3) of Algorithm 5, before enumerating the action plans of the unit, we do not need to generate all of the sequences; that is, for each unit, determination of its order and enumeration of its actions are carried out simultaneously.

4.3. Comparison. First, we compare the time complexities of the two algorithms.

The time consumption of the recursive enumeration algorithm lies in an n times loop and an $n-1$ times recursion, such that the time complexity is $O(n(n-1)(n-2)\cdots 1) = O(n!)$ [23]. It is the same as the time complexity of the dictionary sequence enumeration algorithm [23]. Moreover, the states searched by the two algorithms are also the same.

Theorem 1. *The states searched by Algorithms 2 and 5 are the same.*

Proof. Suppose $S(Ord)$ is the set of the states in the sequence *Ord*, and Pre_a are the sequences beginning with a in Q^A.

According to Algorithm 2, it first determines the order of a sequence *Ord* and then enumerates all of the states S_1 under this sequence:

$$S_1 = \bigcup_{Ord^A \in Q^A} S\left(Ord^A\right). \tag{5}$$

According to the outermost layer of the recursion in Algorithm 5, we can obtain all of the states S_2:

$$S_2 = \bigcup_{a \in A} S\left(Pre_a\right). \tag{6}$$

Because $\cup_{a \in A} Pre_a = Q^A$ and $\cup_{Ord^A \in Q^A} S(Ord^A) = S(Q^A)$, therefore, $S_1 = S_2$. □

The difference between Algorithms 2 and 5 reflects the efficiency of their enumerations. In the searching process, an important atomic operation (ops1) expands each unit's action plan on each position it moves to. This is because (1) the states taken by search are mainly composed of every unit moving to every position and (2) every unit arriving at every position and then attacking or choosing other options for action is a time-consuming operation in the searching process. Suppose the number of ops1 in Algorithms 2 and 5 is H_1 and H_2, respectively. For simplicity, we make the following assumptions.

Assumption 2. Assume that every unit's movement range does not overlap another's, the sizes of which are all equal; that

```
(1) if i > n then
(2)    return
(3) else
(4)    j ← i
(5)    while j ≤ n do
(6)       swap(Ord_i, Ord_j)
(7)       for each action plan of the ith unit
(8)          execute the current plan
(9)          call Plans_Search(i + 1)
(10)         cancel this plan and rollback to the previous state
(11)      end for
(12)      swap(Ord_i, Ord_j)
(13)      j ← j + 1
(14)   end while
(15) end if
```

ALGORITHM 5: Recursive enumeration algorithm: *Plans_Search(i)* (search action plans from *i*th to the last unit).

is, $|R_1| = |R_2| = \cdots = |R_n| = r$, and $R_1 \cap R_2 \cap \cdots \cap R_n = \varnothing$. Moreover, every unit cannot attack after moving (i.e., none of the enemies are inside the attack range).

In the following, we calculate H_1 and H_2, respectively.

In Algorithm 2, in each identified sequence, ops1 corresponds to the nodes of the search tree formed by enumerating states (except the root node, which represents no action). The depth of the tree is n, and each of the branching factors is r; then, the number of nodes is $r^n + r^{n-1} + \cdots + r$. Moreover, the number of all sequences is $P_n^n = n!$ and therefore

$$H_1 = n! \left(r^n + r^{n-1} + \cdots + r \right). \tag{7}$$

In Algorithm 5, suppose that the number of ops1 of n units is h_n. The first unit performing an action according to the order of the current sequence is a. According to Algorithm 5, every time a moves to a tilt, it will make a new state combining the following $n - 1$ units, such that the number of the ops1 is $1 + h_{n-1}$. Because the number of tilts a can move to is r and the recursion operates n times, we can deduce that $h_n = nr(1 + h_{n-1})$, where $h_1 = r$; thus,

$$H_2 = h_n = n! \sum_{i=0}^{n-1} \frac{r^{n-i}}{i!}. \tag{8}$$

Accordingly,

$$H_1 - H_2 = n! \sum_{i=2}^{n-1} \frac{i! - 1}{i!} r^{n-i}. \tag{9}$$

It is easy to see that the number of ops1 of Algorithm 5 is smaller than that of Algorithm 2. Table 2 lists the experimental results, showing H_1 under Assumption 2, H_2 under a general condition, and their differences.

Conclusion. On the premise that the search states are exactly the same, Algorithm 5 is better than Algorithm 2 regarding the consumption of ops1 and actual running time.

5. Experimental Evaluation

In this section, we present our experimental evaluation of the performance of Algorithms 2 and 5 under all types of conditions and their comparison. Because they are both single-round search algorithms, we set only one side's units on the board, ignoring the other side's, whose interference is equivalent to narrowing the range of units' movement. Experiments are grouped based on the following conditions: the number of units, the unit's movement point, and the dispersion of units. The number of units is set to 3 and 4 (setting to 2 is too simple with a lack of universality, while setting to 5 leads to timeout). The movement point is set to 2, 3, and 4, and the movement cost of each tilt is set to 1. The dispersion is set to the most dispersive ones and the most centralized ones. The most dispersive cases mean that the movement ranges of all of the units are independent without overlapping each other, corresponding to the worst case in Section 3.1. The most centralized cases mean that all of the units are put together (Figure 10), which maximizes the overlap degree and corresponds to the best case in Section 3.1. The experimental groups set above cover all of the actual situations. The board used in the experiments is completely open without any boundary and barrier. The case of a board with boundaries and barriers can be classified into cases where a smaller movement point of units is set. The experimental tool is a PC with Intel Core i7-2600@2.40 GHz CPU and 4.00 GB memory, and the program was written with Visual C++ 2005 with optimized running time.

From Table 2, we can see that in all cases the number of ops1 of Algorithm 5 is less than that of Algorithm 2 for different levels. Assuming that the number of units is invariable, the optimization level of Algorithm 5 will become low by increasing the movement point, which can be deduced from (8) and (9): under Assumption 2, $\widehat{D}_{\mathrm{ops1}}$ which shows the reduced percentage of using ops1 in Algorithm 5 instead of in Algorithm 2 is

$$\widehat{D}_{\mathrm{ops1}} = \frac{H_1 - H_2}{H_1} = \frac{\sum_{i=2}^{n-1} ((i! - 1)/i!) r^{n-i}}{\sum_{i=0}^{n-1} r^{n-i}}. \tag{10}$$

TABLE 2: (a) For three units, the comparison of ops1 under different movement points and different dispersions. (b) For four units, the comparison of ops1 under different movement points and different dispersions.

(a)

	Movement point 2		Movement point 3		Movement point 4	
	Dispersed	Compact	Dispersed	Compact	Dispersed	Compact
Algorithm 2	14274	9804	97650	79260	423858	371652
Algorithm 5	14235	9771	97575	79191	423735	371535
D_{ops1}*	0.27%	0.34%	0.077%	0.087%	0.029%	0.031%
$\widehat{D}_{\text{ops1}}$**	0.30%		0.080%		0.030%	

(b)

	Movement point 2		Movement point 3		Movement point 4	
	Dispersed	Compact	Dispersed	Compact	Dispersed	Compact
Algorithm 2	742560	345264	9765600	6394800	69513696	53301744
Algorithm 5	740272	343804	9757600	6388468	69492704	53283548
D_{ops1}*	0.31%	0.42%	0.082%	0.099%	0.030%	0.034%
$\widehat{D}_{\text{ops1}}$**	0.30%		0.080%		0.030%	

*D_{ops1} shows the reduced percentage of using ops1 in Algorithm 5 instead of in Algorithm 2.
**$\widehat{D}_{\text{ops1}}$ shows the estimated value of D_{ops1} under Assumption 2.

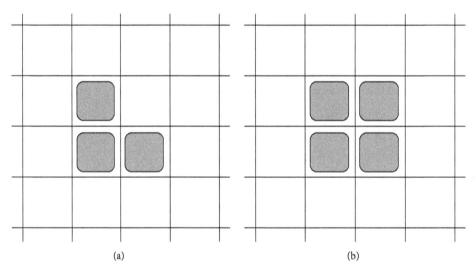

(a)   (b)

FIGURE 10: (a) Compact placement of three units. (b) Compact placement of four units.

In (10), the numerator is the infinitesimal of higher order of the denominator; that is,

$$\widehat{D}_{\text{ops1}} \approx \frac{1}{2} r^{-2}. \qquad (11)$$

Table 2 lists the values of $\widehat{D}_{\text{ops1}}$ when the movement point is 2, 3, and 4, which are consistent with the experimental results.

Under the same conditions of the movement point and the number of units, the value of D_{ops1} with compact units is more than that with dispersed units. This is because the more the units are compact, the stronger the interference the units will cause to each other, which is equivalent to a narrow movement range of r. According to (11), therefore, D_{ops1} will increase correspondingly. Moreover, under the same conditions of the movement point and the degree of units'

dispersion, D_{ops1} will also increase with the increase of the number of units. In summary, the experiments show that, regardless of whether Assumption 2 is satisfied, Algorithm 5 always performs better than Algorithm 2 on the number of ops1, which coincides with $\widehat{D}_{\text{ops1}}$ from (11). Because the degree of optimization is not very prominent, the running times of these two algorithms are almost the same.

6. Conclusions

Based on a modest study of turn-based war chess games (TBW), a common gaming model and its formal description are first proposed. By comparison with other chess type models, the most important feature of TBW has been discussed: the player needs to complete actions for all of his units in a turn, which leads to a huge branching factor. Then, a game tree theory framework to solve this model is proposed. Finally, two algorithms for single-round search from the most complex part of the framework are proposed: Algorithm 2 is the dictionary sequence enumeration algorithm and Algorithm 5 is the recursive enumeration algorithm. Finally, based on theoretical derivations and experimental results, respectively, the completeness of these algorithms is proven. Also, the performance comparison shows that under all conditions the number of opsl of Algorithm 5 decreases to a certain extent compared to that of Algorithm 2.

Although these two algorithms are designed from classical algorithms, they can be used to solve the single-round search problem completely and effectively. Moreover, the research angles of the two algorithms are completely different, which provide two specific frameworks for a further study on TBW.

(1) The dictionary sequence enumeration algorithm is implemented in two steps. The first step consists of the generation of sequences; and the second step consists of the enumeration of action plans under these sequences. Therefore, this algorithm is based on sequences. Different permutation algorithms can be used to generate different orders of sequences, which may be more suitable for new demands. For instance, the orthoposition trade method [23] can minimize the difference of each pair of adjacent sequences. Thus, more action plans from the former sequence can be reused for the next, which can improve the efficiency.

(2) The recursive enumeration algorithm is also implemented in two steps. The first step consists of the enumeration of action plans of the current unit; and the second step consists of the generation of the sequences of the next units. Therefore, this algorithm is based on action plans. Pruning bad action plans in the depth-first search process can easily cut off all the following action sequences and action plans of later units, which will lead to a significant improvement of efficiency.

In the current era of digital entertainment, TBW games have broad application prospects. They also have a profound theoretical research value. However, in this study, TBW theory has been discussed partially. The game model framework we proposed is composed of the combinatorial optimization problem on one hand, and the game tree search problem on the other hand. Thus, our future research will mainly start with the following two points:

(1) Introduce the multiagent collaborative planning approach to efficiently prune the huge branches of the game tree. Moreover, by introducing the independent detection approach [26], we can separate the independent units that have no effect on each other into different groups with the purpose of decreasing the number of units in each group.

(2) Introduce the Monte Carlo Tree Search method to simulate the deep nodes. The single-round search

algorithms proposed in this paper are complete algorithms and can be used to verify the performance of the new algorithm.

Acknowledgments

This work is supported by the National Key Basic Research Program of China (973 Program 2013CB329103 of 2013CB329100), the National Natural Science Foundations of China (NSFC-61173129, 61472053, and 91420102), the Fundamental Research Funds for the Central University (CDJXS11182240 and CDJXS11180004), and the Innovation Team Construction Project of Chongqing Institute of Engineering (2014xcxtd05).

References

[1] L. V. Alus, H. J. van den Herik, and M. P. H. Huntjens, "Go-Moku solved by new search techniques," *Computational Intelligence*, vol. 12, no. 1, pp. 7–23, 1996.

[2] C. Deng, *Research on search algorithms in computer go [M.S. thesis]*, Kunming University of Science and Technology, 2013.

[3] H. C. Neto, R. M. S. Julia, G. S. Caexeta, and A. R. A. Barcelos, "LS-VisionDraughts: improving the performance of an agent for checkers by integrating computational intelligence, reinforcement learning and a powerful search method," *Applied Intelligence*, vol. 41, no. 2, pp. 525–550, 2014.

[4] Y. J. Liu, *The research and implementation of computer games which based on the alpha-beta algorithm [M.S. thesis]*, Dalian Jiaotong University, 2012.

[5] J. Jokić, *Izrada šahovskog engine-a [Ph.D. thesis]*, University of Rijeka, 2014.

[6] N. R. Sturtevant and R. E. Korf, "On pruning techniques for multi-player games," in *Proceedings of the 17th National Conference on Artificial Intelligence and 12th Conference on Innovative Applications of Artificial Intelligence (AAAI-IAAI '00)*, vol. 49, pp. 201–207, Austin, Tex, USA, July-August 2000.

[7] C. Luckhart and K. Irani B, "An algorithmic solution of N-person games," in *Proceedings of the 5th National Conference on Artificial Intelligence (AAAI '86)*, vol. 1, pp. 158–162, Philadelphia, Pa, USA, August 1986.

[8] C. Browne, "A problem case for UCT," *IEEE Transactions on Computational Intelligence and AI in Games*, vol. 5, no. 1, pp. 69–74, 2013.

[9] M. H. M. Winands, Y. Björnsson, and J.-T. Saito, "Monte Carlo tree search in lines of action," *IEEE Transactions on Computational Intelligence and AI in Games*, vol. 2, no. 4, pp. 239–250, 2010.

[10] P. Nijssen and M. H. M. Winands, "Monte carlo tree search for the hide-and-seek game Scotland Yard," *IEEE Transactions on Computational Intelligence and AI in Games*, vol. 4, no. 4, pp. 282–294, 2012.

[11] G. Wang, H. Liu, and N. Zhu, "A survey of war games technology," *Ordnance Industry Automation*, vol. 31, no. 8, pp. 38–41, 2012.

[12] M. H. Bergsma and P. Spronck, "Adaptive spatial reasoning for turn-based strategy games," in *Proceedings of the 4th Artificial Intelligence and Interactive Digital Entertainment Conference (AIIDE '08)*, pp. 161–166, Palo Alto, Calif, USA, October 2008.

[13] S. Paskaradevan and J. Denzinger, "A hybrid cooperative behavior learning method for a rule-based shout-ahead architecture," in *Proceedings of the IEEE/WIC/ACM International Conferences on Web Intelligence and Intelligent Agent Technology (WI-IAT '12)*, vol. 2, pp. 266–273, IEEE Computer Society, December 2012.

[14] S. Wiens, J. Denzinger, and S. Paskaradevan, "Creating large numbers of game AIs by learning behavior for cooperating units," in *Proceedings of the IEEE Conference on Computational Intelligence in Games (CIG '13)*, pp. 1–8, IEEE, Ontario, Canada, August 2013.

[15] G. Badhrinathan, A. Agarwal, and R. Anand Kumar, "Implementation of distributed chess engine using PaaS," in *Proceedings of the International Conference on Cloud Computing Technologies, Applications and Management (ICCCTAM '12)*, pp. 38–42, IEEE, Dubai, United Arab Emirates, December 2012.

[16] X. Xu and C. Xu, "Summarization of fundamental and methodology of computer games," *Progress of Artificial Intelligence in China*, pp. 748–759, 2009.

[17] J. Song and M. Muller, "An enhanced solver for the game of Amazons," *IEEE Transactions on Computational Intelligence and AI in Games*, vol. 7, no. 1, pp. 16–27, 2015.

[18] D. Gesang, Y. Wang, and X. Guo, "AI arithmetic design and practical path of a war-chess game," *Journal of Tibet University (Natural Science Edition)*, vol. 26, no. 2, pp. 102–106, 2011.

[19] X. Xu and J. Wang, "Key technologies analysis of Chinese chess computer game," *Mini-Micro Systems*, vol. 27, no. 6, pp. 961–969, 2006.

[20] B. Bošanský, V. Lisý, J. Čermák, R. Vítek, and M. Pěchouček, "Using double-oracle method and serialized alpha-beta search for pruning in simultaneous move games," in *Proceedings of the 23rd International Joint Conference on Artificial Intelligence*, pp. 48–54, AAAI Press, Beijing, China, August 2013.

[21] A. Guez, D. Silver, and P. Dayan, "Scalable and efficient Bayes-adaptive reinforcement learning based on Monte-Carlo tree search," *Journal of Artificial Intelligence Research*, vol. 48, pp. 841–883, 2013.

[22] R. Sedgewick, "Permutation generation methods," *ACM Computing Surveys*, vol. 9, no. 2, pp. 137–164, 1977.

[23] D. E. Knuth, *The Art of Computer Programming Vol. 4A: Combinatorial Algorithms, Part 1*, The People's Posts and Telecommunications Press, Beijing, China, 2012.

[24] B. R. Heap, "Permutations by interchanges," *The Computer Journal*, vol. 6, no. 3, pp. 293–298, 1963.

[25] F. M. Ives, "Permutation enumeration: four new permutation algorithms," *Communications of the ACM*, vol. 19, no. 2, pp. 68–72, 1976.

[26] G. Sharon, R. Stern, M. Goldenberg, and A. Felner, "The increasing cost tree search for optimal multi-agent pathfinding," *Artificial Intelligence*, vol. 195, pp. 470–495, 2013.

## 9

Pegasus: A Simulation Tool to Support Design of Progression Games

Marcelo Arêas R. da Silva ⓘ[1] and Geraldo Bonorino Xexéo[1,2]

[1]*COPPE/UFRJ, Federal University of Rio de Janeiro, Rio de Janeiro, RJ, Brazil*
[2]*Department of Computer Science, Institute of Mathematics (DCC-IM), Rio de Janeiro, RJ, Brazil*

Correspondence should be addressed to Marcelo Arêas R. da Silva; mareas@gmail.com

Academic Editor: Michael J. Katchabaw

The process of designing a game involves many phases. We can summarize the work of the game designer as satisfactorily converting the idea in their mind to a digital game, which is not a simple task. Therefore, game designers should have a variety of tools to assist them. However, there are not that many specialized tools to support the game design process. Herein, we describe the experience of using Pegasus to design a part of a game. We propose an environment to simulate progression games based on game design patterns. Thus, we described the interaction of the game designer with Pegasus in such an environment, in order to support the process of creating, testing, and refining game elements before proceeding to the programming phase. Each configuration of the game elements corresponded to a simulation that could be performed multiple times, like in discrete event simulation. The results showed that Pegasus has the potential to support game design. Additionally, we presented some support components that were created to facilitate the use of the tool.

1. Introduction

The digital games industry is growing fast. A survey conducted annually in the United States indicated that consumer spending on digital games increased 42% from 2010 to 2016. The same research indicated that there is at least one person in every United States household who plays three or more hours of digital games a wcck [1]. There was a time when people thought that videogames were aimed only at children, but that is a fallacy; there are studies that characterize the profile of older players [2].

Despite such growth, the process of creating a digital game can be as complex as creating an information system. There are many steps—from designing the initial idea to reaching the final product—involved in conceiving a digital game. Several authors have dealt with this subject [3–7]; some for specific types of games (e.g., serious games [8, 9]), but few have attempted to support the design process by using formal methods [10]. In fact, as stated by Neil [11] and Koster [12], there is a lack of tools to support game design.

If the game designer could test scenarios and refine the game prior to the programming phase, it is reasonable to say that product quality would improve and time would be saved. Thus, this paper is part of a thesis [13] and we propose an environment to simulate games that have a progression-based structure.

This paper is organized as follows: Section 2 describes some related works in this research area; Section 3 presents our proposal of an environment to simulate progression games; Section 4 introduces the Pegasus simulation tool; Section 5 reports on the experience using the simulator to support the design of part of a game; and finally, Section 6 presents the conclusions and future work.

2. Literature Review

The *Machinations* framework is a way to represent games by highlighting their internal economy, focusing on the relationships of the game mechanics and the dynamic gameplay that emerges from these relationships [14]. It works as a visual language, composed of diagrams and components, in which the game designer can create, simulate, and test the internal game economy. *Machinations* is satisfactory for simulating

TABLE 1: Patterns in game design and their relationships.

Pattern	Instantiates	Instantiated by
Game world	-	Levels
Levels	Game world	-
Inaccessible areas	Traversing	-
Enemies	Combat	Boss monsters, Avatars, Units, Elimination
Boss monsters	Enemies	Elimination
Obstacles	Inaccessible areas	-
Avatars	Enemies	-
Units	Enemies, Resources	-
Tools	Improved abilities, Rewards	Pick-ups
Pick-ups	Tools	Power-ups, Resources
Power-ups	Pick-ups, Improved abilities	-
Lives	Resources	-
Resources	Pick-ups, Rewards, Penalties	Units, Lives
Combat	Randomness, Resources	Elimination, Enemies
Movement	-	Traversing
Improved abilities	Rewards	Power-ups, Tools
Rewards	Balancing	Improved abilities, Tools
Penalties	-	Elimination, Resources
Elimination	Combat, Penalties, Enemies, Boss Monsters	-
Traversing	Movement	-
Randomness	Balancing	Combat
Balancing	-	Rewards, Randomness

emergence in games, but is not suitable for progression games. Dormans [15] tried to shape emergent mechanics to produce progressive experiences; however, due to limitations of *Machinations*, only an evolution of the same structure of the emergence pattern was achieved to represent the constant increase in difficulty.

The simulation technique is often used in several areas, for example, analysing production processes, optimizing transport networks, evaluating user behaviour, and learning [16, 17]. In the study of Nummenmaa et al. [18], the authors proposed simulating gameplay as a design tool. They described a case study with implementation of a simulation model for a game using a simulation software package.

Evaluating player enjoyment is also a common theme in this area of research; there are works presenting models for analysing game playability [19, 20]. Syriani and Vangheluwe [21] proposed an approach to improve game playability by simulating the movement of characters with simple mechanics as well as by evaluating player behaviour.

Even if it was just a theoretical foundation, Grünvogel [10] introduced formalism for designing games from small submodels, due to complex games being difficult to simulate. Gradually, those models would be combined into more complex systems to represent the game as a whole.

2.1. Progression and Emergence in Games. Among the many genres and subgenres of digital games, a game is classified into these different genres depending on the observer [22]. However, according to Juul [23], we can say that there are two basic structures of games: emergence and progression.

In a game structured by emergence, a small set of rules combine to produce large game variations, and players then create strategies to deal with the random world [23]. We found emergence in strategy, card, and sports games, as well as in chess and tournaments. On the other hand, progression deals with a controlled sequence of events and often tells a story. The game designer plans each level and its challenges. The player must overcome the events in a given sequence to advance in the game [23]. In general, adventure and actions games are based on progression structure.

Most modern digital games fit the two definitions; that is, they contain elements of emergence and progression [14]. For example, *Assassin's Creed*, *Red Dead Redemption*, *GTA*, *The Division*, and *Destiny* are open world games, in which a player controls a character with freedom to explore and perform various activities. However, there are optional and main missions; the latter usually unlock new places when completed. These games contain a progression structure and tell a story, but despite this, each mission has its own emergent elements.

3. Proposal of Environment to Simulate Progression Games

Björk and Holopainen [24] presented a large collection of patterns in game design. We studied patterns and their relationships in order to propose a favourable environment for simulating progression games. Table 1 shows the relationships among some patterns commonly found in games with a progression-based structure.

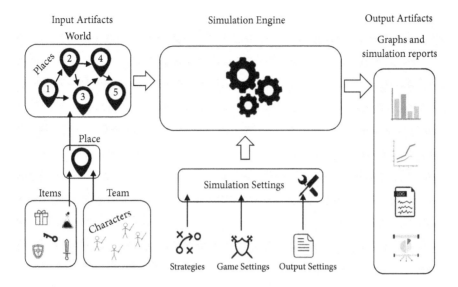

FIGURE 1: The simulation environment.

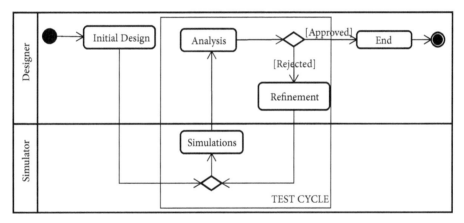

FIGURE 2: Actions of game designer.

3.1. Types of Progression Games Covered.

The proposed environment supports games with elements that are typical of role-playing and adventure games and could involve single-player or multiplayer games. The player controls a character or a team, starts from point A, faces some challenges, and tries to reach point B alive. During the journey, the player visits several places, which may contain enemies, items, and/or obstacles. Places can be mandatory or optional, which results in many possible ways to reach the end. The degree of complexity depends on the player's creativity in combining elements to create the game world.

Games of the *Dungeon Crawl* genre—such as *Rogue*, *Gauntlet*, *Dungeonlike*, and *Diablo*—fit the described characteristics very well. Furthermore, the proposed environment is also suitable for any game which involves entering a place, resolving conflicts, collecting items, and moving on.

3.2. Description of the Environment.

The environment is composed of a *Simulation Engine*, *Input Artifacts*, and *Output Artifacts*; see Figure 1. The *Input Artifacts* are *Team*, *World*, and *Simulation Settings*. *Team* is made up of *Characters*, which can be *Heroes* or *Foes*. *Places* are arranged inside the *World* and may contain *Teams* of *Foes* and collectible *Items*.

The *Simulation Settings* should allow the game designer to adjust and test distinct scenarios to obtain different results. *Output Artifacts* are data collected—in an easy-to-read format—from all of the simulation events performed. Thus, data could be processed to generate valuable information, reports, statistics, summarization, and graphs.

The diagram in Figure 2 illustrates how the game designer should act in the environment. The inspiration of a game designer remains fundamental. The process starts after the game designer constructs the *Input Artifacts* to feed the simulator; we call this *Initial Design*. The designer then starts a test cycle, performing simulations (*Simulations*), analysing the results (*Analysis*), and, if applicable, adjusting some elements and settings to start new simulations (*Refinement*). Once the game designer approves the results, the participation of the simulator is concluded (*End*), and everything is set to move forward to the programming phase of the creation process.

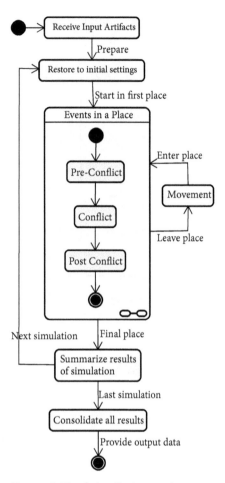

FIGURE 3: Simulation Engine requirements.

3.3. Simulation Engine Requirements. The operations of the *Simulation Engine* must fulfill certain requirements to ensure the proper functioning of the proposed environment (Figure 3). The first step is to receive the *Input Artifacts*, then to restore all of them to their initial conditions. Thereafter, with the *Hero* or *Team* of *Heroes* at the first place, the conflict should be solved in the following order:

(i) *Preconflict*: preparation for the conflict; *Heroes* can use *Items* to improve or restore attributes.

(ii) *Conflict*: resolve the threats—such as battles—at the particular place.

(iii) *Postconflict*: *Heroes* collect pick-up *Items* as rewards, if they exist.

Heroes then move to the next place, and the aforementioned process starts again until one of the following happens:

(a) *Heroes* are in the final place or

(b) all *Heroes* are dead.

In both cases the simulation ends.

During a simulation, the *Simulation Engine* must record all data from each event as it happens. Such events can be battle logs; how the values of each attribute of the characters are modified, items collected, items used, keys found, etc. At the end of a simulation, all the collected data should be summarized.

The described process comprises a single simulation. At this point, the next simulation can be performed or, if it was the last one, the *Simulation Engine* consolidates the results from all previous simulations and provides the data. In the subsequent sections we show some examples of processed data.

4. Pegasus: Progression Game Simulator

We built Pegasus to implement our proposal. It was constructed in the Python programming language [25] to comply with best practices for software design patterns [26]. In this section, we present the architecture, related artifacts, and support components.

4.1. Architecture and Input Artifacts. Pegasus architecture is divided into layers (see Figure 4), as follows:

(a) *Interface*: where all the processes are initiated. The *Input Artifacts* are forwarded to the subsequent corresponding layers.

(b) *Component*: collection of essential and nonessential modules that facilitate usage and give new configuration options to the game designer. It is referred to as the *Component* layer because new modules can be built and incorporated into it.

(c) *Simulation*: the simulation process core was developed respecting the guidelines of our proposal.

(d) *Result Storage*: it stores all simulation results; it works concurrently with the *Simulation* layer.

(e) *Result Processing*: it generates reports and graphs from the collected data.

Grey arrows represent the sequence of events, whereas white arrows indicate that a layer acts upon another.

The *Input Artifacts* are class objects representing the game elements and simulation settings. Figure 5 shows a class diagram with the relationships.

A *Character*, which can be either a *Hero* or *Foe*, is part of a *Team* and has a set of *Attributes* and *Items*. The *Attributes* define the kind of action a *Character* is capable of. There are four distinct types of *Attributes*, all of which affect and are affected by battles: *life*, *attack*, *defense*, and *agility*. The *life* attribute defines if a *Character* is still alive; thus, the absence of this attribute means that a *Character* does not participate in battles. The *attack* attribute is essential to a *Character* inflicting damage on others. The *defense* attribute is the capacity to reduce damage suffered. Finally, the *agility* attribute influences how fast a *Character* can perform actions when in battle.

The *Places* can have *Teams*, *Items*, or nothing. The *Places* connect to each other; a *Team* of *Heroes* tries to find a way from the first to the final *Place*. The *Items* may be weapons or potions for temporarily or permanently improving some of the *Attributes*; for example, a key to a *Place* that would

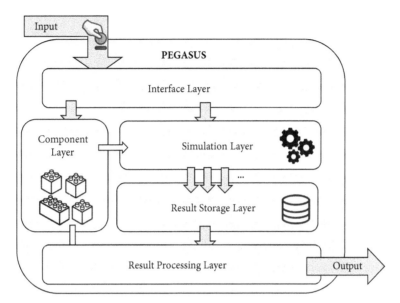

FIGURE 4: Pegasus architecture.

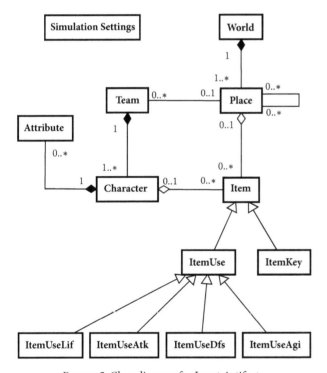

FIGURE 5: Class diagram for Input Artifacts.

otherwise be inaccessible. This key/lock system is frequently found in a large range of games.

Once these elements are prepared, they are all encompassed by the World.

The *Simulation Settings* comprise a set of options to guide the behaviour of some components. More details are introduced in the subsequent subsections.

4.2. Output Artifacts. The *Result Storage* layer records all events that have occurred in the simulations, thus satisfying what was described in our proposal. Subsequently, the *Result Processing* layer generates summary and detailed reports. Figure 6 contains snippets of some reports as examples.

Both the *Summary Report* (a) and the *Detailed Report* (c) contain data from each simulation, composed of the places entered, number of turns in each battle, and items found. At the end of each simulation there is a summary with the following: total number of places visited, names of all items found, number of the place where the simulation ended, total number of turns, average number of turns, and the order of the places visited. The *Detailed Report* (c) also contains logs of each battle; the values of the attributes vary according to each battle.

In each report, the consolidated results (b) contain information on all simulations and are shown after all simulations, at the end of the report. They state the number of times the *Heroes* concluded a simulation, average number of places visited, average number of items found, average number of turns per simulation, average number of turns per place, and the most common order of the places visited.

One of the modules developed in the *Component* layer acts on the *Result Storage* layer to generate graphs from the collected data. Currently, the following graphs can be generated:

(a) Bar chart and pie chart for the number of times a simulation ends in a place.

(b) Scatter plot and Box plot for the variation in a *Hero* attribute at each place, for all simulations.

(c) Line chart for the average value of the attributes of every *Hero* at each place.

(d) Scatter plot for the variation in number of turns at each place, for all simulations.

(e) Line chart for the most common order of places visited.

```
****** STARTING SIMULATIONS ******

*** Starting Expedition #1 ***

Entering Place #1
Battle in Place 1 ends after 18 turns

Entering Place #2
Battle in Place 2 ends after 67 turns
Item(s) found:[keyPlace4 (KEY).
Qty:1]

Entering Place #3
Battle in Place 3 ends after 4 turns

End of Expedition #1. Summary:
Heroes LOST
Places visited: 3
ItemsFound: keyPlace4
Ended in place: 3
Total turns: 89
Turns avg: 29.67
Visit order: 1, 2, 3
```

(a)

```
----------Simulation report after 5000 expeditions:----------
Heroes successes: 1600 (32.0%)
Heroes failures: 3400 (68.0%)
Avg visited places: 4.05
Avg items found: 1.49
Turns avg per expedition: 85.88
Turns avg per places: 24.5
Most common visit order: 1, 3, 5. Per 1250 times (25.0%)
```

(b)

```
Entering Place #3
Heroes data:
Name: Knight. Life:71. Attrib: Sword(ATK):10. Shield(DFS):8. Agi(AGI):10.
Name: Wizard. Life:25. Attrib: Wand (ATK):12. Wand(DFS):6. Agi(AGI):7.
Enemies data:
Name: Goblin 1. Life:25. Attrib: Knife(ATK):6. Dfs(DFS):2. Agi(AGI):10.
Name: Goblin 2. Life:25. Attrib: Knife(ATK):6. Dfs(DFS):2. Agi(AGI):10.
Name: Hunter. Life: 30. Attrib: Axe(ATK):15. Shield(DFS):6. Agi(AGI):7.
Hunter attacks Wizard. Atk pw:20. Dfs pw:7.6. Dam:12.4. Wizard life:12.6
Knight attacks Goblin 2. Atk pw:16. Dfs pw:3.6. Dam:12.4. Goblin 2 life:7.6
 .
 .
 .
Battle in Place 3 ends after 29 turns
No Items
```

(c)

FIGURE 6: Simulation reports: (a) summary report, (b) consolidated results, and (c) detailed report.

(f) Bar chart for the order in which the different places were visited.

(g) Pie chart with the percentage of successes and failures of the *Team* of *Heroes*.

4.3. Support Components. We created an XML format in order to create the elements *World*, *Place*, *Character* and *Item*, as well as an XML reader to read files with this format and to create the corresponding objects. As this reader was not a part of the simulator, we preferred to put it here. The next components are part of the *Component* layer. One of them is the module to support graph generation, which was introduced in the previous subsection. The other modules operate according to the options set in *Simulation Settings*.

TABLE 2: Foes and items at each place.

Place	Foes	Items
1	4 goblins	-
2	5 goblins, 1 orc	Silver key
3	3 goblins, 1 troll	-
4	6 goblins	Defense shield
5	2 goblins, 1 orc, 1 troll	Life potion
6	2 orcs	Silver lock, life potion, and sword
7	Warlock (Boss)	-

TABLE 3: Simulation settings.

Setting	Option chosen
Movement strategy	Random place
Character to attack in battle	Randomly picked
Character to benefit from item	Randomly picked
Battle mechanics	Active time battle system
Randomness generator for attack	Min 0% and max 60%
Randomness generator for defense	Min 0% and max 30%

Here we show a list with the names and options available for each component developed so far:

(a) *Movement strategy*: next place, random place, farthest place, prioritized unvisited places.

(b) *Strategy for choosing character to attack in battle*: pick randomly, pick character with highest value for a particular attribute, and pick character with lowest value for a particular attribute.

(c) *Strategy for choosing character to benefit from item*: same as previous.

(d) *Battle mechanics*: alternating turn system; active time battle system.

(e) *Randomness generator*: choose minimum and maximum bonus value for attacking and defending.

(f) *Output settings*: set the path on the computer to save the *Output Artifacts*.

(g) *Graph generator*: inform the relationship of the graphs to be generated.

Pegasus's architecture was designed to permit the addition of new options. These options are relatively simple and only the first ones created. There are other studies in research areas related to the topics covered in these options that could be adapted and incorporated into our simulation system.

5. Results

In this section we report on the experience using Pegasus to support the design of a level of an adventure type of game. In this game, a group of three heroes with different abilities need to reach the end of the map and defeat the boss who is there. On the way they may encounter some foes and collectible items.

The imagined level has seven different places, and all of them have some enemies to confront. Place 2 has a key. If the heroes do not possess this key it is not possible to enter place 6. Place 4 has a shield to improve defense. Places 5 and 6 have potions to restore life, and place 6 has a sword to improve attack. These places are part of the world, as Figure 7 shows. Table 2 shows the enemies and items at each place, and Table 3 contains the chosen settings for the simulations. The attributes of the characters were not included in order to keep the tables brief.

We performed 10,000 simulations in a computer with an Intel Core i5 processor (5th generation, 8 GB RAM), which

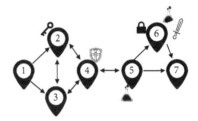

FIGURE 7: World map for the adventure game.

took 9 min 48 s. The following are the consolidated results of the Summary Report: heroes' successes: 985 (9.85%); heroes' failures: 9015 (90.15%); average number of places visited: 6.31; average number of items found: 3.37; average number of turns per simulation: 205.09; average number of turns per place: 35.47; and most common order of places visited: 1, 3, 4, 5, 7–1292 times (12.92%). We assembled some interesting graphs in Figure 8.

Upon analysing (d), we could see that the heroes arrived at the final place 70.5% of the time, which seems to be a good number. However (a) and (c) indicate that they arrived with a low life value.

There are several ways to change the balance of the game. Due to the heroes being successful only 9.85% of the time, we wanted to increase the success rate, but without changing the attributes of the final boss. In order to do this, we thought of some options like adding new power items to the map or decreasing some attribute of the enemies. In the end, we chose to decrease the number of enemies at Place 5, due to it being the place where the battles lasted the longest—see (b)—and where a big drop in life value occurred; see (a) and (c).

Thus, in the new configuration, we removed one goblin and one troll from Place 5. After another 10,000 simulations (in 10 min 4s), the new results were as follows: heroes' successes: 4469 (44.69%); heroes' failures: 5531 (55.31%); average number of places visited: 6.65; average number of items found: 4.11; average number of turns per simulation: 199.65; average number of turns per place: 32.56; and most common order of the places visited: 1, 3, 4, 5, 7–1280 times (12.8%). The new graphs are shown in Figure 9.

Now the heroes reached the final place almost every time (97.4%); see (d). We can see in (a) and (c) that the curve from place 4 to place 5 became smoother. Also, the number of turns at each place decreased, as we had planned.

We considered the results of this iteration to be satisfactory; therefore, we finished the refinement phase. However, a

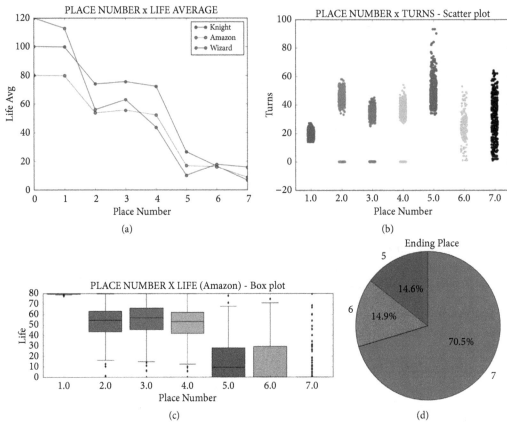

FIGURE 8: Simulation results from the first iteration: (a) average life at each place, (b) number of turns at each place, (c) life of the Amazon *Hero* at each place, and (d) place where simulation ended.

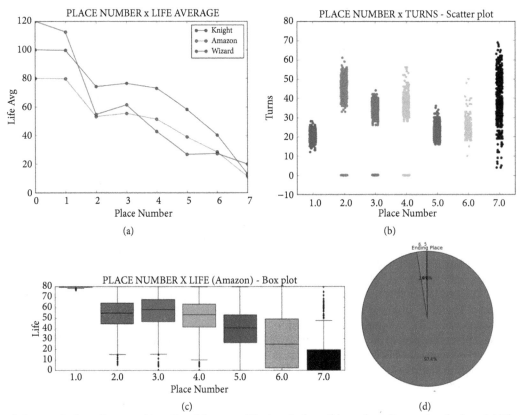

FIGURE 9: Simulation results from the second iteration: (a) average life at each place, (b) number of turns at each place, (c) life of the Amazon *Hero* at each place, and (d) place where simulation ended.

new cycle could be started in order to test other configurations. This process can be repeated extensively until an ideal configuration producing the expected results is achieved.

6. Conclusions and Future Work

In this paper, we proposed an environment to support the design of games with a progression-based structure. We studied the well-known patterns in game design, and highlighted the ones typically found in the kind of games in which we were interested. We introduced Pegasus—a simulation tool created according to our proposal—and described its architecture and how it operates. We also developed some support components that can be improved and expanded.

Pegasus showed potential to be a valuable tool in assisting game designers with their tasks. The ability to test the variation of scenarios—even during the design phase of a game's production—is a great benefit.

In our tests, we noticed that varying the strategy for choosing the character to attack in battle can produce different results to those using characters picked randomly. We believe that the *random* strategy is the most appropriate for evaluating what the behaviour of an ordinary player would be. Moreover, adjusting the strategy gives an idea of how players with more skill could behave. Similarly, it is possible to test different strategies for the behaviour of enemies. Thus, this is a useful feature to discover the best configurations for multiple difficulty levels of the same game.

For future work, we intend to create new modules as well as new options for the existing modules of the *Component* layer, starting with a new battle system. We also intend to make some improvements so that the designer could prepare more than one scenario, which would lead to the simulations producing collections of results.

Acknowledgments

This study was financed in part by the Coordination for the Improvement of Higher Education Personnel (Coordenação de Aperfeiçoamento de Pessoal de Nível Superior (CAPES)), Finance Code 001.

References

[1] Entertainment Software Associaton, *Essential Facts About the Computer and Videogame Industry*, Washington, DC, USA, 2017.

[2] B. De Schutter, "Never too old to play: The appeal of digital games to an older audience," *Games and Culture*, vol. 6, no. 2, pp. 155–170, 2011.

[3] C. Crawford, "The art of computer game design," *Osborne/McGraw-Hill*, 1984.

[4] J. Schell, *The Art of Game Design: A Book of Lenses*, vol. 54, Morgan Kaufmann Publishers Inc., San Francisco, CA, USA, 2008.

[5] A. Rollings and D. Morris, *Game Architecture and Design: A New Edition*, New Riders Publishing, Indianapolis, Indiana, 2004.

[6] E. Bethke, *Game development and production*, Wordware Publishing, Inc., Plano, Texas, USA, 2003.

[7] K. Salen and E. Zimmerman, *Rules of Play: Game Design Fundamentals*, vol. 37, The MIT Press Cambridge, Cambridge, UK, 2004.

[8] A. F. S. Barbosa, P. N. M. Pereira, J. A. F. F. Dias, and F. G. M. Silva, "A New Methodology of Design and Development of Serious Games," *International Journal of Computer Games Technology*, vol. 2014, Article ID 817167, 8 pages, 2014.

[9] F. Bellotti, R. Berta, A. De Gloria, A. D'ursi, and V. Fiore, "A serious game model for cultural heritage," *Journal on Computing and Cultural Heritage*, vol. 5, no. 4, pp. 1–27, 2012.

[10] S. M. Grünvogel, "Formal models and game design," *Game Studies: The International Journal of Computer Game Research*, vol. 5, no. 1, 2005.

[11] K. Neil, "Game design tools: Time to evaluate," in *Proceedings of the 2012 International DiGRA Nordic Conference*, 2012.

[12] R. Koster, "A Theory of Fun 10 years later," in *Proceedings of the Game Developers Conference*, 2012.

[13] M. A. R. da Silva, *PEGASUS: Uma Ferramenta de Simulação para Apoio ao Design de Jogos de Progressão*, Universidade Federal do Rio de Janeiro, 2018, https://www.cos.ufrj.br/index.php/pt-BR/publicacoes-pesquisa/details/15/2850.

[14] J. Dormans, *Engineering Emergence: Applied Theory for Game Design*, Universiteit van Amsterdam, 2012.

[15] J. Dormans, "Integrating emergence and progression," in *Proceedings of the 2011 DiGRA International Conference: Think Design Play*, pp. 1–17, 2011.

[16] J. A. Sokolowski and C. M. Banks, *Principles of Modeling and Simulation: A Multidisciplinary Approach*, John Wiley & Sons, Inc, 2008.

[17] B. D. Ruben, "Simulations, games, and experience-based learning: The quest for a new paradigm for teaching and learning," *Simulation & Gaming*, vol. 30, no. 4, pp. 498–505, 1999.

[18] T. Nummenmaa, J. Kuittinen, and J. Holopainen, "Simulation as a game design tool," in *Proceedings of the International Conference on Advances in Computer Enterntainment Technology - ACE '09*, pp. 232–239, Athens, Greece, October 2009.

[19] P. Sweetser and P. Wyeth, "Gameflow: A model for evaluating player enjoyment in games," *Computing and Entertainment*, vol. 3, no. 3, p. 3, 2005.

[20] J. L. G. Sánchez, F. L. G. Vela, F. M. Simarro, and N. Padilla-Zea, "Playability: analysing user experience in video games," *Behaviour & Information Technology*, vol. 31, no. 10, pp. 1033–1054, 2012.

[21] E. Syriani and H. Vangheluwe, "Programmed graph rewriting with time for simulation-based design," in *Theory and Practice of Model Transformations*, A. Vallecillo, J. Gray, and A. Pierantonio, Eds., vol. 5063, pp. 91–106, Springer Berlin Heidelberg, Berlin, Heidelberg, Germany, 2008.

[22] A. Järvinen, *Games without Frontiers: Theories and Methods for Game Studies and Design*, University of Tampere, Finland, 2009.

[23] J. Juul, "The Open and the Closed: Games of Emergence and Games of Progression," in *Proceedings of the Computer Games and Digital Cultures Conference*, 2002.

[24] S. Björk and J. Holopainen, *Patterns in Game Design*, vol. 54, no. 3, Charles River Media, 2005.

[25] Python, *Python Software Foundation*, 2018, http://www.python .org.

[26] E. Gamma, R. Helm, R. Johnson, and J. Vlissides, *Design Patterns: Elements of Reusable Object-Oriented Software*, Addison-Wesley Longman Publishing Co., Inc, Boston, MA, USA, 1995.

## 10

Evaluating Affective User-Centered Design of Video Games using Qualitative Methods

Yiing Y'ng Ng[ID],[1] Chee Weng Khong[ID],[2] and Robert Jeyakumar Nathan[3]

[1]*School of Computing & Creative Media, KDU University College, Utropolis Glenmarie, 40150 Shah Alam, Malaysia*
[2]*Faculty of Creative Multimedia, Multimedia University, 63100 Cyberjaya, Malaysia*
[3]*Faculty of Business, Multimedia University, 75450 Melaka, Malaysia*

Correspondence should be addressed to Yiing Y'ng Ng; yy.ng@kdu.edu.my

Academic Editor: Yiyu Cai

In recent years, researchers and practitioners in the human-computer interaction (HCI) community have placed a lot of focus in developing methods and processes for use in the gaming field. Affective user-centered design (AUCD) plays an important role in the game industry because it promotes emotional and mental communication, hence improving the interaction modes between users and video games. This paper looks at the development of a suitable AUCD guideline to determine if the expressed emotion, semantics, and mental concept of a tangible and intangible video gaming interface are well received by its intended users. Approaching AUCD in video games requires investigating multiple data to obtain a reliable data especially when assessing and interpreting affect and emotion. They present a challenge due to many ambiguities related to affect definition and measuring affective emotion can be very tedious due to its complexity and unpredictability. In this paper, we describe the methods and techniques used to assess affective user-centered design in video games. We also discuss our approaches within the context of existing affective gaming and user-centered design theory and data gathering procedures, including the factors affecting internal and external validity and the data analysis techniques.

1. Introduction

In recent years, game studies have shown to be worthy of research attention and have become one of the established domains of research within the field of human-computer interaction (HCI) [1]. Evidently, user experience studies have also become more prominent in HCI [2]. The user experience in video gaming tends to go beyond the actual implementation of the game itself. To appreciate and comprehend gaming, there is a need to understand what happens in the act of playing, as well as player and the experience of gameplay [3, 4]. The main intent for any game development is to develop a game with the following factors: fun to play, entertaining, providing surprises, challenging, providing aesthetically pleasing experiences, to support social connectedness, and allowing the player to identify with the game [5]. Hence, the user experience design for video games is highly important [2, 6] to the success of the games.

It is noted that the user experience is closely connected to affect and emotion [4, 7] where affect plays the main role in both entertainment and "serious" games. Player's emotions usually act as mediator for player engagement within the game [8, 9]. *"Emotion"* is often used interchangeably with *"affect"*. However, it does not share the same definition [10]. In Norman's [11] term, *"affect is a general term for judgmental system, whether conscious or subconscious"*. When users are experiencing queasy or uneasy feeling without knowing why, this is called affect. Whereas emotion is the conscious experience of affect [11]. Desmet [12] suggested that *"emotions are best considered as a multifaceted phenomenon which consist of the following components: behavioural reactions (e.g., approaching), expressive reactions (e.g., smiling), physiological reactions (e.g., heart pounding), and subjective feelings (e.g., feeling amused)"*.

Therefore, games should be designed to provide players with a variety of unforeseen changes (visual or auditory) to evoke affective reactions in the players. However, there is a need to understand affect in multiple levels concurrently. The current focus of game research is to design games that provide an equal user experience to all players, irrespective of player motivation, experience, or skill. A number of HCI practitioners and researchers have placed a lot of effort to apply, refine, and invent user-centered design (UCD) techniques to improve the enjoyability of games. Several HCI researchers have pointed that affect plays a vital role in both entertainment and "serious" games, in terms of designing experience for users [5, 13–15] and also in terms of assessing the game design factors and aesthetic discipline which instills certain effect upon the user [5, 16].

2. Affective User-Centered Design

Although usability and design receives a lot of attention, emotions are increasingly seen at the heart of user experience [11, 17]. For all types of games during gameplay, the emotional factor is one of the most important components. Quoted by Hudlicka [9], *"affect plays a key role in user experience, both in entertainment and in serious games."* Therefore, the key is focus on the user-game affective communication, where the user affectiveness will help create believable interaction between players and the gaming interface [9, 18].

This is where both "affective design" and "user-centered design" are needed to improve the user-game experience by addressing the human needs and game design, leading to the term "affective user-centered design" (AUCD) being coined by Ng and Khong [19]. AUCD can be defined as the *"attempt to explore the emotional relationship and the affective properties of both interface and design while addressing the user's needs and desire at the same time"* [19].

3. Affective Evaluation

The ability to measure user affect has become important for the intelligent interfaces in games that aim to establish believable interactions or to alter internal behaviours. It is challenging to capture what users are feeling at a particular moment because every individual expresses and reacts differently under different situations. As a result, satisfying a player's true needs is indeed challenging [20]. According to Wang and Yu [21], players' response to video game is based upon the relationship between the presentation of the game content and the interpretation occurring within the mind of the player. Their characteristic and personality can influence how they think and behave in the real world and should, therefore, also influence their in-game behaviour as well [21]. Hence, it is also important to take into consideration the differences in cultures, age groups, and social and national requirements.

There is an extensive variety of options that exist for evaluating affect and emotion in video games as shown in Figure 1. While much progress has been made in the assessment methods, tools, and techniques to evaluate affect and emotion, several researchers [9, 22–24] pointed out that to gain a more reliable assessment, coexisting use of multiple

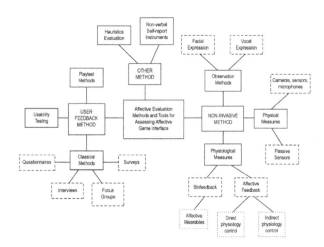

FIGURE 1: Affective evaluation methods and instruments for assessing affective game interface.

methods is required to provide a more holistic result and to obtain more reliable data regarding emotion and affect. Thus, Ng and Khong [19] proposed two types of methods to be employed: (i) user feedback method and (ii) noninvasive method. By merging these two methods, HCI and game researchers are able to obtain data of the player's behaviour and emotional responses, consciously and subconsciously.

For any affective evaluation, attaining user feedback is of the highest importance. Users can provide valuable information about various aspects of a game to help make it more fun to play. Furthermore, they may generate an important information that game designers refer to when designing better features, as well as gaining a better understanding of player thoughts and preferences. The advantage of user feedback method is that it can be used to measure mixed emotions, as well as being adapted to appear as any set of emotions [12]. When collecting feedback from users from the target group, it is important to be assured that the data gathered actually represent the feelings and thoughts of the population. While this method can collect user feedback, they are far from immediate gaming experience. Hence, they may need other types of methods to support them [25].

When evaluating affective game interface, it is essential to find a noninvasive and easily carried-out method to help gain further understanding about the affective state of a person during interface evaluation with users [26]. The biggest possible advantage of noninvasive method is that it can be taken in parallel during interaction rather than interrupting the user or asking him after the task. As Phan [18] pointed out, players disliked being interrupted while playing. However, Picard [27] advised to keep in mind that some people might feel uncomfortable with "parallel communication" of affect, especially with methods involving signals that they do not usually see. Hence, this highlights a limitation of this method which is the lack of accuracy in assessing mixed emotions [12, 26], which is overcome by user feedback method.

However, according to Isbister, Höök, Sharp, and Laaksolahti [28], there are more methods yet to be discovered. Moreover, there are other factors to be considered during affective evaluation for video games. Besides the game characters, game storyline, game mechanics, and game usability, it is also important to consider aspects that may change the results during the evaluation such as the genre, music, difficulty, and environment. It is important to recognise these types of affective video game applications because different applications demand the utilization of different gaming approaches.

4. Methods

Approaching AUCD in video games requires investigating multiple data sources in-depth. For this study, multiple case studies were conducted. This allowed us to analyse within and across each setting. We examined several cases to clarify the similarities and differences between each case. Moreover, the evidence from several case studies added more assurance compared to that of a sole case study. The two research objectives that were identified to help frame the inquiry are (i) to investigate game designers' and gamers' thoughts and feelings on the video game design and (ii) to determine which game design components affected the user behaviour and emotional responses.

For the first objective, we examined the thoughts and feelings on the game design from both the game designers and avid gamers. This enabled us to determine the video game design components that instill affect on the player's emotional state which is likely to influence their gaming experience. More importantly, these factors will determine in what way AUCD can influence the interface design of a game to provide a better gaming experience. By drawing out the affective game design components from the perception of game designers and gamers, a profile of affective game interfaces can be explored, verified, and developed further through the second case study by utilizing a popular video game. This leads to the second objective.

Measuring emotion and affect proves to be challenging; hence, a verbal method and nonverbal method were employed. For the verbal method, interview was conducted to measure subjective feelings. Interviewees can provide valuable information about various game design aspects that can create an engaging video game. As for nonverbal method, observation was chosen to evaluate the participants' affective states during their interaction with the popular video game and to highlight the game design components that instill effect on their behaviour and emotional responses.

4.1. User Feedback Method: Interview. The central research question was formed to determine the video game designers' and gamers' background experiences and their involvement in gaming, which relate back to affective user-centered design. The subquestion was formed to explore their viewpoints and knowledge on the game design components that affected their gaming experience.

The purpose of this interview is to answer the first objective which was to discover game designers and players' thoughts and feelings on the game design in video games as well as their gaming experience. For this interview, a

semistructured approach was used. Semistructured approach can assist in developing a structure for content analysis to promote generalisation of the discoveries [29], while allowing more flexibility for follow-up questions for the interviewees to elaborate on their answers. The selected participants will involve a 45-minute face-to-face interview. The interviews were video recorded to aid the researcher during data analysis. We insisted that the interview dialogue to be descriptive and beneficial and to have a natural flow while gathering information on the interviewee's opinions relating to affective user-centered design in video games.

A sample of eight interviewees were conducted comprising four game designers and four avid gamers. These two groups were selected as they played an important role in AUCD. The game designer role is to guide the players through the game and to create game components that provide opportunities for players to experience emotionally. Besides, they have vast knowledge and experience on designing video games, thus knowing which game design aspect will provide a good gaming experience. Although the game designer can induce emotion through the design, it may not be experienced by the gamer. Hence, expert gamers are needed as well because their involvement may provide richer insights into the game design due to their broad experience in playing video games. They know what to expect from a good game and they can identify the errors and faults in the gameplay. It is essential to gain different viewpoints from game designers and expert gamers to ensure the results will not lead to biasness. Evidently, the most important criteria for selecting the interviewees are that they must have a strong passion towards gaming.

4.2. Noninvasive Method: Observation. Observation is used as a supportive and supplementary method to complement the information obtained through the series of interviews. Observation is used to validate and corroborate the information obtained in the interview [30] to help clarify the game design components which affect the player's emotion, reaction, and gaming experience. In this study, we observed the participants playing a preselected popular video game. The participants were also given the opportunity to provide their feedback after playing the game. The interview took place prior to the observation study. Data collected from the interviews pertaining to the perceptions of the game designers and gamers were referenced to determine if the statements made were evident during the course of the observation study. Interview content and players' observations were attentively compared to determine the similarities and differences.

The observation study was conducted through an expert review and prior to the actual observation we tested the chosen video game to set a guideline of expectations as an aid during the player's observation. Therefore, to use this method effectively, an event coding scheme (see Figure 2) was created to record the participants' activity along their emotional and behaviour responses. According to Robson [30], events can be recorded in many ways but the observer must respond whenever the event occur, using either some complex recording instrument or pencil and paper.

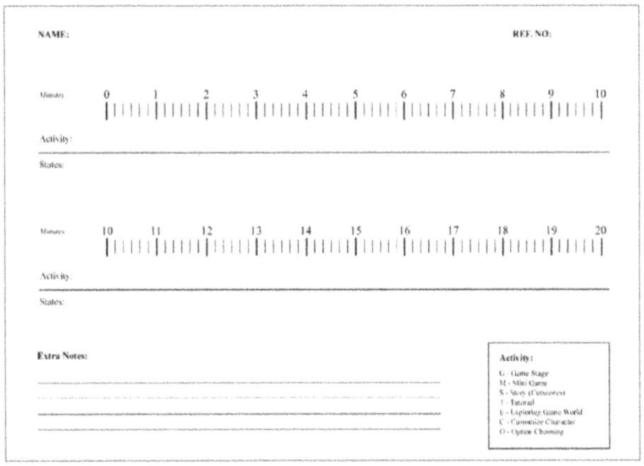

[Figure 2 — event coding scheme form with NAME, REF.NO., Minutes scales 0–10 and 10–20, Activity, States, Extra Notes, and an Activity legend box]

FIGURE 2: Event coding scheme. The event coding scheme can aid the researcher to record the participants' activity and their emotional and behaviour responses.

FIGURE 3: Selected game, LittleBigPlanet2 (Sony Computer Entertainment Europe, 2011).

The observation was coded in two forms: activity and states. There are seven main activities that the participant is likely to carry out in the game: play a game stage, play minigame, watch story (cutscenes), watch tutorial, explore game world, customize character, and choose option settings. States are participants' reaction during gameplay and what prompts them to react in such way. Nevertheless, main focus of this observation in the study is to clarify the affective game design components of a popular game, not the participants' emotional states.

As Barr, Noble and Biddle [6] mentioned that to represent the updated or current state of video games, there is a need to perform in-depth studies on popular and contemporary video games. In addition, a popular video game was selected because it is a game that players enjoy playing and find it appealing. Moreover, players are drawn to popular games because they usually provide good feelings and experience. Thus, LittleBigPlanet2 (see Figure 3) was chosen as the popular video game for this study. LBP2 is listed as one of the top selling game series for PlayStation 3. The LBP series has won numerous awards for its outstanding innovative design and artistic achievement from various gaming press and entertainment community. By knowing the strength and flaw of the popular video game, the researcher was able to verify further the design components of the video game that affects the player's gaming experience and what made the game popular in the first place. In addition, according to the post literature review, puzzle type games are one of the suitable genres for affective evaluation as it requires a player's full, undivided attention to respond rapidly in the gameplay [31, 32]. Furthermore, LBP2 appeals to all types of players where anyone can play LBP2 irrespective of their skills or experience.

The post-activity questionnaire helped the researcher to determine which affective game design component potentially made the LBP2 a popular game. The questionnaire was formed based on data collected from the interview. After the participants have played LBP2, they were given a post-activity questionnaire to complete. Nine males and 7 females were

selected for this observation study. The participants consist of amateur, intermediate, and expert players. Each of the participants was given 20 minutes to play LBP2. After 20 minutes of playing, the participants were then requested to provide their feedback on LBP2 affective design elements, as well as their experience while playing the game.

Written field notes, including chronological and personal notes, were taken during the observation study. Personal notes helped to create a record of the researcher's emotions, behaviour, and reactions during the research process. These notes provided us rich data to understand better the emotions and to formulate new strategies or derive more questions. Thus, it built a stronger validity in the study. Triangulation was engaged via interviews, direct observations, and the synthesis of the literature review. Recurring themes were used as a basis to determine when data saturation has been reached. Member checking was employed in the study as well.

5. Findings and Analysis

The literature review pointed to a number of aspects of affective user-centered design for gaming. These aspects were from the player's affective state while playing a game, including their gaming experience, game genres, type of players, and a combination of these factors. We created a list and definition of a priori codes. The data was assigned codes to identify the data source type. The interviewees were coded "P" with a number to identify the participant in order of the interview sequence. For example, the first interviewee was coded as "P1". Observations were coded "OB" with a number to identify the observations in sequence. For example, the first participant to be observed was coded as "OB1".

After transcribing the interviews, it was carefully read as a whole. Responses were then evaluated for content analysis using matrices to identify the main elements and emergent themes, as well as exploring any emergent components of affective gaming. The aim was to analyse the data and establish common themes, patterns, terms, or ideas that can inform a deeper understanding of relating issues. Once the

TABLE 1: Affective game design components that were aggregated from post literature review.

Affective Game Design Components	Frequency	Percentage
Challenging Gameplay	5/8	62.5%
Pacing difficulty for every stage or level	7/8	87.5%
Clear goals or objectives	5/8	62.5%
Increasing player's capability	8/8	100%
Special rewards	6/8	75%
Interactive game environment	6/8	75%
Interaction between AI actor and player's character	6.5/8	81.25%
Graphic quality	6/8	75%
Creativity	8/8	100%
Fantasy	4/8	50%
Storyline	8/8	100%
Characters	7/8	87.5%
Range of options to customize game settings	4/8	50%
Options to skip-non interactive content	6/8	75%
Interruption during gameplay	4.5/8	56.25%
Not lagging	8/8	100%
Organized menu design	4.5/8	56.25%
Provide tutorial and training session	5.5/8	68.75%
Unobtrusive view	6.5/8	81.25%
Provide help or hint when player is lost	7/8	87.5%
Consistency and non-complex control system	6/8	65%

similarities and differences were found in the data, they are then used to verify patterns in the data and code where cross-case analysis was conducted on affective gaming aspects and how they influence the gaming experience.

5.1. Findings: Interview. The findings of the interview found that each sample has similar and different opinions and perceptions on the design components in games. During the interview, the interviewees were also asked to provide their perception on the game design components and how each component affects player emotional responses and gaming experience. According to Sediq, Haworth, and Corridore [33], it is important to identify and isolate components of a game in order to determine how the particular components affect player's gaming experience. Table 1 shows a list of game design components which emerged from the post literature review. In this table, interviewees have expressed their thoughts and feelings on the importance of these game design components for video games and how it can affect the user's emotional responses and gaming experience. This will aid the researcher to clarify the affective user-centered design elements in video games.

In Table 1, it was found that the interviewees have different viewpoints for each game design component because they experienced each of the design components differently. Even if some design components in games were not important for some, but other users may need them because they supported the overall game design to provide a positive gaming experience. All of the interviewees agreed that increasing players' capability, creativity, story-telling, and no lagging in games are important because these components can affect

the user's gaming experience greatly. Almost the majority of the interviewees found these design components such as challenge, pacing difficulty for every level, clear goals, special rewards, interactive game environment, AI actor interaction, graphic quality, characters, option to skip noninteractive content, unobtrusive view, hints, tutorials, and consistent control system to be important as well in video games because these components do instill affect on user's gaming experience during the course of the game. However, although these game design components are essential, some interviewees mentioned it also depend on the user and the game itself. Some users may not be affected by some of these design components due to their preference or skill wise. Besides that, the video games may be designed in such way that some of these design components have no importance in it.

5.2. Findings: Observation. It seems that there are variation and similarity patterns among the participants that emerged from the data analysis during the observation study. Each participant is apparently different in terms of experience and skills. During the observation study, it was found that even experienced player could not master the gameplay instantly. Some participants had trouble playing LBP2 even though they are seasoned player because they could not master the controls in a short time. They took quite some time to remember the action buttons. In addition, for players who play a genre that they dislike or are bad at, this is likely to affect their overall gaming experience in a negative way. It seems that platform difference can affect users gaming experience as well. Few participants had a hard time familiarizing themselves with the controls of another platform. Every participant

TABLE 2: LittleBigPlanet2 user experience ratings.

Participants	1	2	3	4	5	6	7	8	9	10	11	12	13	14	15	16	Mean	Std.dev
Rate	5	5	5	4	4	4	3	4	4	5	4	5	5	5	5	4	4.44	0.61

Reference: 1 = poor, 2 = fair, 3 = average, 4 = good, and 5 = excellent.

TABLE 3: Affective evaluation on LittleBigPlanet2.

Affective Game Design Components	Frequency	Percentage
Challenging	13/16	81.25%
Pacing difficulty in levels	15/16	93.75%
Provide Goals	15/16	93.75%
Provide Rewards	14/16	87.5%
Interactive game environment	16/16	100%
Good graphic quality	15/16	93.75%
Creativity	16/16	100%
Fantasy	16/16	100%
Good narrative	7/16	43.75%
Interesting characters	13/16	81.25%
Option to adjust game settings	15/16	93.75%
Option to skip non-interactive content	14/16	87.5%
No lagging	12/16	75%
Organized menu design	12/16	75%
Helpful tutorial	15/16	93.75%
Provide hints	13/16	81.25%
Good camera angle	14/16	87.5%
Easy to pick-up controls	12/16	75%

appeared to have different motives when playing LBP2. They were either interested in exploring the game world, wanting to know the story ending, looking for good challenges, or mainly to enjoy and experience the game. Participants who are familiar with the gameplay tend to play spontaneously and seldom falter in the gameplay, thereby completing the level quickly. For participants who are new and unfamiliar with the gameplay, they will hesitate occasionally.

Similar patterns were found in terms of the participants' emotions during certain events of the game including how they choose their level. Participants who felt insecure with their skills usually chose an easier level, whereas those who were confident with their skills chose to play a more difficult level and they tended to feel excited when there is a challenge. Furthermore, while playing through the levels, many participants took their time to enjoy other design components such as the characters, the background animation, interactive objects, cutscenes, graphics, music, and many more. The participants found the characters to be amusing and entertaining. They provide good entertainment and humour to the game. Participants were mostly calm and laid-back when exploring the game world, or during the cutscenes and cinematic scenes, or when the level offers no challenge. When the participants are deeply immersed into the gameplay, they usually have a serious expression. In addition, participants also change many expressions in a short time whenever they stumble upon a difficult obstacle. Most of the participants do become frustrated eventually if they make the same

mistakes repetitively, regardless unintentionally or not. Only few participants found making mistakes was fun when they have successfully overcome the obstacle, they will show a relief expression and delight when they have completed the level. The participants mainly showed a confused expression when they have problem recalling the controls or they were unsure what to do in the game.

After playing LBP2, the participants were requested to complete post-activity questionnaire for feedback on *LittleBigPlanet2*. Besides observing the players behaviour and emotional responses while playing LBP2, the participants feedback also provided us deeper insights into affective user-centered design in video games. The participants' feedback are listed in Tables 2 and 3, respectively.

LBP2 has both strengths and weaknesses in its gameplay even though it is a popular game. Overall, the game received mostly positive views from the participants. From Table 2, it appears that a majority of the participants (15:16) enjoyed the game (M = 4.44; SD = 0.61), except for one participant. He explained that he is not a fan of platform and puzzle genre type of games and did not enjoy playing LBP2. Nonetheless, LBP2 was rated highly by the participants with seven participants rating it as "good" and eight participants rating it as "excellent", with the one participant rating as "average". Many of the participants praised the game mainly on its aesthetics, creativity, challenges, and diverse gameplay. Although the concept of the game is simple, the visual is positively appealing and pleasant. Participants noted that

LBP2 has many quirky design elements which made the whole game bright and jovial. Besides that, the well-designed puzzles in LBP2 actually make them test their intelligence. In fact, participants actually had fun making mistakes because they enjoyed learning new techniques and tricks to get through the levels. Thus, although it was challenging to learn, in the end it was rewarding. Participants found LBP2 entertaining as they enjoyed the many interactivity features in the gameplay. Additionally, it has nonrepetitive gameplay which many participants found refreshing. Elements found to be lacking in LBP2 are the depth in the narrative, and, for some participants, the lag of AI responsiveness and confusing controls.

6. Discussion

Fifteen recommendations of affective user-centered design for video games have emerged from the data analysis. (i) user preference, (ii) user capability, (iii) pacing difficulty, (iv) providing goals, (v) providing rewards, (vi) interactive game environment, (vii) graphic quality, (viii) fantasy, (ix) good narrative, (x) interesting characters, (xi) reducing lagging, (xii) flexible options, (xiii) good game interface, (ivx) tutorials and hints, and (vx) ease of user controls. These recommendations are the main elements that affect users behaviour and emotional responses during the course of the game, which in turn affects their gaming experience. These recommendations are listed under five main groups: (i) Diversity of User, (ii) Challenging Gameplay, (iii) Impressive Visuals, (iv) Creative Gameplay, and (v) Flow in Games. After the list of recommendations was gathered, a framework was formulated (see Figure 4) as a guide to create an engaging affective user-centered design for video games.

For AUCD, it is important to understand the players' wants and needs beforehand because the players will be affected differently while playing due to their biasness. Once the player's characteristics are identified in the earlier stage, it is easier to study their preconceived notions and individual affective states and emotions without judging them because their biasness is already known. The following four groups are based on the main elements of affective user-centered design in games. These game design elements are responsible for instilling affect in player's gaming experience as well as their behaviour and emotional responses.

6.1. Diversity of Users. Several researchers [4, 21] stress that understanding player characteristics or personalities is one of the key components of game design in order to understand both the uses and effects of video game. However, Khalid [34] stated the need for affect differs greatly among people as user population becoming more diverse and it is hard to determine an ideal user. This was supported during the interview and observation study where the interviewees and participants were different individuals with distinct personalities. Players who become immersed in their interaction with the game will experience affective pleasures and hence evaluate their game experience positively, whereas those who fail to become immersed will evaluate their game experience negatively [4].

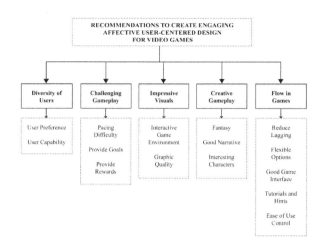

FIGURE 4: List of recommendations to create an engaging affective user-centered design for video games.

Thus, it is essential to pay attention to all types of player when dealing with affect and emotion. Fortunately, LBP2 is playable for all types of player. In the domain for diversity of user, there are two general areas: (i) user preference and (ii) user capability.

6.1.1. User Preferences. The work done by Sacranie [35] highlights the difficulty in measuring user emotion due to the users' preference in the video game. It appeared that all users have their own preference of game genres and game titles they have played. Players hardly play from a single genre as they crave for variations in the video game market. Users taste in video games is always changing. However, users do show loyalty to games that are reputable and provide good gaming experience, as mentioned by Liu, Li, and Santhanam [36].

6.1.2. User Capability. In Gilleade and Dix's [7] work, users' capability must be taken into consideration to ensure the game flows smoothly depending on their motivation, skills, and experience. In addition, Khalid [34] also mentioned that there are certain individuals who possess the need to showcase their skills in games and constantly looking to improve their skills. Based on the observation, expert players seemingly mastered the controls quickly after a few attempts. For amateur and intermediate players, it depends on how fast they can learn to memorise the controls. However, there are cases where expert players have trouble learning the controls if they are playing an unfamiliar different game platform or game genre.

6.2. Challenging Gameplay. The findings have revealed that challenge is an important element in gaming, especially towards motivation. Another reason why challenge is important is because it inspires users to improve themselves until they become masters of the game. The game loses its replay value when the user feels unmotivated to continue playing the game anymore. For challenging gameplay, there are three general areas of interest: (i) pacing difficulty, (ii) provisions of goals during gameplay, and (iii) provisions of rewards.

6.2.1. Pacing Difficulty.

The work done by Desurvire, Caplan, and Toth [37] as well as Juul and Norton [38] highlighted the importance to vary a level's difficulty gameplay to ensure user faces good challenge while developing mastery in gameplay. Thus, it is important to vary a level's difficulty to ensure the user faces a good challenge while developing mastery in the gameplay. However, they should not experience losing streaks all the time because it will discourage them and eventually quit the game as they are unable to progress further.

6.2.2. Provide Goals.

Malone's [39] work emphasized strongly that games without goal are less enjoyable than games with goals. This is supported along with Pagulayan, Keeker, Wixon, Romero, and Fuller [23] work where the main aim in games is to experience everything in it but Desurvire, Caplan, and Toth [37] highlighted the importance of introducing the goals in early stage of the game and should be identified effortlessly. Besides that, secondary goals or minor objectives such as bonus levels should be presented to help the players achieve a further sense of positive affect [40]. It is essential to provide game objectives to the players especially if they are meant to explore the entire game world because players may easily get lost in the game. When a user fails to know how a challenge is to be completed and his progress in reaching the given goal is impeded, his frustration level will start to arise. Gilleade and Dix [7] call this in-game frustration.

6.2.3. Provide Rewards.

Rewards such as power-up, level-up, weapons, armour, and many more should be provided to draw players more deeply into the game and to keep them inspired to return to play [23, 37, 39]. The reward should have the same value as the player's efforts in obtaining it. As the player's character grows stronger, they will need to unlock more capabilities to expand their skills in order to beat the next level. However, it is important to consider that users can eventually become bored once their character reaches the maximum point of its potential and can no longer grow further. This mainly applies for online hard-core levelling games.

6.3. Impressive Visuals.

According to Gilleade, Dix, and Allanson [13], the advancement in the design and aesthetics for games has allowed gaming to produce a more honest emotional experience to the users. Therefore, games should be made as appealing as possible to draw more attention. Visual plays an essential role in capturing people's attention because it is the first thing that they see. For this aspect, there are two general areas of interests: (i) interactive game environment and (ii) graphic quality.

6.3.1. Interactive Game Environment.

According to Bidarra, Schaap, and Goossens [41], human beings are strongly influenced by their environment. Current games are striving to provide a richer gaming experience; thereby improving game environment is essential. In addition, Malone [39] emphasized that the game environment must be novel and surprising but not entirely incomprehensible. It should provide an optimal level of informational complexity just enough for the players to know what to expect while evoking their curiosity. This was supported by the interview and observation findings. Majority agreed that an interactive game environment can improve the overall gameplay because it creates suspense in the gameplay. Gilleade and Allanson [32] also added that game must be able to respond to the players' existence within the game environment. Nonetheless, Norman [11] stressed that players should devote their time and effort towards mastering the game by enjoying the presentations and exploring the whole game domain rather than spending time mastering the controls.

6.3.2. Graphic Quality.

In today's contemporary world, high-quality games are likely to sell better according to Davis, Steury, and Pagulayan [25]. Not only it keeps players engage on the gameplay, but also it allows gaming to produce a more honest emotional experience to the users. This is supported by majority of the interviewees and participants. They agreed that game graphics and animations have enhanced greatly over the years and it is one of the game industry's greatest achievements. According to them, it seemed that every game platform is having a console war as the console has the most impressive graphics. In this modern gaming era, it is unacceptable to have bad graphics. People do not want to play the game that has bad graphics because it is unappealing. Moreover, as Picard [27] stated users tend to feel good when they see something that they like. Therefore, impressive game visual can attract players to play the game because it provides them mostly positive feeling.

6.4. Creative Gameplay.

Malone [39] emphasized the importance of creativity, strong aesthetic, and psychological sensitivity to create more interesting, enjoyable, and satisfying games. Creativity is identified as one of the important main design aspects in affective gaming because it gives users a completely different experience for every game they play. Video games are always innovating [42]. Creativity also aids in making a game more unique than the other. It offers the players a chance to imagine more. For creative gameplay domain, three general areas emerged: (i) fantasy feature, (ii) good narration, and (iii) interesting characters.

6.4.1. Fantasy Elements.

In Malone's [39] work, he stressed that fantasy is an important game feature and it assists a game's routine tasks to be more enjoyable and not repetitive. Majority of the participants disliked playing repetitive gameplay because it tends to be meaningless and boring. In the observation study, all of the participants agree that LBP2 has a strong fantasy element which made the entire gameplay enjoyable, refreshing, and unique. Some of them pointed that a game without fantasy is not really a game, because it is not possible for games to follow the exact facts. Besides that, the main reason why people play games is because they want to explore a world that cannot be found in the real world. However, it is not necessary to have a fantasy or unrealistic environment to catch the user's interest. Malone [39] advised that the game designer needs to be careful when choosing a fantasy that appealed to their target audience.

6.4.2. Good Narrative.

Pagulayan, Keeker, Wixon, Romero, and Fuller [23] stated that every game has a story and game designers should approach the storyline the same way as the conventional authors approach it. Players could not imagine a game without a story because the story is the main factor that drives the gameplay and other elements in the game. Many [6, 43, 44] support that while game narrative is not consistently connected with its nature as a game, it still conveys values to the player which may shape their gameplay and allows them to become emotionally involved with the trials of the game character. This type of fundamental understanding can help assemble the aspects of a true video game.

From the findings, it appeared that the story can bring both great moments and bad moments to the players. Narrative drives players to keep playing further into the game because they are interested to know the ending and to unlock new stories. This statement is supported by all the interviewees. They also believed that the story can affect a good game and the user's experience.

6.4.3. Interesting Game Characters.

In recent video games, the game developers provide players a much deeper insight of the character background. In Bidarra, Schaap, and Goossens' [41] work, they believed that game characters' unique traits and emotional behaviours can enhance the interaction level between the players and the gameplay. There are three main reasons why players are attracted to the game character. Firstly, the character's personality or life story may be very much alike with the player. Secondly, the player may find the character fascinating. Thirdly, the players are interested in the character's growth and development during the course of the game. It appears that both interviewees and participants from the observation study share the same opinions as above. Moreover, since users are in control over their characters, they tend to feel attached to the characters and become emotionally involved. According to Horsfall and Oikonomou [43], players look for in-depth characters that they can relate to. This definitely affects the players' emotions and their gaming experience in the game.

6.5. Flow in Games.

Csikszentmihalyi's [45] notion of "flow" is a state of deep concentration, enjoyment, and total absorption in an activity. Many [11, 34, 40, 46] shared similar views that any game which facilitate flow will be successful because it generates a positive effect, where players have deep involvement and enjoyability during gameplay. For this particular domain, known as flow, five areas of interest emerge: (i) reduce game lag, (ii) flexible options, (iii) good game interface design, (iv) game tutorials and hints, and (v) easy-to-use controls.

6.5.1. Reduce Lagging.

According to Johnson and Wiles [9] work, a common mistake in game design is to make the user

wait. Users should not encounter any pauses or interruptions during gameplay because it might allow time for self-reflection [47]. Lagging is one of the major factors that can easily destroy the game flow and the gaming experience. It appeared that all interviewees agreed that lagging can be very inconvenient especially when the gameplay suddenly does not run as smoothly as they wanted. They will eventually become annoyed and likely to quit the game because they cannot progress further, for instance, after confirming all options and selections at the end of every game event, which was also mentioned by Johnson and Wiles [9]. One of interviewees suggested the loading should be of a more simulative kind where the players can feel that they are not pulled out halfway from the game. This is supported by Whitson, Eaket, Greenspan, Tran, and King [47] where they considered loading screen as one of worst offenders for self-awareness. In terms of multiplayer games, players will appreciate a swift loading time especially if they wished to quickly log in and out of a game.

A majority of interviewees also found that Artificial Intelligent (AI) must be able to respond well if it is designed to aid the player in the game. If the AI responded poorly and interrupted the player's game instead, then it will spoil the whole gaming experience. AI supporting characters are important because they help provide guidance and aid to the player throughout the game.

6.5.2. Flexible Options.

Several authors [13, 34, 48] highlighted the importance of allowing the player to customize the game settings in order for the game to accommodate their individual needs. If all the options in the game are prefixed, it can be a dull experience for the players. From the game developer perspective, they preferred to provide more customization options to suit every player's needs because they do not know what the players want most of the time. In terms of challenging gameplay, there should be an option to choose a different level of difficulty to allow both amateur players and expert players a choice where they can enjoy the gameplay at their own level of skills [13, 34]. The interviewees who are expert gamers shared a similar view as well. Besides that, it is convenient to have difficulty settings for players who are only interested to know the game narrative and experience the gameplay.

From the findings, there should be an option to skip noninteractive content, i.e., cutscenes, especially if players are to play the game repeatedly. Several interviewees emphasized the importance of having the option to save anywhere or anytime in the game. Players do find it a hassle when they have to go only to certain places to save their games especially games that have long hours of gameplay.

6.5.3. Good Gaming Interface.

It is also important to design a good usable game interface [5, 39] to create a compelling experience and provide an overall positive effect on the quality and success of a game. Good games are meant to make tasks easy but at the same time it has to make them difficult enough for players to compete. Games with poorly designed interface are difficulty to use and may easily cause players to be aggravated. A player should experience a consistent user interface but it should be unobtrusive to the player [37]. The interface can include menus, status bars, field of view, and controller buttons.

Based on the findings, players do no mind the interference if it is important or intended in the game. However, they will be frustrated if they are interrupted often especially when they are doing something important in the game that requires their full attention. Thus, the interviewees suggested that the game should have an option to close any task bars or the game automatically pauses when the notification appears for the players' convenience.

Johnson and Wiles [40] also stated that it is important to design a game menu interface with visual consistency and readability to provide convenience for the players to make their selection in the gameplay. Desurvire, Caplan, and Toth [37] asserted that menu layers should be well organized and simple. Many of the interviewees shared the similar view as well where a fluent and organized menu design is essential because it provides convenience for the players to make their selection.

Besides that, the field of view (FOV) is another important aspect in games according to Pinelle, Wong, and Stach [48]. Field of view allows the player to observe the game world to a certain extent on display at any given moment. All the games should allow more flexibility in camera angles rather than prefixed camera. Poor camera angles can ruin the whole gameplay because it is inconvenient and frustrating if the player's FOV is restricted during a critical moment.

6.5.4. Tutorial and Hints. Games required its players to develop a conceptual understanding of the rule of use due to the complexity and steep learning curves [23, 25] pointing to tutorials and help systems within the game interface. Majority of the interviewees also have a similar view that tutorials and training are crucial especially for complex games, or a new genre, new gameplay element, or something unfamiliar. From the observation study, a majority of the participants found the tutorials and training sessions were provided in LBP2. It appears that some of the participants found LBP2 tutorials very enjoyable as they had fun learning the controls and exploring them. Skills that players expect to use later or right before the new skill is needed should be taught early [37]. As the players explored further into the game, the tutorials are slowly disabled because at some point they should be quite familiar with the gameplay.

Lastly, Pinelle, Wong, and Stach [48] also stressed that players should have access to a complete documentation of the game, including how to interpret the visual representation and how to interact with the game elements. Almost all of the interviewees feel that helps or hints should be provided whenever the player is lost in the game. Although a majority of the participants saw the hints provided in LBP2, there were some who were not aware of them because they were solely concentrating to finish the level. One interviewee suggested that when a player gets stuck or stays at one place for too long, the system should eventually learn that the player is unsure of their next objective. Then, a nonplayable character (NPC) will

show up to prompt the player of what they are supposed to do. This helps to keep the players back on track in the game.

6.5.5. Easy-to-Use Controls. Johnson and Wiles [40] asserted that the lesser cognition required for remembering input commands, the better concentration and engagement the player has, thereby generating a flow while completing the task. If the control itself is complex, even experienced players may take a while to actually learn and become familiar with the controls. According to the interviewees, it depends on the players' experience as well. This has been explained earlier in the users' capability section. Experienced players tend to pick up the controls fast, whereas nonexperience players might take a while. This was proven during the LBP2 observation study. Overall, the majority stated that LBP2 control was easy to pick up and they were not required to remember many commands. Besides that, a few participants believed that once the players were familiar with the gameplay, they can eventually guess the controls.

7. Mapping with Other Researcher's Work

All fifteen recommendations were mapped against other researcher's work for comparison, as shown in Table 4. This mapping is to ensure that this study has contributed to the field of research and provide a more holistic view on affective user-centered design (AUCD) for video games. Five research works were selected based on their similarity to this study that is to form a set of guidelines for engaging video games. The *"tick"* in the table (Table 4) means that the AUCD recommendation is covered by other researcher's work under one of their game design categories.

Desurvire, Caplan, and Toth [37] have presented a heuristic to evaluate playability (HEP) for games which is helpful in early game design and user studies. However, there is a lack of in-depth studies on the user preference and user capability which is important for user studies. In addition, fantasy element and reducing lagging in games were not included in their HEP guidelines. Johnson and Wiles [40] research have explored many components of flow in games that can inform affective design as well as highlighting the importance of cross-platform differences in audience and game style. Their research more or less covered majority of the recommendation except for graphic quality, game tutorials, and game narrative and characters. Malone [39] research work has presented a checklist of game design features to design better user interface for engaging games. Malone's work emphasizes the importance of creativity and strong aesthetic in the interface. Although his work was chosen as one of the main references for this study, there are some recommendations he did not cover in his research such as the game narrative, lagging in games, game tutorials, and game controls. Pinelle, Wong, and Stach [48] research work introduced a set of heuristic to identify usability issues in early game. However, their research mainly focuses on the usability principles for video games. Thus, their research did not cover most of the recommendations which are the user studies (user preference; user capability) as well as the game visuals

TABLE 4: Mapping with other researchers' work.

List of affective game components	Desurview, Caplan and Toth (2004)	Johnson and Wiles (2003)	Malone (1982)	Pinelle, Wong and Stach (2008)	Sweetser and Wyeth (2005)	Ng, Khong and Nathan
Player Preferences		✓	✓			✓
Player Skills		✓	✓		✓	✓
Pacing Difficulty	✓	✓	✓		✓	✓
Goals	✓	✓	✓	✓	✓	✓
Rewards	✓	✓	✓	✓	✓	✓
Interactive Environment	✓	✓	✓		✓	✓
Graphic Quality	✓		✓			✓
Creativity		✓	✓		✓	✓
Narrative	✓				✓	✓
Characters	✓		✓		✓	✓
Game Interface	✓	✓	✓	✓	✓	✓
Ease-of-User Controls	✓	✓			✓	✓
Tutorials and Hints	✓				✓	✓
Reduce Lagging		✓				✓
Flexible Options	✓	✓	✓	✓	✓	✓

(interactive environment and graphic quality) and game creativity (fantasy, good narrative, and interesting characters) for video games. Similar to Johnson and Wiles [40] research work, Sweetser and Wyeth [49] also focused on the flow components in video games. They presented a game flow model which aims to build understandable and enjoyable games. However, their work did not cover the user preference as well as graphic quality and reducing lag in video games.

8. Conclusion and Further Work

This paper hopes to clarify the principles and elements of affective user-centered design in gaming that can improve the interaction between the users and video game design components. The overall findings here served to assist game developers in enhancing and creating better quality games. The summary presents a comprehensible clarification of affective user-centered design for video games that will greatly aid game designers to identify the affective problems early on in the game design process.

There are several limitations of this study. Firstly, there were limited sample sizes. However, according to Miles and Huberman [50] as well as Creswell [42], it is typical for qualitative researchers to work with few individuals or cases because larger number of people or cases can become unmanageable, which might result in superficial perspectives. Validity can be strengthened by increasing the sample size with as many conditions of the research. Secondly, this research was firmly grounded in the assumption that the participants' gaming experiences and emotional responses were affected by the game design components of the video games that they have played throughout their life. However, according to Picard [51], it is crucial to always draw

assumptions on the affective and emotional state of the users regardless what they are feeling exactly. Lastly, the limitation in the observation method was that participants were observed in a short amount of time. Observer can only observe and review the participants within a time period. If the time is given longer, participants' feedback and their gaming experience may vary, and the observation on the users' affective state could be more in depth.

The research results also suggest a few implications. However, each of these implications should be considered in light of the research limitation and should be tested further. First of all, researchers should consider popular games as a legitimate site of study for researching users' affective state and gaming experience. This is because contemporary and popular video games are known as the representative of the current state of the art [6]. The results of the research suggest that the participants' affective state changes depending on the design component in the game. Popular games can be used as contexts to evaluate how users feel and how they react while playing which helps to determine whether the current gameplay design is good or bad. Next, game designers should understand that players may play and react differently from what they intended of them. There are some unquestionable explanations on how users make their decision and play a game in their own way. Therefore, it is important to understand and learn how players work through the levels and what inspires them into the course of action and react the way they did. Finally, video games in general may provide insights of individual personality and interest. By understanding deeper the relationship between affective emotions in gaming, it is possible to gain insights of the users personality and interest. When participants expressed their dislike, desire, and opinions on video games, they are partially exposing their interest as well. However, whether they apply in real-life it is still unanswered, but hopefully gaming will one day aid in approaching this study.

We hope that other researchers and practitioners from the HCI community and game industry will continue to pursue this list of recommendations in the future using alternative game genre or game platform to further probe its efficacy and limitations. Further studies in understanding the components of game design that affects user's behavioural and emotional state are necessary as the design of user experience become increasingly important in the development of video games. In addition, we foresee more work in the future in affective user-centered design employing mixed-methodologies and multidisciplinary approaches to obtain a more reliable assessment.

References

[1] P. Cairns, A. Cox, and A. Imran Nordin, "Immersion in Digital Games: Review of Gaming Experience Research," *Handbook of Digital Games*, pp. 339–361, 2014.

[2] E. H. Calvillo-Gámez, P. Cairns, and A. L. Cox, "Assessing the core elements of the gaming experience," in *Game User Experience Evaluation*, Human–Computer Interaction Series, pp. 37–62, Springer International Publishing, Cham, Germany, 2015.

[3] L. Ermi and F. Mäyrä, "Fundamental components of the gameplay experience: analysing immersion," *Worlds in Play: International Perspectives on Digital Games Research*, vol. 37, no. 2, pp. 37–53, 2005.

[4] M. Liljedahl and D. Örtqvist, "Immersion and gameplay experience: a contingency framework," *International Journal of Computer Games Technology*, vol. 2010, Article ID 613931, 6 pages, 2010.

[5] R. Bernhaupt, "User experience evaluation methods in the games development life cycle," in *Game User Experience Evaluation*, Human–Computer Interaction Series, pp. 1–8, Springer International Publishing, Cham, 2015.

[6] P. Barr, J. Noble, and R. Biddle, "Video game values: human-computer interaction and games," *Interacting with Computers*, vol. 19, no. 2, pp. 180–195, 2007.

[7] K. M. Gilleade and A. Dix, "Using frustration in the design of adaptive videogames," in *Proceedings of the the 2004 ACM SIGCHI International Conference*, pp. 228–232, Singapore, June 2005.

[8] A. Z. Abbasi, D. H. Ting, and H. Hlavacs, "Engagement in games: developing an instrument to measure consumer videogame engagement and its validation," *International Journal of Computer Games Technology*, vol. 2017, Article ID 7363925, 10 pages, 2017.

[9] E. Hudlicka, "Affective computing for game design," in *Proceedings of the 4th International North-American Conference on Intelligent Games and Simulation (Game-On NA '08)*, pp. 5–12, August 2008.

[10] L. E. Nacke, S. Stellmach, and C. A. Lindley, "Electroencephalographic assessment of player experience: A pilot study in affective ludology," *Simulation & Gaming*, vol. 42, no. 5, pp. 632–655, 2011.

[11] D. A. Norman, *Emotional Design: Why We Love (or Hate) Everyday Things*, Basic Civitas Books, 2004.

[12] P. Desmet, "Measuring emotion: development and application of an instrument to measure emotional responses to products," in *Funology*, M. Blythe, K. Overbeeke, A. Monk, and P. Wright, Eds., vol. 3 of *Human-Computer Interaction Series*, pp. 111–123, Springer Netherlands, 2005.

[13] K. M. Gilleade, A. Dix, and J. Allanson, "Affective videogames and modes of affective gaming: Assist me, challenge me, emote me," in *Proceedings of the 2nd International Conference on Digital Games Research Association: Changing Views: Worlds in Play (DiGRA '05)*, June 2005.

[14] E. Hudlicka, "Affective game engines: Motivation and requirements," in *Proceedings of the 4th International Conference on the Foundations of Digital Games (ICFDG '09)*, pp. 299–306, April 2009.

[15] J. McCarthy and P. Wright, "Technology as experience," *Interactions*, vol. 11, no. 5, pp. 42-43, 2004.

[16] M. Bødker, M. S. Christensen, and A. H. Jørgensen, "Understanding affective design in a late-modernity perspective," in *Proceedings of the International Conference on Designing Pleasurable Products and Interfaces (DPPI '03)*, pp. 136-137, June 2003.

[17] D. Lottridge, M. Chignell, and A. Jovicic, "Affective interaction: understanding, evaluating, and designing for human emotion," *Reviews of Human Factors and Ergonomics*, vol. 7, no. 1, pp. 197–217, 2011.

[18] M. H. Phan, "Video gaming trends: Violent, action/adventure games are most popular," *Usability News*, vol. 13, no. 2, 2011, http://psychology.wichita.edu/surl/usabilitynews/132/video-games.asp.

[19] Y. Y. Ng and C. W. Khong, "A review of affective user-centered design for video games," in *Proceedings of the 3rd International Conference on User Science and Engineering (i-USEr)*, pp. 79–84, Shah Alam, Malaysia, September 2014.

[20] C. Reynolds and R. W. Picard, "Designing for affective interactions," in *Proceedings of the 9th International Conference on Human-Computer Interaction*, p. 6, 2001.

[21] C. Wang and G. Yu, "The relationship between player's value systems and their in-game behavior in a massively multiplayer online role-playing game," *International Journal of Computer Games Technology*, vol. 2017, Article ID 6531404, 10 pages, 2017.

[22] K. Chu, C. Y. Wong, and C. W. Khong, "Methodologies for evaluating player experience in game play," in *Proceedings of the International Posters Extended Abstracts*, pp. 118–122, Springer Berlin Heidelberg, 2011.

[23] R. Pagulayan, K. Keeker, T. Fuller, D. Wixon, R. Romero, and D. Gunn, "User-centered design in games," in *Human–Computer Interaction Handbook*, Human Factors and Ergonomics, pp. 795–822, CRC Press, Boca Raton, FL, USA, 2012.

[24] C. H. Wu, Y. L. Tzeng, and R. Y. M. Huang, "A conceptual framework for using the affective computing techniques to evaluate the outcome of digital game-based learning," in *Advanced Technologies, Embedded and Multimedia for Human-centric Computing*, pp. 189–196, Springer Netherlands, 2014.

[25] J. P. Davis, K. Steury, and R. Pagulayan, "A survey method for assessing perceptions of a game: the consumer playtest in game design," *Game Studies*, vol. 5, no. 1, 2005.

[26] E. De Lera and M. Garreta-Domingo, "Ten emotion heuristics: Guidelines for assessing the user's affective dimension easily and cost-effectively," in *Proceedings of the 21st British HCI Group Annual Conference: People and Computers XXI HCI.But Not as*

We Know It (HCI '07), vol. 2, pp. 163–166, British Computer Society, Swinton, UK, September 2007.

[27] R. W. Picard, "Toward computers that recognize and respond to user emotion," *IBM Systems Journal*, vol. 39, no. 3-4, pp. 705–719, 2000.

[28] K. Isbister, K. Höök, M. Sharp, and J. Laaksolahti, "The sensual evaluation instrument: developing an affective evaluation tool," in *Proceedings of the CHI 2006: Conference on Human Factors in Computing Systems*, pp. 1163–1172, April 2006.

[29] C. Cassell and G. Symon, "Essential guide to qualitative methods in organizational research," *Sage*, 2004.

[30] C. Robson, *Real World Research: A Resource for Social Scientists and Practitioner-Researchers*, London, UK, Blackwell, 3rd edition, 2002.

[31] T. H. Apperley, "Genre and game studies: toward a critical approach to video game genres," *Simulation & Gaming*, vol. 37, no. 1, pp. 6–23, 2006.

[32] K. Gilleade and J. Allanson, "A toolkit for exploring affective interface adaptation in videogames," in *Proceedings of the IICI International*, pp. 370–374, 2003.

[33] K. Sedig, R. Haworth, and M. Corridore, "Investigating variations in gameplay: cognitive implications," *International Journal of Computer Games Technology*, vol. 2015, Article ID 208247, 16 pages, 2015.

[34] H. M. Khalid, "Embracing diversity in user needs for affective design," *Applied Ergonomics*, vol. 37, no. 4, pp. 409–418, 2006.

[35] J. Sacranie, "Consumer perception of video game sales: a meeting of the minds," *Honors Projects Paper*, vol. 108, 2010, Accessed 8 Jun. 2012, http://digitalcommons.iwu.edu/econ_honpoj/108.

[36] D. Liu, X. Li, and R. Santhanam, "Digital games and beyond: what happens when players compete?" *MIS Quarterly: Management Information Systems*, vol. 37, no. 1, pp. 111–124, 2013.

[37] H. Desurvire, M. Caplan, and J. A. Toth, "Using heuristics to evaluate the playability of games," in *Proceedings of the ACM Conference on Human Factors in Computing Systems (CHI '04)*, pp. 1509–1512, April 2004.

[38] J. Juul and M. Norton, "Easy to use and incredibly difficult: on the mythical border between interface and gameplay," in *Proceedings of the 4th International Conference on the Foundations of Digital Games (ICFDG '09)*, pp. 107–112, April 2009.

[39] T. W. Malone, "Heuristics for designing enjoyable user interfaces: lessons from computer games," in *Proceedings of the 1982 conference on Human factors in computing systems*, pp. 63–68, Gaithersburg, MD, USA, March 1982.

[40] D. Johnson and J. Wiles, "Effective affective user interface design in games," *Ergonomics*, vol. 46, no. 13-14, pp. 1332–1345, 2003.

[41] R. Bidarra, R. Schaap, and K. Goossens, "Growing on the inside: Soulful characters for video games," in *Proceedings of the 2010 IEEE Conference on Computational Intelligence and Games, (CIG '10)*, pp. 337–344, August 2010.

[42] J. W. Creswell, *Educational Research: Planning, Conducting, And Evaluating Quantitative and Qualitative Research*, Pearson Education, Upper Saddle River, NJ, USA, 2005.

[43] M. Horsfall and A. Oikonomou, "A study of how different game play aspects can affect the popularity of role-playing video games," in *Proceedings of the 16th International Conference on Computer Games: AI, Animation, Mobile, Interactive Multimedia, Educational and Serious Games (CGAMES '11)*, pp. 63–69, July 2011.

[44] A. Poplin, "Playful public participation in urban planning: a case study for online serious games," *Computers, Environment and Urban Systems*, vol. 36, no. 3, pp. 195–206, 2012.

[45] M. Csikszentmihalyi, *Flow and the Psychology of Discovery and Invention*, Harper Collins, New York, NY, USA, 1996.

[46] D. Weibel and B. Wissmath, "Immersion in computer games: the role of spatial presence and flow," *International Journal of Computer Games Technology*, vol. 2011, Article ID 282345, 14 pages, 2011.

[47] J. Whitson, C. Eaket, B. Greenspan, M. Q. Tran, and N. King, "Neo-immersion: awareness and engagement in gameplay," in *Proceedings of the 2008 Conference on Future Play: Research, Play, Share (Future Play '08)*, pp. 220–223, November 2008.

[48] D. Pinelle, N. Wong, and T. Stach, "Heuristic evaluation for games: usability principles for video game design," in *Proceedings of the SIGCHI Conference on Human Factors in Computing Systems (CHI '08)*, pp. 1453–1462, April 2008.

[49] P. Sweetser and P. Wyeth, "GameFlow, a model for evaluating player enjoyment in games," *Computers in Entertainment*, vol. 3, no. 3, p. 3, 2005.

[50] M. Miles and A. Huberman, *Qualitative Data Analysis*, SAGE Publications, Thousand Oaks, Calif, USA, 1994.

[51] R. W. Picard and S. B. Daily, "Evaluating affective interactions: alternatives to asking what users feel," in *Proceedings of the CHI Workshop on Evaluating Affective Interfaces: Innovative Approaches*, pp. 2119–2122, New York, NY, USA, April 2005.

## 11

Analyzing the Effect of TCP and Server Population on Massively Multiplayer Games

Mirko Suznjevic,[1] **Jose Saldana,**[2] **Maja Matijasevic,**[1]
Julián Fernández-Navajas,[2] **and José Ruiz-Mas**[2]

[1] Faculty of Electrical Engineering and Computing, University of Zagreb, Unska 3, 10000 Zagreb, Croatia
[2] Communication Technologies Group (GTC), Aragon Institute of Engineering Research (I3A), EINA, University of Zaragoza, 50018 Zaragoza Ada Byron Building, Spain

Correspondence should be addressed to Mirko Suznjevic; mirko.suznjevic@fer.hr

Academic Editor: Alexander Pasko

Many Massively Multiplayer Online Role-Playing Games (MMORPGs) use TCP flows for communication between the server and the game clients. The utilization of TCP, which was not initially designed for (soft) real-time services, has many implications for the competing traffic flows. In this paper we present a series of studies which explore the competition between MMORPG and other traffic flows. For that aim, we first extend a source-based traffic model, based on player's activities during the day, to also incorporate the impact of the number of players sharing a server (server population) on network traffic. Based on real traffic traces, we statistically model the influence of the variation of the server's player population on the network traffic, depending on the action categories (i.e., types of in-game player behaviour). Using the developed traffic model we prove that while server population only modifies specific action categories, this effect is significant enough to be observed on the overall traffic. We find that TCP *Vegas* is a good option for competing flows in order not to throttle the MMORPG flows and that TCP SACK is more respectful with game flows than other TCP variants, namely, *Tahoe, Reno,* and *New Reno*. Other tests show that MMORPG flows do not significantly reduce their sending window size when competing against UDP flows. Additionally, we study the effect of RTT unfairness between MMORPG flows, showing that it is less important than in the case of network-limited TCP flows.

1. Introduction

Massively Multiplayer Online Role-Playing Games (MMORPGs) have become one of the most profitable genres in the gaming industry. The leading MMORPG in the market, namely, *World of Warcraft* (WoW) by *Activision Blizzard*, at its peak, had approximately 12 million players [1], and it reported around one billion US dollars of profit in 2010. MMORPG players demand interactive virtual worlds, so a good underlying network quality is needed. In other words, the traffic generated by virtual worlds of MMORPGs has very high quality of service demands in terms of delay and packet loss. While MMORPGs are real-time multiuser virtual worlds, many of them use TCP for communicating the actions of the player to the server and vice-versa.

The use of TCP as a transport protocol is not very widespread in the area of networked games. Besides flash based web games, TCP is not that common. Most of the games which feature full real time 3D virtual worlds use UDP, including First Person Shooters (FPS), racing, Real Time Strategy (RTS), and Multiplayer Online Battle Arena (MOBA). MMORPGs are one of the few game genres in which the use of TCP is employed (although UDP is used as well, depending on the game [2]). Most MMORPGs use the same client-server architecture with client holding all the application logic and 3D information, while the only thing exchanged with the server is the updates of specific entities in the virtual world. This enables very low requirements of these games on network bandwidth which are common in the whole genre [3]. WoW is, according to [4], still the most popular subscription based MMORPG in terms of number of players with around 8 million active subscribers (even after losing 4 million). Therefore, WoW still holds a very large portion of the market, and its traffic has more impact on the network than the traffic of next ten MMORPGs combined which makes it a logical choice for a study focused on effects of using TCP in an online game.

Using TCP has many implications, taking into account that TCP was initially designed for bulk transfers [5, 6], with the main objective of transmitting an existing amount of data with the maximum throughput, always maintaining fairness between flows. Since the throughput limit of bulk transfers mainly depends on network bandwidth, we can talk about *network-limited traffic*. However, an MMORPG sends information which does not previously exist but is continuously generated according to the player's actions. As a consequence, MMORPGs do not always exhaust their bandwidth share, as sometimes the application has nothing to send (*application-limited traffic*), and this makes some TCP mechanisms inefficient or even counterproductive. As an example, the authors of [6] reported that TCP back-off mechanism did not activate and also that fast retransmissions are very exceptional because of the high inter-packet times, leaving most recoveries to be made by timeout; furthermore, a correctly received TCP packet following a lost packet would be blocked from delivery to the application until the lost packet was eventually retransmitted successfully. In addition, some TCP mechanisms (e.g., delayed acknowledgment mechanism [2]) innately cause quality of service degradation.

While the impact of using TCP on MMORPGs performance has been studied [5], as well as the inspection of different TCP versions [6], limited work has been done on investigating how other TCP flows in a network would impact the MMORPG flows, as well as the analysis of RTT unfairness. MMORPG flows share a large portion of the network path with other flows, both in local networks of the end users (e.g., wireless LAN or DSL connection) as well as in the network operator core network. The rise of these games is modifying the traffic mix present in operator's networks, increasing the rate of small TCP packets which, due to the interactivity requirements of the games, cannot be considered as "best effort" flows. This fact makes it necessary to study the interaction of MMORPG application-limited TCP flows with "traditional" flows, such as TCP bulk transfers and UDP flows.

To perform realistic tests, accurate statistical models of the network traffic are commonly used. Such models are also useful for network capacity planning and optimization. However, the traffic of online games in general is very difficult to model [7] and strongly dependant on player behaviour at the application level [8]. What must be taken into account is that an MMORPG allows a wide range of activities, from picking flowers to fighting dragons with the help of some friends, and logically, the game interactivity and usage of network resources vary significantly depending on the deployed task.

To enable the characterization of the network traffic under different application conditions (i.e., picking flowers against fighting dragons), in previous work we have grouped activities within the game into different behaviour categories: *Questing, Trading, Player versus Player (PvP) combat, Dungeons, Raiding,* and *Uncategorized* [9]. We will follow this classification in the present work. As shown in Figure 1, which has been obtained from empirical traces, the traffic varies

significantly depending on the player's activity. A source-based network traffic model based on defined behavioural categories was presented in [10]. This model comprises two main components: (1) a teletraffic model for each of the proposed categories and (2) player's behaviour (i.e., the probability of a player deploying an activity in a certain moment).

At the same time, one of the major problems for MMORPG's providers is scalability. To calculate the virtual world state when a large number of entities are in a small area of that world is a difficult task in real time [11]. Therefore, game operators often replicate the virtual world into multiple independent "shards" or servers and divide the player base across them. As a consequence, players cannot interact between shards. These techniques combined with Area of Interest (AOI) management (avatars out of the AOI of a player are considered not to interact with him) create significant load reductions. For different reasons, however, some of the shards become highly popular, whereas others are almost "deserted" (e.g., in WoW a highly popular server in Europe is *Outland*, while an almost deserted one is *Jaedenar*). The server population (i.e., the number of players on particular server or shard) has a significant effect on network traffic characteristics, mainly in the server-to-client direction. This is because the server has to send to the client application the updates of the state of all the entities in the AOI of the player, and this information increases in volume if the server is more crowded.

Having in mind the need for an accurate traffic model, we first deploy tests with the proposal of capturing the impact of the number of players in a shard onto the network traffic. In other words, the initial traffic model is extended to be able to modify Application Protocol Data Unit (APDU) sizes and Inter-APDU Arrival Times (IAT) according to the population of a particular server. This mainly affects the activities in which the number of players significantly varies, as *Trading* and *PvP combat*. This relationship between the server traffic and the number of players in the server has been measured for a concrete game, but this phenomenon is expected to happen in other similar games which use sharding.

Once the effect of server population has been statistically characterized, a full traffic model has been implemented in NS2 network simulator and used to deploy a number of tests with the aim to explore the interactions between MMORPG and other traffic flows. The competition between different flows when sharing a bottleneck is studied, including

(i) interaction of MMORPG and network-limited traffic using different TCP variants,

(ii) competition of MMORPG and UDP traffic,

(iii) influence of RTT on the behaviour of MMORPG flows (RTT unfairness),

(iv) global effect of the amount of players in a shard.

All in all, the contribution of this paper is threefold: first, the study of how MMORPG traffic characteristics change depending on the number of players which, to the best of our knowledge, is reported and measured for the first time. Second, once a realistic model is available, several

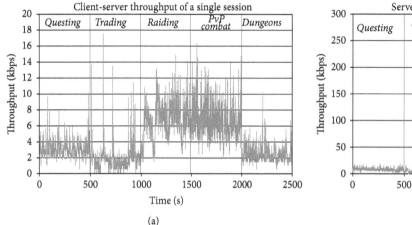

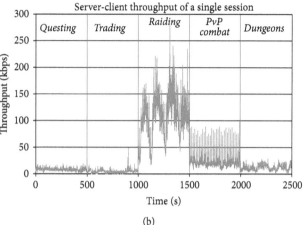

FIGURE 1: Bandwidth usage of the original game for different categories: (a) client-server and (b) server-client (the trace presented in the figure is a set of characteristic fragments obtained from separate captures).

tests exploring interactions between TCP MMORPG flows and other traditional applications have been deployed in order to illustrate the characteristics of competition between MMORPG flows with other network flows. Finally, the proposed model has been fully implemented in NS2. This NS2 script, which allows a wide range of tests, is offered to the research community. As previously stated, the model takes into account the variation of the player behaviour during the hours of the day, modifying the probability of the player's activity and the duration of each activity.

The structure of the paper is as follows: in Section 2, we review the previous work in MMORPG traffic classification, characterization, and interaction with other kinds of traffic. Section 3 addresses the question of obtaining the traffic model depending on the activity and population. Section 4 presents the MMORPG traffic competition tests deployed using the model, and the Conclusions section closes the paper.

2. Related Work

Network traffic of MMORPGs has been a target of a number of studies which are summarized in survey papers [3, 12]. Chen et al. and Wu et al. [2, 5] evaluate performance of TCP for online games in general and discuss whether TCP is in fact a suitable protocol for MMORPGs. They identify some network performance degradation problems derived from the traffic characteristics of this game genre: tiny packets, low packet rate, application-limited traffic generation, and bidirectional traffic. They remark that TCP is normally used by applications which deploy bulk transfers, so the bandwidth is limited by the network. In the case of MMORPGs, there are some moments in which the application has no data to send, and this may produce the effect of the TCP congestion window being reset unnecessarily. In other cases, the window may become arbitrarily large, producing bursts demanding a high amount of bandwidth from the network.

The authors of [6] investigate the performance of different TCP versions with respect to retransmission delay when low-rate, real-time event streams are sent to clients. They tested the existing TCP variants, that is, *New Reno* (plain, with SACK, DSACK, FACK, and with DSACK and FACK), *Westwood*, BIC, and *Vegas* on Linux. They concluded that there are only small differences between TCP variants which are used for MMORPG flows, but also that multiplexing different flows into one TCP connection and a more aggressive timeout retransmission time promise a reduction of the delay perceived at the application level. In addition [13] explored the reservation on part of the path between a game server and a number of clients, discussing the implications of using it for network infrastructure. In our previous work [14] we presented a preliminary study of the coexistence of WoW and network-limited TCP using different variants. The present paper further explores this issue, including the effect of RTT, and it also extends the study to the coexistence with other flows.

In the area of network traffic modelling, WoW has been a use case in several studies, as it is the most popular subscription-based MMORPG. An initial traffic model for this game was presented by Svoboda et al. [15], together with the analysis of a traffic trace captured within a 3G mobile core network, which showed that WoW was one of the ten most popular TCP services in the monitored network. Other MMORPGs have also been modelled: *Lineage* [16] and *World of Legend* [17]. All the previously listed models are based on a methodology proposed in [18]; however, a different traffic model for WoW [19] is based on a transformational scheme developed for the highly erratic network traffic of online games.

While previous approaches focus on modelling the traffic of a game as a whole, another approach for addressing the highly variable network traffic of MMORPGs is based on classification of application level states. In [20] Park et al. applied such approach for MMORPG—WoW and a First Person Shooter (FPS)—*Quake 3*. The actions defined for WoW are *Hunting the NPCs, Battle with players, Moving,* and *No play*. Another classification has been proposed by Wang et al. [21], proposing *Hunting, Battlefield,* and *Downtown*.

The authors also inspect different scenarios of movement for the player (in the real world): subway, bus, and campus. In the following work, the same research group proposed traffic models for each category, which were implemented in NS2 [22].

There are several studies which focus on the number of players in MMORPGs [23–27]. The most in-depth analyses have been performed by means of cooperation between game providers with the research community by providing internal datasets. Such analyses have been performed for *EvE Online* [23] and *EverQuest II* [24].

Another approach to the investigation of the number of players is based on the use of application specific capabilities of clients, in order to obtain more information regarding the state of the virtual world. Through the development of scripts which run within the client, it is possible to obtain a range of information regarding currently active players in the virtual world. Notable studies using this approach are Pittman's [25, 26] and Lee's [27], both performed on WoW. Pittman investigated a number of players on *Aerie Peak,* a North American WoW server labelled as *full.* They noted that the average daily number of users peaks around 3,500 players [26]. The authors also concluded that the spatial distribution of players in the virtual world is not uniform, but there are hot spots in which players gather, while a large portion of the virtual world is empty. On the other side, Lee et al. presented a dataset comprising information regarding players on an Asian WoW server *Light's Hope,* captured for 1,107 days [27]. Lee's dataset only comprises the data about one of the two factions of the game and presents peaks below 500 players. Even if we double that value in an effort to estimate the number of both factions, it is still 3.5 times lower than the values reported by Pittman. Therefore, it is evident that different servers for the same game have significantly different player populations. The causes of this may vary, depending on social dynamics on each particular server, technical difficulties, server migrations, and so forth. The discrepancies in player population cause differences in both computational and network load.

In a previous work, we defined the following action categories: *Questing, Trading, Player versus Player (PvP) combat, Dungeons, and Raiding* [9], and we developed network traffic models for each of the categories, performed player behaviour measurements and modelling [28], and created a software architecture able to generate real traffic using the previously defined model [10].

Some traffic models of other game genres (i.e., FPS games) [29, 30] have considered the effect of the number of players sharing the virtual world. However, the number of concurrent players of these genres is limited to a few tens, whereas an MMORPG shard can host thousands of players, adding a high degree of complexity which requires different techniques like, for example, the definition of the Area of Interest. The specific contribution of the current paper, regarding traffic modelling, is the study of the modification of the MMORPG's patterns for specific action categories which are affected by differences in server population. The most affected category is *Trading,* due to the previously identified phenomena of players grouping in one or more "hubs," which are usually

capital cities [25]. In addition, *PvP combat* traffic shows a strong dependence on the number of players, since this category is designed for a number of players ranging between 4 and 100. To the best of our knowledge, none of the existing traffic models for MMORPGs takes into account the server population (i.e., the number of players on the server).

3. Population and Player-Dependant Traffic Model

As previously shown, the population of different servers in MMORPGs varies significantly. The causes of this phenomenon can be various, but they can mostly be attributed to sociological and game related influences. For example, in WoW, the English speaking server *Outland* in Europe (at the time of writing this paper) is one of the most popular servers and "it is well known" among the player population that this is the server where there are a lot of players focused on *PvP combat.* In addition, some servers are designed for different languages (e.g., German, French, etc.) and this fact can also impact their population. Game mechanics such as division of server by types, instability of certain server hardware, and migrations between shards, also have an impact on overall server population.

We consider that modelling traffic at application level is a more accurate approach than doing it at packet level, adopting the approach in [15]. In addition, this makes the model independent of the underlying network technology. Thus, we characterize APDU size and IAT, instead of working with packets. In addition, we avoid the simplification of considering that the player always generates traffic with the same statistical distribution: as seen in Figure 1, traffic strongly varies depending on player's activities. As a consequence, the advanced traffic model uses two steps: we first model the player's behaviour, and then we devise the parameters which rule the traffic generation. A previous model, including the behavioural parameters as well as the teletraffic statistic distributions for each of the action categories, can be found in [10]. As we have already said, we want to construct an improved model which modifies its statistics according to the population of the server.

3.1. Identification of Action Categories in Which Traffic Depends on Population. We now describe the tests we have deployed in order to identify the activities in which the traffic significantly varies with the number of players in the server. The client generates a traffic flow transmitting the player's actions to the server. At the same time, the server calculates the next state of the virtual world and transmits it to the client. Thus, the server has to communicate to the client the movements and characteristics of the rest of the avatars in its area of Interest. So logically, the population of the server influences server to client traffic, whereas the information sent by the client is not population dependant.

First, the traffic of *Trading* category has shown its strong dependency on the server population. The reason is that *Trading* is mostly performed in capital cities in WoW, which have been proven to be "hot spots" for player gathering [26], so interaction between players is frequent. Also, points in the virtual world in which the players can perform offline trading through auctioning items (i.e., *Auction Houses*) are located in the big cities. On the other hand, *Questing* is performed in very large areas, so even in highly populated servers there are never more than a few players in the vicinity. The results in [31] also indicate that stay time of players in quest areas is dependent on the level for which the questing area has been designed, further lowering the density of the players in those areas.

Regarding the rest of activities, they are based on "instancing." Instances are areas of the virtual world which are replicated for each group of players who enter them, and the number of players is fixed during the activity. As a consequence, they do not depend on the server population but on the number of players in the instance. *Raiding* and *Dungeons* are the categories which are defined with a fixed number of players, so we do not model these action categories as dependant on number of players, and we use the models described in [10].

On the other hand, we have modelled *PvP combat* to be aware of the number of players, as each *PvP* area is designed for a different number of players (from four to eighty). It should be noted that the population of the particular server does not have an effect on *PvP combat*; only the population of the specific area in which the player has been assigned has an influence. All in all, we will model the statistics of *Trading* and *PvP combat* as population dependant. In the next subsections we describe in detail the developed statistical models.

3.2. Measurement Methodology.

3.2. Measurement Methodology. The method for measuring the number of players performing a particular activity is similar to the one proposed in [25]: the use of the "*/who*" call of the WoW command line user interface. This call is used to obtain the list of online players in a certain zone, of specific level, class, or name. As a parameter, we use a name of the zone in which the avatar was located in order to obtain the number of players in the surrounding area.

In order to characterize these activities, we performed measurements of the number of players in two WoW servers with different population: *Bladefist*, a low populated realm, and *Outland,* a server labelled as "full." Measurements were performed between 20:00 and 21:00 hours. This time frame is considered as "prime" time (i.e., when the number of players on the shard is among the highest). The results showed that there are up to six times more players on *Outland*. This difference in the number of players results in significantly different traffic characteristics of server-to-client traffic.

First, we have captured network traces with different numbers of active players in the vicinity. With that aim, we have placed a virtual character in *Stormwind*, a capital city of the *Alliance* faction, and performed trading activities (e.g., browsing auction house, visiting bank, checking mail, etc.); we captured network traffic for 30 minutes and also measured the number of avatars in the area. As a result, we obtained seven traffic traces with different numbers of active players around, from 30 to over 600. We also obtained a trace of a player in a completely deserted area, with no other players around, in order to obtain the characteristics of traffic when only "keep alive" data is sent.

PvP combat in WoW is a quite complex activity, but it always involves two teams who fight to ensure victory through either killing all the members of the opposing team (arenas) or gathering a certain number of points or objectives depending on the map (battlegrounds). The number of players is fixed to brackets which can be 4, 6, and 10 for arenas and 20, 30, and 80 for battlegrounds. For the purposes of player-dependant *PvP combat* modelling, we used 20 traces of arena matches and battlegrounds [28].

3.3. Population-Dependant Teletraffic Model of Trading. It has been previously noted that Weibull distribution shows the best fit for both APDU size and IAT of the general WoW traffic [10, 15]. While we previously modelled *Trading* category with Lognormal distribution [10], we obtained better results with Weibull distribution when performing fitting for a specific number of players. We determined the parameters of the Weibull distribution for each of the captured traces and defined a relationship between those parameters and the number of players. Using nonlinear regression, we estimated the parameters of APDU size dependence of number of players in this way:

$$\alpha = 55.067 * N^{0.357},$$
$$\gamma = 1.02 + 0.000406 * N, \tag{1}$$

where α and γ are the *scale* and *shape* factors of the Weibull distribution and N is the number of active players in the AOI.

Trading IAT is described with the following formulae:

$$\alpha = 118,508 + 298,763 * e^{(-0,0119498*N)},$$
$$\gamma = 1.149 * N^{0.068}. \tag{2}$$

As shown in Figure 2 (where M stands for "Measured" and G stands for "simulation Generated"), the fit is quite good, especially for the APDU (Figure 2(a)), while for IAT the trend is captured (Figure 2(b)), but with more significant discrepancies. For the sake of clarity, we only plot the two measurement cases which we consider borderline (30 and 602 players) and one common case (121 player). The rest of the measurements have between 100 and 500 players average and behave similarly to the depicted curves.

3.4. Statistical Model of PvP Combat. We show the characteristics of both APDU and IAT for every *PvP* activity in Figure 3, as well as the respective statistical models (common for IAT, and based on the number of players for APDU). According to the results shown in Figure 3(b), we have not modelled IAT for *PvP* combat as depending on the number of players, since the IAT distribution has shown to be fairly constant for every *PvP* activity, regardless of the number of players. This is due to the fact that *PvP* is a very dynamic action category with constant movement and use of various abilities, which results in very frequent updates from the server, regardless of the number of players [28].

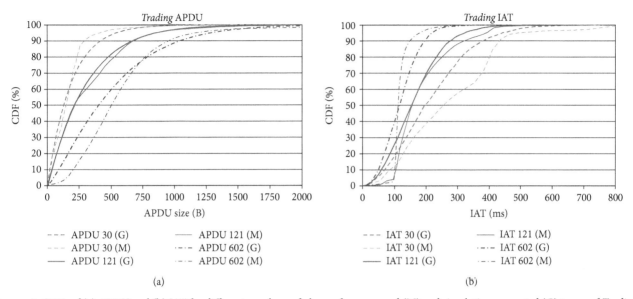

FIGURE 2: CDFs of (a) APDU and (b) IAT for different numbers of players for measured (M) and simulation generated (G) traces of *Trading*.

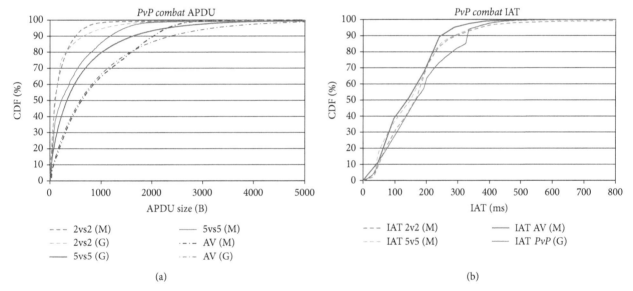

FIGURE 3: CDFs of (a) APDU (b) IAT, for different numbers of players for measured (M) and simulation generated (G) traces of *PvP combat*.

We model APDU size as dependant on the number of players (i.e., the arena bracket or specific battleground). For arenas the modelling procedure is simpler, as they are small areas in which players are constantly in the AOI of the others. Through comparison of arena traces of different brackets, we extracted how much additional data is transferred per additional player, obtaining a mean APDU increase of 38 bytes per player. Thus, we fit the APDU size to a Weibull distribution dependant on the number of players. The formula is as follows:

$$\text{Mean}(N) = \text{Mean}(4) \cdot 38 \cdot (N - 4),$$

$$\alpha = \frac{\text{Mean}(N)}{1.178}, \quad (3)$$

$$\gamma = 0.76,$$

where Mean(i) is the mean of the distribution describing i players and Mean(4) = 258.33 (estimated from the measurements).

For battlegrounds the case is more complex, as they are larger in terms of virtual space, and not all players are always in the AOI of all other players. That is why we first estimate the average number of players in the AOI, depending on the battleground. The estimation is based on the measurement traces of each particular battleground and the values obtained from measurements of arenas in which we know exactly how many players are in the AOI. The estimated values of the average number of users are listed in Table 1.

The formula for battlegrounds has also been slightly modified in comparison with arenas, as in arenas there is constant fight until someone "dies," whereas in battlegrounds there are also time periods in which players wait to be "reborn" after

TABLE 1: Estimated Average Number of Players per Battleground.

Battleground	Average number of players
Alterac Valley	21.32
Arathi Basin	10.90
Warsong Gulch	10.11
Eye of the Storm	13.14
Strand of the Ancients	15.03

they have been killed, time periods in which the player is travelling from one end of the battleground to another, and so forth. These differences reflect on the characteristics of the Weibull distribution. The final battleground formula for server APDU sizes is

$$\text{Mean}(N) = \text{Mean}(4) \cdot 38 \cdot (N - 4),$$

$$\alpha = \frac{\text{Mean}(N)}{1.073}, \qquad (4)$$

$$\gamma = 0.87,$$

where the parameter N is representing an estimated average number of players in the AOI for the battleground and Mean(4) = 258.33. In Figure 3 the results of the model are plotted versus the measured data for cases of *2v2* and *5v5* arenas and for *Alterac Valley* (AV) battleground. As it can be observed, the models tend to slightly overestimate the empirical distribution, but the general trend is captured well.

As *PvP combat* has been fractionated into arenas and battlegrounds and some parameters of the model are dependent on the battleground type, we have to fully adapt the behavioural model. We make two assumptions here: first, we consider the duration of the *PvP* activity as independent of whether it is a battleground or an arena; second, we assume a battleground/arena ratio of 50% : 50%, since there is no reliable empirical data from which the values for this parameter could be extracted.

Our model makes the decision of a player entering a specific bracket of arena or battleground, based on data gathered by WoW add-on census (the dataset and the add-on are further described on http://www.warcraftrealms.com/). The parameters of popularity of each particular arena bracket or battleground are displayed in Tables 2 and 3, respectively. The popularity parameter describes how often players join specific battleground map or specific arena bracket.

3.5. Implementation of the Advanced Model. Once we have obtained the statistics of the traffic for each activity, the model has been fully implemented in NS2. It includes the probability of a player deploying each activity, which varies with the hour of the day. This script, allowing a wide range of tests, is offered to the research community. As an example of the use of the model, Figure 4 shows the daily behavioural variation obtained when simulating 3,000 players during a whole day. It can be seen that it does capture the main trends in player behaviour such as the high rise of *Raiding* in the evening [10]. The slight discrepancies with respect to previous results

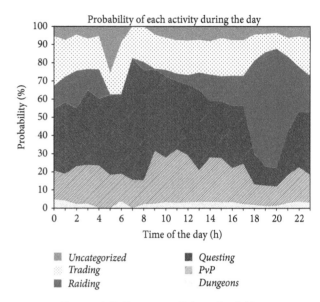

FIGURE 4: Daily pattern of players' activities.

TABLE 2: Popularity of arena brackets.

Arena	Popularity
2v2	45.05%
3v3	45.16%
5v5	9.79%

TABLE 3: Popularity of specific battlegrounds.

Battleground	Popularity
Arathi Basin	24.56%
Warsong Gulch	32.50%
Eye of the Storm	7.96%
Strand of the Ancients	2.08%
Alterac Valley	32.89%

[10] are mainly caused by the fact that we do not model the fluctuation of the players during the day.

All in all, as an example of the results of the developed model, Figure 5(a) shows the client-server traces generated by the NS2 script, for each activity. To illustrate the bandwidth difference depending on the number of players and activity, Figure 5(b) shows the effect of the server population for server-client traffic of *Trading* and the same effect depending on the different scenarios for *PvP combat*. As it can be seen, the script captures the differences in traffic characteristics for particular player behaviour (note that Figure 5(b) is not comparable with Figure 1(b), since it only shows the activities that modify their behaviour with the number of players).

4. Tests and Results

In this section we present the results of different experiments using the complete NS2 traffic model described previously, with the aim of illustrating the behaviour of these flows when they share the network with other traffic. Thus, we

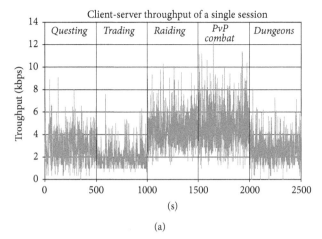

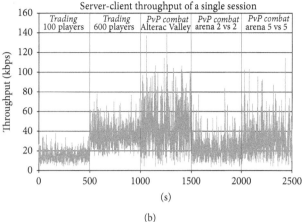

FIGURE 5: Throughput generated by the model for (a) client to server for each category and (b) server to client for *Trading* and *PvP combat* with different options.

will mainly focus on the competition between application-limited TCP game traffic and other flows, and how this competition modifies the communication parameters. The considered competing flows are FTP, which use TCP so as to get as much throughput as possible (network-limited), and UDP Constant Bit Rate (CBR), which generates the same throughput despite the status of the network.

The obtained results will be presented in terms of the most interesting parameter for each kind of traffic.

(i) For the MMORPG TCP traffic we will mainly focus on Round Trip Time (RTT), taking into account that latency is the most important parameter, because the interactivity of the game mainly depends on it. In order to estimate the RTT in NS2, we will use the parameters that govern TCP dynamics (e.g., retransmissions), namely, "smoothed RTT" and "RTT variation," which are calculated and updated frequently, according to the network conditions. They are subsequently used to obtain the value of Retransmission TimeOut (RTO) [32]. If this timeout expires, the packet is retransmitted.

(ii) For the FTP background traffic, we will present the achieved throughput, since these flows try to get as much as possible of the bandwidth share. The size of the sending window of TCP will also be presented if required.

(iii) For the CBR traffic, the results can be presented in terms of bandwidth or packet loss rate which are directly related to this case, since the traffic is sent in an open loop.

In order to create a scenario where the different flows share a bottleneck, we have configured a dumbbell topology (Figure 6): two pairs of client-server connections (*A* and *B*) correspond to game nodes and the other pair is used for generating background traffic.

Regarding the parameters of the simulations, when activity exchange is not explicitly required by the test, we will use

by default *Questing* traffic, one of the most popular activities, which also presents a relatively stable traffic profile. The advantage of using a single activity in those tests is that we avoid the influence of player behaviour, which may obscure the observations. In the last subsection we include activity exchange so as to better observe the characteristics of the realistic traffic generated through the model. Each *Questing* flow generates about 2.2 kbps in the client-server connection and roughly 18 kbps in the server-client one. By default, the bandwidth in the bottleneck is 10 Mbps in both directions. Queue sizes are 100 packets. The Round Trip Time (RTT) delay of the bottleneck (RTT0) is 40 ms. By default, the rest of RTTx delays are set to 0. Each simulation lasts 200 seconds, and a "tick" of 1 second is used to calculate the average RTT or throughput during each interval. The tick is 0.1 seconds for the TCP window size.

4.1. Competition of MMORPG and FTP Flows: The Effect of TCP Variants. In this subsection we will study the competition of application-limited (MMORPG) and network-limited TCP flows (we will use FTP as a typical application). To this aim, 100 MMORPG sessions are established between *client A* and *server A,* and 10 FTP upload and 10 FTP download sessions are set between *background* 1and 2, with a packet size of 1,500 bytes.

In order to correctly imitate the behaviour of WoW, which uses a single session, piggybacking the ACKs in packets in the opposite direction [15], the *Full-TCP* NS2 TCP implementation (using *Reno*) has been used for game sessions. For the FTP sessions, five TCP variants are tested: *Tahoe, Reno, New Reno, SACK,* and *Vegas,* using the standard NS2 implementations for these protocols. Each TCP session is started using a different random delay, in order to avoid the effect of the synchronization of TCP window sizes [30]. Thus, the first seconds of the presented graphs may present a transient behaviour different from the stationary.

The effect of the different TCP variants used for the background flows can be observed in Figure 7 (on behalf of clarity, only *New Reno, SACK,* and *Vegas* are shown), where

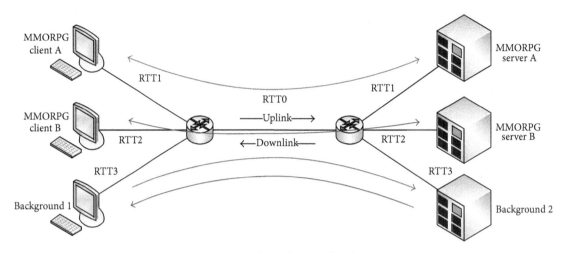

FIGURE 6: Network topology used in the tests.

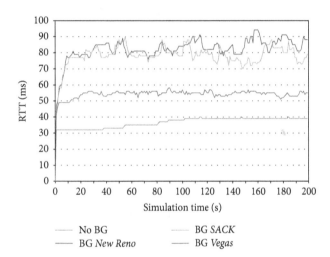

FIGURE 7: Competition of MMORPG versus FTP traffic for different TCP variants: smoothed RTT of a game flow.

TABLE 4: Average RTT between all the game flows when different TCP variants are used for the background traffic.

BG TCP variant	avg smoothed RTT	avg RTT variation
No BG	38.76 ms	3.05 ms
Tahoe	82.61 ms	7.24 ms
Reno	81.23 ms	7.36 ms
New Reno	84.54 ms	6.76 ms
SACK	77.64 ms	6.85 ms
Vegas	54.74 ms	3.65 ms

the smoothed RTTis presented. Table 4 presents the average RTT on each case, between all the game flows. This RTT increase is caused by queuing delay at the bottleneck. These results are complemented with those in Figures 8, 9, and 10, which present the aggregate throughput obtained by the FTP flows and the TCP window size for *New Reno, SACK,* and *Vegas.* Finally, Table 5 summarizes the FTP throughput results for all the tested TCP variants.

TABLE 5: Average throughput obtained by the FTP background flows using different TCP variants.

BG TCP variant	Avg throughput uplink	Avg throughput downlink
Tahoe	871.15 kbps	736.08 kbps
Reno	866.58 kbps	746.53 kbps
New Reno	874.58 kbps	749.85 kbps
SACK	849.84 kbps	717.88 kbps
Vegas	814.76 kbps	672.24 kbps

It can first be observed that when no background traffic is present, the estimated latency is roughly 40 ms. The behaviour of *New Reno* and *SACK* is very similar, but it can be seen that game traffic obtains better results when *SACK* is used for the background traffic: 7 ms are reduced from the RTT, at the cost of a slighter share of the bandwidth of the link for the FTP flows (an average of 849 kbps instead of 874 kbps per flow, i.e., a 3% throughput reduction). The reason for this can be that *SACK* reduces the retransmissions, since its ACK mechanism is able to acknowledge packet ranges, so the behaviour results are a bit less aggressive. The results for *Tahoe* and *Reno* are very similar to those of *New Reno.*

TCP *Vegas* behaves in a very different way, as shown in Figure 10: the window size does not grow aggressively, but it remains constant. Because of this *timid* behaviour [33], when TCP *Vegas* notices the RTT increase, it maintains its sending rate, even in the absence of packet loss. In the uplink, *Vegas* only gets 814 kbps (which means a reduction of 9% with respect to *New Reno*), and in the downlink the reduction is roughly 10%. However, as a counterpart,this is translated into a significant reduction of the RTT of the MMORPG flows: only 14 ms are added to the 40 ms of default RTT, whereas in *New Reno* this figure is 44 ms.

It should be noted that in all these cases the game is still playable, taking into account that the literature has reported that MMORPG players can tolerate up to some hundreds of milliseconds of RTT [34].

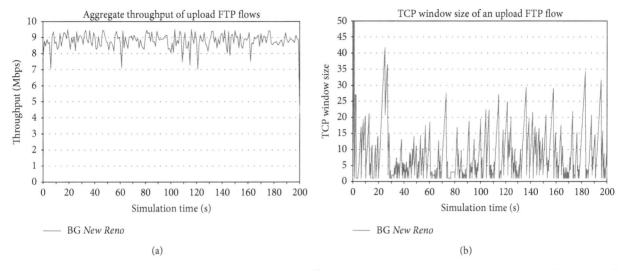

FIGURE 8: Competition between MMORPG and FTP background traffic using TCP *New Reno*: (a) aggregate throughput of the 10 FTP flows and (b) evolution of the TCP window of one of the flows.

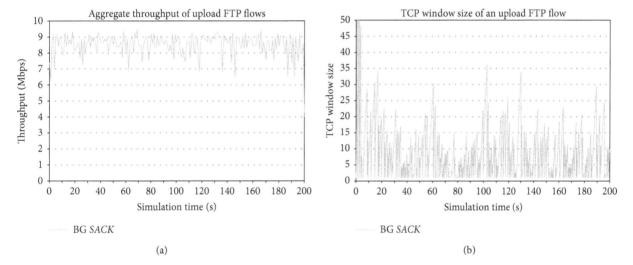

FIGURE 9: Competition of MMORPG and FTP background traffic using TCP *SACK*: (a) aggregate throughput of the 10 FTP flows and (b) evolution of the TCP window of one of the flows.

As a result, we can conclude that the most popular TCP variants (i.e., *New Reno* and *SACK*) can be respectful with competing MMORPG traffic, although they add some latency due to their behaviour trying to get the maximum bandwidth share. On the other hand TCP *Vegas* could be considered as a good option for competing flows in order not to throttle the MMORPG flows and by that to better preserve the quality of game experience for the MMORPG players.

4.2. Competition of MMORPG and UDP Background Traffic. It is normally assumed [35] that, when TCP and UDP flows compete for a shared link, UDP gets all the required bandwidth while TCP uses the remainder of the bandwidth, because of TCP flow control mechanism. However, in the case of MMORPGs, in which the traffic is not limited by the network but is application limited, a different behaviour can be observed.

We have set this scenario: 100 MMORPG *Questing* sessions (roughly 2 Mbps in the server-client direction) are run from *client A* to *server A*. At the same time, three UDP flows are sent between *backgrounds* 1 and 2. The total amount of UDP traffic is the aggregation of these three flows: small packets (40 bytes, 50% of the packets), medium packets (576 bytes, 10% of the packets), and large packets (1,500 bytes, 40% of the packets) [36].

In Figure 11, 7 Mbps of UDP traffic share the link with 100 MMORPG sessions. Since there is enough bandwidth, each flow obtains the required amount. The first row of Table 6 summarizes the results: first, it can be seen that the RTT of the MMORPG connections is not affected, since the obtained value is similar to the result obtained when no background traffic was present (Table 4). In addition, it can be seen that the packet loss rate of the CBR traffic is residual. When 8 Mbps of UDP CBR traffic are sent (Figure 12), the average

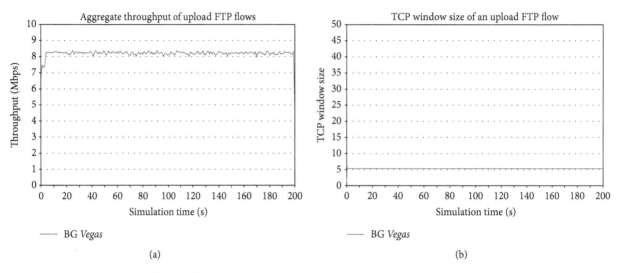

FIGURE 10: Competition of MMORPG and FTP background traffic using TCP *Vegas*: (a) aggregate throughput of the 10 FTP flows and (b) evolution of the TCP window of one of the flows.

TABLE 6: Summary of the tests: average RTT of all the MMORPG flows; packet loss rate in the downlink.

CBR throughput (downlink)	Average RTT MMORPG	Average packet loss rate CBR
7 Mbps	39.35 ms	0.05%
8 Mbps	48.16 ms	0.34%
8.5 Mbps	38.58 ms	4.61%
9 Mbps	76.78 ms	11.67%

RTT rises up to 48 ms. At the same time, the packet loss rate of the UDP flows is slightly increased.

However, when UDP traffic is 8.5 Mbps (Figure 13) and the total offered traffic is above the bandwidth limit, the tendency is that MMORPG traffic maintains its bandwidth use of roughly 2 Mbps, whereas UDP traffic only obtains the remaining throughput.

This is also observed in Figure 14, where the offered UDP traffic is 9 Mbps. The bandwidth obtained by the UDP flows is roughly the same as in the previous case, whereas MMORPG maintains its bandwidth, with a slight increase of 3.22%, caused by duplicate game packets. All in all, it can be seen that MMORPG traffic flows roughly obtain the same throughput, despite the amount of competing UDP traffic.

All in all, this behaviour is the opposite of that normally expected in the TCP-UDP competition [33], where TCP only obtains the traffic not used by UDP. The reason for this is that the bandwidth demand of the MMORPG flows is not governed by the congestion window, since they do not have an amount of traffic ready to be transferred but keep on generating new information while the game evolves. In order to illustrate this, Figure 15(a) shows the TCP window of an MMORPG session, in the case where no background traffic is present (negligible queuing delay), and (Figure 15(b)) in the case of having 8.5 Mbps of UDP background traffic.

Although the size of the TCP window is reduced when background traffic is present, the flows keep on sending their traffic, since they do not need a high value of the TCP window in order to send it. This fits with the two opposed effects reported in [6]: on one hand, the thinness of each stream makes that few packets are sent by RTT, making the window hardly grow. On the other hand, the flows do not correctly react to congestion, so they may keep on sending the same amount of traffic.

4.3. RTT Unfairness Tests. The aim of this subsection is the study of RTT unfairness between different MMORPG TCP flows. As reported in the literature [34], when two TCP flows with different RTTs compete for the same bottleneck link, the one with a smaller RTT has an advantage with respect to the other. The cause of this is that the most popular TCP versions *(New Reno, SACK)* increase their sending windows according to the received ACKs, so different delays will make them increase their rates differently.

However, in the case of MMORPG flows, we cannot expect a modification in the throughput, since the traffic is application limited instead of network limited. As we have already said, the main figure of merit for MMORPGs is RTT. Hence, an increase of the network RTT should be translated into a direct increase of the smoothed RTTseen by TCP. So the aim of this subsection is to check if there is any additional impairment caused by RTT unfairness, leaving apart the RTT increase itself.

In order to answer this question, we have set the parameters of the scenario this way: 100 MMORPG flows are established between *client A* and *server A*, and at the same time, 100 MMORPG flows are active between *client B* and *server B*. Background traffic consists of 10 FTP upload and 10 FTP download sessions using TCP *SACK*, between *background* 1 and *background* 2 nodes. The value of RTT1 (Figure 6) is set to different values, higher than 0, so the flows having a higher RTT, and thus the flows between *client A*

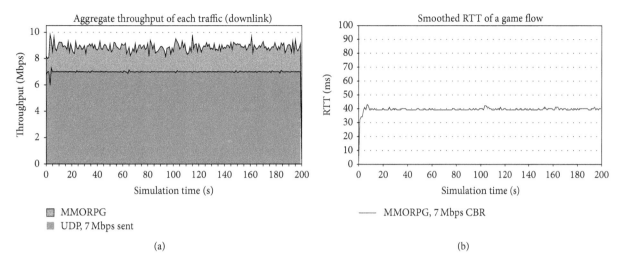

FIGURE 11: Coexistence of 100 MMORPG flows and 7 Mbps of UDP CBR traffic. (a) received throughput in the downlink by each traffic and (b) smoothed RTT of one of the game flows.

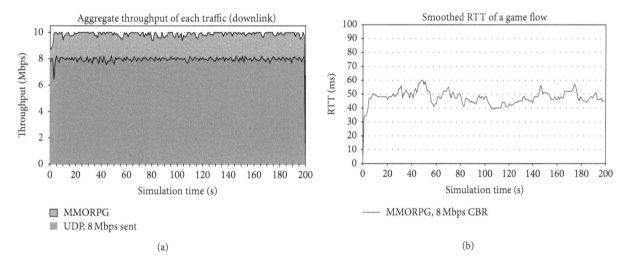

FIGURE 12: Coexistence of 100 MMORPG flows and 8 Mbps of UDP CBR traffic: (a) received throughput in the downlink by each traffic and (b) smoothed RTT of one of the game flows.

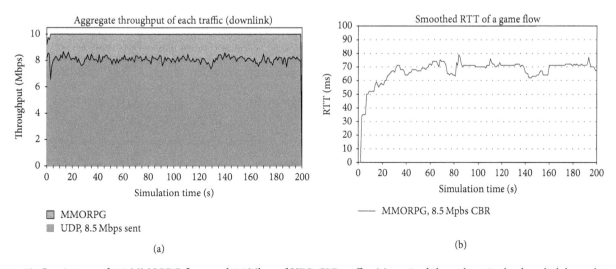

FIGURE 13: Coexistence of 100 MMORPG flows and 8.5 Mbps of UDP CBR traffic: (a) received throughput in the downlink by each traffic and (b) smoothed RTT of one of the game flows.

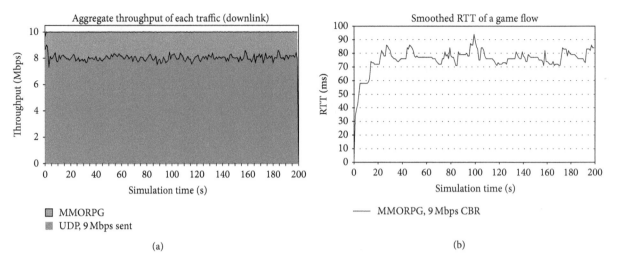

(a)   (b)

FIGURE 14: Coexistence of 100 MMORPG flows and 9 Mbps of UDP CBR traffic: (a) received throughput in the downlink by each traffic and (b) smoothed RTT of one of the game flows.

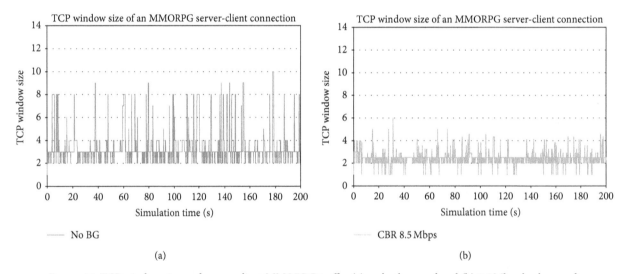

(a)   (b)

FIGURE 15: TCP window size, and server-client MMORPG traffic: (a) no background and (b) 8.5 Mbps background.

and *server A* are at a disadvantage. The RTT of the bottleneck (RTT0) is always 40 ms.

Figure 16 presents the results obtained when 100 game flows from *client A* to *server A*, experiencing different amounts of RTT (from 50 to 90), share the bottleneck with 100 game flows from *client B* to *server B*, always with an RTT of 40 ms. Regarding the value of smoothed RTT, two things can be appreciated in Figure 16(a): first, the difference between the columns is roughly the difference in terms of network RTT: for example, when 100 flows with an RTT of 60 ms share the bottleneck with 100 flows with an RTT of 40 ms, the difference in terms of smoothed RTT is 21.85 ms (i.e., roughly 20 ms). This happens (with very small variations) for all the values. Second: the RTT value for the *client B* to *server B* connections always remains the same.

Regarding the results of RTT *variation* (Figure 16(b)), it can be appreciated that the variation of the RTT is significantly higher for the flows experiencing a higher RTT, which will be translated in high jitter values.

The results of the throughput are not shown here, since the throughput variations between *A-A* and *B-B* flows are negligible (up to 3%), as it could be expected. We can conclude saying that smoothed RTT is not affected by this unfairness, but only RTT *variation* is worse for the flows with a higher RTT.

4.4. The Effect of Server Population on the Aggregate Traffic. We have previously mentioned the importance of the number of players present on a server, since this can have an effect on the global traffic. This subsection uses the proposed model to confirm that the traffic can significantly vary according to the server population, and also depending on the hour of the day. The developed model takes into account both variables.

In the tests of this subsection we have established 100 MMORPG traffic flows between *client A* and *server A*, competing with 10 FTP upload flows, 10 FTP download flows (using TCP *SACK*), and UDP background traffic of 6 Mbps

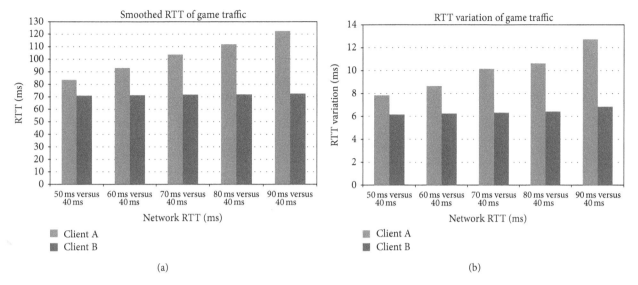

FIGURE 16: Latency of MMORPG flows from *client A* and *client B* (a) Smoothed RTT and (b) RTT *variation*.

in both uplink and downlink. We have considered that the players are using low-populated servers (30 players) in one case, and high-populated ones (600 players) in the other. Taking into account that the two activities in which traffic significantly varies with the server population are *PvP combat* and *Trading*, we have selected three different hours of the day (see Figure 4):

(i) 8:00 as an example of low *PvP combat* and high *Trading*;

(ii) 11:00 where both activities have a high probability of being performed;

(iii) 20:00 where both activities have low probability.

In this case, the aggregate traffic (100 MMORPG flows) is composed of flows corresponding to the six action categories, according to their probabilities, which also depend on the hour of the day. In this way, we investigate if the variation of the APDU and IAT of *Trading* and *PvP combat* has a global effect, which can be observed on the aggregate server-to-client traffic.

The results are shown in Figure 17, where 200 simulation seconds are run for each case. The left figure displays the case of players in low populated servers, while the right displays the case of highly populated servers. During the initial seconds, there is a transient status in which FTP connections need some time in order to increase their sending windows. As a first observation, we see that the throughput of these 100 MMORPG sessions strongly varies with the hour of the day: at 8:00 it can vary from 2 to 2.4 Mbps, depending on the global population of the servers where the players are. However, at 20.00 it varies from 3.5 to 4.1 Mbps. It should be remarked that these variations are not caused by a different number of flows, but only by the global population of the servers to which these players are connected.

At the same time, it can be observed that, at 11.00 (Figures 17(c) and 17(d)), the difference between the traffic

TABLE 7: Average smoothed RTT of all the MMORPG flows.

Hour of the day	Smoothed RTT 30 players	Smoothed RTT 600 players
8:00	91.39 ms	87.69 ms
11:00	90.46 ms	89.23 ms
20:00	93.61 ms	96.32 ms

is significant: 2.18 Mbps with 30 players and 2.96 Mbps with 600 players (35%). At 20:00 (Figures 17(e) and 17(f)), the difference is only from 3.5 to 4.1 (17%). At 8.00 (Figures 17(a) and 17(b)) the traffic ranges from 2 to 2.44 Mbps (22%).

Finally, in order to explore if the variation of the bandwidth with the hour of the day has any influence on the RTT (measured as smoothed RTT), Table 7 shows its average value for the 100 MMORPG flows. It can be seen that the variations are really small (between 1% and 4%), and this fits with another phenomenon that can be observed in Figure 17; that is, we see that in all the cases the UDP flows get reduced their 6 Mbps of bandwidth share, whereas MMORPG flows maintain their throughput. FTP flows are only able to get the bandwidth that the two other kinds of flows leave free. This is in concordance with the results shown in Sections 4.1 and 4.2, and with the effect reported in [6]; that is, the flows do not react to congestion due to their thinness, and they keep on sending the same amount of traffic.

The high variability of MMORPG traffic depending on the hour of the day and on the population of a server makes it difficult to calculate the number of servers required for provisioning an online game. In addition, many other factors have an influence; for example, the release of a new game or of new content of an existing one can cause a traffic rush. Although game developers may experience difficulties when predicting the success of a game, they may be interested in using statistical models in order to predict the demand variations according to the hour of the day.

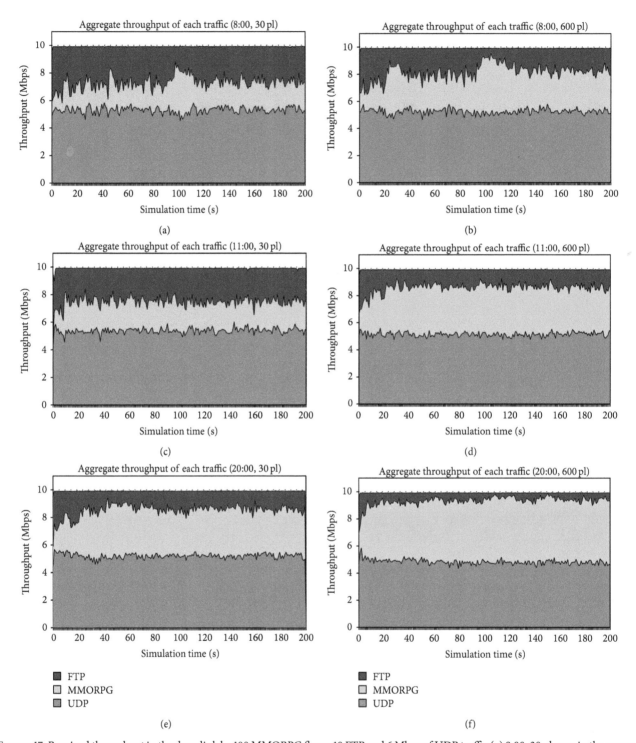

FIGURE 17: Received throughput in the downlink by 100 MMORPG flows, 10 FTP and 6 Mbps of UDP traffic (a) 8:00, 30 players in the servers; (b) 8:00, 600 players in the servers; (c) 11:00, 30 players; (d) 11:00, 600 players; (e) 20:00, 30 players; (f) 20:00, 600 players.

4.5. Discussion of the Results. This subsection summarizes and discusses the results presented in this section. In the first tests, we measured the competition of MMORPG and FTP flows using different variants of TCP. We first observed that the MMORPG flows are able to work properly even with network-limited TCP connections in the background. The most important parameter for players, namely, RTT can be kept low for all the TCP variants. TCP *SACK* shows a more

respectful behaviour with game flows: it increases less the game RTT, at the cost of achieving a slightly lower amount of bandwidth share than *Tahoe, Reno,* and *New Reno.* This tradeoff is more accentuated with TCP *Vegas,* which reduces even more its throughput but as a counterpart adds less delay (up to 30 ms) to the RTT of the game flows.

The second subsection has studied the mutual influence of MMORPG TCP flows and UDP CBR ones. In contrast with what normally happens with TCP flows, which only get the bandwidth share not used by UDP ones, the tests have shown that TCP game flows are able to maintain their throughput despite the amount of UDP traffic. The reason is that the bandwidth demand of the game flows is not governed by the congestion window, since they do not have an amount of predefined data to transfer, but they keep on generating new information according to the player actions and the game evolution.

The third battery of tests has explored the RTT unfairness, normally observed when several TCP flows with different RTTs share a bottleneck. This difference is not as important as for network-limited TCP flows. In this case, the bandwidth obtained does not vary with the RTT, taking into account that the traffic is mostly signalling. In addition, the RTT experienced by the game (measured in terms of TCP smoothed RTT) varies according to the real network RTT. Only the RTT *variation* shows worse results for the flows with a higher RTT, which will be translated into a higher jitter in the game traffic.

Finally, we have used the developed model of the game traffic so as to obtain results illustrating the effect of the number of players in a server (server population). Different hours of the day have been selected, drawing some conclusions that mainly affect server-to-client traffic: the bandwidth may vary up to 35% depending on the population of the server, and this difference may also vary according to the hour of the day. The cause of this phenomenon is that, in some moments, the activities preferred by the players are more server-population dependant. In addition, it has again be observed that game flows are able to maintain their throughput and a reasonable RTT, even in the presence of high amounts of combined FTP and UDP traffic flows.

5. Conclusion

This paper has studied the interactions between application-limited TCP traffic, typical of MMORPGs, and other flows. In order to do this, an advanced traffic model of a popular MMORPG game has been first developed. By using measurements deployed in real servers of the game, we have analyzed how the APDU and IAT of some activities vary with the number of players on the server, and this effect has been included in the statistics that rule the traffic generation in the model. In addition, the model is able to simulate user behaviour, generating traffic according to different activities, which have different probabilities depending on the hour of the day.

The traffic model has also been implemented in a network simulator, and a set of tests of the coexistence between traffic flows have been deployed: the coexistence of the game traffic with FTP using different TCP variants; the competition with UDP flows; the effect of different values of RTT between game flows; and the global effect of the server population on the aggregate traffic. It has been shown that TCP *SACK* is more respectful with game flows than *Tahoe, Reno,* and *New Reno;* that is, it achieves a slightly lower throughput but adds less delay to MMORPG flows. Furthermore, the behaviour of TCP *Vegas* is even better, not throttling the MMORPG flows and causing no growth on their RTT, since it does not increase aggressively its window size. Interestingly, we found

that MMORPG flows are resilient to UDP traffic: since they do not need significant sizes of the TCP window, they are able to maintain their bandwidth share while maintaining their RTT in reasonable limits. The RTT unfairness for application-limited TCP traffic has also been studied, showing that only the RTT variation is affected. Finally, we have confirmed that the player population on the server has significant impact on the overall traffic (up to 30%). Although game developers may experience difficulties when predicting the success of a new game, the use of statistical models able to predict the demand variations according to the hour of the day is seen as very convenient. As future work, we plan to improve the model so as to include players' arrivals and departures. In addition, the influence of different buffer sizes and policies on the coexistence of MMORPG traffic with other flows will be studied.

Acknowledgments

This work has been partially financed by the Project "Content Delivery and Mobility of Users and Services in New Generation Networks," by the Ministry of Science, Education, and Sports of the Republic of Croatia; the European Community Seventh Framework Programme under Grant Agreement no. 285939 (ACROSS); CPUFLIPI Project (MICINN TIN2010-17298); Project TAMA, Government of Aragon; Project Catedra Telefonica, University Zaragoza; European Social Fund in collaboration with the Government of Aragon. The authors would like to thank John Miller for his advice regarding some details of the game traffic. they also want to thank Tanja Kauric for her help in obtaining the traffic traces of the game.

References

[1] Activision Blizzard, "World of Warcraft subscriber base reaches 12 million worldwide," October 2010, http://us.blizzard.com/en-us/company/press/pressreleases.html?id=2847881.

[2] K.-T. Chen, C.-Y. Huang, P. Huang, and C.-L. Lei, "An empirical evaluation of TCP performance in online games," in *Proceedings of the ACM SIGCHI International Conference on Advances in Computer Entertainment Technology (ACE '06)*, Hollywood, Calif, USA, June 2006.

[3] M. Suznjevic and M. Matijasevic, "Player behavior and traffic characterization for MMORPGs: a survey," *Multimedia Systems*, vol. 19, no. 3, pp. 199–220, 2012.

[4] I. V. Geel, "MMOData: Keeping track of the MMORPG scene," August 2013, http://mmodata.net/.

[5] C.-C. Wu, K.-T. Chen, C.-M. Chen, P. Huang, and C.-L. Lei, "On the challenge and design of transport protocols for MMORPGs," *Multimedia Tools and Applications*, vol. 45, no. 1–3, pp. 7–32, 2009.

[6] C. Griwodz and P. Halvorsen, "The fun of using TCP for an MMORPG," in *Proceedings of the 16th Annual International Workshop on Network and Operating Systems Support for Digital Audio and Video (NOSSDAV '06)*, pp. 1–7, New York, NY, USA, May 2006.

[7] K. Shin, J. Kim, K. Sohn, C. J. Park, and S. Choi, "Transformation approach to model online gaming traffic," *ETRI Journal*, vol. 33, no. 2, pp. 219–229, 2011.

[8] K.-T. Chen, P. Huang, and C.-L. Lei, "Game traffic analysis: an MMORPG perspective," *Computer Networks*, vol. 51, no. 3, pp. 19–24, 2007.

[9] M. Suznjevic, O. Dobrijevic, and M. Matijasevic, "MMORPG Player actions: Network performance, session patterns and latency requirements analysis," *Multimedia Tools and Applications*, vol. 45, no. 1–3, pp. 191–214, 2009.

[10] M. Suznjevic, I. Stupar, and M. Matijasevic, "A model and software architecture for MMORPG traffic generation based on player behavior," *Multimedia Systems*, vol. 19, no. 3, pp. 93–101, 2012.

[11] B. De Vleeschauwer, B. van den Bossche, T. Verdickt, F. de Turck, B. Dhoedt, and P. Demeester, "Dynamic microcell assignment for massively multiplayer online gaming," in *Proceedings of the 4th ACM SIGCOMM Workshop on Network and System Support for Games (NetGames '05)*, pp. 1–7, Hawthorne, NY, USA, 2005.

[12] X. Che and B. Ip, "Packet-level traffic analysis of online games from the genre characteristics perspective," *Journal of Network and Computer Applications*, vol. 35, no. 1, pp. 240–252, 2012.

[13] C. Majewski, C. Griwodz, and P. Halvorsen, "Translating latency requirements into resource requirements for game traffic," in *Proceedings of the International Network Conference (INC '06)*, pp. 113–120, Plymouth, UK, 2006.

[14] J. Saldana, M. Suznjevic, L. Sequeira, J. Fernandez-Navajas, M. Matijasevic, and J. Ruiz-Mas, "The effect of TCP variants on the coexistence of MMORPG and best-effort traffic," in *Proceedings of IEEE ICCCN 8th International Workshop on Networking Issues in Multimedia Entertainment (NIME '12)*, pp. 1–5, Munich, Germany, 2012.

[15] P. Svoboda, W. Karner, and M. Rupp, "Traffic analysis and modeling for world of warcraft," in *Proceedings of the IEEE International Conference on Communications (ICC '07)*, pp. 1612–1617, Glasgow, UK, June 2007.

[16] J. Kim, E. Hong, and J. Choi, "Measurement and analysis of a massively multiplayer online role playing game traffic," in *Proceedings of Advanced Network Conference*, pp. 1–8, 2003.

[17] Y. Wu, H. Huang, and D. Zhang, "Traffic modeling for Massive Multiplayer On-line Role Playing Game (MMORPG) in GPRS access network," in *Proceedings of the International Conference on Communications, Circuits and Systems (ICCCAS '06)*, pp. 1811–1815, Guilin, China, June 2006.

[18] V. Paxson, "Empirically derived analytic models of wide-area TCP connections," *IEEE/ACM Transactions on Networking*, vol. 2, no. 4, pp. 316–336, 1994.

[19] K. Shin, J. Kim, K. Sohn, C. J. Park, and S. Choi, "Transformation approach to model online gaming traffic," *ETRI Journal*, vol. 33, no. 2, pp. 219–229, 2011.

[20] H. Park, T. Kim, and S. Kim, "Network traffic analysis and modeling for games," in *Internet and Network Economics*, vol. 3828 of *Lecture Notes in Computer Science*, pp. 1056–1065, Springer, 2005.

[21] X. Wang, H. Kim, A. V. Vasilakos et al., "Measurement and analysis of world of warcraft in mobile WiMAX networks," in *Proceedings of the 8th Annual Workshop on Network and Systems Support for Games (NetGames '09)*, Paris, France, November 2009.

[22] X. Wang, T. Kwon, Y. Choi, M. Chen, and Y. Zhang, "Characterizing the gaming traffic of World of Warcraft: from game scenarios to network access technologies," *IEEE Network*, vol. 26, no. 1, pp. 27–34, 2012.

[23] W.-C. Feng, D. Brandt, and D. Saha, "A long-term study of a popular MMORPG," in *Proceedings of the 6th ACM SIGCOMM Workshop on Network and System Support for Games (NetGames '07)*, pp. 19–24, Melbourne, Australia, September 2007.

[24] J. Kawale, A. Pal, and J. Srivastava, "Churn prediction in MMORPGs: a social influence based approach," in *Proceedings of the International Conference on Computational Science and Engineering*, pp. 423–428, Vanoucer, Canada, August 2009.

[25] D. Pittman and C. G.Dickey, "A measurement study of virtual populations in massively multiplayer online games," in *Proceedings of the 6th ACM SIGCOMM Workshop on Network and System Support for Games (NetGames '07)*, pp. 25–30, Melbourne, Australia, September 2007.

[26] D. Pittman and C. G. Dickey, "Characterizing virtual populations in massively multiplayer online role-playing games," in *Advances in Multimedia Modeling*, vol. 5916 of *Lecture Notes in Computer Science*, pp. 87–97, Springer, 2010.

[27] Y.-T. Lee, K.-T. Chen, Y.-M. Cheng, and C.-L. Lei, "World of warcraft avatar history dataset," in *Proceedings of the 2nd Annual ACM Multimedia Systems Conference (MMSys '11)*, pp. 123–128, San Jose, Calif, USA, February 2011.

[28] M. Suznjevic, I. Stupar, and M. Matijasevic, "MMORPG player behavior model based on player action categories," in *Proceedings of the 10th Annual Workshop on Network and Systems Support for Games (NetGames '11)*, Ottawa, Canada, October 2011.

[29] P. A. Branch, A. L. Cricenti, and G. J. Armitage, "An ARMA(1,1) prediction model of first person shooter game traffic," in *Proceedings of the IEEE 10th Workshop on Multimedia Signal Processing (MMSP '08)*, pp. 736–741, Cairns, Australia, October 2008.

[30] T. Lang, P. Branch, and G. Armitage, "A synthetic traffic model for quake3," in *Proceedings of the ACM SIGCHI International Conference on Advances in Computer Entertainment Technology (ACE '04)*, pp. 233–238, Singapore, June 2005.

[31] X. Zhuang, A. Bharambe, J. Pang, and S. Seshan, "Player dynamics in massively multiplayer online games," Tech. Rep. CMU-CS-07-158, School of Computer Science Carnegie Mellon University, Pittsburgh, Pa, USA, 2007.

[32] T. Issariyakul and E. Hossain, *Introduction to Network Simulator NS2*, Springer, 2011.

[33] G. Marfia, C. E. Palazzi, G. Pau, M. Gerla, and M. Roccetti, "TCP Libra: derivation, analysis, and comparison with other RTT-fair TCPs," *Computer Networks*, vol. 54, no. 14, pp. 2327–2344, 2010.

[34] M. Ries, P. Svoboda, and M. Rupp, "Empirical study of subjective quality for massive multiplayer games," in *Proceedings of the 15th International Conference on Systems, Signals and Image Processing (IWSSIP '08)*, pp. 181–184, Bratislava, Slovakia, June 2008.

[35] H. Sawashima and Y. H. H. Sunahara, "Characteristics of UDP packet loss: effect of TCP traffic," in *Proceeeding of the 7th Annual Conference of the Internet Society (INET '97)*, p. 6, Kuala Lumpur, Malaysia, 1997.

[36] Cooperative Association for Internet Data Analysis (CAIDA), "NASA Ames Internet Exchange Packet Length Distributions," March 2008, http://www.caida.org/research/traffic-analysis/AIX/plen_hist/.

## 12

An Assessment of Serious Games Technology: *Toward an Architecture for Serious Games Design*

Walid Mestadi ⓘ,[1] **Khalid Nafil** ⓘ,[2] **Raja Touahni** ⓘ,[1] **and Rochdi Messoussi** ⓘ[1]

[1]*Ibn Tofail University, Faculty of Sciences, Kenitra, Morocco*
[2]*Mohamed V University, Faculty of Sciences, Rabat, Morocco*

Correspondence should be addressed to Walid Mestadi; mestadi.walid@gmail.com

Academic Editor: Hanqiu Sun

The design of an engaging and motivating serious game (SG) requires a strong knowledge of learning domain, pedagogy, and game design components, which are hard to be found and restrained by an individual or one entity. Therefore and in the light of this statement, the collaboration between domain content, pedagogical, and playful experts is required and crucial. Despite the fact that the existing models that support SG design are intended to have a combination of learning and fun, the design of SG remains difficult to achieve. It would then be appreciated to propose means and guidelines that facilitate this design. To do so, this paper proposes a taxonomy, which classifies models that treat SG design, and then presents an opening as a functional architecture for supporting SG conception, which promotes the separation during the design, the collaboration between different involved experts, and the reuse of prior expert productions.

1. Introduction

The human evolution depends on how much importance is given to knowledge inter-generation transfer by taking into consideration individual characteristics as well as environment changes for each generation (i.e., digital or. com social network, web 2.0, and gaming). Students need a wide education in various fields which is essential for economical outcomes [1]. Researches in educational field require several researchers with different backgrounds. The challenges remain on student's engagement and motivation in traditional education, where engaged and motivated ones persist and investigate in understanding rather than only receiving the educational material. In contrast, disengaged students react to the education offer with less importance and without excitement or commitment. Thus, student's engagement is fundamental and critical for educational success [2–4].

The targeted engagement and motivation factors in education field are naturally available in gaming activities. Video games success and popularity are similar to those of books, movies, television, and other forms of media [5]. Video games are designed to engage players in an interactive environment, which makes them different from those media; also, they are played cooperatively or competitively, alone, with other physically present players, or with thousands of other online players, and they are played on various devices (consoles, computers, and cell phones) [6]. Games and their characteristics [7] have the potential to engage young and adult players naturally. As reported by [6], 91% of children between the ages of 2 and 17 play video games and up to 99% of boys and 94% of girls play these games. In addition, video games brought over $25 billion in 2010, more than Hollywood's 2010 box office. Educational and gaming experts are interested in designing games, which combine the fun factor and the educational content to engage and motivate students while learning. Such games are called serious games (SGs) [6–8].

Serious game is defined as a game [5], a mental contest [9], an interactive computer application [8], a digital game, a simulation, a virtual environment, and a mixed reality/media [10], applied in serious context such as education [5], government or corporate training, health, public policy, and strategic communication objectives [9]. Moreover they are used to impart skills/knowledge/attitude [8] or to deliver information [10], using the fun elements to engage learners [5, 8–10].

More specifically, serious game (SG) for educational purpose works on addressing the engagement issue by using the fun factors to immerse learners in an active learning environment [7, 11] and pushing learners to compete and overcome challenges by actions with immediate feedback [8]. However, because of the lack of standards on how to design SG in the field of education, it will be difficult to judge if the SG design results really meet the purpose for which it is designed. For example, if the domain content is designed by an individual or organization that is unfamiliar with the educational field, which is the case of a game designer, it may slip content errors if it is not validated by domain content and educational expert [12, 13].

However, the major issue relies on combining and balancing game elements (game characteristics, game mechanics, and gameplay) with learning factors (domain content or knowledge, skills, and learning mechanics) while keeping SGs potential promises. Designing and delivering a SG that engages and affects learners require a strong understanding of its filed and theories: game design, learning theories, and domain content. This can be achieved only by investigating how to mix and balance game potential in concert with learning outcomes and pedagogical objectives and how to manage the collaboration of experts with diverse creative and scholarly backgrounds [5, 8, 14, 15].

The current paper provides the main research works in SG design reported in the literature. The study of those proposals aims to understand SG design field, the challenges faced, and the proposed solutions in order to draw a classification and then propose an adequate solution for SG design. Our starting point for going into this in depth is exploring research's works in SG design field. In fact we will explore how SG model can be classified according to the nature of the model proposed, in order to facilitate the field's understanding, and then propose a solution that can help to design SG. As a first step we give an overview on notable works relevant to SG designs, in order to underline what they are trying to improve. Then, a discussion of SG model is given. Furthermore a comprehensive taxonomy of SG model is presented. Next an opening is presented and discussed, and we explain how it could be a best solution and useful for designing SG. Moreover, we study its implementation on two existing serious games. Then a conclusion is presented as a synthesis.

2. State of the Art

Several researches work on modeling their framework to deal with SG challenge from different views, where the challenge is seen as the difficulty in integrating the domain content into the game structure, the technological complexity introduced by game development, the mapping of learning theories and game mechanics, the reusability of prior production of SG, the organizational aspects, and the collaboration between the education and game experts or as framework which proposes a coherent set of structural components, which is used to create the foundations and outlines of the whole or a part

of SG. However, designing SG which integrates and balances education and game requires solid bases to start with, such as a theoretical framework [30, 31].

From the view of integrating the domain content into the game structure, authors in [16] aim to teach software engineering processes by proposing a card game design under the name of "Problems and Programmers", which is a competitive game in which each student plays the role of a project manager; they lead the same project and the player who finishes first is the winner. For this, players have to manage their budget and resources to produce high quality software while meeting software project requirements. In order to achieve this goal, players should use their knowledge of software engineering to avoid any problems. The game imposes the use of the Waterfall development model that requires passing through the following steps: analysis, design, development, integration, and testing. Based on the "Problems and Programmers" design, authors in [25] propose a card game called "PlayScrum" which aims to teach the Scrum Agile Framework. Also, authors in [17] aim to teach programming and computational thinking concepts by proposing a platform's game called "Program your robot", in which player controls a game object which represents a "robot". The player should write an algorithm to order the "robot" to avoid obstacles faced in the platform. From an abstract level the "Program your robot" design is similar to the SG proposed by [18, 20, 22] in terms of "drag and drop" and writing a code by using preprogramming commands. In the same context, authors in [21] propose a SG design that uses domain content and analogical representations, where the learner is asked to complete a task such as comparing between real cases and analogical ones that are presented side-by-side. Authors in [29] focus on domain content integration into SG design by proposing a model, which is composed of two components. The first one represents a main game while the second one represents a set of separated "mini-games", "puzzles", and "quizzes" which are related to the main game. The main game is composed of a set of quests/missions, in which the educational objectives are represented by Non-Player Characters (NPC) in addition to the resources to be collected. Those resources are required to interact with "mini-games", in which we incorporate domain content to teach. Based on their model, the authors design a game called "Clean World" which aims to teach "Recycling and Renewable Energies".

From an organizational aspect and the collaboration between the education and game experts view, authors in [12] propose a structure of SG design composed of six phases under the name of "facets": "pedagogical objectives", "domain simulation", "interactions with the simulation", "problems and progression", "decorum", and "conditions of use". Additionally the authors provide a process model that specifies how pedagogical experts (domain content, pedagogy, knowledge, etc.) and playful experts (game designers, level designers, game producers, storyboard writers, artistic directors, actors, graphic designers, sound managers, etc.) collaborate according to the proposed structure. Each phase underlines a specific problem related to SG design and the needed expertise. However, in pedagogical objectives phase, pedagogical experts collaborate in order to represent domain content, educational objectives, and domain errors interpretation ("define problems where players can fail") into a valid domain model. Afterward, the pedagogical experts build a domain simulation with a game engine in compilation with the valid domain model. The aim of the simulator is to validate the domain model and to enumerate the player's action by testing the simulator responses to the player's actions including the domain errors interpretation. Then, the playful experts should represent simulator interactions by playful interactions (analogical representation), in addition to other interactions that are pure for game world. In the problems and progression phase, the pedagogical and playful experts collaborate to design problems (based on domain errors interpretation) challenging player and how he progresses in each level. The decorum phase is the complement of the previous phase, where the playful experts envelop or represent playful interactions with art, graphics, and also the introduction of music, avatar, etc., in addition to calling advice from pedagogical experts. In the last phase, the conditions of use represent how and when to use the targeted SG. Similarly, authors in [13] propose a knowledge management approach, which focuses on early stages of conception and development of a SG aiming to satisfy the requirement of customers from financial institutions. Those customers are interested in teaching new hired employees about the organization, the group structure, its functions, and corporate values. The knowledge management approach goes through four main stages. The first one consists of classifying knowledge according to a structured typology: (a) nature of the knowledge which refers to knowledge characteristics (e.g., confidentiality and degree of relevance) used to communicate with customers for validation and prioritization, (b) type of knowledge which refers to knowledge classification (e.g., factual, declaratory, and procedural), and (c) pedagogical objectives specification which refers to hierarchical view of knowledge type with its pedagogical objectives. The second step deals with game design decision making about the pedagogical objectives integration into game story or gameplay; as suggested by those authors, factual knowledge type should be integrated into game story and procedural knowledge type into gameplay or game mechanics; also this step works on guiding game designer during the definition of game rules. In addition, the creation of a cognitive model step represents domain objects, actions, properties, rules, and their internal interactions to build an expert system. The expert system will be used by the game designer in the final stage to make decision on which variables the player is going to control, the consequences of good/bad actions, rewards, conditions of failure/victory, and frequency of messages or cut-scenes.

From the theoretical framework view, authors in [7] propose an "Input-Process-Output" model underlining the relation between game features (fantasy, curiosity, competitiveness, control, and visual and sound effects), instructional content, and the player, from a motivational and engagement perspective. The model underlines the fact that game features should be mixed with instructional content in order to design an instructional program. These features trigger game cycle to keep the player motivated and engaged while achieving a learning objective, which should be maintained by feedback of player's progression. Also, the model highlights the need for matching game features or game events with learning outcomes, in the cases that game features do not represent directly the instructional content. Finally, the "Input-Process-Output" indicates that SG should propose the mechanics to be played several times. This model could be considered as a metamodel [32] for SG design and has been extended by [24] into a conceptual framework. The proposed framework highlights two perspectives for SG design. The first one focuses on the structure which requires the definition of pedagogical objective and instructional content to design intended learning outcome mixed with game attributes that support learning (i.e., feedback) in order to design learning activities. Based on these activities, the authors believe that the game genre with its mechanics will be easy to choose; while the second one focuses on SG behaviors in order to maintain player motivated and engaged. In addition, authors in [33] propose an iterative cyclic process focusing on leisure game called the "Mechanics, Dynamics, and Aesthetics" framework MDA. The MDA framework aims to design a game from two perspectives; the first one deals with the three components of the game design and their relations, and the second one focuses on how player's interactions are affecting those components. However, the MDA framework focuses only on gameplay. Authors in [30] proposes "Design, Play, and Experience" DEP framework by extending the MDA framework to be explored in SG design context. The DEP framework is defined by five layers: "learning", "storytelling", "gameplay", "user interface", and "technology". Each layer is structured by three interconnected components: "design", "play", and "experience" similar to MDA framework. Also, each layer targets a specific objective in SG design, which goes through design, play, and experience in an iterative way. Also, DEP framework is proposed to underline the influences among those layers.

From mapping of learning theories and game mechanics view, aiming to support educational theories with SG design, authors in [34] propose a highest level mapping between games and learning mechanics called "SG mechanics". The SG mechanics is structured according to bloom's taxonomy cognitive functions, namely, remembering, comprehending, applying, analyzing, synthesizing, and evaluating. In more specified level, authors in [32] propose a taxonomy which links learning functions and game design patterns considered as a technical solution; they investigate inter-patterns relations such as strong dependence "instantiation, composition", a low dependence "modulation, aggregation", and the logical presence in game genre "conflict". On the other hand, authors in [35] aim to use SG design patterns to support communication between various experts during SG game design. Moreover, authors in [36] discussed a matching between existing games genre such as "First-Person-Shoot" (FPS) and learning outcomes. They stated that FPS characteristics are suitable for improving learning function [6].

According to the reusability of prior production of SG view, authors in [27] attempt to standardize prior production into a central repository. They propose a technical architecture to adapt existing and new components in serious context in order to be reused during the SG design. Also,

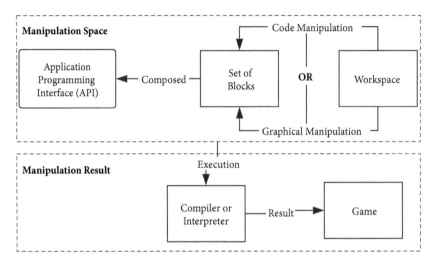

FIGURE 1: Abstract presentation of the adopted design for teaching computational thinking.

the architecture provides a mechanic that allows the communication (information exchange) between components. In contrast, authors in [28] intend to allow game designer building SG which can interact with existing virtual learning environment without being distracted by standards related to learning via middleware which unifies the communication procedure.

From a complexity technological side, authors in [26] propose high-level tool which provides guidance to educators to design SG via a graphical interface. The tool generates a game for specific platforms (flash, XNA console, etc.) by using a Role-Playing Game (RPG) model.

3. State of the Art Discussion

Although those research works are not exhaustive, their multiple views may quite well represent the SG design aspects relevant to our context. Also, for the classification perspective there is the desire for finding a reduced terminology that represents those and similar works.

Going deeper into the direction of classifying SG design approach, the card game "Problems and Programmers" designed for teaching specific domain content with a deep look, gives clues about how to explore the concepts used in its structure and rules in order to integrate new content; from an abstract view, the programmer card represents a human resource with its personal data such as name and professional data, namely, skills, personality, and salary; based on these data, the players can take decision about what this resource can produce and with what level of quality, the personality to manage collaboration conflict, and the salary to manage budget. For example, the concept presented by the programmer, problems, and concepts cards could embed domain content like manufacture or similar one, and if there is domain content differentiation, it could make an adaptation as presented by "PlayScrum" card game which extends "Problems and Programmers" from teaching "Waterfall model" to teaching "Scrum Agile Framework". In

the game "Program your robot", as well as the game proposed by [18] and the web platforms in [37, 38], the authors aim to teach computational thinking; they adopt the same design as that presented in Figure 1, where the Manipulation Space contains specific tools for programming such as Application Programming Interface (API), which exposes a set of functions (preprogramming commands such as "move" and "jump") forming a set of blocks. The player manipulates those functions in order to elaborate an algorithm to complete missions and achieve goals by designing an algorithm into the Workspace, either by code manipulation (e.g., programming language) or by graphical manipulation (drag and drop). The player's algorithm is interpreted or compiled (depending on the proposed solution), and then the result is reflected into the game (see, for example, [18]).

Also, in the "Clean World" game, the mini-game "garbage collection" represents the concept of "items collections" which means that we can collect any items from any domain content (for example, coins, words, potatoes, etc.) and then separate them according to given features, and the mini-games can be changed by any other game only if its game mechanics embedded items collection and items separation concepts. Such a design simplifies the SG design and also investigates the domain content integration into game and it could be considered as architecture; in contrast, it limits the field of use or application and targets one game genre only. Moreover, designing a technical framework is not always investigating domain content integration into game [27, 28].

Mapping between learning theories and game in SG design, that is, the mapping procedure investigating which game aspects can support learning, is quite common. The investigation underlines links between learning theories and game from two views, technical, functional, or both:

(i) functional: abstract level, such as learning function [32, 34, 36], game attributes [24], and game mechanics [34];

(ii) technical: concrete level, such as teaching practices [35], game design pattern [32], and game genre [36].

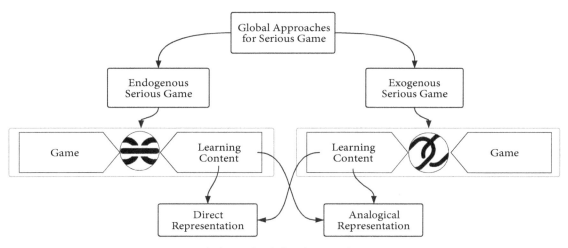

FIGURE 2: The hierarchical classification of serious games.

However, the mapping of learning theories and game does not consider domain content and, more importantly, they need contextualization where they could be explored efficiently such as a process model [35] besides a functional or a technical architecture (Figure 3):

(i) A process model defines the way of collaboration between different experts, in which we focus on external structure of SG design (analogically, car production process); see, for example, a comparative study of process model of serious game design [39]. However, the presence of all various experts (heavy and high cost) is mandatory at every time it is needed to design a SG, which limits the reusability of the proposed structure and organization.

(ii) A technical architecture aims to simplify the SG design and limits the field of application—in most cases targeting one game genre.

(iii) A functional architecture consists of describing in a symbolic and schematic manner the different elements of the system, their interrelations, and their interactions in order to meet the system specifications, emphasize intention and objectives, provide functional decomposing, influence the process model, limit the intervention of stakeholders by providing guidance, simplify translating into a technical architecture, and most importantly improve the reusability; in contrast, it has a high complexity in realization [40–42].

4. Toward a Comprehensive Taxonomy to Classify Research Works Dealing with Serious Game Design

Relying on the work of [43], SG can be classified into the following principal categories:

(i) market: the kind of market that uses them such as healthcare;

(ii) purpose: the purpose they are designed to serve.

Also, a combination of criteria can be adopted to categorize SG, providing more specified hybrid taxonomy based on market and purpose of the SG, which cannot be clearly classified. Moreover, the authors introduced their own model combining the gameplay, purpose, and scope, believing that SGs are composed of both "serious" and a "games" dimensions.

According to researchers in the field, designing SG could be done by two global approaches, exogenous and endogenous [7, 12, 13, 30, 44, 45]. The endogenous or intrinsic approach claims that domain content and game should be naturally embedded or tied. It consists of integrating the domain content into game structure and rules, where the gameplay represents the learning content which is necessary for game goal achieving. In addition, as the game is interesting, the content becomes interesting, and it is considered as a good approach to create better SG requiring to start by a blank board and to make the domain content in the centre of the design process; also it may target SG with more complex learning goals. In contrast, the exogenous or extrinsic approach considers that the domain content and the game are unrelated, which means that the game represents a simple wrapper for domain content. The gameplay does not represent the domain content and it is separated from the learning content. Such games use preexisting game structure and rules [7, 12, 13, 30, 44, 45].

Exploring the two general approaches discussed earlier (the exogenous and the endogenous) seems to be a good start for going into the proposition of a new classification; they split approaches addressing SG design into two distinct categories (Figure 2). The exogenous category represents SG in which the learning content is separated from game representing a heterogeneous entity—the gameplay is indirectly related to the learning content. In contrast, the endogenous category represents SG in which the learning and the game representing a homogeneous entity—the gameplay is directly related to the learning content.

Both categories (the exogenous and the endogenous) definitions do not specify learning content representation into the game world, which leads to a freedom in learning

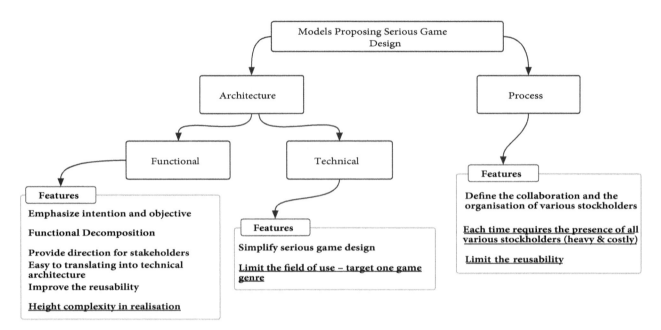

FIGURE 3: The hierarchical classification of models approaching SG design.

content design; as stated by [7] "students may learn about physics by piloting a spaceship on reentry to earth's orbit"; from this statement it is difficult to claim that the learning content is directly represented in the game world or it is represented differently. In contrast, authors in [12] state that "the students must defend a territory (the metaphor of the body) by adjusting the defences (metaphor of the immune system)"; it is clear that the learning content is represented by an analogical representation, as both statements refer to endogenous approach. In the same way of the exogenous approach, authors in [7] state that "children may learn fractions and by doing so slay a dragon in an enchanted forest", which refers to an analogical representation. In contrast, authors in [13] report an experience which consists of using a SimCity-style building game accompanied by a knowledge base; in order to play the game the learner should earn points by responding to questions proposed outside the game; also, authors in [19] propose how to explore the Angry Birds game with video analysis and modeling software (Tracker) for teaching kinematics and dynamics in physics field. This fact leads us to subdivide learning content element into two subcategories: direct representation and analogical representation.

As stated before, exogenous and endogenous approaches both represent a general solution for SG design, but for exogenous approach, the solution is limited to the reuse of preexisting successful games and the learning content could be either inserted or related by another means to the game world. By contrast, for endogenous approach, the solution defines the intention of designing an engaged and an effected SG, which means that the SG design challenge is ongoing. As presented earlier in the State of the Art Discussion, several models emerged approaching the challenge by the proposition of either of three categories: a process model, a technical architecture, or a functional architecture. In order

to complete our taxonomy, SG design should be classified also according to the three categories as a second level classification (Figure 3).

In order to classify existing research works dealing with serious games design, we propose a grid which examines these works according to some questions as summarized in Table 1. The grid is divided into two levels; the first one concerns works proposing serious game implementation, and the second one concerns those who are proposing model to design serious game accompanied or not by implementation.

As mentioned before, the endogenous approach is considered as a good one to create better SG and proved by models presented in the State of the Art targeting such category, except the works that support SG design such as the mapping approach. The proposed taxonomy will be adopted to classify those models according to endogenous approach (Table 2). The sequences of this table can be explained as follows: The first column represents models presented in the State of the Art which discuss only SG design. The second column identifies the domain content representation directly or analogically or both into the game world ("Yes" or "No" and "Yes!" or "No!", probable). The third column shows the nature of the models which could be a process model or a functional or a technical architecture or all of them ("Yes" or "No" and "Yes!" or "No!", probable).

The solution we want to present to design serious games (see the next section) is entirely based on the concept of the functional separation of the design of playful aspects from serious aspects; instead, in the authors' proposal [24] the definition of pedagogical objective and instructional content to design intended learning outcome are designed separately, but these last are mixed with game attributes in order to design learning activities. Moreover, we found in the authors' proposal [12] that the definition of problems and progression phase requires the presence of pedagogical

TABLE 1: The grid of questions used during the classification.

Level one: works proposing serious game implementation			
Questions	Clues	Examples	Criteria
How to play the Serious Game?	Playing the Game requires knowledge of the teaching content.	Playing the Game proposed by the authors in [16–18] requires knowledge of the teaching content.	Endogenous
	Playing the Game is the reward after completing a serious activity where the game is used to teach content.	Playing the game ("SimCity-style building" [13]) is the reward after completing a serious activity (exploring the knowledge base) or the game ("Angry Birds" [19]) is used to teach content (kinematics and dynamics in physics field).	Exogenous
How teaching content is represented in the serious game?	The serious game clearly presents the teaching content.	The games presented in [16–18] clearly represent the teaching content, except the case of two games [17, 18] which incorporate symbolic representations (the reader is invited to consult the experience on the advantage of symbolic representations for learning [20]).	Direct Representation
	The serious game represents the teaching content with different elements from another domain.	As suggested by the authors in [12], to teach the immune system (the source domain) is like teaching the defence of the territory (the target domain); also, the authors in [7] mention that when fighting a dragon the children can learn fractions; more precisely the authors in [21] clearly specify the use of analogies in serious game design. However, in order to gain insight into the importance of using analogical representations in the learning process, the reader is invited to read our recent work on analogical representations [22].	Analogical Representation
Level two: model to design serious game accompanied or not by an implementation			
How does the model structure the serious game design?	The model proposes a set of **organized activities** that interact to achieve a result (often refers to a product)	The model proposed by the authors in [12, 13] presents a set of organized activities to conceive a serious game.	Process
	The model proposes an **implementation** that targets a single type of game that accepts the integration of a single content type.	As we pointed out in the Discussion, the game structure "Problems and Programmers" [16] can be used to integrate content from the manufacturing domain. Other examples can be found in Google Play Store at the web address referenced in [23] in which we can find two serious games that have the same structure and mechanics, where the first one aims to help children memorize the "Basic Music Notes" and the second one for memorizing the "Tifinagh Alphabet", which is the writing used by Berbers in North Africa.	Technical architecture
	The model proposes a set of **functionality** for designing serious games.	The model proposed by the authors in [24] presents a set of functionality for designing serious games.	Functional Architecture

and playful experts. Strong separation reduces constraints on the concern of both aspects during SG design. In order to achieve this goal, we will first separate the playful and serious aspects; then we propose functional decomposition of the serious aspects independently of the playful aspects; and then we will present how the two aspects interact with each other.

5. Toward an Architecture for Serious Games Design

5.1. The Architecture Description: Overview. All the works discussed so far lead to an important conclusion: education is a sensible field and SG design (if not well-defined) will not solve all of its challenges. However, researches and

TABLE 2: Synthesis which presents the classification of serious game and models addressing SG design discussed in state of the art according to the endogenous approach.

Works	Content representation into the game		Models proposed for serious game design		
			Process	Architecture	
	Directly	Analogical		Functional	Technical
An experimental card game for teaching software engineering processes [16].	Yes	No	No	No	Yes
PlayScrum - A Card Game to Learn the Scrum Agile Method [25].	Yes	No	No	No	Yes
A serious game for developing computational thinking and learning introductory computer programming [17].	Yes	No	No	No	Yes
A Platform Independent Game Technology Model for Model Driven Serious Games Development [26].	Yes	No	No	No	Yes
RAGE Architecture for Reusable Serious Gaming Technology Components [27].	Yes	No	No	No	Yes
A general architecture for the integration of educational videogames in standards-compliant virtual learning environments [28].	Yes	No	No	Yes	Yes
A New Methodology of Design and Development of serious game [29].	Yes	No	No	No	Yes
The design of an analogical encoding tool for game-based virtual learning environments [21].	Yes	Yes	No	No	Yes!
The six facets of serious game design [12].	Yes!	Yes	Yes	No	No
Knowledge Management Approach to Support a Serious Game Development [13]	Yes	Yes!	Yes	No	No
Games, motivation, and learning: A research and practice model [7].	Yes	No	No	Yes	No
A conceptual framework for serious games [24].	Yes	No	No	Yes	No
The design, play, and experience framework [30].	Yes	No	No	Yes	No

professional working in SG design agree that SG is composed of three main components: domain content, game, and learning theories. Each component requires several stakeholders or experts from different background/creativity. Therefore, the design of a SG with respect to expert concerns makes a SG process as hard as a complex system, or even more. However, due to the heterogeneousness fields of knowledge implied in the design of SG, communication may influence the collaboration between these experts. And, it is obvious that when the extent and the complexity of the domain content become important, each expert sees the game from a given angle and communicates with others using a specific language of his own field of expertise; therefore confusion in the achievement of the objectives is likely to happen and, hence, results may be dominated by either the learning aspect or the playful one. However, there is a necessity to develop a process model or architecture oriented application (a functional architecture) or technical one which is not

highly recommended. The architecture oriented application or functional architecture is the adequate base to start with. It provides a functional decomposing by defining clearly which functionalities are required to conceive a SG, and each functionality represents a container delimited by a clear edge, which naturally limits the intervention of all various stakeholders/experts most importantly it emphasizes intention and objectives by defining clearly how SG could be made (global vision), based on the right decisions and questions that could be drawn. The architecture should contain functionalities (most presented in literature and not exhaustive) like domain content and learning theories, pedagogy, learner profile, and game (Figure 4).

However, the domain content and learning theories, the pedagogy, and the learning profile have a common context representing serious sides which make them grouped into one entity called educational robot; on the other hand, all game aspects will be represented into one entity called game.

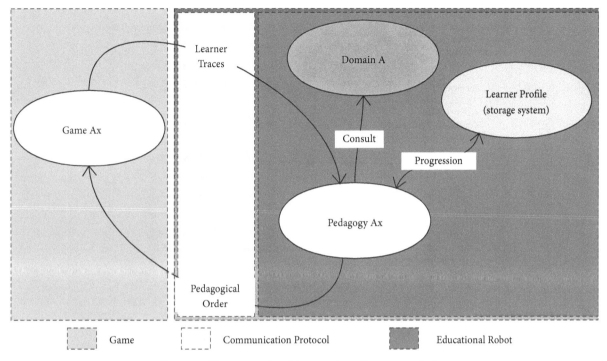

FIGURE 4: The proposed architecture for serious games design.

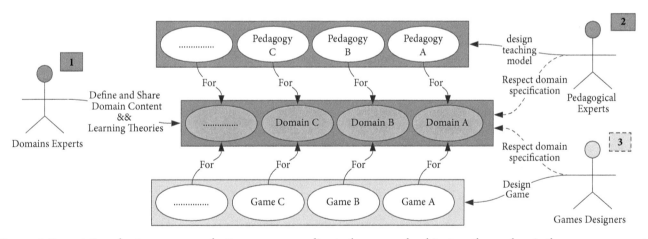

FIGURE 5: Presentation of serious games production process according to the proposed architecture; the numbers in the squares represent intervention order.

The educational robot and the game should exchange data or information; the game knows what the learner/player is doing, and by communicating relevant information (learner traces) to the educational robot, the last one knows what the player has done, and by analyzing learner's traces a decision is communicated back to the game (pedagogical order) to be applied such as repeating the same level with less or higher complexity, going to next level, and going back to previous level. The proposed architecture promotes the reusability, meaning functionality can be replaced or improved without or with miner influence on other functionalities, and provides guidance and influences the process by specifying how experts collaborate, Figure 5, as follows:

(i) The domain content and learning theories are the responsibility of domain expert, in which he defines domain content specifications (an example is presented in Figure 6), and then the domain content can be shared with pedagogical and playful experts.

(ii) The pedagogy is the responsibility of pedagogical expert. Based on the shared domain content specifications, he can draw a learning model which takes into consideration how to teach content in addition to all decisions required to help learners to overcome the faced difficulty to validate each part from domain content and to keep track of learner progression during several sessions, for example, by designing a

```
<?xml version="1.0" encoding="UTF-8"?>
<structure name="optional_name" id="unique_identifier" version="1.0.0" domain="Domain_Title">
  <level id="unique_identifier" desc="Chapter_Title">
    <layer id="unique_identifier" desc="Section_Title">
      <block id="unique_identifier" desc="Content_Title" >
        <cognitive>
          <remember complexity="1 ... 5" score="1 ... 20" type="conceptual;...;principle">
              Content Description.
          </remember>
          <understand complexity="1 ... 5" score="1 ... 20" type="conceptual;...;principle" >
              Content Description.
          </understand>
          <apply complexity="1 ... 5" score="1 ... 20" type="conceptual;...;principle">
              Content Description.
          </apply>
        </cognitive>
      </block>
      <block id="unique_identifier" desc="Content_Title">
        <cognitive>
          <analyze complexity=" 1 ... 5" score="1 ... 20" type="conceptual;...;principle" >
              Content Description.
          </analyze>
          <evaluate complexity="1 ... 5" score="1 ... 20" type="conceptual;...;principle">
              Content Description.
          </evaluate>
          <create complexity="1 ... 5" score="1 ... 20" type="conceptual;...;principle">
              Content Description.
          </create>
        </cognitive>
        <dependances>
          <level id="Level_Id" />
          <layer id="Layer_Id" />
          <block id="Bloc_Id" />
        </dependances>
      </block>
    </layer>
  </level>
  <level id="unique_identifier" desc="Chapter_Title" >
      ........................................
  </level>
</structure>
```

FIGURE 6: A proposal for domain content specifications, designed using XML (Extensible Markup Language) to represent domain content specifications, in which the hierarchy is structured by level close to chapter, layer to section, and block to subsection. The block is composed of a cognitive tag that contains the required learning function and its attributes in addition to the dependences tag which refers to the previous block, layer, or level; in the case that the block depends on a given layer or level, it is necessary to review all blocks that contain these dependences.

pedagogical expert system or a pedagogical agent [11], or see our example in Figure 7.

(iii) The game is the responsibility of playful expert or game designer. Based on the shared domain, he can design a game that respects content specifications.

5.2. The Architecture Description: Conceptual Level. In order to illustrate how SG game could be designed according to the proposed architecture, we propose an example (varying depending on the involved experts) of domain content specifications, Figure 6, and then we present how educational robot works and how it communicates with the game by using flowchart (a type of diagram that represents an algorithm), Figure 7.

The design of domain content specifications should make the domain content meaningful, understandable, and easy to read, in which the domain expert defines the structure of the content to be taught (e.g., the hierarchy) and then indicates

for each content the learning function that is required [46], the content type (e.g., conceptual, fact, procedural, and principle) [46], the complexity or difficulty according to a specific standard scale (e.g., from 1 to 5), dependences between domain content hierarchy components, and finally a min score (e.g., from 1 to 20). The domain content hierarchy represents how learner should progress into the domain content, the learning function and the content type underline how content should be learned, the min score represents the minimal score to validate the associated part of content, the complexity or difficulty highlights the associated part of content useful for content representation, and finally the dependences refer to prerequisite activities for a given activity in the domain content hierarchy (e.g., activity N depends on activities N-1, N-4,...). The term activity is used to represent a position in the domain content hierarchy. The design of game should respect the domain content specification such as the hierarchy (e.g., level design or game activity such as

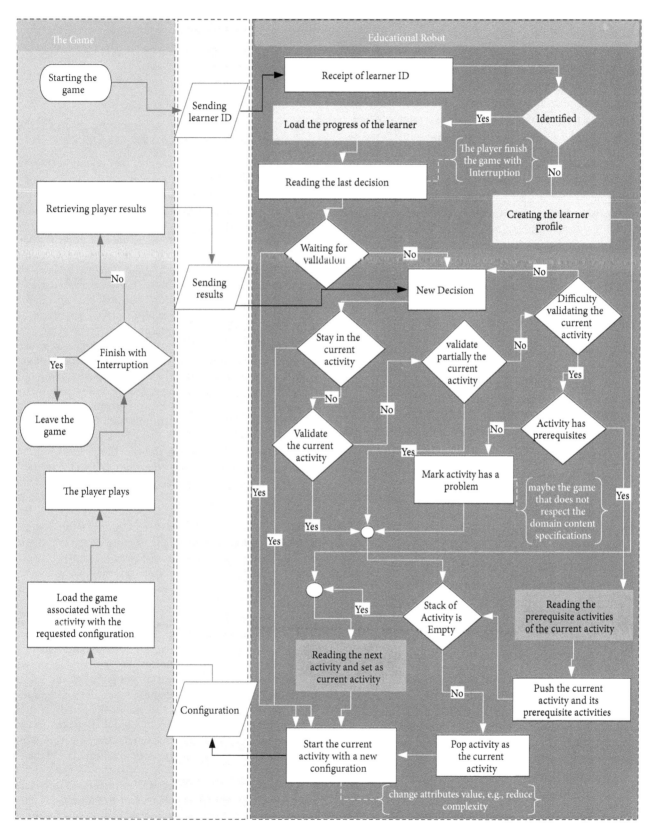

FIGURE 7: An example that shows implementation of the educational robot and how it communicates with the game.

mini-game), the learning function required and the content type (e.g., game mechanics), and the complexity (e.g., game adaptation).

5.3. The Architecture Description: Practical Level. The proposed architecture offers many advantages and benefits. In order to demonstrate that it is relevant and can handle real situations related to the serious game design, we proposed to use a case from two developed serious games which are "Problems and Programmers" [16] and "SimSE" [47] as a running example. Therefore, the objective relies on implementing these two games based on the proposed architecture. The two games which are described below share the same educational objective, teaching the software project management and the life cycle model, specially Waterfall. However, each game uses a different presentation and gameplay (game card and game based simulation). As pointed out in State of the Art, the "Problems and Programmers" [16] game represents a competitive game in which each student plays the role of a project manager, but the "SimSE" [16] game aims to teach project management in a single player mode. Moreover, the player drives the process by, among other things, hiring and firing developers, assigning tasks to them, monitoring their progress, and purchasing tools. At the end of the game, the player receives a score indicating how well they performed. Based on this description, we brief in the following points the main elements which describe how the domain content is represented in these two games.

At the start of SimSE game, the player reviews the resources and assesses what they have to work with. All resources have predefined values which constitute the current context or configuration. The resources are listed below:

(i) The project is characterized by description, budget, money spent, allotted time, and time used.

(ii) The customer is characterized only by name.

(iii) The purchased tools are characterized by name and cost and organized by categorizing their use.

(iv) The employee is characterized by name, energy, mood, pay rate, and expertise's years in requirement, design, coding, and testing.

In the first step of "Problems and Programmers" game, the player starts with picking up a card from the project deck and then five cards from the main deck which contains cards representing programmers, concepts, and problems. Then, in each turn the player is required to take two cards from the documentation deck which contains code cards. All the picked cards and those in the decks have predefined values which constitute the current context or configuration. The card types are listed below:

(i) The project card is characterized by name, budget, quality, length, and complexity.

(ii) The problem card is characterized by name, condition, and description to show consequences.

(iii) The concept card is characterized by name and description showing the effect, decisions which a player can make.

TABLE 3: Example of three mission configurations.

Difficulty level	Time	Quality	Budget	Length
Simple	Max	Min	Max	Min
Intermediate	[Min, Max]	[Min, Max]	[Min, Max]	[Min, Max]
Difficult	Min	Max	Min	Max

(iv) The programmer card is characterized by name, short expertise description, salary, personality, and skill.

The architecture underlines the fact that domain expert will be the first to design the teaching content. We use two existing serious games as a running example; we will provide generalized example of the structure of teaching subject (project manager), in which the project to be managed will be represented by a mission structured by several phases following the Waterfall model. Each mission is characterized by several constraints (time, quality, budget, etc.) and it requires managing several resources represented by collaborators. The collaborators also are characterized by expertise regarding each phase, degree of collaboration, and other factors. Each phase contains obstacles referring to the problems that may occur. Note that the subject represents an atomic entity, meaning that we cannot teach an element (e.g., that collaborators chose) without its relations with other elements (e.g., project). As presented by those two games, all elements have predefined values, which represent the current context or configuration based on which the player/learner make decisions/actions.

The atomic aspect necessitates that the learner progresses from a simple configuration to a more difficult one. Tables 3, 4, and 5 represent our example of domain design, which shows some basic configurations of the mission, collaborators, and obstacles. Each characteristic could accept a value within a [Min, Max]. Figure 8 represents a basic design of learner progression from simple to more difficult configuration, by using combination from Tables 3, 4, and 5.

By applying the architecture on the two games, we separate the design of the serious aspect, which is in our case the educational robot, from the playful aspect (the game). The educational robot uses the hierarchical domain content design (Figure 8) to identify how learner should progress from a simple configuration to a complicated one. The educational robot establishes the communication with the game as follows: (1) Select a configuration and ask the game to apply it. (2) The game applies the configuration and sends back the result at the end of the activity. (3) The educational robot checks the result and then makes decision (selecting the next configuration or retrying the previous one) as shown in Figure 9(a). This process is repeated until the end of the content hierarchy.

The same domain content will be integrated into different games: card game "Problems and Programmers", game based simulation "SimSE", and strategy games that share the same concept of domain design (analogical representation) as illustrated in Figure 9(b). In this running example of applying the proposed architecture in two existing serious games, the implementation was backward contrarily to the

TABLE 4: Example of collaborators configurations.

Quality level	Name	Collaboration degree	Consumption	Power	Productivity			
					Phase a	Phase b	Phase c	Phase d
Low	Coll 1	Min	Min	Min	Min	Min	Min	Min
Intermediate	Coll 2	[Min, Max]	[Min, Max]	[Min, Max]	[Min, Max]	[Min, Max]	[Min, Max]	[Min, Max]
Hot	Coll 3	Max	Max	Max	Max	Max	Max	Max

```xml
<?xml version="1.0" encoding="UTF-8"?>
<structure name="optional_name" id="1" version="1.0.0" domain="Project_Manager">
  <level id="1" desc="Chapter_Title">
    <layer id="1" desc="overall educational objective">
      <block id="1" desc="educational objective" complexityLevel ="simple" "Validationscore="" >
          Difficulty level simple mission, obstacles
                          and Quality level low collaborators
      </block>
        <block id="2" desc="educational objective" complexityLevel ="intermediate" " Validationscore="" >
          Difficulty level intermediate mission, obstacles
                          and Quality level intermediate collaborators

          <dependances>
                <block id="1" />
          </dependances>
        </block>
        <block id="3" desc="educational objective" complexityLevel ="complexes" " Validationscore="" >
          Difficulty level complexes mission, obstacles
                     and Quality level hot collaborators

          <dependances>
                <block id="2" />
          </dependances>
        </block>
      </layer>
    </level>
</structure>
```

FIGURE 8: An example of the hierarchical domain content design.

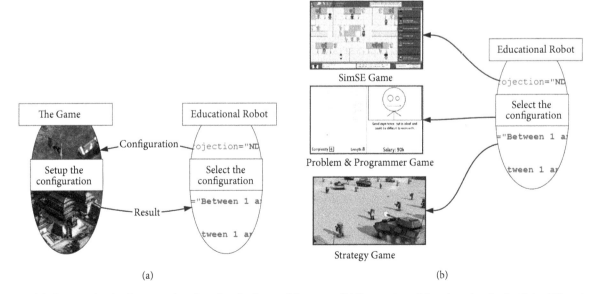

(a) (b)

FIGURE 9: (a) Communication between the educational robot and the game. (b) Integration of the educational robot into different games.

TABLE 5: Example of problems/obstacles configurations.

Difficulty level	Number	Complexity Phase a	Complexity Phase b	Complexity Phase c	Complexity Phase d
Simple	Min	Min	Min	Min	Min
Intermediate	[Min, Max]	[Min, Max]	[Min, Max]	[Min, Max]	[Min, Max]
Difficult	Max	Max	Max	Max	Max

architecture process. We started by identifying the elements which constitute the domain content and then we designed an abstracted domain content that was encapsulated in the educational robot. This robot mapped successfully with the two games. This success demonstrated the feasibility of the proposed architecture. Based on the reusability aspect of this architecture, the educational robot can be also integrated into other games respecting the elements of the abstracted domain content. The proposed architecture is designed to work according to the presented process, Figure 5, in which the domain expert designs domain content and shares it (in public repository). The pedagogical expert designs a teaching model for the shared domain content encapsulated into an educational robot, which can be implemented as an API (Application Programming Interface) or as a Web Service. The playful experts design a game for the shared domain content and integrated educational robot. The main advantages can be briefed in the following points:

(i) modifying decisions of the educational robot without affecting the game;

(ii) responding to new educational robot updates by simple game improvements;

(iii) reusability of the educational robot with new designed games.

6. Conclusion

The presented taxonomy represents a guide to new SG researchers; they will be capable of analyzing state of the art of proposed SG design models, overcoming the lack of standards in classifying these models. The other advantage realized by the proposed taxonomy is helping SG designers to choose the adequate category/model according to their perspective (endogenous/exogenous). Also, the proposed architecture indicates how stockholders collaborate and how SG game is made, allowing domain experts to focus on defining their knowledge without worrying about the playful aspects, and the game designers to focus on building the game without having deep knowledge of the domain content and more importantly the pedagogical aspects. Such architecture presents the following benefits:

(i) Separation during the SG design reduces the dependences and the overlaps of the various expert's concerns and encapsulates expert's intellectual production in a computer component such as an expert system, which replaces the intervention of the human expert. When we need specific domain knowledge, we use the expert's product without its presence.

(ii) Collaboration during the use with less constraints reduces the effort and integration time of game and serious expert's production.

(iii) Reuse of both serious and game expert's production develops several serious games for one domain content, allowing the change or the improvement of a serious component with less changes in the game component and vice versa.

All these features (separation, collaboration, and reuse) lead to an open market of SG based on the reusability without implying expert's presence "commercial off-the-shelf" [48, 49]. In the open market places, in which we can find that SG components encapsulate expert's knowledge specific to the learning theories, the domain content, and the game, the SG is designed as separate components and in each one specific concern is encapsulated (expertise production), so that the SG can be produced by combining those components. In future work we will design a simple serious game that presents implementation of the proposed architecture.

References

[1] J. M. Allen, S. Wright, N. Cranston, J. Watson, K. Beswick, and I. Hay, "Raising levels of school student engagement and retention in rural, regional and disadvantaged areas: is it a lost cause?" *International Journal of Inclusive Education*, pp. 1–17, 2017.

[2] F. M. Newmann, *Student engagement and achievement in American secondary schools*, vol. 1234, Amsterdam Avenue, New York, NY, USA, Teachers College Press, 1992.

[3] J. A. Fredricks, P. C. Blumenfeld, and A. H. Paris, "School engagement: Potential of the concept, state of the evidence," *Review of Educational Research*, vol. 74, no. 1, pp. 59–109, 2004.

[4] D. J. Shernoff, M. Csikszentmihalyi, B. Schneider, and E. S. Shernoff, "Student engagement in high school classrooms from the perspective of flow theory," *Applications of Flow in Human Development and Education: The Collected Works of Mihaly Csikszentmihalyi*, pp. 475–494, 2014.

[5] D. R. Michael and S. L. Chen, *Serious games: Games that educate, train, and inform*, Muska & Lipman/Premier-Trade, 2005.

[6] I. Granic, A. Lobel, and R. C. M. E. Engels, "The benefits of playing video games," *American Psychologist*, vol. 69, no. 1, pp. 66–78, 2014.

[7] R. Garris, R. Ahlers, and J. E. Driskell, "Games, motivation, and learning: a research and practice model," *Simulation & Gaming*, vol. 33, no. 4, pp. 441–467, 2002.

[8] B. Bergeron, *Developing serious games*, game development series, 2006.

[9] M. Zyda, "From visual simulation to virtual reality to games," *The Computer Journal*, vol. 38, no. 9, pp. 25–32, 2005.

[10] T. Marsh, "Serious games continuum: Between games for purpose and experiential environments for purpose," *Entertainment Computing*, vol. 2, no. 2, pp. 61–68, 2011.

[11] D. A. Lieberman, "What can we learn from playing interactive games?" *Playing Video Games: Motives, Responses, and Consequences*, pp. 447–469, 2006.

[12] B. Marne, B. Huynh-Kim-Bang, and J.-M. Labat, "Articuler motivation et apprentissage grâce aux facettes du jeu sérieux," in *EIAH 2011-Conférence sur les Environnements Informatiques pour l'Apprentissage Humain*, pp. 69–80, Editions de l'UMONS, Mons, 2011.

[13] B. C. Ibáñez, V. Boudier, and J.-M. Labat, "Knowledge management approach to support a serious game development," in *Proceedings of the 9th IEEE International Conference on Advanced Learning Technologies, ICALT '09*, pp. 420–422, Latvia, July 2009.

[14] J. Kirkley, S. Kirkley, and J. Heneghan, "Building bridges between serious game design and instructional design," *The design and use of simulation computer games in education*, vol. 2, p. 74, 2007.

[15] S. De Freitas and S. Jarvis, *A framework for developing serious games to meet learner needs*, 2006.

[16] A. Baker, E. O. Navarro, and A. Van Der Hoek, "An experimental card game for teaching software engineering processes," *The Journal of Systems and Software*, vol. 75, no. 1-2, pp. 3–16, 2005.

[17] C. Kazimoglu, M. Kiernan, L. Bacon, and L. Mackinnon, "A Serious Game for Developing Computational Thinking and Learning Introductory Computer Programming," *Procedia - Social and Behavioral Sciences*, vol. 47, pp. 1991–1999, 2012.

[18] M. Muratet, P. Torguet, J.-P. Jessel, and F. Viallet, "Towards a serious game to help students learn computer programming," *International Journal of Computer Games Technology*, vol. 2009, Article ID 470590, 12 pages, 2009.

[19] M. Rodrigues and P. Simeão Carvalho, "Teaching physics with angry birds: Exploring the kinematics and dynamics of the game," *Physics Education*, vol. 48, no. 4, pp. 431–437, 2013.

[20] V. M. Sloutsky, J. A. Kaminski, and A. F. Heckler, "The advantage of simple symbols for learning and transfer," *Psychonomic Bulletin & Review*, vol. 12, no. 3, pp. 508–513, 2005.

[21] D. Williams, Y. Ma, S. Feist, C. E. Richard, and L. Prejean, "The design of an analogical encoding tool for game-based virtual learning environments," *British Journal of Educational Technology*, vol. 38, no. 3, pp. 429–437, 2007.

[22] W. Mestadi, K. Nafil, R. Touahni, and R. Messoussi, "Knowledge Representation by Analogy for the Design of Learning and Assessment Strategies," *International Journal of Modern Education and Computer Science*, vol. 9, no. 6, pp. 9–16, 2017.

[23] https://play.google.com/store/apps/developer?id=Maxware.

[24] A. Yusoff, R. Crowder, L. Gilbert, and G. Wills, "A conceptual framework for serious games," in *Proceedings of the 9th IEEE International Conference on Advanced Learning Technologies, ICALT '09*, pp. 21–23, Latvia, July 2009.

[25] J. M. Fernandes and S. M. Sousa, "PlayScrum - A card game to learn the scrum agile method," in *Proceedings of the 2nd IEEE International Conference on Games and Virtual Worlds for Serious Applications, VS-GAMES 2010*, pp. 52–59, Portugal, March 2010.

[26] S. Tang, M. Hanneghan, and C. Carter, "A platform independent game technology model for model driven serious games development," *Electronic Journal of E-Learning*, vol. 11, no. 1, pp. 61–79, 2013.

[27] W. Van Der Vegt, W. Westera, E. Nyamsuren, A. Georgiev, and I. M. Ortiz, "RAGE Architecture for Reusable Serious Gaming Technology Components," *International Journal of Computer Games Technology*, vol. 2016, 3 pages, 2016.

[28] Á. Del Blanco, J. Torrente, P. Moreno-Ger, and B. Fernández-Manjón, "A general architecture for the integration of educational videogames in standards-compliant Virtual Learning Environments," in *Proceedings of the 9th IEEE International Conference on Advanced Learning Technologies, ICALT '09*, pp. 53–55, Latvia, July 2009.

[29] A. F. S. Barbosa, P. N. M. Pereira, J. A. F. F. Dias, and F. G. M. Silva, "A New Methodology of Design and Development of Serious Games," *International Journal of Computer Games Technology*, vol. 2014, Article ID 817167, 8 pages, 2014.

[30] B. M. Winn, "The design, play, and experience framework," in *Handbook of research on effective electronic gaming in education*, pp. 1010–1024, IGI Global, 2009.

[31] P. Rooney, "A theoretical framework for serious game design: exploring pedagogy, play and fidelity and their implications for the design process," *International Journal of Game-Based Learning*, vol. 2, no. 4, pp. 41–60, 2012.

[32] S. Kelle, R. Klemke, and M. Specht, "Design patterns for learning games," *International Journal of Technology Enhanced Learning*, vol. 3, no. 6, pp. 555–569, 2011.

[33] R. Hunicke, M. Leblanc, and R. Zubek, "MDA: A formal approach to game design and game research," in *Proceedings of the 19th National Conference on Artificial Intelligence*, pp. 1–5, USA, July 2004.

[34] N. Suttie, S. Louchart, T. Lim et al., "In persuit of a 'serious games mechanics' : A theoretical framework to analyse relationships between 'game' and 'pedagogical aspects' of serious games," in *Proceedings of the 4th International Conference on Games and Virtual Worlds for Serious Applications, VS-GAMES 2012*, pp. 314–315, Italy, October 2012.

[35] B. Marne, J. Wisdom, B. Huynh-Kim-Bang, and J. Labat, "The Six Facets of Serious Game Design: A Methodology Enhanced by Our Design Pattern Library," in *21st Century Learning for 21st Century Skills*, vol. 7563 of *Lecture Notes in Computer Science*, pp. 208–221, Springer Berlin Heidelberg, Berlin, Heidelberg, 2012.

[36] J. Sherry and A. Pacheco, "Matching computer game genres to educational outcomes," *Electronic Journal of Communication*, vol. 16, no. 1, p. 2, 2006.

[37] https://scratch.mit.edu.

[38] https://code.org/learn.

[39] L. Bennis and S. Benhlima, "Comparative study of the process model of Serious Game Design through the generic model DICE," in *Proceedings of the 1st International Conference on Intelligent Systems and Computer Vision, ISCV 2015*, Morocco, March 2015.

[40] M. Mancona Kandé and A. Strohmeier, "On the role of multi-dimensional separation of concerns in software architecture," in *OOPSLA Workshop on Advanced Separation of Concerns in Object-Oriented Systems*, Minneapolis, Minnesota, USA, 2000.

[41] L. Bass, P. Clements, and R. Kazman, *Software Architecture in Practice*, Addison-Wesley Professional, 2003.

[42] I. Jacobsson, M. Christerson, P. Jonsson et al., *Object-Oriented Software Engineering*, 1992.

[43] D. Djaouti, J. Alvarez, and J. Jessel, "Classifying Serious Games," in *Handbook of Research on Improving Learning and Motivation through Educational Games*, Advances in Game-Based Learning, pp. 118–136, IGI Global, 2011.

[44] M. P. J. Habgood, S. E. Ainsworth, and S. Benford, "Endogenous fantasy and learning in digital games," *Simulation & Gaming*, vol. 36, no. 4, pp. 483–498, 2005.

[45] C. Fabricatore, *Learning and videogames: An unexploited synergy*, 2000.

[46] L. W. Anderson, D. R. Krathwohl, P. W. Airasian et al., *A taxonomy for learning, teaching, and assessing: A revision of Blooms taxonomy of educational objectives , abridged edition*, Longman, White Plains, NY, 2001.

[47] E. O. Navarro and A. Van Der Hoek, "Software process modeling for an educational software engineering simulation game," *Software Process: Improvement and Practice*, vol. 10, no. 3, pp. 311–325, 2005.

[48] E. Folmer, "Component based game development—A solution to escalating costs and expanding deadlines?" in *Component-Based Software Engineering*, H. W. Schmidt, I. Crnkovic, G. T. Heineman, and J. A. Stafford, Eds., vol. 4608 of *Lecture Notes in Computer Science*, pp. 66–73, Springer Berlin Heidelberg, Berlin, Germany, 2007.

[49] T. Susi, M. Johannesson, and P. Backlund, *Serious games: An overview*, 2007.

## 13

The Interplay between Real Money Trade and Narrative Structure in Massively Multiplayer Online Role-Playing Games

Byungchul Park and Duk Hee Lee

School of Business and Technology Management, College of Business, Korea Advanced Institute of Science and Technology (KAIST), Daejeon, Republic of Korea

Correspondence should be addressed to Duk Hee Lee; dukheelee@kaist.ac.kr

Academic Editor: Michael J. Katchabaw

A narrative structure is one of the main components to constitute the genre of Massively Multiplayer Online Role-Playing Games (MMORPGs). Meanwhile Real Money Trade (RMT) enables a player to adjust an ex post level of challenge by skipping the narrative structure of a game. However, RMT may concurrently disturb a player who enjoys game following the narrative structure hierarchically. In pursuance of developing the knowledge about the relationship between RMT and the usage of MMORPG, we investigate the role of the strictness of predetermined narrative structure. We present the dual structure of societies to describe a player that arbitrarily decides to reside in a virtual society. Then we adopt the social nominalism to explain how individual motif of playing a game is expanded to the nature of game. Finally, we argue that a game with weakly predetermined narrative structure is more positively associated with RMT volume, since these games arouse a player's sentiment of fun by relying more on their socially oriented motivation. With empirical evidence from the Korean MMORPGs market, we proved the hypothesis.

1. Introduction

The phenomenon of Real Money Trade (RMT) has appeared in Massively Multiplayer Online Role-Playing Game (MMORPG). RMT is an action where digital in-game goods (e.g., items and virtual currency) are traded with real money by player to player. It has been studied since Castronova [1] initially advocated virtual economies. Since the phenomenon of RMT itself is externally identical for many games, existing RMT research studied the relationship between playing time and RMT volume, disregarding the effect of the narrative structure [2, 3]. However, narrative structures of each game make motivations of RMT diverse and therefore considering narrative structures is crucial to include in the analysis. Hence the purpose of this study is to present the role of narrative structure in the association between playing time of MMORPGs and RMT volume.

We studied MMORPG based on the concept of "flow" [4] and the "puzzle of puzzles model" [1] and the twofold structure between reality and virtual reality. Then we expand individual motives for RMT into a game's heterogeneous properties according to its narrative structure. When players want to live in an MMORPG with strictly predetermined narrative structure, they want to enjoy the preorganized storyline of the game, while players who choose a game with weakly predetermined narrative structures do not. Therefore, RMT volume is less associated with the total usage of the game in the case of MMORPG with strictly predetermined narrative structure because RMT intrinsically makes players skip the preliminarily constructed steps and hindered in enjoying the hierarchical achievement structure. We demonstrate empirical evidence from the Korean MMORPGs market to verify the influence of narrative structure on the relationships between RMT and the usage of MMORPG. We gather the RMT volume and total time usage data for four years from the PC-Bang user database and collect narrative scores based on one of the representative online MMORPG user communities. Consequently, we prove the hypothesis that there is a different relationship for RMT with the games which are observed based on the strength of game's narrative structure.

The remainder of this article is organized as follows. The next section introduces a framework to understand MMORPGs. The third section analyzes the importance of the narrative structure in an MMORPG unlike other game genres which drives the dual structure of societies. The fourth section introduces the theory about personal motivations in RMT and deduces virtual reality based on the narrative structure. For demonstration, we adopt the viewpoint of social nominalism that has idiosyncratic properties including arbitrariness of individual decision on being oneself in the certain society. In the fifth section, we demonstrate empirical evidence from the Korean MMORPG market using the Korean PC-Bang database. The last section summarizes the research, states the overall conclusion, and discusses the limitations of this study.

2. Theoretical Background

MMORPG is similar to other genres such as First-Person Shooter (FPS) games like "Call of Duty," Real Time Strategy (RTS) games like Warcraft, or Multiplayer Online Battle Arena (MOBA) games like "League of Legends" in that several different players join each other online. However, an MMORPG is different from the rest in that a permanent avatar represents a player. In other words, players find "fun" from short competitions in other genres, but in MMORPG, a player is entertained by living another life through an avatar in virtual reality [5]. To create similar kind of fun in MMORPG, games of other genres have adopted a ladder system or sale of items for ornamental purposes, but these items are merely external factors that cannot fundamentally affect the results of the games. For example, League of Legends sells a variety of "skins" which decorates the characters in the game; if these "skins" affect the result of the "battle arena," the game would be decided by money and not by skill, which would hinder the pleasure originated from the game.

2.1. Flow Channel. MMORPG has distinct characteristics as compared with other genres, especially in terms of items. Collecting items to decorate and strengthen an avatar's power is an important source of fun by progression and becomes a player's primary motivation. Researchers [6, 7] found the source of fun by progression from positive psychology and refer to the concept of "flow" of Csikszentmihalyi [4]. Csikszentmihalyi [4] defined flow as the status of complete concentration with multidimensional joy and satisfaction. When gamers develop skills and execute activities, they feel anxious if the challenge is larger than their skills, or they feel boredom if the challenge is too easy [4]. Thus an equilibrium where continuing balance between skill and challenge existed is the flow channel, and when a gamer plays games within this flow they feel enjoyment and joy with exhilaration. Consequently, avatar's skills and items are supposed to accumulate, and corresponding challenges are supposed to be provided so that the gamer is intrinsically motivated.

2.2. The Puzzle of Puzzles Model. The Puzzle of Puzzle Model devised by Castronova [1] is the first economic approach to

virtual reality. The model is as follows:

$$S = \alpha R - \beta (C - \Omega)^2. \tag{1}$$

Let S be emotional satisfaction of player, let R be available reward, let C be actual challenge level, let Ω be ideal challenge level of the player, and let α and β be parameters. From (1), it is evident that a player's emotional satisfaction increases as the available reward increases and the separation distance between ideal challenge level and the actual challenge level increases. If actual challenge level is assumed to be dependent on the player's skill, the player reaches the highest emotional satisfaction at ideal challenge level; thus the point is equivalent to the flow channel [3]. MMORPGs continuously repeat a challenging puzzle with the proper difficulty level for the player to be satisfied and rewarded so that the intrinsic motivation of the game can be sustained. These steps begin with a tutorial where a player develops her skills (player versus avatar); after she is familiarized (united as one), the avatar develops its skills to solve objects to face virtual reality (avatar versus in-game environment); in some games it leads to an avatar versus avatar challenge at the end. These puzzles are supposed to contain a narrative structure and are one of the factors by which MMORPGs keep the players on the flow channel.

3. Narrative Structure of MMORPGs

MMORPG is a game genre that consists of avatars, opponents, maps, items and money, and a narrative structure [8]. Among these components the narrative structure, the literary concept of the structural composition between hierarchical events that follows a plot [9], makes a distinction between MMORPG and the other genres. A certain fiction can only be presented to or interact with readers who follow the intention of the author's design. Since the narrative structure originates in the literature, there has been a conflict between narratology and ludology, preceded by Huizinga [10] about the possibility of understanding game. The former argues that traditional Aristotelian dramatic experience consists of characters, background, and events analyze the game, while ludology places emphasis on the simulation. For example, an old puzzle genre such as Tetris does not have a story, but rules, results, and the interactive experience that matters the most cannot be explained by narratology [11]. However, in the perspective of recent game studies, Juul [11] argues that a game cannot exist where the game stresses on just a current simulation, denying the roll and possibility of narrative in the game. For example, if an RPG is viewed as successive puzzles, narrative can be placed according to Csikszentmihalyi's flow channel in the interaction called puzzle. Therefore, we define the concept of narrative structure as a hierarchical storyline mainly composed of compulsory quests that logically differ from game to game.

Several genres other than RPG or MMORPG, including adventure, RTS, MOBA, and shooting, are compelled to contain a narrative structure. A representative example would be World of Warcraft (WoW), which was once most popular MMORPG in the world. The WoW was based on an RTS game, Warcraft series, which was first released in 1994 and recently released again in 2003. The Warcraft, a kind of RTS, contains a fantasy-based background, but a player does not need to know about narrative structure to play an RTS. In other words, the Warcraft contains storyline and, however, does not create any cyberspace. On the other hand, MMORPG WoW inherited the background of the Warcraft to the virtual world [12]. In WoW, players chose character growth through the "quest" system [13], which forces them to follow the storyline strictly to proceed with the game. The degree of importance for players to follow storyline varies depending on characteristics of MMORPGs. For instance, Lineage, a Korean MMORPG, is less dependent on narrative structures and thus a novice can proceed in the game by merely leveling by hunting as the quests are optional in the game. Meanwhile such "blood pledges" of Lineage are able to obtain a kind of sovereignty by siege warfare in game [14]. An operator of the game adheres to a laissez-faire policy about their hierarchical governance structure to maximize random, accidental, or happenchance story. For example, in Lineage 2, a coalition of blood pledges began a liberation war and rioted against one blood pledge that had monopolized politico-economic power of the entire server and exerted its authority and reign on potentates [15]. The game operator NC Soft did not intervene for over four years of the liberation war, while it maximized the voluntary configuration of conflict [16].

A game's narrative structure is diversified according to genre of the game as discussed in advance. Overall a game that is overly dependent on narrative tends to restrict a players' freedom to keep them stay on the flow channel that maximizes a player's emotional satisfaction. The restriction is not an exogenous condition to overcome, as is generally regarded in the contemporary economic theory, but rather a source of utility. An individual makes a payment to obtain more freedom from restriction in the general case; on the other hand, she pays a price to be confined in a puzzle-like game [1]. That is, being voluntarily confined is compensated with a new experience that is only possible in a virtual reality. A player can only act within a controlled space, with controlled skill, and with controlled methods that are designed to be enjoyable by the developers of the game. Thus the narrative structure is able to create many different types of games. In an MMORPG, a player as a consumer can choose the virtual reality she wants to live in that is different from thrown projections of real life [17]. Consequently a developer's goal is to maximize a player's subjective freedom by creating narrative as a nature that imposes restrictions on a player's objective freedom. A game developer needs to understand the dual structure of societies to successfully implement this strategy.

While playing a game, certain type of players may acquire more freedom and is less dependent on the narrative structure. That kind of game consumers or players could prefer a game that allows more objective freedom since even games that are less dependent on narrative structures can provide different types of rewards that other games dependent on narrative structure can provide. This could be conceptualized as an extrinsic reward. One of the reasons for the success of

Lineage, one of the popular Korean MMORPG, is that the game can provide new forms of enjoyment even after the avatar has reached the maximum level at which the player is familiarized with all the skills. Even after all of the quests are completed, instead of letting players reach the tip of flow channel and feeling burdensome, Lineage provides another type of enjoyment by siege warfare between blood pledges [18]. Steinkuehler [14] described that the narrative and history of Lineage could be created by within- and between-pledge activities.

Yee [19] proposes three categories for motivations for playing online games: achievement, social, and immersion with ten elements. It is natural that each component has weak correlations with the other and no motivation is more important than the others [19], and eventually all factors play roles for any game. However, under the assumption that achievement is the general motivation of playing any games [7], a combination of achievement and immersion is mainly the motivations behind playing games more dependent on narrative structures.

Niman [7] argued that fiery from triumph at the end of an intrinsic reward [20] and Csikszentmihalyi's flow channel is a necessary condition and that the sufficient condition is an incorporation of extrinsic rewards inspired by self-esteem from comparison to others. Therefore, a combination of social factors such as achievement, socializing, relationship, and teamwork can be the motivation for playing a game that is less dependent on narrative structure. Thus enjoyment can be provided to a player through the extrinsic reward from forming communities, mutual competition, and pride from comparison. Lineage's blood pledge and siege warfare system can help a hardcore user who can be bored to take one more step at the end of the intrinsic reward.

4. RMT, Narrative Structure, and Playing MMORPGs

Since RMT plays the role of a bridge between reality and virtual reality, affecting motives and rewards of playing game, there have been attempts to explain this phenomenon by not only game researchers, but also social scientists studying e-business and policy [21–24]. Though the marginal cost of producing the virtual product is almost zero, the products are different from nonrival information goods as that they are not instantaneously reproduced [25]. At this moment, since MMORPG is the online platform in which the most available data were accumulated, most researches deduced results from MMOPRG data. Meanwhile, more users need to enjoy a game for an MMORPG's virtual reality to be massive. Therefore, the number of users is important for sustainability of MMORPG and for developers who earn profit from the users, as profits of an online game come from its playing time [26]. Thus, like the existing literature, we focus on the effect of RMT on game usage.

4.1. RMT in MMORPGs. Simpson [27] introduced the MMORPG Ultima Online as a closed economy and suggested that the entire economy consisting of NPC, players, and resources can collapse from inflation caused by overproduction. Nowadays, economic aspect became crucial factor to manage the virtual world so thus patches or updates have been dedicated to manage economic problems as well as traditional gameplay issues [28]. In this context, RMT can be seen as international trade between the real and the virtual economy; that is, the real economy affects the virtual economy thorough RMT as a foreign economy influences the domestic economy. On the other hand, RMT also seems to disclose contradictory natures of game consumption. A game as amusement is obviously a field of leisure in labor economics. Thus, voluntarily spending time on MMORPG must be an action of generating more utility. However, Kelly [29] emphasized that most games contain costs and boredom from repetitive activities for skillfulness though almost time spent playing an MMORPG can be rewarded as enjoyment. Thus, RMT could directly affect the enjoyment of a player. A player can utilize RMT to actively change their enjoyment based on their motivation for game usage and can be passively affected from other player's RMT. This is the motivation for analyzing the effect of RMT on MMORPG depending on the narrative structure. Since RMT is a factor that is external to the game, we should first look into the internal factors that determine the marketability of an MMORPG. Since MMO-RPG is an RPG before being an MMO, the game's narrative structure is the internal factor that produces entertainment. Thus, we need to consider each game's narrative structure to understand the influence of RMT on MMORPGs.

Some of the existing literature argues a negative relationship between RMT and MMORPG usage. Castronova [30] analyzed the negative externalities of an RMT using traditional economic supply-and-demand analysis. From this foundation, several strands of the literature on human-computer interaction presented a method to detect a player who plays "gold farming," a behavior to produce in-game items and currency for real-world profit, or who is an automatic program called a bot [31–33]. Other studies show that RMT has a positive effect on game usage. Huhh [34] and Huhh [2] showed with a model that RMT can lower the minimum number of players required to meet the critical mass that ensures the sustainability of the MMORPG because MMORPG has a network effect. This result contradicts Castronova [30], arguing that utilizing RMT enables game publishers to differentiate service price for consumers to increase profitability. Additionally, gold farming only appears in popular games, thus signaling that the game is well-made.

The existing literature about RMT and MMORPG usage has analyzed games in various perspectives; however, the studies have ignored the degree of dependency on narrative structure of each game. Additionally, most literature discussed the issue using data from only one specific game. Hence, we tried to reveal that narrative structure affects the relationship between RMT volume and MORPG usage with the data from multiple games.

Just as practical considerations affect the real economy, the virtual society of each MMORPG could be affected by narrative structures as an institution that restricts the objective freedom of players. Therefore, we should analyze

motives at the microlevel of RMT, taking into consideration the heterogeneous narrative structure of MMORPGs.

4.2. Motives of RMT. Spending time on a game as leisure provides utility, while utility is also generated by decreasing grinding time as a cost since time is a typical economic resource. Because the efficient execution of quests suggested by the MMORPG produces utility, enjoyment occurs when a player saves time [7]. Extant literature investigates personal motivation in RMT to understand different desires. Lehdonvirta [35] theoretically related the playing motivation model by Yee [36] to the motivation behind RMT and argued for the validity of the framework through individual case studies on four types of MMORPG. Lehdonvirta [35] found that achievement and immersion oriented players generally have negative perspectives on RMT as compared to socially oriented players. However Lehdonvirta [35] also showed that if the structure of hierarchical achievement in a game is not clear, an achievement oriented player does not have a negative perspective on RMT. To understand this, the puzzle of puzzles framework can be used.

Starodoumov [3] described the case where a player reaches their ideal quest by adopting RMT to the puzzle of the puzzles model [1] with Figure 2. This means that players with and without the sufficient skills for a quest can achieve higher satisfaction by adjusting the difficulty of the quests using RMT. In other words, if the hierarchical achievement structure represented by the narrative structure does not exist, a player can proceed in a game by searching for their ideal challenge level using RMT and subsequently reaching the state of "flow."

4.3. Effects of RMT Depending upon Narrative Structure. Therefore, the different effects of RMT based on the narrative structure of a game can be understood by developing a player's motivation on RMT. For the study, we need the underlying assumption that social oriented players are the majority in the game that produces enjoyment from social functions and that achievement oriented players that have a negative perspective on RMT are the majority in the game that produces enjoyment from a hierarchical achievement structure. For this assumption we have to cognize the virtual societies that each MMORPG constructs from the viewpoint of methodological individualism. As described in Figure 1, virtual reality is clearly different from reality where projected individuals exist. Individuals of the virtual society voluntarily decide to exist in the virtual society. Therefore, unlike the ontology of the real-world society, where there is sharpening conflict between the stance of social nominalism and social realism, the ontology of virtual reality clearly supports social nominalism.

MMORPGs need avatars of each player to form a virtual society, but the game's essential characteristics and the strength of narrative structure are predetermined by game developers, as sovereignty transferred leviathan [37]. Thus a virtual society is formed through "time-reversed social contract." Before individuals (players) who transferred sovereignty to leviathan exist, leviathan (developer) or the

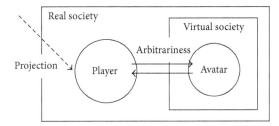

FIGURE 1: The dual structure of societies.

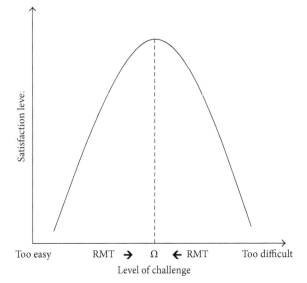

FIGURE 2: RMT influence on the satisfaction of the player [3].

autocrat acquired sovereignty by transfers created in the society that restricts the objective freedom of individuals. Then, the individuals (players) decided to be (play) or not. Once virtual reality is formed, the decision whether to exist in the virtual reality as an avatar is made in the real world by the player as seen in Figure 1. From the viewpoint of the real world, virtual reality is a good or product to enjoy leisure, and a player would consume based on their needs in an exclusive market with differentiated products. Consequently, for the achievement oriented player who has a negative view of RMT plays a game with strong hierarchical achievement structure, RMT disturbs the flow of the narrative structure. The social oriented player who does not have a negative view of RMT plays a game in which RMT does not disturb the flow, without strictly predetermined narrative structure in the same vein. We conclude that the characteristic of time-reversibility of social composition and arbitrariness for individual's decision on existence makes the majority of the individuals in a virtual society resemble the innate nature of society. For example, an avatar of a social oriented player would exist in a game that produces enjoyment through social functions and maintains the flow of players. In other words, an avatar derives enjoyment through the narrative structure and the sustenance of the flow of players. As a result, we can expand the individual micromotives of RMT to the virtual society.

In this respect, the model in Starodoumov [3] only describes games where the narrative structure is less important. In such a game where players focus more on social functions, RMT can have a positive influence on overall game usage. However, in case of games with strictly predetermined narrative structures, players can maximize enjoyment by proceeding in games with sophisticated stories without breaking away from immersion. In this case, RMT can distract a player's immersion, and if they skip the narrative time line by RMT, the intrinsic reward of enjoyment can be reduced. This is consistent with the argument that an achievement and immersion oriented player has negative view of RMT if there is a clear hierarchical achievement structure.

Therefore, we hypothesize that there is a difference between the effects of RMT depending upon the intensity of narrative structure. We inductively test the hypothesis to present empirical evidence.

Hypothesis. The playing time of games with weakly predetermined narrative structure is more positively associated with the RMT volume than the playing time of games with strictly predetermined narrative structure.

5. Empirical Evidence

We present empirical evidence from the Korean MMORPGs market since Korean MMORPG had become a standard design in the Asian online game market until early 2000s. In terms of consumption, the Korean game culture is characterized by PC-Bang. The IT initiative of the Korean government made broadband Internet available throughout the entire country, which contributed to the development of online games, and PC-Bang served as a catalyst to this phenomenon. PC-Bang was available where fast Internet could be used for a low price, especially by young Koreans, and a de facto community where they socially interact with acquaintances emerged [38]. On the other hand, it seems paradoxical that an offline-local form of game usage pattern called PC-Bang was formed during this time. Huhh [39] explained that PC-Bang complemented the online culture that allowed for building relationships; especially, MMORPG gamers could play a variety of online games for low prices due to the IP-Pricing system (IP-Pricing means that each PC-Bang is charged a price in accordance with the number of fixed IP addresses by the game publisher [35]). It is important to note that computer hardware technology could not keep up with people's expectation and desire. Generally, PC-Bang was furnished with computers with better performance than those of home PCs, and therefore, users tended to utilize PC-Bang.

5.1. Data. We use the database gathered from Gametrics (this description is on http://www.gametrics.com/services/gametrics_guide.pdf) that collects statistical data with respect to its clients of PC-Bangs. The data was gathered from a daily random sample of 4,000 PC-Bangs using the management software that Gametrics had distributed to predict the total usage of every PC-Bang in South Korea.

We collected the data for total time usage and total quantity of RMT items of Korean MMORPG markets for four years (208 weeks) from 2011-05-03 to 2015-04-27 on a weekly basis. Then we arranged the MMORPGs in descending order by aggregating four years of time usage data to select the most used games on a sustained basis during the 208 weeks for analysis, which means that we selected the games that were launched before 2011-05-03 and sustained their service at least until 2015-04-27. To classify the MMORPGs based on the intensity of the narrative structure, we referred to MMORPG.com, which is one of the most popular communities to assess the game elements among game players. On the basis of the highest total playing time, the following top eight games are selected among assessed games in Cyber Creations (MMORPG.com): Aion, Lineage 2, World of Warcraft, Maple Story, TERA, MU Online, Mabinogi, and Rohan in order.

5.2. Method and Results. We supposed that a game highly rated in terms of narrative has a strictly predetermined narrative structure. In the same vein, we assumed that a game lowly rated has a weak predetermined narrative structure. Since only eight games were available, existing in both Gametrics and Cyber Creations, we relatively evaluated the games and separated the games into two groups depending on the degree of predetermination related to narrative structure. As the number of games is not enough to apply statistical methods, we tried to decide an objective branch point. Hence, we counted the games rated lower than 6.9 as a low-rated group and the other games rated over than 7.0 as high-rated group. Among the eight games selected, Lineage 2 (6.8), TERA (6.8), MU Online (6.8), and Aion (6.9) have low ratings in the narrative subsection (among the 8 sections of ratings in MMORPG.com, we use the score of "Role-Playing" subsection). World of Warcraft (7.2), Maple Story (7.2), Mabinogi (7.4), and Rohan (7.1) belong to the high-rated group. We compare the ratio of the playing time to the RMT volume, which is a proxy of the influence of RMT, between the groups with high and low ratings. Table 1 provides the general information of each game.

Since the purpose of analysis is to examine the difference between usage of the high-rated games and usage low-rated games, we adopt an ANOVA process. The time/RMT variable is a unit of time usage of the game while the RMT is executed; that is, its expression is the slope of the time usage over the RMT volume. According to our hypothesis, the high-rated games are played with very little RMT. On the other hand, the low-rated games are played with more RMT. Table 2 presents the descriptive statistics and the results. The first row shows the result of the hypothesis using ANOVA analysis. The low-rated narrative group has a significantly higher influence of RMT. Therefore, we conclude that the playing time of games with weakly predetermined narrative structure is more positively correlated with the RMT volume than the playing time of games with strictly predetermined narrative structure. There is a significant difference between two groups, which supports our hypothesis.

We extend the data sample to 12 games to check the robustness. The Kingdom of the Wind (7.1), Dekaron (7.1), and Ragnarok Online (7.2) are added to the high-rated group,

and Hero Online (5.9) is added to the low-rated group. The second row of Table 2 displays the results. The difference of two types of groups is significant and low-rated group has the higher association. It is consistent with the first analysis and the hypothesis.

6. Conclusion

We discuss the characteristics of the narrative structure of MMORPGs during the process of development and RMT during management process after they are launched. We deduce results based on the dual structure of societies, in which a person in the real world decides whether to exist in the virtual society. This considers virtual reality as created in the viewpoint of time-reversed social nominalism. This study contributes to developing an understanding of RMT on MMORPGs in the way that we recognized the role of narrative structure with regard to extend previous literature [2, 3]. We find that the effects of RMT have differences in overall game usage according to narrative structures that confine players in the "flow" and provide players' enjoyment. Since achievement and immersion oriented players have a negative opinion of RMT, there is a less positive impact on the games with strictly predetermined structure than those with weakly predetermined narrative structure. We verified the conclusion using Korean PC-Bang data and empirically found that the deductive conclusion is inductively supported. In addition, we showed that the past RMT literature has neglected MMORPG's heterogeneity of narrative structures.

There are several limitations in our research. First, the importance of MMORPG's narrative structure could change over time. Most MMOPRGs, excluding ones that serve as social network service, contain a type of narrative structures necessarily and players are to follow the structure in the beginning of the game after launched. Importantly the significance of narrative structure is based on whether developers continuously add new stories through patches or updates. In this context, our research has a shortcoming since we used a single rating for the narrative structure of each game, while analyzing four years of playing time and the quantity of RMT. Second, this research used Korean PC-Bang data on only 12 games in the Korean MMORPGs market that could be identified by the authors. This PC-Bang database is not a complete enumeration and it does not include the behavior of individual gamers at home. It means that Gametrics, the Korean PC-Bang database, used the sample PC-Bangs and estimated the population of playing time. If the statistics of Gametrics are biased, we cannot guarantee the empirical results of ANOVA analysis. In addition, there are underlying assumption that there is no difference in consumption behavior between gamers in PC-Bang and gamers at home. Future research should verify if this is the case. Furthermore, we choose the games that had been serviced during the sample period. It could generate survival bias, accordingly the results could undergo influence when we include the games interrupted before the end of sample period. We should also mention that the cut-off criteria used in separating group were not decided by a statistical method but a relatively evaluation among the sample. Finally, the

TABLE 1: Descriptive information.

Ranking	Game	Publisher	The date of issue (Korea standard)	Ratings (role-playing)
1	Aion	NC Soft (Korea)	2008-11-25	6.9
2	Lineage 2	NC Soft (Korea)	1998-09-01	6.8
3	World of Warcraft	Blizzard (US)	2004-11-23	7.2
4	Maple Story	NEXON (Korea)	2003-04-29	7.2
5	TERA	Bluehole (Korea)	2011-01-25	6.8
6	MU Online	Webzen (Korea)	2001-11-19	6.8
7	Mabinogi	NEXON (Korea)	2004-06-22	7.4
8	Rohan	Playwith INC (Korea)	2006-03-07	7.1
9	Kingdom of the wind	NEXON (Korea)	1996-04-01	7.1
10	Dekaron	Dekaron Project (Korea)	2005-05-03	7.1
11	Ragnarok Online	GRAVITY (Korea)	2002-07-29	7.2
12	Hero Online	MGAME (Korea)	2005-01-25	5.9

TABLE 2: Descriptive statistics and empirical results.

(Time/RMT)	High-rated		Low-rated		p value
	Mean	SD	Mean	SD	
8 games	193.82	475.01	251.51	463.53	.013*
12 games	125.75	369.16	310.46	502.08	.000***

$*$ and $* * *$ denote $p < .05$, and $p < .001$, respectively.

empirical results are based on the Korean MMORPG market and therefore, we cannot generalize the conclusions to other markets. We believe that the future research will need to prove the mediating effect of narrative structure on the association between RMT and the usage of MMORPG. It will extend our result that proves the existence of difference. Moreover, we suggest that future research with international MMORPG market data would generalize the results of our findings.

Nexon, who developed the world's first MMORPG, announced that it may adopt exchange system (this description is on http://www.mmobux.com/articles/320/what-nexons-s-groundbreaking-universal-currency-exchange-means-for-the-publisher-and-mmorpg-industry). Using "Nexon stars" as key currency issued by Nexon platform, it will create a system where items and game money can be exchanged between different MMORPGs provided by Nexon. It is certain that both game developers and researchers need to understand the importance of managing RMT as well as creation of MMORPG as virtual world [40]. Thus we believe that our conclusion, the effect of RMT is different based on MMORPG's narrative structure, provides managerial implications to game developers.

Acknowledgments

This work was supported by the National Research Foundation of Korea Grant funded by the Korean Government (2014S1A3A2044459).

References

[1] E. Castronova, "On virtual economies," CESifo Working Paper, 2002.

[2] J. Huhh, "Simple economics of real-money trading in online games," SSRN Electronic Journal, 2008.

[3] A. Starodoumov, Real Money Trade Model in Virtual Economies, Institute of International Business (IIB), Stockholm School of Economics, 2005.

[4] M. Csikszentmihalyi, Beyond Boredom and Anxiety, Jossey-Bass Publishers, San Francisco, Calif, USA, 1st edition, 1975.

[5] C. Kolo and T. Baur, "Living a virtual life: social dynamics of online gaming," Game Studies, vol. 4, no. 1, 2004.

[6] P.-L. P. Rau, S.-Y. Peng, and C.-C. Yang, "Time distortion for expert and novice online game players," Cyberpsychology & Behavior, vol. 9, no. 4, pp. 396–403, 2006.

[7] N. B. Niman, "The allure of games: toward an updated theory of the leisure class," Games and Culture, vol. 8, no. 1, pp. 26–42, 2013.

[8] E. Seko, Professional Ni Naru Tame No Game Planning No Kyokasho <Kiso> (The Textbook of Game Planning for Beginners), Gijutsu-Hyoron Co., Tokyo, Japan, 2012.

[9] M. Bal, Narratology: Introduction to the Theory of Narrative, University of Toronto Press, Buffalo, NY, USA, 1985.

[10] J. Huizinga, Homo Ludens; A Study of the Play-Element in Culture, Routledge & K. Paul, London, UK, 1949.

[11] J. Juul, "Games telling stories? A brief note on games and narratives," The International Journal of Computer Game Research, vol. 1, no. 1, 2001.

[12] L. T. Graham and S. D. Gosling, "Personality profiles associated with different motivations for playing world of warcraft," Cyberpsychology, Behavior, and Social Networking, vol. 16, no. 3, pp. 189–193, 2013.

[13] J. Moon, M. D. Hossain, G. L. Sanders, E. J. Garrity, and S. Jo, "Player commitment to massively multiplayer online role-playing games (MMORPGs): an integrated model," *International Journal of Electronic Commerce*, vol. 17, no. 4, pp. 7–38, 2013.

[14] C. A. Steinkuehler, "Learning in massively multiplayer online games," in *Proceedings of the 6th International Conference on Learning Sciences (ICLS '04)*, pp. 521–528, Santa Monica, Calif, USA, June 2004.

[15] Y. S. Cho, *Playing for resistance in MMORPG: oppositional reading, emergence, and hegemony in the lineage II "Bartz Liberation War" [M.S. thesis]*, Georgia State University, 2012.

[16] I. Yi, *Korean Digital Storytelling: The Story of Bartz Liberation War in the Lineage II*, Sallimbooks, Paju, South Korea, 2009.

[17] M. Heidegger, *Being and Time*, SCM Press, London, UK, 1962.

[18] K. Nagygyörgy, R. Urbán, J. Farkas et al., "Typology and sociodemographic characteristics of massively multiplayer online game players," *International Journal of Human-Computer Interaction*, vol. 29, no. 3, pp. 192–200, 2013.

[19] N. Yee, "Motivations for play in online games," *Cyberpsychology & Behavior*, vol. 9, no. 6, pp. 772–775, 2006.

[20] J. McGonigal, *Reality Is Broken: Why Games Make Us Better and How They Can Change the World*, Jonathan Cape, London, UK, 2011.

[21] R. Heeks, "Understanding 'gold farming' and real-money trading as the intersection of real and virtual economies," *Journal of Virtual Worlds Research*, vol. 2, no. 4, 2010.

[22] S. Papagiannidis, M. Bourlakis, and F. Li, "Making real money in virtual worlds: MMORPGs and emerging business opportunities, challenges and ethical implications in metaverses," *Technological Forecasting & Social Change*, vol. 75, no. 5, pp. 610–622, 2008.

[23] A. K. Shelton, "Defining the lines between virtual and real world purchases: second Life sells, but who's buying?" *Computers in Human Behavior*, vol. 26, no. 6, pp. 1223–1227, 2010.

[24] E. Castronova, I. Knowles, and T. L. Ross, "Policy questions raised by virtual economies," *Telecommunications Policy*, vol. 39, no. 9, pp. 787–795, 2015.

[25] J. A. T. Fairfield, "Virtual property," *Boston University Law Review*, vol. 85, pp. 1047–1102, 2005.

[26] G. Jung, B. Lee, B. Yoo, and E. Brynjolfsson, "Analysis of the relationship between virtual goods trading and performance of virtual worlds," *SSRN Electronic Journal*, 2011.

[27] Z. B. Simpson, "The in-game economics of ultima online," in *Proceedings of the Computer Game Developer's Conference*, San Jose, Calif, USA, 2000.

[28] M. El-Shagi and G. von Schweinitz, "The diablo 3 economy: an agent based approach," *Computational Economics*, vol. 47, no. 2, pp. 193–217, 2016.

[29] J. N. Kelly, Play Time: The Problem of Abundance in MMORPG, pp. 1–13, 2004.

[30] E. Castronova, "A cost-benefit analysis of real-money trade in the products of synthetic economies," *Info*, vol. 8, no. 6, pp. 51–68, 2006.

[31] R. Thawonmas, Y. Kashifuji, and K.-T. Chen, "Detection of MMORPG bots based on behavior analysis," in *Proceedings of the International Conference on Advances in Computer Entertainment Technology (ACE '08)*, pp. 91–94, ACM, Yokohama, Japan, December 2008.

[32] A. Fujita, H. Itsuki, and H. Matsubara, "Detecting real money traders in MMORPG by using trading network," in *Proceedings*

of the 7th AAAI Conference on Artificial Intelligence and Interactive Digital Entertainment (AIIDE '11), pp. 26–31, Stanford, Calif, USA, October 2011.

[33] Y. Mishima, K. Fukuda, and H. Esaki, "An analysis of players and bots behaviors in MMORPG," in *Proceedings of the 27th IEEE International Conference on Advanced Information Networking and Applications (AINA '13)*, pp. 870–876, March 2013.

[34] J. Huhh, "Effects of real-money trading on MMOG demand: a network externality based explanation," *SSRN Electronic Journal*, 2006.

[35] V. Lehdonvirta, "Real-money trade of virtual assets: ten different user perceptions," *Proceedings of Digital Art and Culture*, pp. 52–58, 2005.

[36] N. Yee, Model of Player Motivations, 2005.

[37] T. Hobbes, A. Crooke, J. Nodin, and Oliver Wendell Holmes Collection (Library of Congress), *Leviathan, or, The Matter, Forme, & Power of a Common-Wealth Ecclesiasticall and Civill*, Printed for Andrew Ckooke i.e. Crooke , at the Green Dragon in St. Pauls Church-yard, London, UK, 1651.

[38] D. Y. Jin and F. Chee, "Age of new media empires: a critical interpretation of the Korean online game industry," *Games and Culture*, vol. 3, no. 1, pp. 38–58, 2008.

[39] J.-S. Huhh, "Culture and business of PC bangs in Korea," *Games and Culture*, vol. 3, no. 1, pp. 26–37, 2008.

[40] M. Nazir and C. Lui, "A brief history of virtual economy," *Journal of Virtual Worlds Research*, vol. 9, no. 1, pp. 1–26, 2016.

## 14

Visualization of Tomato Growth based on Dry Matter Flow

Hongjun Li,[1] Xiaopeng Zhang,[2] Weiliang Meng,[2] and Lin Ge[3]

[1]*College of Science, Beijing Forestry University, Beijing 100083, China*
[2]*NLPR-LIAMA, Institute of Automation, CAS, Beijing 100190, China*
[3]*Department of Biostatistics and Computational Biology, University of Rochester, Rochester, NY 14620, USA*

Correspondence should be addressed to Hongjun Li; lihongjun69@bjfu.edu.cn

Academic Editor: Soraia Raupp Musse

The visualization of tomato growth can be used in 3D computer games and virtual gardens. Based on the growth theory involving the respiration theory, the photosynthesis, and dry matter partition, a visual system is developed. The tomato growth visual simulation system is light-and-temperature-dependent and shows plausible visual effects in consideration of the continuous growth, texture map, gravity influence, and collision detection. In addition, the virtual tomato plant information, such as the plant height, leaf area index, fruit weight, and dry matter, can be updated and output in real time.

1. Introduction

Crop growth simulation is useful for constructing virtual scenes used in 3D computer games and virtual gardens, evaluating crop behaviors [1] and supporting the management of crops [2]. As a kind of widespread crop, numerous varieties of tomatoes are ubiquitously planted across the world. In recent years, tomato growth simulation in computer has been gaining more and more attention.

In the view of tomato growth theories, the physiological analysis of plant [3] gets attention. The growth period, environment condition, and architectural traits had been studied. Both the temperature and the nonstructural carbohydrate level (dry weight) are used to predict the influences on the growth of tomato [4, 5]. For exploring the influence between the plant growth and the environment, Functional-Structural Plant Models (FSPM) are brought up which shows great performance in the past years. A mechanistic Functional-Structural Plant Model, GreenLab model [6], is used to analyze tomato crops [7, 8]. Recently, Fan et al. [9] proposed a novel knowledge-and-data-driven modeling (KDDM) approach for simulating plant growth. A GreenLab model used as the knowledge-driven and a radial basis function network used as the data-driven were integrated together.

Researchers have built many convenient crop simulation systems, for example, FAST [10], TOMSIM [11, 12], TOMGRO [13, 14], TOMPOUSSE [15], and CROPGRO-Tomato [16, 17]. Besides these systems, the reference axis model [18] and the web-based interactive system [1] also show numerical results of tomato virtual growth.

All above mathematical models and those simulation systems focus on the accuracy of simulation, which can be evaluated by comparing the experiments measuring data to the simulation results with statistical indexes. The outputs of most of these theory models are numbers or statistical charts, which can not be used for intuitive computer visual applications. For example, those models gave the number of tomato fruits but did not tell their positions. In order to simulate the tomato growth in the view of computer graph application, we in this paper should make some detailed technologies clear.

In the view of visualization, most popular methods of simulating tomato growth depend on the parametric L-system [19–21] which is a parallel rewriting system with formal grammar [22]. Parameters used in their visualization systems are measured from real plant or estimated with image and video technology [23]. However, these existing systems have some deficiencies for visualization. For example, leaf shape and leaf phyllotaxis are still not suitable for the constantly changing leaf shape during the growing process [19]. Besides, in some cases the plant shows artificial figure using regular L-system grammar [21].

TABLE 1: Parameters used in published papers.

Par.	C°	LAI	DM	CO$_2$	GR	FW	LN	Ph	Re	LW	Pa	Ra
[2]	√											
[4]	√	√			√		√	√	√			
[9]	√	√	√	√	√				√	√	√		√
[10]											√	
[11]			√	√		√	√					
[13]	√		√		√							
[17]		√										
[19]	√											
[26]	√	√	√	√				√	√			
[29]		√				√	√		√	√		
[30]	√	√	√			√	√			√		
[31]		√						√	√	√	√	√
[32]		√	√		√	√						
[33]	√			√	√							
[34]	√	√										
[35]						√			√		√	
[36]	√		√	√			√					√
[37]	√					√						
N	11	9	7	6	5	5	5	5	5	4	3	3

In order to improve the visual effect of tomato growth simulation system, we construct a general visual platform in this paper. There are three contributions in our work: (1) Several key parameters and growth functions are selected and designed, respectively. (2) Growth functions including LAI and dry matter partitioning formulae are converted to new patterns which are adapt to our system. For example, the formula about dry matter acquiring is revised from average estimation to leaf by leaf. (3) A new general visual platform is designed. The geometry of each leaf, fruit, and flower grows and expands corresponding to the age of the plant and resource provision. In addition, collision detection and gravity influence are taken into account. Compared to most previous literatures [19, 24], the realistic effect significantly improves in our system.

With realistic visual effect and those classical growth theories, our visual system can be used in 3D computer games, tomato growth analysis, computer graphic modeling, three dimensional animations, computer virtual gardens, popular science, and so forth. In the following, several parameters and the growth functions are constructed (Section 2), and a visual system is built (Section 3). At last, the system is evaluated by some experiment results (Section 4), and conclusion is given in Section 5.

2. Growth Functions and Modeling

Tomato growth is a very complex phenomenon, so its simulation involves a lot of parameters and growth functions, which is the basis of our visual system.

2.1. Model Parameters. Model parameters are important factors for the simulation, and reasonable selection from commonly used parameters for computation can speed up the

simulation result while meeting the accuracy requirements of the simulation. By investigating 18 published literatures (Table 1), about 130 parameters are employed in those models. Among those parameters, the most popular 12 variables in the order of frequency number N from large to small are air temperature (C°), leaf area index (LAI), dry matter weight (DM), CO$_2$, growth rates (GR), fruit weight (FW), leaf number (LN), photosynthesis (Ph), respiration (Re), leaf weight (LW), partitioning (Pa), and radiation level (Ra). For the simplification of modeling but keeping the key parameters, our simulation system employs all those 12 variables.

2.2. Variables and Symbols. In order to make clear the related simulation theories and our visualization approach, some terminologies, variables, and symbols are summarized here. Symbols are mainly the same as GreenLab [4, 6, 9]. Besides parameters listed in Table 1, there are several other parameters that contribute to the simulation. These parameters can be classified into three categories as follows.

The first category parameters are related to environment, that is, *environmental variables*. They are measurable and represent the growth conditions inside a greenhouse.

   (i) T: average daily air temperature.

   (ii) CO$_2$: carbon dioxide concentration inside, gm^{-3} (constant).

   (iii) I: solar radiation level.

   (iv) PAR: photosynthetically active radiation.

The second category is *tomato crop parameters*.

   (i) P_α: physiological age of α, where $\alpha \in \Omega = \{w, \text{leaf}, \text{flower}, \text{fruit}, \text{node}\}$, denoting the plant itself, leaves, flowers, fruits, and internodes.

(ii) E_x: efficiency factor, $x \in \{\text{ph}, m, g\}$, in which ph, m, and g denote photosynthesis, maintenance respiration, and growth respiration, respectively.

(iii) K_α: coefficient which is related to the growth rate.

(iv) N_α: the number of α.

(v) $\text{Area}_{\text{leaf}}$: a single leaf area.

(vi) V_α: the volume of organ α.

(vii) Q: acquired dry matter.

(viii) D: partitioned dry matter.

(ix) r_α: the rate of growth of organ α, varied with time and temperature.

(x) $T_{\min}$: the lower bound of temperature for growing.

(xi) $T_{\max}$: the upper bound of temperature for growing.

The third category involves the *simulation parameters* which are used for visualization.

(i) ι: the growing unit.

(ii) R_0: the minimum radius of a node when it shots.

(iii) N_y: the number of segments of an edge, denoting the resolution of a leaf mesh, $y \in \{\text{wid}, \text{hei}\}$. The element wid denotes the width of a leaf and hei denotes the length of the leaf.

2.3. Growth Functions. Traditionally, functions use the average leaf area [4] which is a function of leaf age or use the representative leaf area [25]. Different from traditional methods, our model obtains the total leaf area by summing the area of leaves one by one. Therefore, those formulae in previous literatures should be revised as follows for our model.

2.3.1. Dry Matter Acquisition. There are a lot of mathematical models which simulate the acquisition of dry matter. Most of them believe that maintainable dry matter is related to light, temperature, and CO_2 [4, 9, 26]. Among them, a mathematical model [4] is the most closed to our investigating result (Section 2.1). Therefore, the mathematical model is changed to (1) which can deal with the area of leaves one by one. The environmental factors, CO_2 and light radiation level I, are incorporated in the equation.

$$Q_{n,\text{acq}} = E_{\text{Ph}} \sum_{k=1}^{N_{\text{leaf},t}} Q_0 \cdot f\left(I, CO_2, T\right)$$
$$\cdot \text{Area}_{\text{leaf},k}(t), \tag{1}$$

$$f\left(I, CO_2, T\right) = \frac{I(t)}{I_0 + I(t)} \frac{CO_2(t)}{C_0 + CO_2(t)} \frac{T(t)}{T_0 + T(t)}, \tag{2}$$

where $Q_{n,\text{acq}}$ is the acquired dry matter during the nth growth stage (i.e., the nth day after sowing in our experiment). In (1) and (2), $Q_0 = 12.0, I_0 = 50, C_0 = 300, T_0 = 12$. These parameters are assigned the same values as in [4].

2.3.2. Maintenance Respiration. As in [4], the index of maintenance respiration denoted as $D_{n,\text{maint}}$ in the nth day is also taken into account in our model. The total demand is the sum of consumption by all organs (internodes, leaves, flowers, and fruits), denoted as

$$D_{n,\text{maint}} = D_{\text{node},m} + D_{\text{leaf},m} + D_{\text{flower},m} + D_{\text{fruit},m} \tag{3}$$

with

$$D_{\text{leaf},m} = E_m K_{\text{leaf},m} \sum_{k=1}^{N_{\text{leaf}}} \text{Area}_{\text{leaf},k}(t) \cdot h(T),$$
$$D_{\alpha,m} = E_m K_{\alpha,m} \sum_{k=1}^{N_{\alpha,t}} V_{\alpha,k}(t) \cdot h(T), \tag{4}$$

where $\alpha \in \{\text{node}, \text{flower}, \text{fruit}\}$ and

$$h(T) = e^{-\beta \cdot |T(t)-25|}. \tag{5}$$

Note that, in literature [4], $h(T) = e^{\beta(T(t)-23)}$ which is a monotonically increasing function and does not meet the assumption that a tomato plant grows best when the environment temperature is around 25°. But the assumption can be met with our new equation (5).

2.3.3. Growth Respiration. If the acquired dry matter is more than the demand of maintenance respiration, the remaining dry matter partitioning will be recalculated for growing. Referring to the equation about growth respiration [4], both maintenance respiration and growth respiration use the same exponential function if $T_{\min} \leq T \leq T_{\max}$. We use the same exponential function but with different equation by introducing internode growth and organs expanding, respectively:

$$D_{\alpha,g} = E_g K_{\alpha,g} \sum_{k=1}^{N_{\alpha,t}} \Delta V_{\alpha,k}(t) \cdot h(T), \tag{6}$$

where $\Delta V_{\alpha,k}(t) = r_\alpha \Delta t$ is the growing amount of internode and organs. For flowers, internodes, and fruits, their volume will increase continuously. For leaves, the growth will lead to the geometry surface expansion as the method in [27].

It has been proven that the total PAR received during the days from sowing to flowering is strongly correlated with the number of days [2], which means that it is reasonable to use growth timeline to simulate the plant growth [19]. In our simulation system, the growth rate r_α is a variable which reflects the organ's state. It is zero if the environment temperature is lower than $T_{\min}$ or greater than $T_{\max}$.

As for the stem branching and the new buds generating, the demanding of dry matter is the same as (6).

3. Visualization System

Our visual system for simulating tomato growth *(TomatoVis)* is an effective integration for geometry computation and visual analysis methods. A tomato grows based on dry matter flow and is constrained by environment factors. Therefore, our system inherently supports both growth visualization and environmental information analysis.

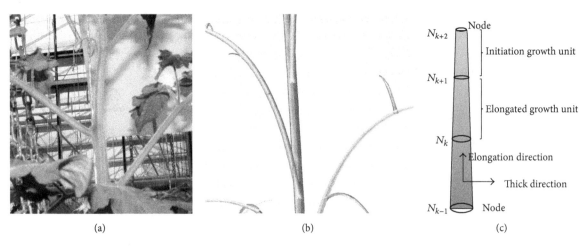

FIGURE 1: Modeling tomato stems with cylinders. (a) Stem photo. (b) Stem model. (c) Growth units and growth directions.

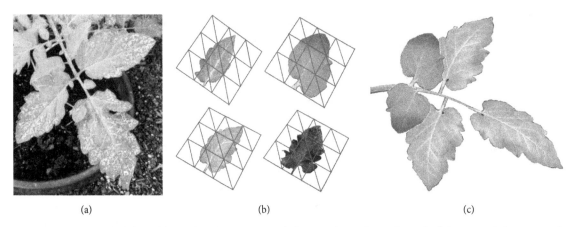

FIGURE 2: Modeling leaves with deformable meshes. (a) A tomato phyllotaxy photo. (b) Different leaf shapes in different growth stages. (c) Building a phyllotaxy with two different shape leaves.

3.1. Generating Geometry of the Stem and Organs. The stem and organs are modeled based on the balance between the complexity and the realistic effect in the user interactive frame rate.

3.1.1. The Stem Modeling. Guided by real photo (Figure 1(a)), we use skeletons and cylinders [19, 20] to represent stems (Figure 1(b)). This is a straightforward method. Here a small trick is that the internode is divided into N_{unit} growth units for simulating the continuous growth of the stem as shown in Figure 1(c). For visualization, a growth unit has the initial length l_0 and radius r_0 at the end point when it was born and a maximum length l_{max} and radius r_{max} when it matures. Each growth unit can increase continuously in the length and the thickness (its radius) until it gets maturity. Both the growth rates of elongating direction and expansion direction are linear functions of growth time if it obtains enough resources (dry matter) and meets the requirement of temperature.

3.1.2. Leaf Modeling. Leaf growth analysis helps us to better understand the relationship between the plant growth and the leaf geometry (shape and size), especially for gene or tissue analysis [27, 38, 39]. We use a simple textured mesh

model [40] to represent the relationship and simulate the leaf growth, and different from existing tomato visual system [19] where all leaves are of the same shape, we use multiple leaves texture images to improve the realistic effect.

For example, a tomato phyllotaxy usually consists of 5 leaves or more, as shown in Figure 2(a). Those leaves are usually different in sizes and shapes. We model several representative leaves and each leaf is modeled with a $N_{wid} \times N_{hei}$ mesh mapped with a real leaf image (Figure 2(b)) for realistic display. Figure 2(c) shows the result that is modeled by two kinds of leaf shapes. The area of each leaf is the mapping texture image area on the mesh.

3.1.3. Flower Modeling. A representative virtual tomato flower consists of 4 parts: pedicel, sepal, petal, and pistil (Figure 3(a)). The pedicel landed to the stem is modeled with cylinders as the same as used for stem. Each tomato flower has 5 sepals and 5 petals and can be changed according to the types of tomatoes. Both a sepal and a petal are modeled with a mesh, respectively. Tomato pistil located centrally in the flower is also constructed with cylinders (Figure 3(b)). After texture mapping, the virtual tomato flower is modeled as Figure 3(c).

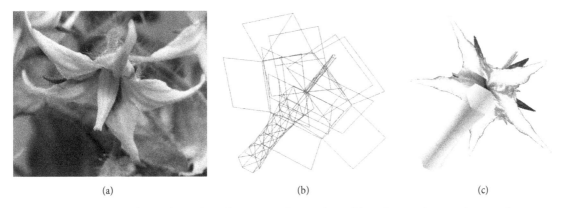

FIGURE 3: Modeling flowers with deformable meshes. (a) A tomato flower photo. (b) Each part of a virtual tomato flower is modeled with mesh. (c) A virtual tomato flower model.

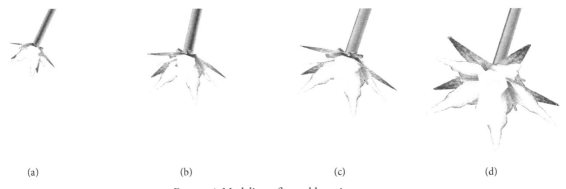

| (a) | (b) | (c) | (d) |

FIGURE 4: Modeling a flower blooming.

For simulating flower blooming, the vertex P_0 representing the petal base position is fixed in the simulation as [41]. Then the growth of the pedicel, sepal, and petal is calculated with a mathematical formulae

$$P_i^{(n)} = P_0 + (1 + \iota_\tau) \left| \overrightarrow{P_0 P_i} \right| \frac{\vec{d}}{\left| \vec{d} \right|},$$

$$\vec{d} = \vec{a}^o + (1 + \theta_\tau) \left(\frac{\overrightarrow{P_0 P_i}}{\left| \overrightarrow{P_0 P_i} \right|} - \vec{a}^o \right), \tag{7}$$

where P_i is the old position on the pedicel, sepal, and petal and $P_i^{(n)}$ is the new position; $\vec{a}^o$ is the unit growth direction of the pistil. The parameter ι_τ is different for the pedicel, sepal, or petal, which means the growth rate in radius of different parts of the flower. Another parameter θ_τ represents the growth rate of open angle of the pedicel, sepal, or petal. The effect of experiment is illustrated in Figure 4.

3.1.4. Fruit Modeling. A simple virtual tomato fruit consists of 3 parts: stalk, sepal, and pericarp (Figure 5(a)). For simulating the flower-to-fruit process, the former two parts, that is, stalk and sepals, use the meshes from flowers, while the pericarp is modeled with a general ellipsoid, denoted with $E(P, \overrightarrow{Px}, \overrightarrow{Py}, \overrightarrow{Pz}, a, b, c)$ by specifying the values of three semiaxes parameters (Figure 5(b)), a, b, c. P is the land point which the ellipsoid links to the stalk at, and $\overrightarrow{Px}, \overrightarrow{Py}, \overrightarrow{Pz}$ is the local

coordinate system. Here we do not use the rotation method presented in [19], because it is easy to detect collision between tomatoes with our ellipsoid models. Referring to the photo (Figure 5(a)), a hanging fruit is modeled vividly as shown in Figure 5(c).

For simulating the process of a fruit expansion (Figure 6), we use expansion mathematical formulae as those used in Section 3.1.3.

3.2. Simulation Flowchart. Tomato growth is simulated by following the flow of carbon (total nonstructural carbohydratc) [4] which is related to CO_2, environment temperature, and light flux density (Formula (1)). The growth processing is illustrated with a flowchart, as shown in Figure 7. At first, the tomato plant obtains the carbon or dry matter (DM) by leaves photosynthesis. The amount of DM is estimated with (1) with input environment information. Then, the plant consumes a part of DM because of maintaining the dark respiration of all stems and organs. The consumption is estimated by (3) to (4). Next, the growth respiration is calculated if there is remaining DM and the environmental factors are approved. At last, the plant geometry is developed.

If needed, the plant height, the number of fruits or flowers, the total dry matter, LAI, and yield can all be exported.

3.3. Gravity Influence. The tomato stem is so thin that its shape is easily influenced by gravity. Given each substem

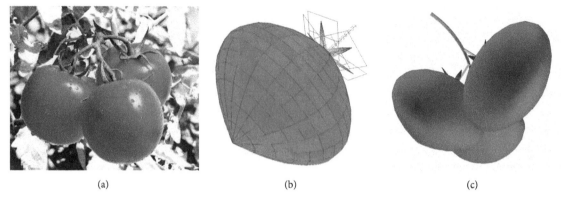

(a)   (b)   (c)

FIGURE 5: Modeling fruits with deformable meshes. (a) A hanging fruit. (b) Building a fruit mesh. (c) Modeling a hanging fruit.

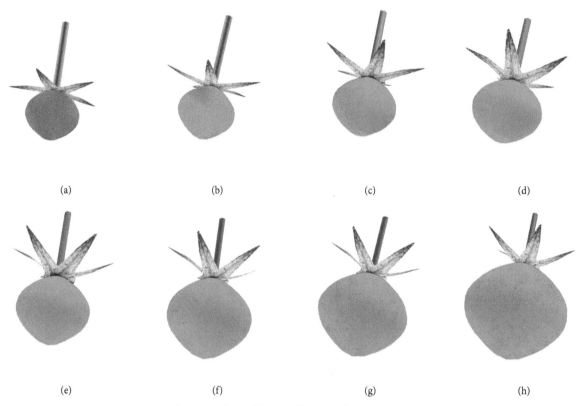

(a)   (b)   (c)   (d)

(e)   (f)   (g)   (h)

FIGURE 6: Several frames illustrate a fruit expansion.

drags the main stem a little bias, a linear function (8) is used to the main skeleton point that is linked to the substem.

$$d_t = C_g \cdot \iota \cdot \Delta D_{s,g} \cdot t, \tag{8}$$

where C_g is the coefficient representing the support force and $\Delta D_{s,g}$ is the amount of increased dry matter of the substem.

The gravity force on leaves, flowers, and fruits is also taken into the substem, which is increased linearly proportionally to the organ area (leaf) and the volume (flower or fruit). Comparing the results without the gravity influence (Figures 8(a) and 8(c)) to the results with gravity influence (Figures 8(b) and 8(d)), the latter obviously show better visual effect.

3.4. Collision Detection. The realistic effects of models can be improved by detecting collision and taking necessary

responses. The fruit is modeled with an ellipsoid, so we just need to check the distance between two ellipsoid center points and the half axis length (a, b, c in Section 3.1.4). Figure 9 is the visual comparison of a tomato plant with and without fruits collision detection.

4. Experiments

Our modeling and simulation algorithms are written in C/ C++ language with OpenGL GLUT library and implemented on a PC with Intel(R)Core(TM)i7-4700MQ CPU@2.40 GHz and 8 G memory.

We focus on the visualization effect influenced by temperature variation. As a result, except for temperature, the light strength, PAR, and CO_2 are set constant values. By referring

TABLE 2: Results of simulating the growing of tomato planted in different dates.

Date	TotalDM	LeavesDM	OrgansDM	LAI	Height
50th	22.33	6.72 (30.1%)	0.0 (0.0%)	1.91	4.70
120th	564.1	145.8 (25.8%)	354.7 (62.88%)	3.81	19.78
190th	444.9	123.4 (27.7%)	244.4 (54.93%)	3.29	21.09
260th	62.2	29.1 (46.8%)	11.9 (19.1%)	5.9	12.2

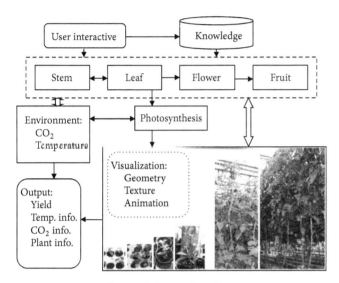

FIGURE 7: System flowchart.

to [2], the time period from sowing to the final harvest stage was 105 days; PAR 5–25 mol/m^2 day and total in production is 300–1200 mol/m^2. By referring to [4], β = 0.0693, CO_2 = 300, and the solar radiation level I = 43. By experiment tests, we set the stop growth temperature T_{min} = 10°C, T_{max} = 32°C; the growth parameter K_g is 0.03, 0.05, 0.06, and 0.07 for leaf, stem, flower, and fruit, respectively.

4.1. Visual Growth Simulation. For a greenhouse environment, the indoor temperature can be set according to the growth demand. We set the greenhouse temperature at the optimal temperature for the tomato growing 25°C and let the daily average temperature T = 25 + ϵ in the growing days. ϵ is from the continuous uniform distribution $U(-5.0, 5.0)$.

The experiment result is partly shown in Figure 10. At the 105th day as shown in Figure 10(j), there are 45253 polygons, 201 leaves, and 56 fruits. The plant height at last is 2.27m.

During the tomato growth process, the accumulate dry matter (DM) of the plant (TotalDM), leaves (LeavesDM), and fruit (FruitsDM) is all in small amounts or zero at the beginning and gradually increases, respectively, as shown in Figure 11(a). At the last day, the ratio of FruitsDM to TotalDM is about 75.8%, which is slightly over some observed results (about 70%, the observed "Sunny" data, in 1992 and 1994 in [17]). The ratio of LeavesDM to TotalDM is about 12.3%. The leaf area index (LAI, Figure 11(b)) in the simulation period increases before the flowering time and then decreases. The curve shape of LAI is the same as the observed data of

"Agriset 761" (1995), "Solarset" (1995), and "Florida 47" (2006) reported in [17].

4.2. Simulation with Real Temperatures. It has very important significance to evaluate the sensitivity to temperature of a simulation system and to compare the prediction results of the accumulate dry matter and fruit yield as done in [4, 13, 17]. We take the comparison experiment by using the daily average temperature in 2014 of California, USA. The temperature data (Figure 12) is from Carbon Dioxide Information Analysis Center (CDIAC, http://cdiac.ornl.gov/epubs/ndp/ushcn/daily_doc.html).

Avoiding those days with lower temperatures that are not suitable for tomato growing, we let the planting date be the 50th, 120th, 190th, and the 260th in 2014. After 105 days of growing, the experiment results are shown in Figure 13. From Figure 13(a), we can find that the plant is short because of low temperature days in its early stage, which influences the flowering and bearing fruits. By contrast, because of the low temperature days in the later stage, the plant grows but its fruits bearing is failure in Figure 13(d). Among the four planting dates, the best planting date is the 120th and 47 large fruits are harvested (Figure 13(b)). Although a highest plant is generated by planting on the 190th day and 65 small fruits are obtained (Figure 13(c)), the total fruits dry matter is not the highest among the four cases. The plant height, dry matter, and LAI information are listed in Table 2 in which the "OrgansDM" includes fruits and flowers dry matter.

4.3. Visual Comparison. We give a visual comparison of our results with two earlier works. Figure 14(a) is generated by sketch-based method and incorporated with BP Neural Network [28]. The tomato model shows good realistic effect and the model is approximate to real one. Figure 14(b) is from a tomato plant modeling system [19] which is based on the growth laws, the topological structure, and parametric L-system. Figure 14(c) is created in the ideal environment (see Section 4.1) by our visual simulation system, and flowers are randomly changed to fruits for showing a visual effect the same as Figure 14(b). Comparing to the tomato photo (Figure 14(d)), all the three virtual models do not show the wither shape, which is a limitation of all these methods. In the view of a vivid visualization, our model is more convincible to those models created by the existing methods [19, 28].

We also make a comparison between our tomato growth process and the plant growth process in Unity3D (Figure 15). In Unity3D, we need to set different growth models in different growth stage based on our modeling goals without any growth principles. These models should be generated in advance, and the adjusting work is a tedious process in

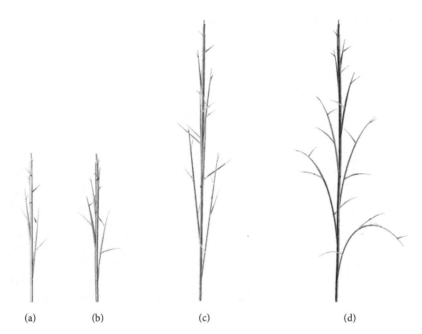

(a)   (b)   (c)   (d)

FIGURE 8: Comparing modeling effect with gravity or not. (a) Day 50 without gravity. (b) Day 50 with gravity influence. (c) Day 80 without gravity. (d) Day 80 with gravity influence.

(a)   (b)

FIGURE 9: Comparison modeling tomato plant with or without collision detection. (a) Without collision detection. (b) With collision detection.

order to keep the continuous growing process. For tomatoes growth, the topology of the plant changes a lot during the growth cycles, and it is difficult to achieve smooth transition based on Unity3D manually. Our method is designed based on biomechanism and the growth transition is more natural. Although we considered many parameters during the tomato growth process, only the temperature is the core factor for the tomato growing, and other parameters can use the default values, as these values are set based on biology knowledge unless the user wants to get some bizarre effects. Usually, it is enough to implement our tomato growth automatically by setting the temperature factor for the computer game application.

The whole growth process can be simulated in real time. As different tomato growth stages will have different topologies, the growing and rendering time maybe increase along with the complexity. Figure 16 shows the growing

and rendering time for the whole life cycle of one tomato plant. The highest time cost is 0.0065 seconds-per-frame (in the 132nd day) as the tomato begins to mature. In all, the rendering rate can be rendered more than 150 frames-per-second for one tomato plant. Figure 17 gives the change state of vertices and faces numbers during the growth process, and the maximum vertices number and faces number are 8064 and 6501, respectively, under our default parameter settings. Our current *TomatoVis* system does not consider the wither and artificial pruning cases, so the number of vertices and faces will not decrease during the tomato life cycle.

For the computer game application, usually there are many plants in the scene. We can use our algorithm to generate one tomato plant mesh model and obtain many instances on GPU based our hardware instancing method [42], making the whole growth process faster.

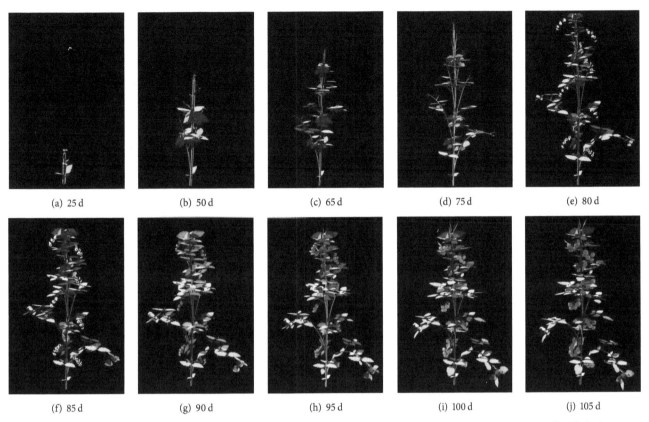

(a) 25 d   (b) 50 d   (c) 65 d   (d) 75 d   (e) 80 d

(f) 85 d   (g) 90 d   (h) 95 d   (i) 100 d   (j) 105 d

FIGURE 10: A visual tomato growing series frames generated with our method (in the subfigure title, id means the ith day).

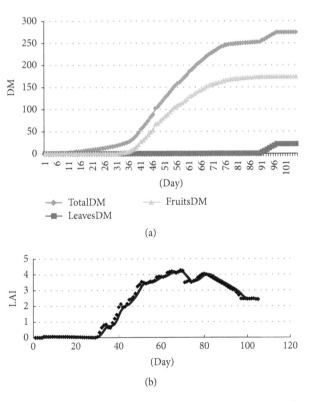

(a)

(b)

FIGURE 11: The simulated data of tomato growing. (a) Accumulate dry matter (DM) of the plant (TotalDM), leaves (LeavesDM), and fruit (FruitsDM). (b) Leaf area index (LAI).

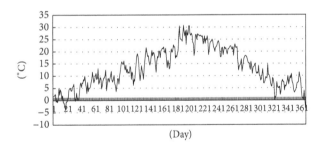

FIGURE 12: Daily average temperature in 2014 in California.

5. Conclusion

In this paper, a visualization system for simulating tomato growth (*TomatoVis*) is built. The system is light-and-temperature-dependent and is developed based on the growth theory with measurable parameters. In our system, the calculation equations of dry matter acquirement and partition are redesigned, and the dry matter flow can be tracked on each node and organ in turn to display the constraints of dry matter and environmental temperature on plant growth. Several nature influence factors, plant growing days, environmental temperature, texture map, gravity influence, and collision detection are taken into account in the simulation for the realistic effects of dynamic growth. Besides, the tomato plant information, including plant height,

(a)   (b)   (c)   (d)

FIGURE 13: The simulated results (after planting 105 days) of tomato growing in different seasons according to CA daily average temperature. Planting on the 50th day (a), the 120th (b), the 190th (c), and the 260th day (d) of the year.

(a) From [28]   (b) From [19]   (c) Ours   (d) Photo

FIGURE 14: Comparison in the view of visualization.

FIGURE 15: Four states of one tree in growth in Unity3D software. Each model must be set manually, and some branches maybe appear suddenly as the discrete setting environment in Unity3D. Referring to Figure 10, our *TomatoVis* system can generate the models continually without any special settings for any growth stage.

leaf area index, fruit number, and dry matter, can be updated and output in real time, which is helpful for visual analysis, greenhouse environment monitoring, and so forth.

However, *TomatoVis* has some limitations. For example, it cannot simulate the leaf wither phenomenon; it contains many parameters but cannot reveal the relation among them; the factors such as water and nitrogen are not included. All these limitations should be considered in our future works. And in the coming days, the scale of growth time should be decreased from a day to an hour. As pointed by [18], leaf

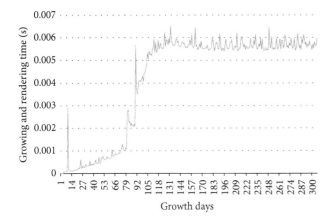

FIGURE 16: The time statistics in a growth cycle of a tomato plant in our *TomatoVis* system. The longest growth cycle for tomato is nearly 304 days in the greenhouse. In most cases, the growth cycle for tomatoes is 4–6 months. In any case, the growing and rendering time for one plant in our system is less than 0.007 seconds-per-frame, which means the growth process can be displayed in real time.

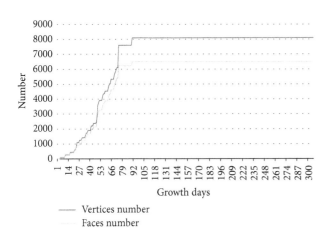

FIGURE 17: The vertices and faces numbers statistics in a growth cycle of a tomato plant in our *TomatoVis* system. As in most cases, the growth cycle for tomatoes is 4–6 months, and from the 91st day, the vertices and faces numbers are not increased anymore.

orientation and insertion angle should also be taken into account. We will try to improve our *TomatoVis* system to conquer the above limitations in future.

Acknowledgments

This work is partly supported by the National High Technology Research and Development Program (863 Program) of China with no. 2013AA10230502 and partly supported by National Natural Science Foundation of China with Project nos. 61571400, 61372190, 61561003, and 61571439. The authors would like to thank Lei Yi, Jia Liu, Jing Hua, and Lihong Xu for their expert contributions to the studies described in this manuscript.

References

[1] E. Fitz-Rodriguez, *Decision support systems for greenhouse tomato production [Ph.D. thesis]*, The University of Arizona, 2008.

[2] M. S. Giniger, R. J. McAvoy, G. A. Giacomelli, and H. W. Janes, "Computer simulation of a single truss tomato cropping system," *Transactions of the American Society of Agricultural Engineers*, vol. 31, no. 4, pp. 1176–1179, 1988.

[3] C. Soler, F. X. Sillion, F. Blaise, and P. De Reffye, "A physiological plant growth simulation engine based on accurate radiant energy transfer," Tech. Rep. RR-4116, INRIA, 2001.

[4] M. P. Gent and H. Z. Enoch, "Temperature dependence of vegetative growth and dark respiration: a mathematical model," *Plant Physiology*, vol. 71, no. 3, pp. 562–567, 1983.

[5] L. E. Marín Vaca, M. L. Domínguez Patiño, N. Lara Ruiz, and M. Aguilar Cortes, "Simulaccion processes of a mathematical model to determine the growth of tomato under plastic cover," *Agricultural Sciences*, vol. 06, no. 12, pp. 1532–1537, 2015.

[6] P. De Reffye and B. Hu, "Relevant qualitative and quantitative choices for building an efficient dynamic plant growth model: greenlab case," in *Proceedings of the International Symposium on Plant Growth Modeling, Simulation, Visualization and their Applications (PMA '03)*, pp. 87–107, Springer and Tsinghua University Press, Beijing, China, 2003.

[7] Q. Dong, G. Louarn, Y. Wang, J.-F. Barczi, and P. De Reffye, "Does the structure-function model GREENLAB deal with crop phenotypic plasticity induced by plant spacing? A case study on tomato," *Annals of Botany*, vol. 101, no. 8, pp. 1195–1206, 2008.

[8] M. Kang, L. Yang, B. Zhang, and P. De Reffye, "Correlation between dynamic tomato fruit-set and sourcesink ratio: a common relationship for different plant densities and seasons?" *Annals of Botany*, vol. 107, no. 5, pp. 805–815, 2011.

[9] X.-R. Fan, M.-Z. Kang, E. Heuvelink, P. de Reffye, and B.-G. Hu, "A knowledge-and-data-driven modeling approach for simulating plant growth: a case study on tomato growth," *Ecological Modelling*, vol. 312, pp. 363–373, 2015.

[10] L. Madden, S. P. Pennypacker, and A. A. MacNab, "FAST, a forecast system for alternaria solani on tomato," *Phytopathology*, vol. 68, no. 9, pp. 1354–1358, 1978.

[11] L. Wilson, R. Tennyson, A. Gutierrez, and F. Zalom, "A physiological based model for processing tomatoes: crop and pest management," in *Proceedings of the in 2nd International Symposium on Processing Tomatoes*, vol. XXII IHC 200, pp. 125–132, Davis, Calif, USA, 1986.

[12] N. Bertin and E. Heuvelink, "Dry-matter production in a tomato crop: comparison of two simulation models," *Journal of Horticultural Science*, vol. 68, no. 6, pp. 995–1011, 1993.

[13] J. Jones, E. Dayan, H. Van Keulen, and H. Challa, "Modeling tomato growth for optimizing greenhouse temperatures and carbon dioxide concentrations," in *Proceedings of the International Symposium on Models for Plant Growth, Environmental Control and Farm Management in Protected Cultivation*, vol. 248, pp. 285–294, 1988.

[14] J. W. Jones, E. Dayan, L. H. Allen, H. Van Keulen, and H. Challa, "Dynamic tomato growth and yield model (TOMGRO)," *Transactions of the American Society of Agricultural Engineers*, vol. 34, no. 2, pp. 663–672, 1991.

[15] Z. Pék and L. Helyes, "The effect of daily temperature on truss flowering rate of tomato," *Journal of the Science of Food and Agriculture*, vol. 84, no. 13, pp. 1671–1674, 2004.

[16] J. M. Scholberg, K. J. Boote, J. W. Jones, and B. L. McNeal, "Adaptation of the CROPGRO model to simulate the growth of field-grown tomato," in *Applications of Systems Approaches at the Field Level*, vol. 6 of *Systems Approaches for Sustainable Agricultural Development*, pp. 135–151, Springer, Dordrecht, Netherlands, 1997.

[17] K. J. Boote, M. R. Rybak, J. M. S. Scholberg, and J. W. Jones, "Improving the CROPGRO-tomato model for predicting growth and yield response to temperature," *HortScience*, vol. 47, no. 8, pp. 1038–1049, 2012.

[18] Q. Dong, Y. Wang, J. Barczi, P. De Reffye, and J. Hou, "Tomato growth modeling based on interaction of its structure-function," in *Proceedings of the 1st International Symposium on Plant Growth Modeling, Simulation, Visualization and Their Applications (PMA '03)*, pp. 13–16, Tsinghua University Press, Beijing, China, 2003.

[19] W.-L. Ding, H.-J. Jin, Z.-J. Cheng, and Q. Chen, "A visualization system for tomato plant modeling," in *Proceedings of the 8th International Conference on Computer Graphics, Imaging and Visualization (CGIV '11)*, pp. 160–165, IEEE, Singapore, August 2011.

[20] L. Xin, L. Xu, D. Li, and D. Fu, "The 3d reconstruction of greenhouse tomato plant based on real organ samples and parametric l-system," in *Proceedings of the 6th International Conference on Digital Image Processing (ICDIP '14)*, pp. 915904:1–915904:5, International Society for Optics and Photonics, Cherbourg, France, 2014.

[21] C. Lu, L. Deng, and M. Fei, "An improved visualization modelling method of greenhouse tomato plants based on L-system," in *Proceedings of the Chinese Automation Congress (CAC '15)*, pp. 480–485, November 2015.

[22] G. Rozenberg and A. Salomaa, *Mathematical Theory of L Systems*, Academic Press, 1980.

[23] D. Li, L. Xu, C. Tan, E. D. Goodman, D. Fu, and L. Xin, "Digitization and visualization of greenhouse tomato plants in indoor environments," *Sensors*, vol. 15, no. 2, pp. 4019–4051, 2015.

[24] W. Ding, H. Jin, L. Xu, and Z. Cheng, "Realistic simulation of tomato garden based on GPU," in *AsiaSim 2012*, pp. 365–372, Springer, 2012.

[25] T.-W. Chen, T. M. N. Nguyen, K. Kahlen, and H. Stützel, "Quantification of the effects of architectural traits on dry mass production and light interception of tomato canopy under different temperature regimes using a dynamic functional-structural plant model," *Journal of Experimental Botany*, vol. 65, no. 22, pp. 6399–6410, 2014.

[26] A. Kano and C. Van Bavel, "Design and test of a simulation model of tomato growth and yield in a greenhouse," *Journal of the Japanese Society for Horticultural Science*, vol. 58, pp. 406–416, 1988.

[27] M. Bar and N. Ori, "Leaf development and morphogenesis," *Development*, vol. 141, no. 22, pp. 4219–4230, 2014.

[28] J. Liu, Z. Jiang, H. Li, W. Ding, and X. Zhang, "3D plant modeling based on BP neural network," in *Transactions on Edutainment XII*, vol. 9292 of *Lecture Notes in Computer Science*, pp. 109–126, Springer, Berlin, Germany, 2016.

[29] E. Heuvelink, "Evaluation of a dynamic simulation model for tomato crop growth and development," *Annals of Botany*, vol. 83, no. 4, pp. 413–422, 1999.

[30] E. Heuvelink, "Growth, development and yield of a tomato crop: periodic destructive measurements in a greenhouse," *Scientia Horticulturae*, vol. 61, no. 1-2, pp. 77–99, 1995.

[31] T. Li, E. Heuvelink, and L. F. M. Marcelis, "Quantifying the source-sink balance and carbohydrate content in three tomato cultivars," *Frontiers in Plant Science*, vol. 6, article 416, 2015.

[32] E. Dayan, H. Van Keulen, J. W. Jones, I. Zipori, D. Shmuel, and H. Challa, "Development, calibration and validation of a greenhouse tomato growth model: I. Description of the model," *Agricultural Systems*, vol. 43, no. 2, pp. 145–163, 1993.

[33] L. Bacci, P. Battista, and B. Rapi, "Evaluation and adaptation of TOMGRO model to Italian tomato protected crops," *New Zealand Journal of Crop and Horticultural Science*, vol. 40, no. 2, pp. 115–126, 2012.

[34] L. Wilson and W. Barnett, "Degree-days: an aid in crop and pest management," *California Agriculture*, vol. 37, no. 1, pp. 4–7, 1983.

[35] L. F. M. Marcelis, E. Heuvelink, and J. Goudriaan, "Modelling biomass production and yield of horticultural crops: a review," *Scientia Horticulturae*, vol. 74, no. 1-2, pp. 83–111, 1998.

[36] S. Xiao, A. van der Ploeg, M. Bakker, and E. Heuvelink, "Two instead of three leaves between tomato trusses: measured and simulated effects on partitioning and yield," *Acta Horticulturae*, vol. 654, pp. 303–308, 2004.

[37] D. L. Ehret, B. D. Hill, T. Helmer, and D. R. Edwards, "Neural network modeling of greenhouse tomato yield, growth and water use from automated crop monitoring data," *Computers and Electronics in Agriculture*, vol. 79, no. 1, pp. 82–89, 2011.

[38] E. E. Kuchen, S. Fox, P. B. de Reuille et al., "Generation of leaf shape through early patterns of growth and tissue polarity," *Science*, vol. 335, no. 6072, pp. 1092–1096, 2012.

[39] A.-G. Rolland-Lagan, L. Remmler, and C. Girard-Bock, "Quantifying shape changes and tissue deformation in leaf development," *Plant Physiology*, vol. 165, no. 2, pp. 496–505, 2014.

[40] H. Li, X. Zhang, W. Che, and M. Jaeger, "Smooth transition between different plant leaves models," in *Proceedings of the 3rd International Symposium on Plant Growth Modeling, Simulation, Visualization and Applications (PMA '09)*, pp. 376–383, IEEE, Beijing, China, November 2009.

[41] J. Li, M. Liu, W. Xu, H. Liang, and L. Liu, "Boundary-dominant flower blooming simulation," *Computer Animation and Virtual Worlds*, vol. 26, no. 3-4, pp. 433–443, 2015.

[42] G. Bao, W. Meng, H. Li, J. Liu, and X. Zhang, "Hardware instancing for real-time realistic forest rendering," in *Proceedings of the SIGGRAPH Asia 2011 Sketches (SA '11)*, pp. 16:1–16:2, ACM, Hong Kong, China, 2011.

## 15

Automated Analysis of Facial Cues from Videos as a Potential Method for Differentiating Stress and Boredom of Players in Games

Fernando Bevilacqua ⓘ,[1,2] **Henrik Engström** ⓘ,[1] **and Per Backlund** ⓘ[1]

[1]*University of Skövde, Skövde, Sweden*
[2]*Federal University of Fronteira Sul, Chapecó, SC, Brazil*

Correspondence should be addressed to Fernando Bevilacqua; fernando.bevilacqua@his.se

Academic Editor: Michael J. Katchabaw

Facial analysis is a promising approach to detect emotions of players unobtrusively; however approaches are commonly evaluated in contexts not related to games or facial cues are derived from models not designed for analysis of emotions during interactions with games. We present a method for automated analysis of facial cues from videos as a potential tool for detecting stress and boredom of players behaving naturally while playing games. Computer vision is used to automatically and unobtrusively extract 7 facial features aimed at detecting the activity of a set of facial muscles. Features are mainly based on the Euclidean distance of facial landmarks and do not rely on predefined facial expressions, training of a model, or the use of facial standards. An empirical evaluation was conducted on video recordings of an experiment involving games as emotion elicitation sources. Results show statistically significant differences in the values of facial features during boring and stressful periods of gameplay for 5 of the 7 features. We believe our approach is more user-tailored, convenient, and better suited for contexts involving games.

1. Introduction

The detection of the emotional state of players during the interaction with games is a topic of interest for game researchers and practitioners. The most commonly used techniques to obtain the emotional state of players are self-reports (questionnaires) and physiological measurements [1]. Questionnaires are practical and easy to use tools; however, they require a shift in attention, hence breaking or affecting the level of engagement/immersion of users. Physiological signals, on the other hand, provide uninterrupted monitoring [2, 3]; however, they are uncomfortable and intrusive, since they require a proper setup in the person's body. Additionally sensors might restrict player's motion abilities; for example, a sensor attached to a finger prevents the use of that finger.

Facial analysis is a promising approach to detect the emotional state of players unobtrusively and without interruptions [4]. The use of computer vision for player experience detection is feasible and visual inspection of gaming sessions has shown that automated analysis of facial expressions is sufficient to infer the emotional state of players [5, 6]. Automatically detected facial expressions have been correlated with dimensions of game experience [7] and used to enhance player's experience in online games [8, 9]. Automated facial analysis has become mature enough for affective computing; however, there are several challenges associated with the process. Facial actions are inherently subtle, making them difficult to model, and individual differences in face shape and appearance undermine generalization across subjects [4]. Schemes such as the Facial Action Coding System (FACS) [10, 11] aim to overcome those challenges by standardizing the measurements of facial expression by defining highly regulated procedural techniques to detect facial Action Units (AU).

While previous work explored the use of manual or automated facial analysis as a mean to detect the emotional state of players, aimed at creating emotionally adapted games [12] or tools for unobtrusive game research, they lack an easier and more user-tailored approach for studying and detecting facial behavior in the context of games. The use of FACS, for instance, is a laborious task that requires trained coders and several hours of manual analysis of video recordings. When automated facial analysis is used, it is often tested on contexts not related to games, or they rely on facial cues derived from models not designed for analysis of emotional interactions in games, such as the MPEG-4 standard [13]. Such standard specifies representations for 3D facial animations, not emotional interactions in games. Automated facial analysis is also commonly performed on images or videos whose subjects are acting to produce facial expressions, which are likely to be exaggerated in nature and not genuine emotional manifestations. Those are artificial reactions that are unlikely to happen in a context involving subjects interacting with real games, where emotional involvement between subject and game is stronger. Another limitation of previous work is the common focus on detecting facial expressions per se, for example, 6 universal facial expressions [14], not necessarily detecting isolated facial actions, for example, frowning, associated with emotional reactions in games. Finally people are different and elements as age and familiarity with a game influence the outcome of automated facial analysis of behavioral cues [15], and different games might induce different bindings of facial expressions [7]. As a consequence, a more user-tailored contextualization is essential for any study involving facial analysis, particularly involving games. Empirical results of manual annotations of facial behavior in gaming sessions have indicated more annotations during stressful than during boring [16] or neutral [17] parts of games. Further investigation of such findings using an automated analysis instead of a manual approach is a topic of interest for game researchers and practitioners, who can benefit from improved tools related to facial behavior analysis.

In this paper, we introduce our method for automated analysis of facial cues from videos and present empirical results of its application as a potential tool for detecting stress and boredom of players in games. Our method is based on Euclidean distances between automatically detected facial points, not relying on prior model training to produce results. Additionally the method is able to cope with face analysis under challenging conditions, such as when players behave naturally, for example, moving and laughing while playing games. We applied our method on video recordings of an experiment involving games as emotion elicitation sources, which were deliberately designed to cause emotional states of boredom and stress. During the game session, subjects were not instructed to remain still, so captured corporal and facial reactions are natural and emerged from the interaction with the games. Subjects perceived the games as being boring at the beginning and stressful at the end with statistically significant differences of physiological signals, for example, heart rate (HR), in those distinct periods [18]. This experimental configuration allows the evaluation of our method in a situation involving game-based emotion elicitation, which contextualizes our automated facial analysis in a more game-oriented fashion than previous work. Our main contribution is twofold: firstly we introduce a novel method for automated analysis of facial behavior, which has

the potential to be used to differentiate emotional states of boredom and stress of players. Secondly we present the results of an automated facial analysis performed on subjects of our experiment, who interacted with different games under boring and stressful gameplay conditions. Our results show that values of facial features detected during boring periods of gameplay are different from values of the same facial features detected during stressful periods of gameplay. Even though the nature of our games, that is, 2D and casual, and the sample size ($N = 20$) could be limiting factors for the generality of the evaluation of our method, we believe our population of experimental subjects is diverse and our results are still promising. Our study contributes with results that can guide further investigation regarding emotions and facial analysis in gaming contexts. It includes information that can be used to create nonobtrusive models for emotion detection in games, for example, fusion of facial and body features (multimodal emotion recognition) which is known to perform better than using either one alone [19].

The rest of this paper is organized as follows. Section 2 presents related work on manual and automated facial analysis focused on emotion detection. Section 3 presents our proposed facial features, the experimental setup, and the methodology used to evaluate them. Sections 4 and 5 present, respectively, the results obtained from the evaluation of the facial features and a discussion about it. Finally, Sections 6 and 7 present the limitations of our approach, a conclusion, and future work.

2. Related Work

The analysis of facial behavior commonly relies on data obtained from physical sensors, for example, electromyography (EMG), or from the application of visual methods to assess the face, for example, feature extraction via computer vision [20]. The approach based on EMG data uses physical sensors attached to subjects to measure electrical activity of facial muscles, such as the zygomaticus, the orbicularis oculi, and the corrugator supercilii muscles (Figure 1), associated with smiling, eyelids control, and frowning, respectively. Hazlett [21] presents evidence of more frequent corrugator activity when positive game events occur. Tijs et al. [3] show increased activity of zygomatic muscle associated with self-reported positive emotions. Similarly, Ravaja et al. [22] show that positive and rewarding game events are connected to increase in zygomatic and orbicularis oculi EMG activity. Approaches based on EMG are more resilient to variations of lighting conditions and facial occlusion; however, they are obtrusive since physical sensors are required to be attached to the subject's face.

Contrary to the obtrusiveness of EMG-based approaches, analysis of facial behavior based on automated visual methods can be performed remotely and without physical contact. The process usually involves face detection, localization of facial features (also known as landmarks or fiducial points), and classification of such information into facial expressions [23]. A common classification approach is based on distances and angles of landmarks. Samara et al. [24] use the Euclidean

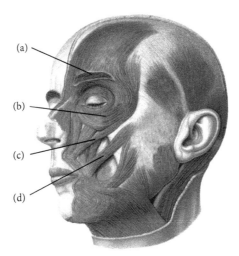

FIGURE 1: Facial muscles. (a) Corrugator supercilii. (b) Orbicularis oculi. (c) Zygomaticus minor. (d) Zygomaticus major. Adapted from "Sobotta's Atlas and Text-book of Human Anatomy," by Dr. Sobotta (Illustration: Hajek and Schmitson), 1909, in the public domain [35].

distance among face points to train a Support Vector Machine (SVM) model to detect expressions. Similarly Chang et al. [25] use 12 distances calculated from 14 landmarks to detect fear, love, joy, and surprise. Hammal et al. [26] use 5 facial distances calculated from lines in key regions of the face derived from the MPEG-4 animation standard [13], for example, eyebrows, for classification of expressions. Tang and Huang [27, 28] use up to 30 Euclidean distances among facial landmarks also obtained from MPEG-4 based 3D face models to recognize the 6 universal facial expressions. Similarly Hupont et al. [29] classify the same emotions by using a correlation-based feature selection technique to select the most significant distances and angles of facial points. Finally Akakn and Sankur [30] use the trajectories of facial landmarks to recognize head gestures and facial expressions.

Some visual methods rely on manual or automated FACS-based analysis as a standard for categorization and measuring of emotional expressions [31]. Kaiser et al. [17] demonstrate that more AU were reported by manual FACS coders during the analysis of video recordings of subjects playing the stressful part of a game when compared to its neutral part. Additionally authors report lip pull corner and inner/outer brow raise as more frequent AUs during gaming sessions. Wehrle and Kaiser [32] use an automated, FACS-based facial analysis aggregated with data from game events to provide an appraisal analysis of subjects emotional state. Similarly Grafsgaard et al. [33] use an automated, FACS-based analysis to report a relationship between facial expression and aspects of engagement, frustration, and learning in tutoring sessions. Contrary to previous work, Heylen et al. [34] do not rely on FACS, but instead use an empirical, manual facial analysis based on the authors' interpretation of the context. Heylen et al. [34] found that most of the time subjects remain with a neutral face.

The use of facial expressions as a single source of information, however, is contested in the literature. Blom et al. [36] report that subjects present a neutral face during most of the time of gameplay and frustration is not captured by face expressions, but by head movements, talking, and hand gestures instead. In a similar conclusion, Shaker et al. [37] show that head expressivity, that is, movement and velocity, is an indicator of how experienced one is on games. Additionally high frequency and velocity of head movements are indicative of failing in the game. Finally Giannakakis et al. [38] reported increased blinking rate, head movement, and heart rate during stressful situations.

Facial analysis based on physical sensors, for example, EMG, provides continuous monitoring of subjects and is not affected by lighting conditions or pose occlusion by subject's movement. However the sensors are obtrusive and the use of sensors increases user's awareness of being monitored [39–41]. Approaches based on video analysis, for example, FACS and computer vision, are less intrusive. Despite the fact that FACS has proven to be a useful and quantitative approach for measuring facial expressions [31], its manual application is laborious and time-consuming and requires certified coders to inspect the video recordings. The application of FACS also has downsides, including different facial expression decoding caused by misinterpretation in specific cultures [42]. Facial analysis from visual methods, such as the previously mentioned feature-based approaches relying on computer vision, is quicker and easier to deploy. However previous works commonly focus on analyzing images or videos whose subjects performed facial expressions on guidance. Those are artificial circumstances that do not portray natural interactions of users and games, for instance. When the analysis is performed on videos of subjects interacting with games, usually the aim is to detect a very specific set of facial expressions, for example, 6 universal facial expressions, disregarding head movement and subtle changes in facial behavior.

Our approach focuses on performing facial analysis on subjects interacting with games with natural behavior and genuine emotional reactions. The novel configuration of our experiment provokes two distinct emotional states on

FIGURE 2: Experimental procedure. *Game$_i$* represents the *i*th interaction of a subject with a game, *Q* is when the subject answered a questionnaire, and *Rest* is a 138-second period when the subject rested.

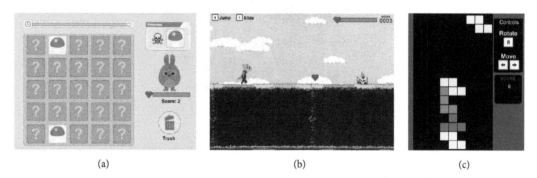

FIGURE 3: Games used in the experiment. From (a) to (c): Mushroom, where the player must sort bad from good mushrooms by analyzing color patterns; Platformer, where the player must jump over or slide below obstacles while collecting hearts; Tetris, which is a clone of the original version of the game, however without hints about the next piece to enter the screen.

subjects, that is, boredom and stress, which are elicited from interaction with games, not videos or images. Additionally our method focuses on detecting facial nuances from calculations based on the Euclidean distances between facial landmarks instead of categorizing predefined facial expressions. We empirically show that such features have the potential to differentiate emotional states of boredom and stress in games. Our calculated facial features can be used as one of the inputs of multimodal emotion detection models.

3. Method

3.1. Experimental Setup. Twenty adult participants of both genders (10 female) with different ages (22 to 59, mean 35.4, SD 10.79) and different gaming experience gave their informed and written consent to participate in the experiment. The study population consisted of staff members and students of the University of Skövde, as well as citizens of the community/city (see [16] for more information about subjects). Subjects were seated in front a computer, alone in the room, while being recorded by a camera and measured by a heart rate sensor. The camera was attached to a tripod placed in front of the subjects at approximately 0.6 m of distance; the camera was slightly tilted up. A spotlight, tilted 45° up and placed at a distance of 1.6 m from the subject and 45 cm higher than the camera level, was used for illumination; no other light source was active during the experiment.

Participants were each recorded for about 25 minutes, during which they played three different games (described in Section 3.1.1), rested, and answered questions. Figure 2 illustrates the procedure. *Game$_i$* represents the *i*th interaction of a subject with a game. The order of the three games which were played was randomized among subjects. Each game was followed by a questionnaire related to the game and stress/boredom. The first two games were followed by a 138-second rest period, where subjects listened to calm classical music. Before starting the experiment, participants received instructions from a researcher saying that they should play three games, answer a questionnaire after each game, and rest; they were told that their gaming performance was not being analyzed, that they should not give up in the middle of the games, and that they should remain seated during the whole process.

3.1.1. Games and Stimuli Elicitation. The three games used in the experiment were 2D and casual-themed, played with mouse or keyboard in a web browser. When keyboard was used as input, the keys to control the game were deliberately chosen to be distant from each other, requiring subjects to use both hands to play. It reduces the risk for facial occlusion during game play, for example, hand interacting with the face. The games were carefully designed to provoke boredom at the beginning and stress at the end, with a linear progression between the two states (adjustments of such progression are performed every 1 minute). The game mechanics were chosen based on the capacity to fulfill such linear progression, along with the quality of not allowing the player to kill the main character instantly (by mistake or not), for example, by falling into a hole. The mechanics were also designed/selected in a way to ensure that all subjects would have the same game pace; for example, a player must not be able to deliberately control the game speed based on his/her will or skill level, for instance. Figure 3 shows each one of the games.

The *Mushroom* game, shown in Figure 3(a), is a puzzle where the player must repeatedly feed a monster by dragging and dropping mushrooms. Boredom is induced with fewer mushrooms to deal with and plenty of time for the task, while stress is induced with increased number of mushrooms and limited time to drag them. The *Platformer* game, shown in Figure 3(b), is a side-scrolling game where the player must control the main character while collecting hearts and avoiding obstacles (skulls with spikes). Boredom is induced

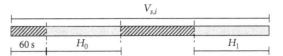

FIGURE 4: Extraction of video segments H_0 and H_1 containing boring and stressful game interactions, respectively. Initial 60 seconds of any video $V_{s,i}$ are ignored and the remaining is divided into three pieces, from which the first and the last ones are selected. Stripes highlight discarded video segments.

with a slow pace and almost no hearts or obstacles appearing on the screen, while stress is induced with a faster pace, several obstacles, and almost no hearts to collect. Finally the game *Tetris*, shown in Figure 3(c), is a modified version of the original Tetris game. In our version of the game, the next block to be added to the screen is not displayed and the down key, usually used to speed up the descendant trajectory of the current piece, is disabled, preventing players from speeding up the game. Boredom is induced by slow falling pieces, while stress is induced by fast falling pieces. All games used the same seed for random calculations, which ensured subjects received the same sequence of game elements, for example, pieces in Tetris. For a detailed description of the games, refer to [16].

Previous analysis conducted on the video recordings of the experiment [18] supports the use of three custom-made games with linear and constant progression from a boring to a stressful state, without predefined levels, modes, or stopping conditions as a valid approach for the exploration of facial behavior and physiological signals regarding their connection with emotional states. Previous results confirm with statistical significance that (1) subjects perceived the games as being boring at the beginning and stressful at the end; (2) the games induced emotional states, that is, boredom and stress, and caused physiological reactions on subjects, that is, changes in HR. Analyses of such changes indicate that HR mean during the last minute of gameplay (perceived as stressful) was greater than during the second minute of gameplay (perceived as boring). An exploratory investigation suggests that HR mean during the first minute of gameplay was greater than during the second minute of gameplay, probably as a consequence of unusual excitement during the first minute, for example, idea of playing a new game. Finally manual and empirical analyses of the video recordings show more facial activity in stressful parts of the games compared to boring parts [16].

Our experimental configuration and previous analysis provide a validated foundation for the application and evaluation of our method for automated analysis of facial cues from videos. Our intent is to test it as a potential tool for differentiating emotional states of stress and boredom of players in games, which can be evaluated with our experimental configuration, since such information can be categorized according to the induced (and theoretically known) emotional states of subjects.

3.1.2. Data Collection. During the whole experiment, subjects were recorded using a Canon Legria HF R606 video camera. All videos were recorded in color (24-bit RGB with three channels × 8 bits/channel) at 50p frames per second (FPS) with pixel resolution of 1920 × 1080 and saved in AVCHD-HD format, MPEG-4 AVC as the codec. At the same time, their heart rate (HR) was measured by a TomTom Runner Cardio watch (TomTom International BV, Amsterdam, Netherlands), which was placed on the left arm, approximately 7 cm away from the wrist. The watch recorded the HR at 1 Hz.

3.2. Data Preprocessing. The preprocessing of video recordings involved extraction of the parts containing the interaction with the games and the discard of noisy frames. Firstly we extracted from the video recordings the periods where subjects were playing each one of the available games. It resulted in three videos per subject, denoted as $V_{s,i}$ where s is the sth subject and $i \in \{1, 2, 3\}$ represents the game.

As previously mentioned, the games used as emotional elicitation material in the experiment induced variations of physiological signals on subjects, who perceived them as being boring at the beginning and stressful at the end. Since our aim is to test the potential of our facial features to differentiate emotional states of boredom and stress, we extracted from each video $V_{s,i}$ two video segments, named H_0 and H_1, whose subject's emotional state is assumed to be known and related to boredom and stress. In order to achieve that, we performed the following extraction procedure, illustrated in Figure 4. Firstly we ignored the initial 60 seconds of any given video $V_{s,i}$. The remaining of the video was then divided into three pieces, from which the first and the last were selected as H_0 and H_1, respectively.

The reason why we discarded the initial part of all game videos is because we believe the first minute might not be ideal for a fair analysis. During the first minute of gameplay, subjects are less likely to be in their usual neutral emotional state. They are more likely to be stimulated by the excitement of the initial contact with a game soon to be played, which interferes with any feelings of boredom. Additionally subjects need basic experimentation with the game to learn how to play it and judge if it is boring or not. Such claim is supported by empirical analysis of the first minute of the video recordings that show repeated head and eye movements from and towards the keyboard/display. As per our understanding, the second minute and onward in the videos is more likely to portrait facial activity related to emotional reactions to the game instead of facial activity connected to gameplay learning. Regarding the division of the remaining part of the video into three segments, from which two were selected as H_0 and H_1, we followed the reasoning that the emotional state of subjects was unknown in the middle part of $V_{s,i}$. Based on self-reported emotional

TABLE 1: Information regarding calculated facial features.

Name	Notation	Description
Mouth outer	F_1	Sum of the Euclidean distance between the mouth contour landmarks and the anchor landmarks. It monitors the zygomatic muscle.
Mouth corner	F_2	Sum of the Euclidean distance between the mouth corner landmarks and the anchor landmarks. It monitors the zygomatic muscle.
Eye area	F_3	Area of the regions bounded by the closed curves formed by the landmarks in contour of the eyes. It monitors the orbicularis oculi muscle.
Eyebrow activity	F_4	Sum of the Euclidean distance between eyebrow landmarks and the anchor landmarks. It monitors the corrugator muscle.
Face area	F_5	Area of the region bounded by the closed polygon formed by the most external detected landmarks.
Face motion	F_6	Average value of the Euclidean norm of a set of landmarks in the last N frames. It describes the total distance the head has moved in any direction in a short period of time.
Facial COM	F_7	Average value of all detected landmarks. It describes the overall movement of all facial landmarks.

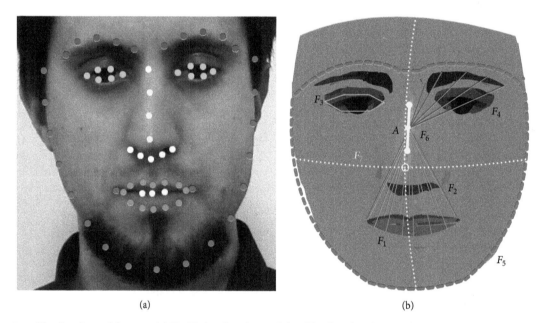

(a)   (b)

FIGURE 5: Facial landmarks and features. (a) Highlight of 68 detected facial landmarks. (b) Visual representation of our facial features.

states, subjects reported the beginning part of the games as boring and the final part as stressful; additionally there are significant differences in the HR mean between the second and the last minute of gameplay in the games [18]. Consequentially we understand that video segments H_0 and H_1 accurately portray interaction of subjects during boring and stressful periods of the games, respectively.

The preprocessing of the recordings resulted in 6 video segments per subjects: 3 segments H_0 (one per game) and 3 segments H_1 (one per game). A given game i contains $N = 20$ pairs of H_0 and H_1 video segments (20 segments H_0, one per subject, and 20 segments H_1, one per subject). When considering all subjects and games, there are $N = 60$ pairs of H_0 and H_1 video segments (3 games $\times$ 20 subjects, resulting in 60 segments H_0 and 60 segments H_1). Subject 9 had problems playing the Platformer game, so segments H_0 and H_1 from subject 9 in the Platformer game were discarded.

Consequentially the Platformer game contains $N = 19$ pairs of H_0 and H_1 video segments; regarding all games and subjects, there are $N = 59$ pairs of H_0 and H_1 video segments.

3.3. Facial Features.

The automated facial analysis we propose is based on the measurement of 7 facial features calculated from 68 detected facial landmarks. Table 1 presents the facial features, which are illustrated in Figure 5(b). Our facial features are mainly based on the Euclidean distances between landmarks, similar to some works previously mentioned; however, our approach does not rely on predefined expressions, that is, 6 universal facial expressions, training of a model, or the use of the MPEG-4 standard, which specifies representations for 3D facial animations, not emotional interactions in games. Additionally our method does not use an arbitrarily selected frame, for example, the 100th frame [38], as a reference for calculations, since our features are derived from each frame (or a small set of past frames). Our features are obtained unobtrusively via computer vision analysis focused on detecting activity of facial muscles reported by previous work involving EMG and emotion detection in games. We believe our approach is more user-tailored, convenient, and better suited for contexts involving games.

The process of extracting our facial features has two main steps: face detection and feature calculation. In the first step, computer vision techniques are applied to a frame of the video and facial landmarks are detected. In the second step, the detected landmarks are used to calculate several facial features related to eyes, mouth, and head movement. The following sections present in detail how each step is performed, including details regarding the calculation of features.

3.3.1. Face Detection.
The face detection procedure is performed for every frame of the input video. We detect the face using a Constrained Local Neural Field (CLNF) model [43, 44]. CLNF uses a local neural field patch expert that learns the nonlinearities and spatial relationships between pixel values and the probability of landmark alignment. The technique also uses a nonuniform regularized landmark Mean Shift fitting technique that takes into consideration patch reliabilities. It improves the detection process under challenging conditions, for example, extreme face pose or occlusion, which is likely to happen in game sessions [16]. The application of the CLNF model to a given video frame produces a vector L of 68 facial landmarks:

$$L = [p_0, p_1, p_2, \ldots, p_{67}]^T, \tag{1}$$

where p_i is a detected facial landmark that represents a 2D coordinate (x_i, y_i) in the frame. Facial landmarks are related to different facial regions, such as eyebrows, eyes, and lips. Figure 5(a) illustrates the landmarks of L in a given frame.

3.3.2. Anchor Landmarks.
The calculation of our facial features involves the Euclidean distance among facial landmarks. Subsequently the Euclidean distance between two landmarks $a_1 = (x_1, y_1)$ and $a_2 = (x_2, y_2)$ is given as follows:

$$d(a_1, a_2) = \sqrt{(x_2 - x_1)^2 + (y_2 - y_1)^2}. \tag{2}$$

Landmarks in the nose area are more likely to be stable, presenting fewer position variations in consecutive frames [38]. Consequently they are good reference points to be used in the calculation of the Euclidean distance among landmarks. In order to provide stable reference points for the calculation of our facial features, we selected 3 highly stable landmarks located in the nose line, denoted as the anchor vector $A = [p_{28}, p_{29}, p_{30}]^T$. The landmarks of the anchor vector A are highlighted in yellow in Figure 5(a).

3.3.3. Feature Normalization.
Subjects moved towards and away from the camera during the gaming sessions. This movement affects the Euclidean distance between landmarks, as it tends to increase when the subject is closer to the camera, for instance. Additionally subjects have unique facial shapes and characteristics, which also affect the calculation and comparison of the facial features between subjects. To mitigate that problem, we calculated a normalization coefficient K as the Euclidean distance between the upper and lower most anchor landmarks in A. In other words, K represents the size of the subjects nose line. Since all features are divided by K, their final value is expressed as normalized pixels (relative to K) rather than pixels per se.

3.3.4. Mouth Related Features.
Mouth related features aim to detect activity in the zygomatic muscles, illustrated in Figures 1(c) and 1(d), which are related to changes in the mouth, such as lips activity (stretch, suck, press, parted, tongue touching, and bite) and movement (including talking). We calculate two facial features related to the mouth area: mouth outer and mouth corner.

Mouth Outer (F_1). Given vector $M = [p_{48}, p_{49}, \ldots, p_{60}]^T$ containing the landmarks in the outer part of the mouth (highlighted in orange in Figure 5(a)). The mouth outer feature is calculated as the sum of the Euclidean distance among the landmarks in M and the anchor landmarks in A:

$$F_1 = \frac{1}{K} \sum_{i=1}^{12} \sum_{j=1}^{3} d(A_j, M_i), \tag{3}$$

where A_j and M_i are the jth and ith element of A and M, respectively.

Mouth Corner (F_2). Given vector $C = [p_{48}, p_{54}]^T$, containing the two landmarks representing the mouth corners (highlighted in pink in Figure 5(a)). The mouth corner feature is the sum of the Euclidean distance among the landmarks in C and A:

$$F_2 = \frac{1}{K} \sum_{i=1}^{2} \sum_{j=1}^{3} d(A_j, C_i), \tag{4}$$

where A_j and C_i are the jth and ith element of A and C, respectively.

3.3.5. Eye Related Features.
Eye related features aim to detect activity related to the orbicularis oculi and the corrugator muscles, illustrated in Figures 1(b) and 1(a), respectively, which comprehend changes in the eyes region, including eye and eyebrow activity. We calculated two facial features related to the eyes: eye area and eyebrow activity.

Eye Area (F_3). Given vector $Y_l = [p_{36}, p_{37}, \ldots, p_{41}]^T$ containing the landmarks describing the left eye, highlighted in green in Figure 5(a), and vector $Y_r = [p_{42}, p_{43}, \ldots, p_{47}]^T$ containing the landmarks describing the right eye, highlighted in green in Figure 5(a). The eye area feature is the area of the regions bounded by the closed curves formed by the landmarks in Y_l and Y_r, divided by K. We calculated the area of the curves using OpenCV's contourArea() function, which uses Green's theorem [45].

Eyebrow Activity (F_4). It is calculated as the sum of the Euclidean distances among the eyebrow landmarks and the anchor landmarks in A. Given the vector $W_l = [p_{17}, p_{18}, \ldots, p_{21}]^T$ containing the landmarks describing the left eyebrow, highlighted in blue in Figure 5(a), and the set $W_r = [p_{22}, p_{23}, \ldots, p_{26}]^T$ containing the landmarks describing the right eyebrow, highlighted in blue in Figure 5(a). The eyebrow activity feature is calculated as follows:

$$F_4 = \frac{1}{K} \sum_{i=1}^{5} \sum_{j=1}^{3} \left[d\left(A_j, W_{l,i}\right) + d\left(A_j, W_{r,i}\right) \right], \quad (5)$$

where A_j, $W_{l,i}$, and $W_{r,i}$ are the jth, ith, and ith element of A, W_l, and W_r, respectively.

3.3.6. Head Related Features. Head related features aim to detect body movements, in particular variations of head pose and amount of motion that the head/face is performing over time. We calculated three features related to the head: face area, face motion, and facial center of mass (COM).

Face Area (F_5). During the interaction with a game, subjects tend to move towards (or away from) the screen, which causes the facial area in the video recordings to increase or decrease. Given vector $F = [p_0, p_1, \ldots, p_{16}]^T$ containing the landmarks describing the contour of the face, highlighted in red in Figure 5(a). The face area feature is the area of the region bounded by the closed curves formed by the landmarks in $F \cup W_r \cup W_l$, divided by K. Similar to the eye area, we calculated the area under the curves using OpenCV's `contourArea()` function.

Face Motion (F_6). It accounts for the total distance the head has moved in any direction in a short period of time. For each frame of the video, we save the currently detected anchor vector A, which produces vector $D = [A_1, A_2, \ldots, A_n]^T$, where A_i is the vector A detected in the ith frame of the video and n is number of frames in the video. We then calculate the face motion feature as follows:

$$F_6 = \frac{1}{K} \sum_{j=1}^{3} \sum_{t=1}^{Z-1} \left\| D\left(f-t, j\right) - D\left(f-Z, j\right) \right\|, \quad (6)$$

where Z is the amount of frames to include in the motion analysis, $D(i, j)$ is the jth element of $A_i \in D$, f is the number of the current frames, and $\| \cdot \|$ is the Euclidean norm. In our analysis, we used $Z = 50$ (50 frames, equivalent to 1 second).

Facial COM (F_7). It describes the overall movement of all facial landmarks. A single 2D point, calculated as the average of all landmarks in L, is used to monitor the movement. The COM feature is calculated as follows:

$$F_7 = \frac{1}{K} \frac{1}{N} \sum_{i=1}^{N} \left\| p_i \right\|, \quad (7)$$

where N is the total number of detected landmarks (elements in L) and $\| \cdot \|$ is the Euclidean norm.

TABLE 2: Mean of differences ($\pm$SD) of features between periods H_0 and H_1 ($N = 59$). Units expressed in normalized pixels.

Feature (notation)	
Mouth outer (F_1)	$-20.59 \pm 57.36^{**}$
Mouth corner (F_2)	$-3.90 \pm 10.16^{**}$
Eye area (F_3)	$-0.019 \pm 0.064^{*}$
Eyebrow activity (F_4)	$-15.59 \pm 49.71^{*}$
Face area (F_5)	$-2.60 \pm 7.90^{*}$
Face motion (F_6)	-44.97 ± 326.74
Facial COM (F_7)	-0.029 ± 0.113

$^{*}p < 0.05$; $^{**}p < 0.01$.

3.4. Feature Analysis. The previously mentioned features can be calculated for each frame of any given video; however, facial cues might be better contextualized if analyzed in multiple frames. For that reason, we applied our facial analysis to all frames of all video segments H_0 and H_1. We then calculated the mean value of each facial feature in each video segment. As a result, any facial feature F_i has $N = 59$ pairs of mean values (59 from H_0 and 59 from H_1). From now on, we will refer to the set of mean values in H_0 or H_1 of a given feature F_i simply as feature value in H_0 or H_1, respectively.

Based on a previous manual analysis of facial actions of the video recordings [16] and findings of related work, values of facial features during boring periods of the games are expected to be different than those during stressful periods. Since subjects perceived the games as boring at the beginning and stressful at the end, we assume that values in H_0 and H_1, for all features, are likely to correlate with an emotional state of boredom and stress, respectively. Consequentially we state the following overarching hypothesis: the mean value of features in H_0 is different than the mean value in H_1, for all subjects and games. More specifically, we can describe the overarching hypothesis as 7 subhypotheses, denoted as u_i, where $i \in \{1, 2, \ldots, 7\}$. Hypothesis u_i states that the true difference in means between the value of a given feature F_i in H_0 and H_1, for all subjects, is greater than zero. The dependent variable of u_i is F_i and the null hypothesis is that the true difference in means between H_0 and H_1 for feature F_i, for all subjects and games, is equal to zero.

We tested hypothesis u_i by performing a paired two-tail t-test on the values H_0 and H_1 of feature F_i. We performed 7 tests in total: u_1 (mouth outer), u_2 (mouth corner), u_3 (eye area), u_4 (eyebrow activity), u_5 (face area), u_6 (face motion), and u_7 (facial COM).

4. Results

Table 2 presents the mean of differences of all features between periods H_0 and H_1, calculated for all subjects in all games according to the description in Section 3.3 and analyzed according to the procedures described in Section 3.4. The mean of differences of all features shows a decrease from H_0 to H_1. Comparing the mean difference of a feature to its mean value in H_0, the decrease from H_0 to H_1 was 10.7% for mouth outer (F_1), 11.8% for mouth corner (F_2), 10.4% for eye area (F_3), 8.1% for eyebrow activity (F_4), 9.4% for face area (F_5), 8.2% for face motion (F_6), and 11% for facial COM (F_7). Changes related to F_6 and F_7 were not statistically significant. All remaining features presented statistically significant changes from H_0 to H_1. The highest decrease with statistical significance was associated with mouth corner, followed by mouth outer, eye area, face area, and eyebrow activity. Those numbers support our experimental expectations that the values for facial features are different when compared between two distinct parts of the games, that is, boring and stressful ones.

The two facial features related to mouth, that is, mouth corner and mouth outer, presented a combined average decrease of 11.24% from H_0 to H_1. The change was the highest compared to all other features. The mean of differences of F_1 and F_2 between periods H_0 and H_1 was $T(59) = -20.59$ (SD 57.36, $p < 0.01$) and $T(59) = -3.9$ (SD 10.16, $p < 0.01$), respectively. Both features had a statistically significant change from H_0 to H_1, which supports the claim that they are different in those periods. Additionally, both features presented SD considerably greater than the mean, which indicates that differences of such features for each subject between periods H_0 and H_1 are likely to be spread out rather than being clustered around the mean value. Features related to eyes, that is, eye area and eyebrow activity, presented a combined average decrease of 9.28% from H_0 to H_1. The mean of differences of F_3 and F_4 between periods H_0 and H_1 was $T(59) = -0.019$ (SD 0.064, $p < 0.05$) and $T(59) = -15.59$ (SD 49.71, $p < 0.05$), respectively. Similar to mouth related features, eye related features had a statistically significant change from H_0 to H_1, indicating that they are different in those periods. Following the same pattern of change of F_1 and F_2, both features F_3 and F_4 also presented a SD considerably greater than the mean, also suggesting that differences of such features for each subject between periods H_0 and H_1 are likely to be spread out rather than being clustered around the mean value.

Finally features related to the whole face, that is, face area, face motion, and facial COM, presented a combined average decrease of 9.52% from H_0 to H_1. The mean of differences of F_5, F_6 and F_7 were $T(59) = -2.60$ (SD 7.90, $p < 0.05$), $T(59) = -44.97$ (SD 326.74, $p = 0.29$), and $T(59) = -0.029$ (SD 0.113, $p = 0.052$), respectively. Face area was the only feature in this category to present a change that was statistically significant between periods H_0 and H_1, supporting the idea that F_5 is different in those periods. On the contrary, F_6 and F_7 lack statistical significance in their differences between periods H_0 and H_1. Similar to facial features related to mouth and eyes, features F_5, F_6, and F_7 presented SD considerably greater than the mean, also suggesting that differences of such features between period H_0 and H_1 are likely to be spread out rather than being clustered around the mean value.

5. Discussion

5.1. Feature Analysis. The overarching hypothesis states that the mean value of features in H_0 is different than the mean value in H_1. The overarching hypothesis is composed of 7 subhypotheses, that is, u_i, one for each feature F_i, where u_i states that the true difference in means between the value of a given feature F_i in H_0 and H_1 is greater than zero. The majority of the calculated facial features, that is, mouth outer (F_1), mouth corner (F_2), eye area (F_3), eyebrow activity (F_4), and face area (F_5), presented statistically significant differences in their mean values when compared between two distinct parts of the games, that is, H_0 and H_1. As previously mentioned, subjects perceived the first part of the games, that is, H_0, as being boring and the second part, that is, H_1, as being stressful. Results support the claim of subhypotheses u_1 to u_5, which indicate that facial features F_1 to F_5 can be differentiated between periods H_0 and H_1 and consequentially have the potential to unobtrusively differentiate emotional states of boredom and stress of players in gaming sessions. Our results refute subhypotheses u_6 and u_7, since features F_6 and F_7 lack statistical significance to be differentiated between periods H_0 and H_1.

Mouth related facial features, that is, mouth outer (F_1) and mouth corner (F_2), presented statistically significant differences between boring and stressful parts of the games. Both features are calculated based on the distance between mouth and nose related facial landmarks, which presented a decrease in stressful parts of the games. Such decrease could be attributed to landmarks in the upper and lower lips being closer to each other, which could be associated with lips pressing, lips sucking, or talking, for instance. Particularly to the mouth corner feature, a decrease in distance is the result of the two mouth corners being placed closer to the nose area, which could be associated with smiles or mouth deformation, for example, mouth corner pull to left/right. Consequentially, a decrease in the mean value of both features suggests higher mouth activity that involves the approximation of mouth landmarks to the nose area in stressful parts of the games compared to boring parts. Such results are aligned with previous studies that show lip pull corner as a frequent facial behavior during gaming sessions [17] and talking as an emotional indicator [36]. Additionally, stating that our mouth related features were constructed after the zygomatic muscle activity, our results are connected with previous studies that show increased activity of the zygomatic muscle related to self reported emotions [3] and its connection to changes in a game [22].

Eye related features, that is, eye area (F_3) and eyebrow activity (F_4), also presented statistically significant differences between boring and stressful parts of the games. They presented a decrease in the mean value from H_0 to H_1, which points to landmarks detected in the eyes contour becoming closer to each other in H_1. It suggests that more pixels in the eyes area were detected during H_0 (boring part) and then H_1 (stressful part). Such numbers might indicate less blinking activity or more wide-open eyes during boring parts of the games. Additionally it could indicate more blinking and eye tightening activity (possibly related to frowning) during stressful parts. Both indications are aligned with previous findings, which show increased blinking activity (calculated from eye area) in stressful situations [38]. Regarding the eyebrow feature, its calculation is based on the distance between facial landmarks in the eyebrow lines and the nose. A decrease in value indicates a smaller distance among eyebrows and nose, which could be explained by frowning, suggesting that subjects presented more frowning action during stressful moments of the game. The mean value of eyebrow activity during H_0 is greater than during H_1, which indicates that the distance between eyebrows and nose was greater during boring parts of the games compared to stressful parts. It could also be the result of more eyebrow risings, for example, facial expressions of surprise, in boring periods compared to stressful periods. Our eye related features were constructed to monitor the activity of the orbicularis oculi and the corrugator supercilii muscles, and our results are connected with previous work that report game events affecting the activity of the orbicularis oculi [22] and the corrugator [21] muscles.

Finally features related to the whole face, that is, face area (F_5), face motion (F_6), and facial COM (F_7), are partially conclusive. Those features are affected by body motion, for example, head movement and corporal posture, so a decrease in value might indicate less corporal movements during H_1 compared to H_0. Face area was the only feature in this category to present a change that was statistically significant. The value of the face area feature is directly connected to subjects' movement towards and away from the camera. A decrease in face area from H_0 to H_1 suggests that subjects were closer to the computer screen more often during boring parts of the games and then during stressful parts. The facial COM feature also presented a decrease from H_0 to H_1. Such feature is connected to vertical and horizontal movements performed by subject's face, being anchored to a fixed reference point and less influenced by head rotations. Despite presenting a change that is not statistically significant ($p = 0.519$), the decrease of facial COM might be an indication that subjects were more still during stressful periods than during boring periods. The face motion feature also presented a decrease from H_0 to H_1 that is not statistically significant ($p = 0.294$). This feature accounts for the amount of movement a subject's face performs in a period of 50 frames (dynamic reference point), which is directly affected by vertical, horizontal, and rotational movements of the head. A decrease could be associated with subjects moving/rotating the head less often during the analyzed 50 frames periods in H_1 than H_0. However, absence of statistical significance suggests the change is not related to subject's emotional state, but other factors such as the inherent behavior associated with game mechanics, that is, head movement caused by observation of cards in the Mushroom game. Our results lack the statistical significance to replicate the findings of previous work, which connect head movements to changes in games, that is, failure [37] and frustration [36], or to stressful situations [38].

It could be argued that the characteristics of each game mechanic influence the mean change of features between the two periods. Such argument is particularly true to features that are calculated based on subject's body movement, that is, face area, face motion, and facial COM. In that case, subjects could move the face as a result of in game action, that is, inspecting mushrooms, rather than being an emotional

TABLE 3: Percentage of change of features from period H_0 to H_1 in the Mushroom game ($N = 20$).

Feature (notation)	Mean	Min.	Max.
Mouth outer (F_1)	−12.9	−69.1	22.1
Mouth corner (F_2)	−15.0	−71.6	15.5
Eye area (F_3)	−8.9	−76.9	8.2
Eyebrow activity (F_4)	−8.0	−72.3	9.6
Face area (F_5)	−11.3	−74.5	18.2
Face motion (F_6)	47.2	−61.3	253.8
Facial COM (F_7)	−12.9	−81.0	9.8

TABLE 4: Percentage of change of features from period H_0 to H_1 in the Platformer game ($N = 19$).

Feature (notation)	Mean	Min.	Max.
Mouth outer (F_1)	−7.4	−54.0	16.9
Mouth corner (F_2)	−8.2	−55.9	15.5
Eye area (F_3)	−6.8	−30.4	20.0
Eyebrow activity (F_4)	−4.9	−31.1	7.8
Face area (F_5)	−5.9	−43.8	14.2
Face motion (F_6)	0.9	−60.2	112.7
Facial COM (F_7)	−3.6	−42.1	23.1

TABLE 5: Percentage of change of features from period H_0 to H_1 in the Tetris game ($N = 20$).

Feature (notation)	Mean	Min.	Max.
Mouth outer (F_1)	−1.5	−27.8	39.0
Mouth corner (F_2)	−2.1	−26.5	26.9
Eye area (F_3)	−2.6	−19.0	26.1
Eyebrow activity (F_4)	−3.3	−16.2	21.1
Face area (F_5)	−1.4	−24.3	26.7
Face motion (F_6)	−11.3	−85.8	114.3
Facial COM (F_7)	−2.7	−24.7	21.8

manifestation. Additionally the mean change of features between the two periods presented SD considerably greater than the mean value, indicating that differences between periods are likely to be spread out. It suggests significant between-subject variations for each feature or game. In order to further explore such topics, we analyzed the changes of all features on a game level. Tables 3, 4, and 5 present the mean, minimum, and maximum change presented by features, in percentages, from period H_0 to H_1, calculated from all subjects in the Mushroom, Platformer, and Tetris game, respectively.

Mouth and eye related features, that is, F_1 to F_4, presented, on average, a decrease from H_0 to H_1 in all three games. However, the decrease does not apply to all subjects, since at least one presented an increase from H_0 to H_1, as demonstrated by the positive values in the Max column in Tables 3, 4, and 5. Comparatively, the mean, minimum, and maximum change of mouth (F_1, F_2) and eye (F_4, F_5) related features are similar in the three games. Consequentially, it is our understanding that features F_1 to F_4 are not affected by the game mechanics; however, they do differ on a subject basis. On the other hand, features related to the whole face, that is, F_5 to F_7, seem to be affected by game mechanics. Both F_5 and F_7 presented, on average, a decrease in the three games. Contrarily F_6 presented, on average, an increase in the Mushroom and the Platformer game. A disproportional mean increase of 47.2% from H_0 to H_1 for feature F_6 in the Mushroom game compared to the Platformer (0.9% increase) and Tetris (11.3% decrease) suggests that the feature is highly influenced by the mechanic of the Mushroom game. In such game, subjects are likely to move the head to facilitate saccadic eye movements used to inspect the cards. As the difficulty of the game increases, the number of cards to be inspected on the screen also increases, which could potentially lead to more (periodic) head movements towards the stressful part of the game.

Finally all features presented changes from periods H_0 to H_1 whose SD is considerably greater than the mean value, as presented in Table 2. The considerable heterogeneous variation of features, as demonstrated by columns *Min* and *Max* in Tables 3, 4, and 5, supports the claim that differences of features between periods are spread out rather than being clustered around the mean. Even though further analysis is required, the high SD and the broad interval of percentage change of all features in the three games, showing decrease of 76.9% and increase of 8.2% for the same feature in the same game, for instance, highlighting the between-subjects behavioral differences. Our interpretation is that a more user-tailored, as opposed to a group-oriented, use of our facial features is more likely to portray such subject-based differences in a context involving emotional detection and games.

5.2. Comparison with Previous Work. The approach presented by this paper differs from other computer facial expression analysis systems by focusing on the detection of basic elements that comprise complex facial movements rather than on classifying facial expressions. It is aligned with previous work focused on studying the relation between those detected basic elements and emotional states, for example, work by Bartlett et al. [31] and Asteriadis et al. [15]. A direct comparison of our approach with existing facial expression recognition solutions is misleading. Following the direction of Bartlett et al. [31] and Asteriadis et al. [15], this paper intends to investigate facial changes happening in real gaming sessions and the process to detect them. The data related to such changes can then be used to potentially differentiate emotional states, in our case boredom and stress, of players in a gaming context. We present plausible statistical results that support the method and such potential. Previous work focuses on detecting facial expressions per se, including the six universal facial expressions of emotion, typically reporting accuracy rates of machine learning models used to detect those predefined facial expressions. A significant number of those approaches train the models using datasets with images and videos of actors performing facial expressions

[24, 26–28, 46], subjects watching video clips [25, 29, 38], or subjects undergoing social exposure [38]. As previously mentioned, those are artificial situations that are significantly different from an interaction with a game. We evaluated our method on a challenging game-oriented context, showing with statistical significance that there are differences between facial activity, not necessarily facial expressions, in two distinct game periods which are associated with particular emotional states, that is, boredom and stress. The process does not rely on a reference point, for example, neutral face, to operate as the majority of previous work. We believe the context of our experiment is sufficiently different from existing work and our results contribute to guide further investigations regarding automated detection and use of basic facial elements as a source of information to infer emotional states of players in games.

6. Limitations

Some limitations of the experimental procedure and analysis should be noted. Firstly our sample size ($N = 20$) is a relatively small number to derive conclusions that can be generalized. A larger sample for the analysis could produce more conclusive results regarding facial activity that could be applied in contexts other than the one presented in our experiment. Our aim, however, is not to standardize the facial behavior of subjects nor to detect particular facial expressions, but to remotely detect basic facial elements and support the claim that they are different in particular moments of the games. As demonstrated with statistical significance, our features present differences at key moments of the games, that is, boring and stressful parts. Those differences were derived from the facial activity of subjects and they do not necessarily rely on the identification of a particular facial expression, for example, joy (smiles). For the context of our experiment, the analysis conducted on those differences shows the potential of our features to differentiate emotional states of boredom and stress. Another limitation is the nature of the games used in the experiment, which are casual and 2D games. Games with different characteristics, for example, 3D games requiring navigation, could produce different results. However we believe our games do have the characteristics expected of a game, such as a sense of challenge and reward, and its 2D nature is not detrimental. The mechanics of the three games are quite different, requiring subjects to perform distinct patterns of eye saccades and head movement to play. The Mushroom, Platformer, and Tetris game require visual attention on the whole screen, on the left side of the screen, and on the top and bottom parts of the screen, respectively. It is our understanding that those elements cover a significant range of different head and eye movement patterns. Those patterns even interfered with some features, for example, face motion (F_6) and facial COM (F_7), as discussed in Section 5.1. Additionally the use of 2D games for studies involving player experience and emotions is recurrent in the literature, for example, an adapted version of Super Mario has been used to create a personalized gaming experience [36], to analyse player behavior [37], and to discriminate player styles based on visual and gameplay cues [15].

7. Conclusion

This paper presented a method for automated analysis of facial cues from videos with an empirical evaluation of its application as a potential tool for detecting stress and boredom of players. The proposed automated facial analysis is based on the measurement of 7 facial features (F_1 to F_7) calculated from 68 detected facial landmarks. Facial features are mainly based on the Euclidean distance of landmarks and they do not rely on predefined expressions, that is, 6 universal facial expressions, nor training of a model nor the use of standards related to the face, for example, MPEG4 and FACS. Additionally, the method does not use an arbitrarily selected frame as a reference for calculations since features are derived from each frame (or a small set of past frames). Features are obtained unobtrusively via computer vision analysis focused on detecting the activity of facial muscles reported by previous work involving emotion detection in games.

The method has been applied to video recordings of an experiment involving games as emotion elicitation sources, which were deliberately designed to cause emotional states of boredom and stress. Results show statistically significant differences in the values of facial features detected during boring and stressful periods of gameplay for features: mouth outer (F_1), mouth corner (F_2), eye area (F_3), eyebrow activity (F_4), and face area (F_5). Features face motion (F_6) and facial COM (F_7) presented variations that were not statistically significant. Results support the claim that our method for automated analysis of facial cues has the potential to be used to differentiate emotional states of boredom and stress of players. The utilization of our method is unobtrusive and video-based, which eliminates need of physical sensors to be attached to subjects. We believe our approach is more user-tailored, convenient, and better suited for contexts involving games. Finally, the information produced by our method might be used to complement other approaches aimed at emotion detection in the context of games, particularly multimodal models.

Currently, work is ongoing to use the proposed method as one of several sources of information in a nonintrusive, multifactorial user-tailored emotion detection mechanism for games. We intend to further investigate the applicability of our method in a new experiment with a larger sample size and the addition of a new game to the experimental setup, for example, commercial off-the-shelf (COTS) game. The facial analysis described here, particularly the differences found in the boring and stressful parts of the games, will be combined to remote photoplethysmographic estimations of heart rate to train a model to identify emotional states of boredom and stress of players. The results presented here will be improved upon and form the basis for a remote emotion detection approach aimed at the game research community.

Acknowledgments

The authors would like to thank the participants and all involved personnel for their valuable contributions. This work has been performed with support from Conselho Nacional de Desenvolvimento Científico e Tecnológico (CNPq), Brazil; University of Skövde; EU Interreg ÖKS Project Game Hub Scandinavia; Federal University of Fronteira Sul (UFFS).

References

[1] E. D. Mekler, J. A. Bopp, A. N. Tuch, and K. Opwis, "A systematic review of quantitative studies on the enjoyment of digital entertainment games," in *Proceedings of the 32nd Annual ACM Conference on Human Factors in Computing Systems, CHI 2014*, pp. 927–936, May 2014.

[2] P. Rani, C. Liu, N. Sarkar, and E. Vanman, "An empirical study of machine learning techniques for affect recognition in human-robot interaction," *Pattern Analysis and Applications*, vol. 9, no. 1, pp. 58–69, 2006.

[3] T. J. Tijs, D. Brokken, and W. A. IJsselsteijn, "Dynamic game balancing by recognizing affect," in *Fun and Games*, vol. 5294 of *Lecture Notes in Computer Science*, pp. 88–93, Springer, Berlin, Germany, 2008.

[4] J. F. Cohn and F. De la Torre, *Automated Face Analysis for Affective*, The Oxford handbook of affective computing, 2014.

[5] C. T. Tan, D. Rosser, S. Bakkes, and Y. Pisan, "A feasibility study in using facial expressions analysis to evaluate player experiences," in *Proceedings of the 8th Australasian Conference on Interactive Entertainment: Playing the System, IE 2012*, July 2012.

[6] C. T. Tan, S. Bakkes, and Y. Pisan, "Inferring player experiences using facial expressions analysis," in *Proceedings of the 10th Australian Conference on Interactive Entertainment, IE 2014*, pp. 1–8, ACM Press, December 2014.

[7] C. T. Tan, S. Bakkes, and Y. Pisan, "Correlation between facial expressions and the game experience questionnaire," in *Proceedings of the Entertainment Computing-ICEC 2014: 13th International Conference*, vol. 8770, p. 229, Springer, Sydney, Australia, October 2014.

[8] X. Zhou, X. Huang, and Y. Wang, "Real-time facial expression recognition in the interactive game based on embedded hidden markov model," in *Proceedings of the Computer Graphics, Imaging and Visualization*, pp. 144–148, Penang, Malaysia, 2004.

[9] C. Zhan, W. Li, P. Ogunbona, and F. Safaei, "A real-time facial expression recognition system for online games," *International Journal of Computer Games Technology*, vol. 2008, pp. 1–7, 2008.

[10] P. Ekman and W. V. Friesen, 1977, Facial action coding system.

[11] J. F. Cohn, Z. Ambadar, and P. Ekman, "Observer-based measurement of facial expression with the facial action coding system," *The handbook of emotion elicitation and assessment*, pp. 203–221, 2007.

[12] T. Saari and M. Turpeinen, "Towards psychological customization of information for individuals and social groups," in *Designing Personalized User Experiences in eCommerce*, vol. 5 of *Human-Computer Interaction Series*, pp. 19–37, Springer, 2004.

[13] G. A. Abrantes and F. Pereira, "MPEG-4 facial animation technology: survey, implementation, and results," *IEEE Transactions on Circuits and Systems for Video Technology*, vol. 9, no. 2, pp. 290–305, 1999.

[14] P. Ekman and W. V. Friesen, "Constants across cultures in the face and emotion," *Journal of Personality and Social Psychology*, vol. 17, no. 2, pp. 124–129, 1971.

[15] S. Asteriadis, K. Karpouzis, N. Shaker, and G. N. Yannakakis, "Towards detecting clusters of players using visual and game-play behavioral cues," in *Proceedings of the 4th International Conference on Games and Virtual Worlds for Serious Applications, VS-GAMES 2012*, pp. 140–147, October 2012.

[16] F. Bevilacqua, P. Backlund, and H. Engström, "Variations of facial actions while playing games with inducing boredom and stress," in *Proceedings of the 8th International Conference on Games and Virtual Worlds for Serious Applications, VS-Games 2016*, September 2016.

[17] S. Kaiser, T. Wehrle, and P. Edwards, "Multi-modal emotion measurement in an interactive computer game: A pilot-study," in *in Proceedings of the VIII conference of the international society for research on emotions*, pp. 275–279, ISRE Publications Storrs, 1994.

[18] F. Bevilacqua, H. Engström, and P. Backlund, "Changes in heart rate and facial actions during a gaming session with provoked boredom and stress," *Entertainment Computing*, vol. 24, pp. 10–20, 2018.

[19] H. Zacharatos, C. Gatzoulis, and Y. L. Chrysanthou, "Automatic emotion recognition based on body movement analysis: A survey," *IEEE Computer Graphics and Applications*, vol. 34, no. 6, article no. 106, pp. 35–45, 2014.

[20] C. Schrader, J. Brich, J. Frommel, V. Riemer, and K. Rogers, "Rising to the challenge: an emotion-driven approach toward adaptive serious games," in *Serious Games and Edutainment Applications*, pp. 3–28, Springer, 2017.

[21] R. L. Hazlett, "Measuring emotional valence during interactive experiences: boys at video game play," in *Proceedings of the SIGCHI Conference on Human Factors in Computing Systems*, pp. 1023–1026, 2006.

[22] N. Ravaja, T. Saari, M. Salminen, J. Laarni, and K. Kallinen, "Phasic emotional reactions to video game events: a psychophysiological investigation," *Media Psychology*, vol. 8, no. 4, pp. 343–367, 2006.

[23] A. A. Salah, N. Sebe, and T. Gevers, "Communication and automatic interpretation of affect from facial expressions," *Affective Computing and Interaction: Psychological, Cognitive and Neuroscientific Perspectives*, pp. 157–183, 2010.

[24] A. Samara, L. Galway, R. Bond, and H. Wang, "Sensing affective states using facial expression analysis," in *Ubiquitous Computing and Ambient Intelligence*, Lecture Notes in Computer Science, pp. 341–352, Springer International Publishing, 2016.

[25] C.-Y. Chang, J.-S. Tsai, C.-J. Wang, and P.-C. Chung, "Emotion recognition with consideration of facial expression and physiological signals," in *Proceedings of the 2009 IEEE Symposium on Computational Intelligence in Bioinformatics and Computational Biology, CIBCB 2009*, pp. 278–283, April 2009.

[26] Z. Hammal, L. Couvreur, A. Caplier, and M. Rombaut, "Facial expression classification: An approach based on the fusion of facial deformations using the transferable belief model," *International Journal of Approximate Reasoning*, vol. 46, no. 3, pp. 542–567, 2007.

[27] H. Tang and T. S. Huang, "3D Facial expression recognition based on automatically selected features," in *Proceedings of the 2008 IEEE Computer Society Conference on Computer Vision and Pattern Recognition Workshops, CVPR Workshops*, pp. 1–8, June 2008.

[28] H. Tang and T. S. Huang, "3d facial expression recognition based on properties of line segments connecting facial feature points," in *Proceedings of the Automatic Face & Gesture Recognition, 8th IEEE International Conference on IEEE*, pp. 1–6, 2008.

[29] I. Hupont, S. Baldassarri, and E. Cerezo, "Facial emotional classification: from a discrete perspective to a continuous emotional space," *PAA. Pattern Analysis and Applications*, vol. 16, no. 1, pp. 41–54, 2013.

[30] H. Ç. Akakn and B. Sankur, "Spatiotemporal-boosted DCT features for head and face gesture analysis," in *Human Behavior Understanding*, pp. 64–74, Springer Nature, 2010.

[31] M. S. Bartlett, J. C. Hager, P. Ekman, and T. J. Sejnowski, "Measuring facial expressions by computer image analysis," *Psychophysiology*, vol. 36, no. 2, pp. 253–263, 1999.

[32] T. Wehrle and S. Kaiser, "Emotion and facial expression," in *Affective Interactions*, vol. 1814 of *Lecture Notes in Computer Science*, pp. 49–63, Springer, Berlin, Germany, 2000.

[33] J. F. Grafsgaard, J. B. Wiggins, K. E. Boyer, E. N. Wiebe, and J. C. Lester, "Automatically recognizing facial expression: Predicting engagement and frustration," in *EDM*, pp. 43–50, 2013.

[34] D. Heylen, M. Ghijsen, A. Nijholt, and R. Op Den Akker, "Facial signs of affect during tutoring sessions," *Lecture Notes in Computer Science (including subseries Lecture Notes in Artificial Intelligence and Lecture Notes in Bioinformatics): Preface*, vol. 3784, pp. 24–31, 2005.

[35] Wikimedia Commons, *Sobotta's Atlas and Text-book of Human Anatomy 1909*, J. Sobotta, K. Hajek, and A. Schmitson, Eds., 2013, https://commons.wikimedia.org/wiki/File:Sobo_1909_260.png.

[36] P. M. Blom, S. Bakkes, C. T. Tan et al., "Towards personalised gaming via facial expression recognition," in *Proceedings of the 10th AAAI Conference on Artificial Intelligence and Interactive Digital Entertainment, AIIDE 2014*, pp. 30–36, October 2014.

[37] N. Shaker, S. Asteriadis, G. N. Yannakakis, and K. Karpouzis, "A game-based corpus for analysing the interplay between game context and player experience," *Lecture Notes in Computer Science (including subseries Lecture Notes in Artificial Intelligence and Lecture Notes in Bioinformatics): Preface*, vol. 6975, no. 2, pp. 547–556, 2011.

[38] G. Giannakakis, M. Pediaditis, D. Manousos et al., "Stress and anxiety detection using facial cues from videos," *Biomedical Signal Processing and Control*, vol. 31, pp. 89–101, 2017.

[39] T. Yamakoshi, K. Yamakoshi, S. Tanaka et al., "A preliminary study on driver's stress index using a new method based on differential skin temperature measurement," in *Proceedings of the 29th Annual International Conference of IEEE-EMBS, Engineering in Medicine and Biology Society, EMBC'07*, pp. 722–725, August 2007.

[40] M. Yamaguchi, J. Wakasugi, and J. Sakakima, "Evaluation of driver stress using biomarker in motor-vehicle driving simulator," in *Proceedings of the Conference Proceedings. Annual International Conference of the IEEE Engineering in Medicine and Biology Society*, pp. 1834–1837, New York, NY, August 2006.

[41] J. A. Healey and R. W. Picard, "Detecting stress during real-world driving tasks using physiological sensors," *IEEE Transactions on Intelligent Transportation Systems*, vol. 6, no. 2, pp. 156–166, 2005.

[42] R. E. Jack, "Culture and facial expressions of emotion," *Visual Cognition*, vol. 21, no. 9-10, pp. 1248–1286, 2013.

[43] T. Baltrusaitis, P. Robinson, and L.-P. Morency, "Constrained local neural fields for robust facial landmark detection in the wild," in *Proceedings of the 14th IEEE International Conference*

on Computer Vision Workshops (ICCVW '13), pp. 354–361, Sydney, Australia, December 2013.

[44] T. Baltrusaitis, P. Robinson, and L.-P. Morency, "OpenFace: An open source facial behavior analysis toolkit," in *Proceedings of the IEEE Winter Conference on Applications of Computer Vision, WACV 2016*, pp. 1–10, March 2016.

[45] J. Stewart, "Calculus," 2011, Cengage Learning.

[46] P. Wang, F. Barrett, E. Martin et al., "Automated video-based facial expression analysis of neuropsychiatric disorders," *Journal of Neuroscience Methods*, vol. 168, no. 1, pp. 224–238, 2008.

## 16

A Method for Fast Leaderboard Calculations in Massive Online Game-Based Environments

Julian Moreno Cadavid ⓘ **and Hernán Darío Vanegas Madrigal**

Universidad Nacional de Colombia, Bogotá, Colombia

Correspondence should be addressed to Julian Moreno Cadavid; jmoreno1@unal.edu.co

Academic Editor: Michael J. Katchabaw

Leaderboards and other game elements are present in many online environments, not just in videogames. When such environments have relatively few users, the implementation of those leaderboards is not usually a problem; however, that is no longer the case when they have dozens of thousands or more. For those situations we propose a method that is easy and cheap to implement. It is based on two particular data structures, a Self-Balanced Ordering Statistic Tree and a hash table, to perform proper leaderboard calculations in a fast and cheap way. More specifically, our proposal has $O(\log_2 N)$ time complexity, whereas other approaches also based on in-memory data structures like linked lists have $O(N)$, and others based on Hard Disk Drive operations like a relational database have $O(N\log_2 N)$. Such improvement with regard to the other approaches is corroborated with experimental results for several scenarios, also presented in this paper.

1. Introduction

The online games industry is in constant growth. According to NewZoo [1], between China and the US only, there were more than 1 billion online gamers in 2016, who represented altogether almost $48 billion in revenues from the $99.6 billion worldwide, up 8.5% compared to 2015. Just as example, according to SteamCharts [2], Dota 2, a Multiplayer Online Battle Arena (MOBA) game for the Steam platform, had a peak of over a million players in January 2017. That number seems a lot but it looks pale compared with League of Legends (LoL), another MOBA game for Microsoft Windows and MAC OS, which in January 2014 had up to 67 million monthly players, with 27 million playing daily [3].

But not only games themselves are a force to consider, also other online environments are now adopting game-based features to improve users' experiences. A clear example of that is the use of gamification, that is, the use of game elements within nongame contexts, in a great diversity of contexts [4, 5] including education [6, 7], health [8], and marketing [9].

One particular element of game-based environments, and therefore of gamified environments, is leaderboards, a common mechanism to rank players according to their relative success. Leaderboards measure players against a particular criterion, usually the underlying score, and are thus indicators of progress that relate the player's performance to the performance of others looking for intrinsic motivation [10–14].

Most games and gamified environments use leaderboards and, in order to implement them, as well as for solving persistence, a common solution is using a database approach. A database, or more precisely a Data Base Management System (DBMS) generally stores data in the Hard Disk Drive (HDD) using certain data structures, typically *n*-ary trees of several types, which allows for fast insertion, deletion, and search, but not so much for ordering (referring specifically to the ORDER BY clause). When the number of players is low, that is, up to hundreds or few thousands, this does not represent a problem for online environments. However, when they have dozens or even hundreds of thousands of players, the response times become a major issue. As an anecdotic reference, that was exactly what motivated this research in the first place: we were working on a gamified learning environment called TICademia (https://ticademia.com) and when the number of users only came to a thousand, the leaderboard based on a relational data base approach worked just fine. However, when such a number raised to the several dozens of thousands, a lot of response time problems started to appear. In rush hours, with almost 25000 active students in the course "pre-calculus," the response time for the leaderboard page was larger than a minute. It might not sound like too much for most users, but it certainly is for the more "enthusiastic." Of course, such response time would depend on the technology used in the online environment but, any case, it would never scape the intrinsic time of the ORDER BY task.

A very similar situation happened to Applibot, one of the major social apps providers in Japan. With popular games like Legend of the Cryptids and Gang Road, they were able to scale smoothly and handle the massively growing traffic but found some troubles to maintain up-to-date player rankings or, at least, with their initial database approach [15].

An alternative, not necessarily to replace but to complement the database approach, is to store particular information in faster memory schemes like in the Random-Access Memory (RAM) and use efficient data structures to manipulate it. What we propose is exactly the following: to use an order-statistic tree jointly a hash table, both in RAM, to obtain considerably lower response times.

The rest of the paper is structured as follows. In Section 2, we present some related works. In Section 3, we describe our proposal and then in Section 4 we show and discuss some experimental results. Finally, in Section 5, we present the conclusions of this research.

2. Related Works

When we searched the scientific literature about how other researchers addressed the leaderboard implementation problem, we found three main obstacles. First, we did not find anything in games themselves, nor commercial, neither other kinds. That does not mean they do not deal with the problem. Our educated guess is that they are not interested in showing it, or at least in that context. Second, what we did find were some works on gamified learning environments that use leaderboards, but most of them focused on the motivational or learning outcomes, not in implementation details. Third, just a few of those works present validation scenarios with real users, but in all cases with a reduced number of them, dozens or hundreds at most.

In the case of ALEPS, for example, a gamified learning environment for physics problem solving, the leaderboard shows the top students based on the results of various game elements such as the score, levels, experience, and number of badges. Even if they did not explicitly state using a database approach for the leaderboard calculation, they did state using SQL Server as DBMS for manipulating all user data [16].

The same happened with a gamified learning environment for solving computer programming assignments. Here, they implemented two leaderboards, one that shows the overall score and one that shows the score for the current week. In this case, they mention that the system incorporates a leaderboard calculation service in the application layer. Again, they did not explicitly state the database approach, but they did report the use of Hibernate for data storage,

an Object-Relational Mapping (ORM) library that supports multiple relational database systems, such as HSQLDB and MySQL [17].

Another example is a gamified online course for multimedia content production, implemented in the Moodle Learning Management System. In this case, they use a leaderboard to display all enrolled students sorted in descending order by level and then by experience points (XP). Because they used Moodle instead of creating their own system, they do not present any implementation details. However, looking into Moodle's documentation, it turns out that it uses XMLDB, a library in the abstraction layer that lets Moodle interact with and access the database, which may be managed by several DMBS like Postgres, MySQL, MSSQL, and Oracle [18].

Outside the scientific literature, it is possible to find some interesting works. In [15], for example, they rightly point out that maintaining a real-time leaderboard is not an easy task because (a) the game environment may have hundreds of thousands players; (b) whenever a player fights enemies or performs other activities, their score changes; and (c) you want to show the latest ranking for the player usually on a web page. They even contrast the simplicity of the implementation with a relational database approach to its poor performance as the scale grows. As a solution, they use an algorithm with similar time complexity as the one we propose in the next section, $O(\log_a N)$. We tried to use this work as a reference in Section 4, but there are two main difficulties. Conceptually, they only use the player score for the ranking function so, unlike our proposal, multiple players may have the same rank. Technically, its throughput has a limitation of about 300 updates/second due to its cloud architecture.

There are also other commercial approaches with similar time complexity, like Amazon ElastiCache for Redis, but they work only in the cloud and are not necessarily cheap.

3. Method Proposed

In order to handle a leaderboard, we first assume that players have at least two attributes, one related to their identifiers and another related to their scores. The identifier, that we will call from now on id, may be numeric or alphanumeric, but in any case, unique. The score may come from a single or multiple data, but in any case, must be comparable. Particularly, we assume that it refers to a single numeric value and that the higher, the better. These two attributes should be stored together in RAM into two different data structures: a Self-Balanced Order-Statistic Tree (SBOST) and a hash table [19–22]. In both cases, the two attributes are part of an object that we will call player. The same two attributes, in addition to all other relevant information like name, alias, avatar, and so on should be stored separately in a database.

A SBOST is a particular kind of a binary search tree. A binary search tree stores nodes, in this case of player type, and each node is linked at most to two subtrees, commonly denoted left and right. A node with no subtrees is called leaf, and the unique top of the whole tree is called root. Now, besides these features, a binary search tree must fulfill a condition: each node must be greater than all nodes in its left subtree, and not greater than any in the right subtree. There

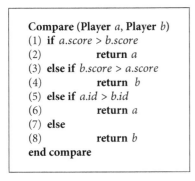

```
Compare (Player a, Player b)
(1)  if  a.score > b.score
(2)            return a
(3)  else if b.score > a.score
(4)            return b
(5)  else if a.id > b.id
(6)  else
(7)            return a
(8)            return b
end compare
```

ALGORITHM 1

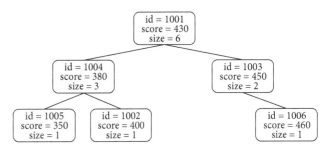

FIGURE 1: Order-statistic tree.

must be, of course, a way to determine which of two nodes is greater than the other. In our case, this comparison is made according to Algorithm 1.

Notice that this algorithm returns the player with the higher score and, in case of a tie, it uses as an untying criterion the higher id. The reason for doing so is that we assume that a higher id means that such a player started later the game or at least checked in later so he/she had less advantage. Of course, this criterion is completely subjective and may be altered according to the designer needs just by adjusting Algorithm 1. For instance, it might use extra information of the player like time spent on the game or time since the last login, and so on. It might also use more information of the score in the case that it refers to multiple, instead of single, data.

For being balanced, a binary search tree must fulfill another condition: the difference between the heights of the left and right subtrees of any node must be at most 1. The height of a subtree is the maximum number of jumps between the root of the subtree and its deepest leaf. Being balanced has a critical repercussion: considering the binary layout of the tree, as well as the relation of each node with its two subtrees, all the basic operations insertion, deletion, and search can be achieved in $O(\log_2 N)$ time complexity where N is the number of elements stored.

Now, for addressing self-balancing, there are several alternatives, being two of the most popular the Adelson-Velsky and Landis (AVL) tree and the Red-Black Tree. In the second, formerly known as symmetric binary B-tree [23], each node has an extra bit which is often interpreted as the color red or black of the node, so that explains its name. Despite all the particular algorithms for doing so, these color bits are used to ensure the tree remains balanced during insertions and deletions without affecting the $O(\log_2 N)$ complexity.

Finally, being an order-statistic tree means that it supports two additional operations beyond the three mentioned above: selection and ranking. The first one refers to finding the ith smallest element stored in the tree, whereas the second one refers to the opposite, finding the rank, or position in a linear order, of a given element in the tree. For our proposal, we are only interested in the ranking operation. Nevertheless, both can also be performed in $O(\log_2 N)$ when a self-balancing tree is used. However, for doing so, all nodes must store one additional attribute, which is the size of the subtree starting at that node. In other words, it refers to the number of

nodes below and including it. All operations that modify the tree (insertion and deletion, knowing that update may be implemented as a composite function of the two) must consider this attribute and preserve the relation presented in the following without altering the time complexity:

$$node.size = (node.left).size + (node.right).size + 1. \quad (1)$$

An example of an order-statistic tree, using the comparison between nodes according to Algorithm 1, is presented in Figure 1.

Considering the previous structure, we can compute the *ranking* operation as presented on Algorithm 2. Notice that besides the *left* and *right* attributes, each node contains a reference to its *parent*. All nodes have a *parent* except for the *root*. Here, we assume that *search()* returns the node of the player we are looking for and that NULL.*size* = 0.

To demonstrate that Algorithm 2 works correctly, we may think of node x's rank as the number of nodes preceding x in an in-order tree walk, plus 1 for x itself. Then, Algorithm 2 maintains the following loop invariant.

At the start of each iteration of the while loop of lines (8)–(13), r is the rank of x in the subtree rooted at node y.

And we use this loop invariant to show that the algorithm works correctly as follows [19].

Initialization. Prior to the first iteration, line (6) sets r to be the rank of player x within the subtree rooted at x. Setting $y = x$ in line (7) makes the invariant true the first time the test in line (8) executes.

Maintenance. At the end of each iteration of the **while** loop, we set $y = y.parent$. Thus we must show that if r is the rank of x in the subtree rooted at y at the start of the loop body, then r is the rank of x in the subtree rooted at $y.parent$ at the end of the loop body. In each iteration of the **while** loop, we consider the subtree rooted at $y.parent$. We have already counted the number of nodes in the subtree rooted at node y that precede x in an in-order walk, and so we must add the nodes in the subtree rooted at y's sibling that precede x in an in-order walk, plus 1 for $y.parent$ if it, too, precedes x. If y is a right child, then neither $y.parent$ nor any node in $y.parent$'s left subtree precedes x, and so we leave r alone. Otherwise, y is a left child and all the nodes in $y.parent$'s right subtree precede x, as does $y.parent$ itself. Thus, in line (10), we add $y.parent$: *right*:*size* + 1 to the current value of r.

```
ranking (Integer score, Integer id)
(1)  Let x be a node
(2)  x = search(score, id)
(3)  if x = null
(4)            return −1
(5)  end if
(6)  r = (x.right).size + 1
(7)  y = x
(8)  while y ≠ root:
(9)            if y = (y.parent).left:
(10)                     r = r + ((y.parent).right).size + 1
(11)            end if
(12)            y = y.parent
(13) end while
(14) return r
end ranking
```

ALGORITHM 2

Termination. The loop terminates when $y = root$, so that the subtree rooted at y is the entire tree. Thus, the value of r is the rank of x in the entire tree.

Now, if the tree is self-balanced, we already discuss that *insertion*, *deletion*, and *search* operations are performed in $O(\log_2 N)$. Now, notice that, in the previous algorithm, once the node x is found it goes up to the *root* one level at the time, which means that the running time is proportional to the tree height. Therefore, that is why the *ranking* operation also runs in $O(\log_2 N)$.

Now, this *ranking* operation requires both attributes *score* and *id*. In a typical situation, however, we would have only the *id* of the player, and that is where that hash table enters the scene. A hash table is a data structure that can map keys to values using a hash function and is able of doing so in $O(1)$ amortized time. In this case, the key refers to the *id* and the value to the corresponding *score*.

If these two data structures are stored in the RAM (of the environment server) and contain the relevant information of all players, performing a complex task as "increment the score of the player with *id* 1002 in 50 points and determine how many positions he/she gained and the corresponding final position in the leaderboard" could be made in the following manner.

Steps 1 and 5 have $O(1)$ time complexity, whereas steps 2, 3, and 4 have $O(\log_2 N)$; therefore, the entire operation requires $O(\log_2 N)$. Of course, in a real game environment, some of this data should be stored additionally in the database which has a complexity on its own. We are not actually discarding this task, what we are doing is performing the most "expensive" operations, that is, inner ordering and therefore ranking, in a lot more efficient way.

In order to clarify all the algorithms presented so far, consider the next hypothetical situation. There are six players with *scores* and *ids* as shown in Figure 1. Then, as described in Algorithm 3, the player with *id* 1002 increments its *score* in 50 points. Before the increasing, and considering the comparison criteria described in the Algorithm 1, the corresponding leaderboard would stand as presented in Table 1.

TABLE 1: Leaderboard before increasing.

Position	id	Score
1	1006	460
2	1003	450
3	1001	430
4	1002	400
5	1004	380
6	1005	350

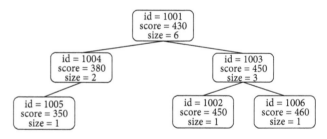

FIGURE 2: Order-statistic tree after increasing.

Once the increasing has been done, the corresponding order-statistic tree stands as shown in Figure 2, whereas the corresponding leaderboard changes as presented in Table 2.

Notice that player 1002 moved up one position in the leaderboard. Checking Algorithm 2, it passes from position 4 to 3. It is important however to make a clarification. The *ranking* operation returns the current position of a player given its *id* and *score* (the *score* may be obtained from the *id* with the hash table), but there is no need of running it N times to get the whole leaderboard. Instead, taking advantage of the binary search structure of the tree, it is possible to just traverse the tree in backward "in-order" as in Algorithm 4.

4. Experimental Results

To validate the method proposed, we performed a comparison against two other approaches. The first of those

Step 1. Search for the score *s* of the player *id* in the Hash Table
Step 2. Use *ranking* (s, id) to obtain current position *p*
Step 3. Update score $s' = s + 50$ for player *id* in both structures, tree and Hash Table
Step 4. Use *ranking* (s', id) to obtain new position p'
Step 5. Return $p' - p$, and p'

ALGORITHM 3

Step 1. Set the *root* as the current node
Step 2. Check if the current node is null, if not, proceed to step 3
Step 3. Traverse the right subtree by recursively calling the in-order function
Step 4. Display information of the current node
Step 5. Traverse the left subtree by recursively calling the in-order function

ALGORITHM 4

TABLE 2: Leaderboard after increasing.

Position	id	Score
1	1006	460
2	1003	450
3	1002	450
4	1001	430
5	1004	380
6	1005	350

TABLE 3: Average running time (in seconds).

Input size	SBOST	Linked list	Database
1,000	0.0272	0.0591	1.280
2,000	0.0442	0.1426	3.610
5,000	0.0726	0.6631	21.0
10,000	0.1083	2.764	95.2
20,000	0.2738	13.6	342.0
50,000	0.5106	164.6	3,398
100,000	0.8825	844.1	13,555

approaches, as we stated earlier, corresponds to the typical solution used in most online game-based environments, which is a database. More specifically, we use a relational database assuming that all relevant information, that is, player's *score* and *id*, is stored in a single table, so no additional operations like joins are required. As for DBMS we used PostgreSQL 9.6. As for the second approach, we used a linked list data structure running in RAM. As in the method proposed, it does not require HDD operations. However, it differs in several aspects. From the technical point of view, its implementation is a lot easier. In fact, just a few Java code lines are needed considering that a native class *LinkedList* is available, including methods for the insertion, deletion, update, and search. From the algorithms point of view, the time complexities of the required operations are entirely different. The native insertion is $O(1)$ if made at the beginning or end of the structure. However, with a few modifications, it can be done orderly in $O(N)$. When doing so, the ranking operation can take place also in $O(N)$, as well as deletion and search.

For the method proposed, we made the corresponding implementation also in Java. For the hash table we used native classes, but for the SBOST we implemented it from scratch. More specifically, we used a Red-Black Tree scheme to achieve self-balancing of the binary search tree and performed the SBOST operations according to the algorithms described in the previous section.

Now, to compare the three approaches, we arranged a scenario in which there are *N* players, each one with a unique *id* and an initial *score*. After that, there are up to *N* queries. Similar to the example presented in the previous section, a query refers to the increment of an individual player *score*, expecting as a result the corresponding new position in the leaderboard, as well as the number of positions gained. With the aim of determining the scalability of each alternative, we used random values for queries using *N* from 1,000, to 2,000, 5,000, 10,000, 20,000, 50,000, and 100,000. For a more robust statistical comparison, we run each case at least ten times and then present the corresponding mean. All runs were made using the same conditions and equipment: Java SE1.8 with Eclipse 4.5.0 in an Intel Core i7-4710HQ at 2.50 GHz, 8 Gb RAM, and 64-bit Windows 8.1.

The results obtained are presented in Table 3. Even with the lower input size, there is a considerable difference between "in-memory" approaches and the HDD-based, that is, between the data structures running in the RAM and the database solution. The difference between the SBOST and the linked list is not too high at the beginning but, as the input size raises, such a difference becomes bigger and bigger. With $N = 100,000$, the SBOST solution is almost $1,000 : 1$ faster than the linked list and $15,000 : 1$ faster than the database.

To visualize these results, but particularly the relation with the input size, Figure 3 presents them as a chart. For the SBOST solution, this chart bears out that running time exhibits a $O(N \log_2 N)$ behavior, whereas the linked list exhibits $O(N^2)$ behavior and the database $O(N^2 \log_2 N)$

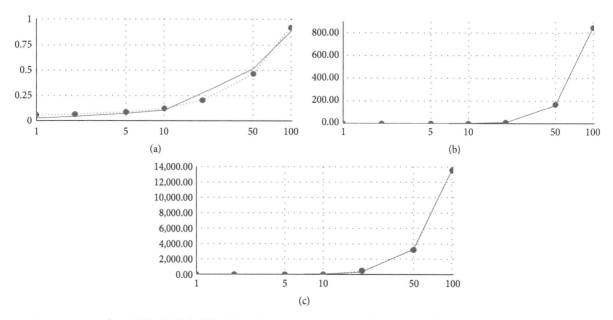

FIGURE 3: Running times for SBOST (a), linked list (b), and database (c). x-axis is for number of queries (in thousands and in logarithmic scale), and y-axis is for average running time (in seconds).

TABLE 4: Multiple linear regression results.

Method	Model	R^2	ANOVA's P value
SBOST	$aN\log_2(N) + b$	0.9823	<0.0001
Linked list	$aN^2 + bN + c$	0.9998	<0.0001
Database	$aN^2\log_2(N) + b$	0.9996	<0.0001

behavior. Even when the shapes in the three cases seem similar, the scales show how different they are. In fact, when running multiple linear regressions for the outcomes of the three solutions, the results presented in Table 4 are obtained whereas the dots on Figure 3 represent the predicted values. In other words, there is empirical evidence for the theoretical time complexity of the three approaches evaluated, including the one of our proposal.

Using those models to extrapolate running times, it results in the fact that, with an input size N = 1 million (nothing too outlandish considering the game related numbers presented at the very beginning of the introduction), the SBOST would obtain nearly 10 seconds, whereas the linked list solution would obtain approximately 28 hours and the database 19 days.

5. Concluding Remarks

Leaderboards are a common element of both online games and game-based environments. Even if there is a lot of evidence of their psychological effects on users, we in this research did not focus on that aspect. Instead, considering such importance, what we proposed is an efficient way to implement them.

Our method has three main features. First, it runs "in-memory," so it exploits fast data access, unlike slower HDD

solutions. Although it might sound as a disadvantage as well, because the reduced space may limit how many users you can have, it is not so problematic considering that in its basic form only the user score and its identifier are needed. For instance, if a four-byte unsigned integer is used for both attributes, a scenario with 100,000 players would require 800,000 bytes, which is less than 1 Mb. Second, it uses specific data structures, so no ordering at all is actually needed for obtaining players positions. More specifically, it uses an SBOST jointly with a hash table which allows for performing all important operations in $O(\log_2 N)$ time complexity. The SBOST was implemented from a Red-Black Tree, but other alternatives for Self-Balanced Binary Search Trees could be adopted as well. Third, the comparison criterion, which ultimately defines the rank of a player, may be easily modified in order to adjust to the designer needs. For instance, it could incorporate more information about the player, rather than just a single score and an identifier.

From the algorithmic point of view, such a proposal surpasses typical solutions as the ones based on databases, as well as other "in-memory," simpler, alternatives as ordered linked lists. As presented in the experimental results section, we achieved speedups on all the scenarios we tested. In fact, the more difficult the scenario, the higher the speedup. For example, such a speedup with an input size N = 100,000 was nearly 1,000:1 and 15,000:1 compared to the other two approaches presented. With the forecast coming from a multiple linear regression with N = 1 million (actual running of such a scenario would be impractical) the corresponding speedups would be nearly as large as 10,000:1 and 160,000:1. This finding turns out to be very relevant in massive environments where dozens or even hundreds of thousands of users are common.

References

[1] NewZoo, "2016 Global games market report," http://resources.newzoo.com/hubfs/Reports/Newzoo_Free_2016_Global_Games_Market_Report.pdf.

[2] SteamCharts, "Dota 2," http://steamcharts.com/app/570.

[3] Forbes, "Riot Games Reveals 'League of Legends' Has 100 Million Monthly Players," https://www.forbes.com/sites/insertcoin/2016/09/13/riot-games-reveals-league-of-legends-has-100-million-monthly-players.

[4] K. Seaborn and D. I. Fels, "Gamification in theory and action: A survey," *International Journal of Human-Computer Studies*, vol. 74, pp. 14–31, 2015.

[5] G. Zichermann and J. Linder, *The gamification revolution: How leaders leverage game mechanics to crush the competition, , McGraw-Hill Education*, McGraw-Hill Education, New York, NY, USA, 1st edition, 2013.

[6] M. Morales, H. R. Amado-Salvatierra, R. Hernández, J. Pirker, and C. Gutl, "A practical experience on the use of gamification in MOOC courses as a strategy to increase motivation," *Communications in Computer and Information Science*, vol. 620, pp. 139–149, 2016.

[7] R. N. Landers, "Developing a Theory of Gamified Learning: Linking Serious Games and Gamification of Learning," *Simulation & Gaming*, vol. 45, no. 6, pp. 752–768, 2014.

[8] B. A. Jones, G. J. Madden, and H. J. Wengreen, "The FIT Game: Preliminary evaluation of a gamification approach to increasing fruit and vegetable consumption in school," *Preventive Medicine*, vol. 68, pp. 76–79, 2014.

[9] J. Hamari, "Transforming homo economicus into homo ludens: a field experiment on gamification in a utilitarian peer-to-peer trading service," *Electronic Commerce Research and Applications*, vol. 12, no. 4, pp. 236–245, 2013.

[10] C. Butler, "The Effect of Leaderboard Ranking on Players' Perception of Gaming Fun," in *Online Communities and Social Computing*, vol. 8029 of *Lecture Notes in Computer Science*, pp. 129–136, Springer Berlin Heidelberg, Berlin, Heidelberg, 2013.

[11] C. Christy and J. Fox, "Leaderboards in a virtual classroom: A test of stereotype threat and social comparison explanations for women's math performance," *Computers & Education*, vol. 78, pp. 769–785, 2014.

[12] R. N. Landers and A. K. Landers, "An Empirical Test of the Theory of Gamified Learning: The Effect of Leaderboards on Time-on-Task and Academic Performance," *Simulation & Gaming*, vol. 45, no. 6, pp. 769–785, 2014.

[13] S. Nebel, M. Beege, S. Schneider, and G. D. Rey, "The higher the score, the higher the learning outcome? Heterogeneous impacts of leaderboards and choice within educational videogames," *Computers in Human Behavior*, vol. 65, pp. 391–401, 2016.

[14] M. Sailer, J. U. Hense, S. K. Mayr, and H. Mandl, "How gamification motivates: An experimental study of the effects of specific game design elements on psychological need satisfaction," *Computers in Human Behavior*, vol. 69, pp. 371–380, 2017.

[15] Google Cloud Platform, "Fast and Reliable Ranking in Datastore," https://cloud.google.com/datastore/docs/articles/fast-and-reliable-ranking-in-datastore/.

[16] Z. Rasool, A. Bimba, N. F. Mohd Noor, H. Affal, M. N. Ayub, and N. Husin, "Gamification of Web Based Learning Environment for Physics Problem Solving," in *Proceedings of the Second Asian Conference on Society, Education and Technology (ACSET)*, Osaka, Japan, 2014.

[17] C. Rasmussen and D. Ase, *A Web-Based Code-Editor For Use in Programming Courses [Dissertation thesis for the Master of Science in Computer Science]*, Norwegian University of Science and Technology, 2014.

[18] G. Barata, S. Gama, J. Jorge, and D. Goncalves, "Engaging engeneering students with gamification," in *Proceedings of the 2013 5th International Conference on Games and Virtual Worlds for Serious Applications, VS-GAMES 2013*, UK, September 2013.

[19] T. H. Cormen, C. E. Leiserson, R. Rivest, and C. Stein, *Introduction to Algorithms*, The MIT Press, Cambridge, UK, 2009.

[20] D. Knuth, *The Art of Computer Programming*, vol. 1, Addison-Wesley, Mass, USA, 3rd edition, 1997.

[21] M. Goodrich and R. Tamassia, *Data Structures and Algorithms in Java*, John Wiley & Sons, Hoboken, USA, 5th edition, 2010.

[22] S. S. Skiena, *The Algorithm Design Manual*, Springer-Verlag, London, UK, 2008.

[23] R. Bayer, "Symmetric binary B-Trees: Data structure and maintenance algorithms," *Acta Informatica*, vol. 1, no. 4, pp. 290–306, 1972.

Permissions

The contributors of this book come from diverse backgrounds, making this book a truly international effort. This book will bring forth new frontiers with its revolutionizing research information and detailed analysis of the nascent developments around the world.

We would like to thank all the contributing authors for lending their expertise to make the book truly unique. They have played a crucial role in the development of this book. Without their invaluable contributions this book wouldn't have been possible. They have made vital efforts to compile up to date information on the varied aspects of this subject to make this book a valuable addition to the collection of many professionals and students.

This book was conceptualized with the vision of imparting up-to-date information and advanced data in this field. To ensure the same, a matchless editorial board was set up. Every individual on the board went through rigorous rounds of assessment to prove their worth. After which they invested a large part of their time researching and compiling the most relevant data for our readers.

The editorial board has been involved in producing this book since its inception. They have spent rigorous hours researching and exploring the diverse topics which have resulted in the successful publishing of this book. They have passed on their knowledge of decades through this book. To expedite this challenging task, the publisher supported the team at every step. A small team of assistant editors was also appointed to further simplify the editing procedure and attain best results for the readers.

Apart from the editorial board, the designing team has also invested a significant amount of their time in understanding the subject and creating the most relevant covers. They scrutinized every image to scout for the most suitable representation of the subject and create an appropriate cover for the book.

The publishing team has been an ardent support to the editorial, designing and production team. Their endless efforts to recruit the best for this project, has resulted in the accomplishment of this book. They are a veteran in the field of academics and their pool of knowledge is as vast as their experience in printing. Their expertise and guidance has proved useful at every step. Their uncompromising quality standards have made this book an exceptional effort. Their encouragement from time to time has been an inspiration for everyone.

The publisher and the editorial board hope that this book will prove to be a valuable piece of knowledge for researchers, students, practitioners and scholars across the globe.

List of Contributors

Firas Safadi, Raphael Fonteneau and Damien Ernst
Université de Liège, Grande Traverse 10, Sart Tilman, 4000 Liège, Belgium

Priscilla Haring
Media psychology, Amsterdam, Netherlands

Harald Warmelink
NHTV Breda University of Applied Sciences, Netherlands

Marilla Valente
Dutch Game Garden, Netherlands

Christian Roth
HKU University of the Arts, Utrecht, Netherlands

Suphanut Jamonnak and En Cheng
Department of Computer Science, College of Arts and Sciences, University of Akron, Akron, OH 44325-4003, USA

Erik Geslin
UCO Laval 3Di, LICIA, 25 rue du Mans, 53000 Laval, France
Arts et Métiers ParisTech, LAMPA, 2 Boulevard du Ronceray, 49000 Angers, France

Laurent Jégou
Maître de Conférences, Department of Geography and UMR LISST, Toulouse Jean-Jaurès University, 5 allée Antonio Machado, 31058 Toulouse Cedex 9, France

Danny Beaudoin
Psychology Department, Faculty of Social Sciences, Université Laval, Pavillon Félix-Antoine-Savard, 2325 rue des Bibliothèques, Quebec City, QC, Canada G1V 0A6

Chaoguang Wang and Gino Yu
Digital Entertainment Lab, Hong Kong Polytechnic University, Hung Hom, Kowloon, Hong Kong

Marvin T. Chan, Christine W. Chan and Craig Gelowitz
Software Systems Engineering Program, Faculty of Engineering and Applied Science, University of Regina, Regina, SK, Canada S4S 0A2

Yogi Udjaja
Computer Science Department, School of Computer Science, Bina Nusantara University, Jl. K. H. Syahdan, No. 9, Kemanggisan, Palmerah, Jakarta 11480, Indonesia
Ekspanpixel, Jl. K. H. Syahdan, No. 37R, Kemanggisan, Palmerah, Jakarta 11480, Indonesia

Hai Nan
College of Computer Science, Chongqing University, Chongqing 400044, China
Department of Software Engineering, Chongqing Institute of Engineering, Chongqing 400056, China

Bin Fang
College of Computer Science, Chongqing University, Chongqing 400044, China

Guixin Wang
Department of Software Engineering, Chongqing Institute of Engineering, Chongqing 400056, China

Weibin Yang
College of Automation, Chongqing University, Chongqing 400044, China

Emily Sarah Carruthers
College of International Education, Chongqing University, Chongqing 400044, China

Yi Liu
PetroChina Chongqing Marketing Jiangnan Company, Chongqing 400060, China

Marcelo Arêas R. da Silva
COPPE/UFRJ, Federal University of Rio de Janeiro, Rio de Janeiro, RJ, Brazil

Geraldo Bonorino Xexéo
COPPE/UFRJ, Federal University of Rio de Janeiro, Rio de Janeiro, RJ, Brazil
Department of Computer Science, Institute of Mathematics (DCC-IM), Rio de Janeiro, RJ, Brazil

Yiing Y'ng Ng
School of Computing & Creative Media, KDU University College, Utropolis Glenmarie, 40150 Shah Alam, Malaysia

Chee Weng Khong
Faculty of Creative Multimedia, Multimedia University, 63100 Cyberjaya, Malaysia

Robert Jeyakumar Nathan
Faculty of Business, Multimedia University, 75450 Melaka, Malaysia

Mirko Suznjevic and Maja Matijasevic
Faculty of Electrical Engineering and Computing, University of Zagreb, Unska 3, 10000 Zagreb, Croatia

Julián Fernández-Navajas, Jose Saldana and José Ruiz-Mas
Communication Technologies Group (GTC), Aragon Institute of Engineering Research (I3A), EINA, University of Zaragoza, 50018 Zaragoza Ada Byron Building, Spain

Walid Mestadi, Raja Touahni and Rochdi Messoussi
Ibn Tofail University, Faculty of Sciences, Kenitra, Morocco

Khalid Nafil
Mohamed V University, Faculty of Sciences, Rabat, Morocco

Byungchul Park and Duk Hee Lee
School of Business and Technology Management, College of Business, Korea Advanced Institute of Science and Technology (KAIST), Daejeon, Republic of Korea

Hongjun Li
College of Science, Beijing Forestry University, Beijing 100083, China

Xiaopeng Zhang and Weiliang Meng
NLPR-LIAMA, Institute of Automation, CAS, Beijing 100190, China

Lin Ge
Department of Biostatistics and Computational Biology, University of Rochester, Rochester, NY 14620, USA

Fernando Bevilacqua
University of Skövde, Skövde, Sweden
Federal University of Fronteira Sul, Chapećo, SC, Brazil

Henrik Engström and Per Backlund
University of Skövde, Skövde, Sweden

Julian Moreno Cadavid and Hernán Darío Vanegas Madrigal
Universidad Nacional de Colombia, Bogotá, Colombia

Index

Printed in the USA
CPSIA information can be obtained
at www.ICGtesting.com
JSHW051413221024
72173JS00006B/1350

9 781632 409461